ALASKA
A History of the 49th State

ALASKA
A History of the 49th State

by
Claus-M. Naske
and
Herman E. Slotnick

WILLIAM B. EERDMANS PUBLISHING COMPANY
GRAND RAPIDS, MICHIGAN

We are grateful to Claus-M. Naske for supplying pictures of the following for the colored-insert section: Mendenhall Glacier, Juneau (I-3), Dog sled on ice pack near Barrow (I-20), Children of Barrow (I-20), Landing a whale near Barrow (I-21), and Spring whaling near Barrow (I-30 and 31).

We are also grateful to the United States Geographical Survey for supplying the following pictures for the colored-insert section: Mosaic of mainland Alaska (I-1), Prudhoe Bay oilfield (I-2), and Mt. McKinley (I-2).

And we are indeed grateful to the State of Alaska, Division of Tourism, for supplying slides of the following for the colored-insert section: Kenai Mountains (I-4), Halibut Cove (I-4), Whittier (I-5), Kenai Mountains (I-5), One of Alaska's many glaciers (I-6), Nome (I-6), Thompson Pass near Valdez (I-7), Katmai National Monument (I-7), Caribou (I-8), Moose (I-8), Dall sheep (I-9), Buffalo, Delta Junction (I-9), Grizzly bear (I-10), Brown bears (I-10), Polar bear (I-11), Fur seals, Pribilof Islands (I-11), Barrow (I-12), Ketchikan (I-12), Nome (I-13), Fairbanks (I-13), Petersburg (I-14), Nenana (I-14), Seward (I-15), Tuntuliak (I-15), Wrangell (I-16), Shaktoolik (I-16), Halibut (I-17), King crab (I-17), Ice fishing near Akiachak (I-18), Ketchikan fishing fleet (I-18), Ketchikan old timer (I-19), Couple from Kotzebue (I-21), Woodcarver, Sitka (I-22), Totem poles near Ketchikan (I-23), Eskimo drummers and dancer (I-23), Cook Inlet oil drilling platform (I-24), Gold dredge, Nome (I-25), Independence Mine near Palmer (I-25), Sitka Russian dancers (I-26), Tlingit canoe, Haines (I-26), Alaska state ferry (I-27), Fishing boat, Homer (I-27), Lumberjack (I-28), Ketchikan pulp mill (I-28), Fishwheel on the Tanana River (I-29), Drying salmon (I-29), and Netting fish, Juneau (I-32).

Library of Congress Cataloging in Publication Data

Naske, Claus-M.
   Alaska, a history of the 49th State.

   Includes index.
   1. Alaska—History. I. Slotnick, Herman,
1916–   joint author. II. Title.
F904.N37 979.8 79-1354
ISBN 0-8028-7041-4

Typography and layout by Greg Kupris

For
Dinah Ariss Naske
and
Mary Slotnick

Contents

Illustrations (duotone)

Illustrations (full-color insert)

Subjects

Maps

Standard False-Color Controlled Landsat Mosaic of Mainland Alaska

Prudhoe Bay oilfield

Mt. McKinley

Mendenhall Glacier, Juneau

Kenai Mountains

Halibut Cove

Whittier

Kenai Mountains

One of Alaska's
many glaciers

Nome

Thompson Pass
near Valdez

Katmai
National Monument

Caribou

Moose

Dall sheep

Buffalo, Delta Junction

Grizzly bear

Brown bears

Polar bear

Fur seals, Pribilof Islands

Barrow

Ketchikan

Nome

Fairbanks

Petersburg

Nenana

Seward

Tuntutuliak

Wrangell

Shaktoolik

Acknowledgments

HISTORIANS, contemplating the writing of a book, believe that they are able to offer something that does not yet exist in published form. Perhaps too much has already been written about Alaska. Even a casual survey of the available literature is overwhelming. There are, for example, the accounts of Russian, English, American, French, Spanish, and German explorers, secondary accounts dealing with Russian America, and many volumes describing Alaska as the American possession acquired in 1867. Voluminous federal governmental reports examine everything from the number of salmon to the conditions of the aborigines. The literature of the Klondike gold rush alone is vast, and eager writers in all fields have added substantially to this body of written work about Alaska.

Still, in spite of all that has been written, the authors feel—or know, depending on their frame of mind at the moment—that yet another book on Alaska is both desirable and necessary. This book is designed to present a narrative account of Alaska's major historical developmental strands from early times to the present, with an emphasis on major developments in the twentieth century. The authors consulted works both lengthy and authoritative but did not attempt to survey all of the available literature.

The works of many specialists contributed to this volume. The holdings of the Skinner Collection at the University of Alaska, Fairbanks were particularly useful.

The authors are grateful to Dr. Robert Carlson, director of the university's Institute of Water Resources, and Charles Hartman, the institute's executive officer, who, as on other occasions, gave encouragement and staff support throughout.

Our good friend and colleague, Dr. William R. Hunt, contributed ideas and carefully read the manuscript. We are most grateful for his assistance.

We also appreciate the typing help of Judith Smith. We are particularly grateful to Marian Tompkins, who again contributed efforts beyond the call of duty. She speedily and cheerfully typed the final version of this manuscript.

As always, our wives, Dinah and Mary, helped with valuable suggestions, careful editing, and encouragement. We would also like to thank Renee Blahuta of the University of Alaska Archives in Fairbanks for her valuable help. Most importantly, authors benefit from the help of a good editor. Reinder Van Til is one of the best. We thank him for his labors.

·1·
Introduction

Geologic History of Alaska

AMERICANS became aware of the great natural resources of the North as early as the 1840s, when New England whalers ventured into the Bering Sea in pursuit of their prey. After the United States acquired Alaska from Russia in 1867, restless and adventurous men came north in search of fortune. They soon found gold, and by 1890 Alaska's mineral production was valued at nearly $800,000. By 1904 gold production exceeded $9,000,000 in value. This relatively rapid development attracted public attention and led to demands for government-sponsored and -financed explorations, surveys, and other investigations. In a few years both public and private enterprise combined to produce a great amount of material on the geography, geology, and mineral resources of Alaska.[1] In short, Alaskans were becoming aware of the land and its natural resources. They knew that the North promised fabulous wealth for the hardy but also that it offered potential dangers.

Alaskans were harshly reminded of these dangers on June 6, 1912, when snow-covered, glaciered, and seemingly dormant Mount Katmai, on the Alaska Peninsula, blew up in a series of violent explosions that threw more than 5½ cubic miles of debris into the air. For hundreds of square miles around, the eruptions destroyed the country. The city of Kodiak, 100 miles away, was plunged into total darkness for sixty hours while volcanic ashes covered everything to a depth of several feet. The accompanying thunder and lightning convinced the terrified residents that the end of the world had come. In Juneau, some 750 miles distant, the explosive sounds of the erupting mountain were plainly heard. In towns such as Seattle and Port Townsend in the Pacific Northwest, over 2,000 miles away from Katmai, cloth fabrics disintegrated from the effects of the sulphuric acid particles, which fell like rain for days.[2]

Alaskans were again reminded of the unstable geologic nature of their land at 5:36 p.m. on Good Friday, March 27, 1964, when one of the greatest earthquakes of all time struck south-central Alaska. Measuring between 8.4

Good Friday earthquake, 1964. Devastation on north side of 4th Avenue between C & D Streets, Anchorage
(*U.S. Army Photograph*)

and 8.6 on the Richter scale, it released at least twice as much energy as the 1906 earthquake which destroyed San Francisco, and it was felt over almost a half-million square miles. The motions lasted longer than for most recorded earthquakes, and more land surface was vertically and horizontally dislocated than by any previously known tremor. The earthquake left 114 dead or missing, and Alaska's governor estimated property damages at between one-half and three-quarters of a billion dollars.

Even at that, Alaskans had been lucky. Had the earthquake occurred during the school and business day, many more lives would have been lost. And had the seismic sea waves accompanying the earthquake struck the coastal communities of south-central Alaska at high rather than low tide, the loss of life and property would have been even greater. As it was, the sea waves traversed the entire Pacific. The seismic vibrations indicated that a huge segment of the earth's crust along a deeply buried fault—the nature and exact location of which are still subjects for speculation—had been dislocated. Not only was the land surface tilted, but an enormous mass of land and sea floor moved several tens of feet horizontally toward the Gulf of Alaska.[3]

A compilation by geophysicist T. Neil Davis of the Geophysical Institute at the University of Alaska at Fairbanks shows that between July 1788 and August 1961 some 880 earthquakes measuring five points or more on the Richter scale occurred in Alaska.[4] The foregoing examples make it obvious that Alaska's geological setting, while promising great wealth in mineral resources, also holds great danger. Despite the fact that geologists have worked in Alaska since the latter part of the nineteenth century, this huge landmass is not well known geologically. Complete geological mapping on a scale of four miles to the inch, comparable to that done in much of the lower forty-eight contiguous states, would require more than a century of intensive work.

The older geological history of Alaska is vague and poorly known, very complex, and thus difficult to summarize. There are extensive areas of ancient rocks and large regions of shallow seas. At present geologists are in the process of rethinking old concepts. Until about 1971 there existed a fairly simple geological picture; but that has now disappeared.

During the Cretaceous period, about 125 million years ago, the major crustal plates coalesced and shaped Alaska's major features. The fusion of these crustal plates, however, profoundly confused the old geological history because geologists have not been able to determine the location of the crustal plates prior to coalescence. Furthermore, only bits and pieces of the old geological history have been collected so far, and these have not been correlated. The

Earthquake 1964, Seward damage scene after *tsunami* hit
(*U.S. Army Photograph*)

events since the Cretaceous period are much clearer. About that time the seas withdrew from the region for the last time, and Alaska emerged pretty much in its present form. Rocks that have accumulated since then are of a nonmarine nature. Alaska's mountain ranges, except for the Brooks Range, are of fairly recent origin.

During the last few million years Alaska's surface features were, to a large degree, sculpted by the advancing and retreating glaciers. When the glaciers retreated for the last time 10,000 years ago, their retreat was accompanied by a rise in the sea levels. Alaska's present climatic patterns were also created during that period, endowing much of the region north of the southern coastal areas with permafrost—a layer of permanently frozen earth a few feet below the surface. Geologists agree that permafrost conditions have profoundly affected the weathering and erosion of the rocks and helped produce the characteristic topography of interior and northern Alaska.

The arctic and subarctic climates have affected not only the formation of glaciers and permafrost, but by controlling the vegetative cover have also affected the erosion process. Much of the state's land is above or even beyond the timberline and is covered by low bushes, herbs, grasses, and mosses, while other parts are so high and cold as to be barren rock deserts.[5]

In recent years scientists have done much work that has thrown new light on the history of the earth. They have shown that the earth's surface is composed of about a dozen moving plates, colliding and brushing past each other, with one sometimes sliding beneath another. These insights are called the "new global plate tectonics," a radically different way of looking at the earth. In Alaska, the Pacific plate is slipping under the North American continental plate along the deep Aleutian trench. When the submerging plate reaches a depth of approximately sixty miles, melting occurs, and the molten material rises and often triggers volcanic eruptions in the Aleutian chain of islands.

Although evidence of the tectonic evolution of Alaska is still very fragmentary, much work is being done here and elsewhere. In 1974 the geologist H. Glenn Richards suggested a new picture of Alaskan tectogenesis. His research indicates that Alaska may be composed of two continental plates that once were separate. These plates drifted toward each other during the Paleozoic and early Mesozoic eras and finally collided and coalesced in the late Jurassic–early Cretaceous time. Richards further subdivides each of the plates into two segments with apparently different geologic histories.[6]

Scientists consider Alaska a key to understanding the geologic correlations around the northern Pacific and the geology of the circumarctic areas. Besides being a link between North America and Eurasia, Alaska also is crucial in evaluating the ancient histories of the Arctic and the northern Pacific Oceans through the study of its continental margins and in testing various theories of continental drift and seafloor spreading in the Arctic.[7]

Matanuska Glacier north
of Palmer
(Claus-M. Naske)

The Regions and Climates of Alaska

The Aleuts call this subcontinent *alaxsxag*, which literally means "the object toward which the action of the sea is directed." The Russians called their American possession *Bolshaia Zeml'a*, the "Great Land," and justifiably so.[8] Sweeping across four time zones, it encompasses 586,112 square miles, 2.2 times the area of Texas, the largest of the lower forty-eight states. Surrounded by fellow Americans from the Southwest working on the Trans-Alaska Pipeline, Alaskans often counter Texas boastings of size by threatening to "split in two and make you third in size."

Alaska extends from 51° to 71° 25′ northern latitude and from 129° 58′ west longitude to 172° 22′ east longitude, thus occupying both the Western and Eastern hemispheres. A map of Alaska superimposed on a map of the contiguous United States would touch the Atlantic and Pacific Oceans and the Canadian and Mexican boundaries. Barrow, Alaska's northernmost settlement, would be located near Lake of the Woods in northern Minnesota, while Ketchikan, Alaska's southernmost city, would be located in the vicinity of Charlestown, South Carolina. From north to south, Alaska measures about 1,400 miles, and from east to west, about 2,700 miles. The Aleutian Islands drape westward well into the Eastern Hemisphere, and together with the Komandorski Islands they form the stepping stones to Kamchatka which were used by the Russian fur hunters in their quest for the sea otter.[9] Alaska is the only state that forms part of the land area surrounding the North Pole and Arctic Basin, the latter, in the late explorer Vilhjalmur Stefansson's words, "the

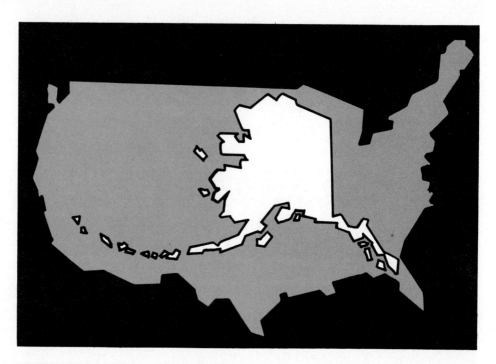

Mediterranean of the twentieth century."

Because the forty-ninth state is of such immense proportions, citizens of the "lower forty-eight" have difficulty comprehending it, and even many Alaskans are somewhat ignorant of their state's geography. The diversity of this lonely and lovely subcontinent is just as incredible as its size. Alaska possesses arctic plains, great forests, swamps, glaciers, ice fields, broad valleys and fjords, the highest mountain of North America, active volcanoes, twelve major river systems, three million lakes, and countless islands. Alaska boasts 50 percent more seacoast than all of the continental United States—some 33,904 miles—and its coasts are washed by two oceans and three major seas. Yet the entire state has little more than 410,000 people, far fewer than Oakland, California.

The overwhelming majority of Alaskans are urban dwellers, and more than half of them live in the Anchorage and Fairbanks boroughs, 175,603 in the former and approximately 60,227 in the latter. Roughly 300,000 Alaskans live in urban centers scattered from Barrow in the Arctic to Ketchikan in southeastern Alaska. Thus, 75 percent of Alaskans are urbanites, and more are moving to the cities and towns each year.

Geographically, there are six regions, each with a distinctive topography and climate. The climates range from the temperate to the frigid and from a desert-like aridity to almost continuous rainfall and snowfall. Barrow, Alaska's northernmost settlement, is not as cold as Fairbanks in the interior, though it is only a comparatively short distance from the Arctic ice pack and the North Pole. Alaska's southernmost point in the Aleutians is at about the same latitude as London, England, and shares a similar climate.

Approaching Alaska from Seattle by ship, the traveler enters the so-called Panhandle, a very narrow, 400-mile-long strip of land that crowds closely against the coast of British Columbia. It is cut off from the main body of the Alaskan landmass by the great St. Elias mountain range. Juneau, Alaska's capital, is located in the Panhandle, as is Ketchikan, self-proclaimed "Salmon Capital of the World" and also the site of one of the region's two pulp mills. Sitka, the former capital of Russian America, is situated on Baranov Island amid forested mountains overlooking the sound. It is the home of the second of the region's pulp mills. At the upper end of the Panhandle lies Skagway, where thousands of argonauts disembarked in 1898 for their difficult climb over the Chilkoot Pass and subsequent journey down the Yukon River to Dawson.

Many islands, steep valleys, and rugged peaks ranging to 10,000 feet stretch all along the Panhandle, dropping to a main shore teeming with marine life. The climate is moderate, with warmer temperatures than most of Alaska and a good deal of rain and cloudiness. Temperatures seldom dip below 10° F and often climb to the 60s and 70s during the summer. Annual rainfall varies from 25 inches to 155 inches, which produces lush forest growth. As a result, the region contains most of the state's commercially marketable timber, western hemlock and Sitka spruce being the two major species.

The southern side of Alaska confronts the Pacific Ocean in a wide-sweeping arc of some 700 miles, flanking some of the highest mountains in

Moore's Wharf in Skagway, at the head of the inland passage
(Price Collection, Archives, University of Alaska, Fairbanks)

North America. Within this arc lies the Gulf of Alaska. One of the arms of this arc is formed by the Alaska Peninsula, while the other is formed by the Panhandle and the coast of Canada. At the very center of this geographical formation lies the Kenai Peninsula, where Alaska's modern oil boom began in the middle 1950s. Set off from the mainland by Cook Inlet, this peninsula is mountainous, dotted with lakes and indented with fjords. Resurrection Bay is long, deep, and completely sheltered. At the head of the bay lies Seward, the starting point of the Alaska Railroad. For many years Seward was the shipping and rail terminus for cargo coming into Alaska from the "outside." In recent years it has been superseded in importance by the port of Anchorage.

Since the 1950s Anchorage has been the economic and social center of south-central Alaska. It also has become Alaska's largest city, with a population of approximately 175,603 in the larger borough. Situated on Cook Inlet, Anchorage began its existence as a tent city in 1915, when construction of the Alaska Railroad began.

Cordova, on Prince William Sound, is a small fishing town today; but it was once the terminus of the Copper River and Northwestern Railroad, which carried copper ore 200 miles from the Alaska Syndicate mine in the Chitina Valley to tidewater. Across the bay from Cordova is Valdez. Completely devastated in the Good Friday earthquake of 1964, Valdez was relocated on stable ground and has since become famous as the terminus of the 789-mile Trans-Alaska Pipeline originating at Prudhoe Bay on Alaska's North Slope. Kodiak

Main Street of Cordova on Election Day, April 7, 1914
(Mackay Collection, Archives, University of Alaska, Fairbanks)

Island is a mountainous region located within the rich fishing waters of the North Pacific. Home of the gigantic Kodiak brown bear, it also processes millions of pounds of king and tanner crabs, as well as shrimp, halibut, and salmon.

Southwestern Alaska includes the Alaska Peninsula, Katmai National Monument, and the great sweeping arc of the Aleutian Island chain. It is a region of contrasts, stretching from the lightly wooded hillsides and rugged mountains of the Alaska Peninsula some 2,000 miles south and west through the barren and volcanic Aleutians almost to Siberia and Japan. The Aleutians are foggy and stormy, forming a dividing arc between the Pacific and Bering seas. The distance from Katmai Mountain at the head of the Alaska Peninsula to Attu, westernmost of the Aleutians, is 1,500 miles. The International Date Line makes a sharp angle to the west to take in the last of the Aleutian Islands and keep Alaska all within the same day. There are actually only a few large islands in the Aleutian chain. They are, in descending order in a southwesterly direction down the chain, Unimak, Unalaska, Umnak, Atka, Adak, and Attu. Thousands of rocks and islets dot the ocean between Unimak and Attu Island.

The foggy Aleutians are stormy and rainy, swept alternately by the cold winds of the Arctic and the humid winds of the Pacific. Close to the Aleutian Islands flows the Japan Current, which brings a warm front from the south into conflict with the cold winds from the north and accounts for the continuous fog, rain, and snow of the region. There is no major vegetation on the Aleutians other than grasses and moss. The islands are mostly of volcanic origin.

Russian church and school, Unalaska, ca. 1910
(Selid-Bassoc Collection, Archives, University of Alaska, Fairbanks)

Spread along the Aleutians are a number of military installations, weather stations, airports, and fish-processing and supply settlements.

Western Alaska is a remote area stretching from Kvichak Bay, at the head of Bristol Bay, north along the coast to Shishmaref on the Seward Peninsula near the Arctic Circle, and includes St. Lawrence, Nunivak, St. Matthew, and various other islands. In addition, it encompasses an immense treeless flatland with thousands of lakes, ponds, and sloughs, and almost unmoving rivers such as the muddy mouths of the Kuskokwim and Yukon Rivers. Cool, rainy, and foggy weather characterizes the summers, while the winters feature high winds and humidity.

Alaska's interior lies south of the Brooks Range and generally north of the Alaska Range and extends west from the Canadian border to an imaginary line anywhere from 40 to 200 miles from the Bering Sea coast. A central plain along the valley of the 2,000-mile-long Yukon River rises high up in Canada's Yukon Territory and flows westward across the entire breadth of Alaska into the Bering Sea. Along this river and its tributaries are located most of the settlements and towns of interior Alaska. Fairbanks lies on the Tanana River, a tributary of the Yukon. Fairbanks and its environs has a population of approximately 60,000. It is the metropolis and supply center for interior and northwest Alaska, particularly in the 1970s with the North Slope oil boom.

Temperatures in the interior vary between 99° F and −66° F. Winters are cold and summers generally hot and dry, with light rainfall of approximately twelve inches per year. Snowfall, because of the extreme cold, often consists of dry, powdery flakes that blow and drift easily. Fairbanks, however, has much fair weather and enjoys long hours of splendid daylight during the spring and summer months, which balances the long, dark winter when days seem grimly short.

The true Arctic extends from Kotzebue, north of the Seward Peninsula, to the Canadian border. It is a place of nightless summers and sunless winters. The climate is extreme: in the winter temperatures drop to below-zero averages, and they climb to the 40s and 50s in the summer. The Arctic includes the Norton and Kotzebue Sound districts and the arctic plain north of the Brooks Range. On the south side the Seward Peninsula faces the Bering Sea, and on the northern side it faces the Chukchi Sea. Both are cold, shallow seas with few good harbors. A harsh, semiarctic climate prevails. The land along these coasts is low. Scattered hills rise several miles back from the shore, and inland the country rises to a low, rolling plateau. There is no timber growth for some distance back from the Bering Sea, except around Norton Sound, but there is an abundance of stunted willow trees. The Seward Peninsula is largely drained by the Fish and Kaviruk rivers. It is a low-lying area and the soil is permanently frozen, only thawing a few inches on the surface every summer. The Kobuk and Noatak rivers carry the waters from the southern and western slopes of the arctic ranges and empty into Kotzebue Sound. The Bering Sea coastal area summers are short and cool. The winters are long, cloudy, and stormy. Temperatures are not as severe as those of the interior and rarely reach −40° F, but dampness and wind make the cold penetrating.

North of Kotzebue begins the Arctic Slope, separated from the interior by the Brooks Range, which rises to elevations of 10,000 feet and forms a mighty barrier. The slope, approximately 750 miles long and about 250 miles wide, consists of large areas of rolling uplands and coastal plains which stretch northward from the Brooks Range. The whole Arctic Slope region is devoid of all timber except for the small stands of willows that grow along streams. Mosses, lichens, and low willows grow over most of the area, and during the short summer months the profusion of flowering plants makes the Arctic a place of beauty. Temperatures are low because of the prevailing northerly winds during all seasons of the year. The average July temperature at Barrow is 40° F, while the average January temperature is −17° F. Total annual precipitation averages about five inches, making the area a desert. The Arctic also is a place of nightless summers and sunless winters, and the shores are ice-locked for much of the year. The North Slope achieved sudden fame when several oil companies discovered vast oil and gas deposits at Prudhoe Bay. The region has now become the potentially most wealthy one in the state.[10]

Alaska Prehistory and the Peoples of the Great Land

Nobody knows just when the human race discovered America, and the subject continues to be debated by many scholars. The disagreements arise anew with the unearthing of skulls, bones, primitive burial grounds, hunting camps, and utensils. Some used to believe that Egyptians first saw America, while others supported the various claims of the Greeks, Etruscans, Hindus, Chinese, Buddhists, Japanese, and the Irish. The Mormons believe that the Indians are descendants of "remnants of the House of Israel." On L'Anse aux Meadows, a grassy plain on the north coast of Newfoundland, the Norwegian anthropologist Helge Ingstad uncovered remnants of Norse dwellings dating back to the year 1000, nearly 500 years before Columbus discovered America.[11]

These controversies, however, are of concern mainly to archaeologists and anthropologists. The present consensus is that the first people who saw what is called America today were following ice-age mammals migrating east from Siberia into what is today Alaska in search of more food and escape from their predators. In time these hunters, still following the game, wandered into the grasslands of the American interior, then east to the Atlantic shores of Canada, south across the deserts, through Central America, and finally to Tierra del Fuego, the tip of South America.

These early hunters entered Alaska via the so-called Bering Sea Land Bridge, some 1,000 miles wide when, in prehistoric times, glacial ice sheets locked up much of the earth's supply of water and lowered the sea levels. As the ice receded, the sea levels rose again until, about ten thousand years ago, Alaska and Siberia were parted once and for all by the waters. How long the Americas have been inhabited by humans is simply informed guesswork, but most agree that it has been at least 15,000 years. In any event, excavations south of Alaska have confirmed this approximate date. Perhaps it can be safely stated that long after mankind had settled the continents of Asia, Africa, and

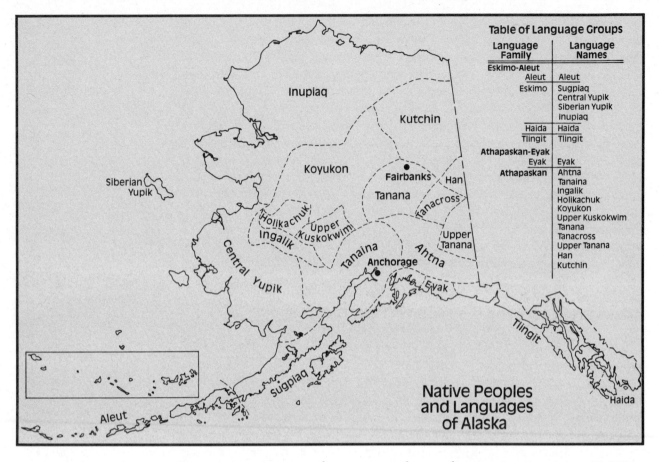

Table of Language Groups	
Language Family	Language Names
Eskimo-Aleut	
Aleut	Aleut
Eskimo	Sugpiaq
	Central Yupik
	Siberian Yupik
	Inupiaq
Haida	Haida
Tlingit	Tlingit
Athapaskan-Eyak	
Eyak	Eyak
Athapaskan	Ahtna
	Tanaina
	Ingalik
	Holikachuk
	Koyukon
	Upper Kuskokwim
	Tanana
	Tanacross
	Upper Tanana
	Han
	Kutchin

Native Peoples
and Languages
of Alaska

Map designed by Michael E. Krauss, director, Native Language Center, University of Alaska, Fairbanks, 1974

Europe, America was unknown to any human beings. At some point, 15,000 to 40,000 years ago, humans began to live in the Americas after they had crossed the Bering Sea Land Bridge.

Today, a mere fifty-six miles of stormy waters separate Siberia's Chukchi Peninsula from the Seward Peninsula of Alaska at the point where the United States and the Soviet Union confront each other most closely.

Similarities between Asians and American Indians

In the last few years American and Russian scientists have been involved in research which has shown that, in the ABO blood group system, the predominant Asian blood type is B. Since these blood groups are determined by separate genes and are not directly affected by the environment, one would expect to find a continuation of the high percentage of the B type east of Bering Strait all the way to Tierra del Fuego. However, this is not the case. Only small numbers with the B type have been found in the recent native populations on the eastern side of the strait, and practically none occurs south of Alaska, where the types O and A are found instead. Still, the majority of genetic and morphologic traits reflect the biological affinities of Asians and American Indians. Biological evidence also suggests that there were several migratory waves across the land bridge.[12]

Among the first to migrate were those who later were called Indians. Of particular interest were those who eventually settled along the shores of northwestern North America from Yakutat Bay in southeastern Alaska to Trinidad Bay in present northern California. All developed and participated in a unique and rich culture based on the tremendous wealth of the natural resources of their area. These consisted of the five species of Pacific salmon, halibut, cod, herring, smelt, and the famous oil-rich olachen, or "candlefish," among others. The sea also furnished large quantities of edible mollusks in addition to marine mammals such as the hair seal, sea lion, sea otter, porpoise, and occasional whales. Land game abounded, and various vegetable foods were easily obtainable. Nature provided in abundance what in most other parts of the world people had to work out of the earth through agriculture and raising livestock. There was, in short, a surplus of foodstuffs which allowed these people much leisure time to devote to the improvement and elaboration of their cultural heritage.

Aleut hunters of Unalaska
(Historical Photograph Collection, Archives, University of Alaska, Fairbanks)

Coastal Indians

Three distinct native groups occupied an area in Alaska which lies approximately between Yakutat in the north and Ketchikan in the south. The Tlingit, the most numerous, were scattered throughout in numerous permanent villages; they spoke a language believed to be related to the Athapaskan of the

Interior of Tlingit
dwelling
(*Historical Photograph
Collection, Archives,
University of Alaska, Fairbanks*)

interior. Consisting of some fourteen tribal divisions, the Tlingit had been pressing westward just before contact with Europeans. The Yakutat Tlingit probably had driven the Chugachmiut Eskimo off Kayak Island, and they, or some related tribe, established an outpost among the linguistically related Eyak at the mouth of the Copper River. Tradition has it that the Tlingit originally migrated north to Alaska from the Skeena River, while other tribes moved from the interior to the coast following the Stikine River.

The Haida inhabited the Queen Charlotte Islands and the southern part of Alaska's Prince of Wales Island. They spoke a language also believed to be related to Athapaskan. Tradition has it that the Alaska Haida, moving north, had driven out some of the Tlingit tribes some 200 years before European contact occurred.

Finally there were the Tsimshian, divided into three major subdivisions, each speaking a slightly different dialect. They lived on the mainland and the islands south of southeastern Alaska. Those tribes wintering in villages along Metlakatla Pass near the modern town of Prince Rupert shifted their quarters to Fort Simpson, which was built by the Hudson's Bay Company in 1834. In 1887 a large group primarily from Fort Simpson, led by the energetic Anglican missionary William Duncan, moved to Annette Island in Alaska after some church-related disagreements.

The Tlingit, Haida, and Tsimshian all shared certain physical characteristics. They averaged 5 feet 8 inches in height, were stocky with broad, muscular chests and shoulders; they usually had broad foreheads and faces and light skin color; their hair was very dark brown and coarse. All three groups had adapted themselves extremely well to coastal life. They used fish traps, nets, and dip nets for fishing; and they used harpoons with detachable heads connected to the shaft by a short line, which also served for sea mammal hunting. They also used hooks for angling, particularly for cod and halibut. All three groups constructed fine canoes of various sizes for different purposes. For land hunting the bow and arrow was standard equipment, but snares and deadfalls were used as well.

The Indians used wood as a primary material for most of their manufactures, which were distinguished by fine workmanship and elaborately carved and painted decorations. The cutting blades of their tools were made from stone and shell, while the tough, hard, bright-green nephrite stones were used for adze blades. They built large rectangular gable-roof houses, occupied by several families, in which the individual timbers were carefully joined together.

Tlingit dwelling,
Ketchikan
(*Woods Collection, Archives,
University of Alaska, Fairbanks*)

The matrilineal type of organization—where descent is traced exclusively through the maternal line—was the social framework among the Tlingit, Haida, and Tsimshian. The Tlingit and Haida tribes each had two major moieties (subdivisions), and each individual had to marry a person of the opposite moiety. The moieties in some tribes, such as the Tlingit, were composed of clans—smaller unilateral social divisions, whose members traced their relationship from a legendary common ancestor.

All these matrilineal societies, however, were built up around lineages consisting of a nucleus of males related through females. They were composed of a group of brothers and some maternal cousins, their sisters' sons, and the sons of the sisters of the second generation. This social unit usually was politically independent; it claimed fishing, hunting, and berrying grounds; it had its own houses and chiefs; and it operated socially—and usually ceremonially as well—as an independent unit. It also had its own crest, personal names, and songs and dances for entire ceremonial occasions.

These matrilineal societies also separated individuals into a series of higher or lower statuses, such as the chiefs, nobles, commoners, and slaves. It was a flexible system, however, because there was a good deal of mobility between levels. Warfare was a well-established practice aimed at driving out or even exterminating another lineage, or family, in order to acquire its lands and material possessions.

Religious belief played an important part in everyday life. The fundamental principles that characterized these religions included a value notion of a disinterested supreme being or beings; the immortality of certain economically important animals together with ritual practices designed to ensure the return of these creatures; and the possibility of lifelong assistance from a personal

Sitka dancers at
Klukwan potlatch
*(Historical Photograph
Collection, Archives,
University of Alaska, Fairbanks)*

guardian spirit. But the religions lacked systematization of beliefs in creation, cosmology, and deities.

The elaborately carved "totem poles," actually comparable to crests, have become famous. There were several varieties of totems, with varying functions. Memorial poles usually were erected by the heir of a deceased chief as part of the process of assuming his predecessor's titles and prerogatives. Mortuary poles and house-portal poles were other varieties. All consisted of symbols that belonged to a particular lineage or family and referred to events in its past.[13]

The Athapaskans

While the coastal Indians enjoyed nature's bounty, the Athapaskan Indians occupied the difficult and demanding expanse of arctic and subarctic lands stretching across the northern edge of the American continent. This vast area, greatly varied in topography, is not richly endowed with sustenance for life, and humans had to search for the particular resources on which to survive.

The northern Athapaskans inhabited the drainages of the Yukon River just short of where it empties into the Bering Sea and those parts of northern Canada drained by the Mackenzie River. Mountainous and for the most part covered by northern coniferous forests, this huge area has great environmental contrasts and many natural barriers between groups. Long, cold winters and short, warm summers characterize the region. The archaeological evidence seems to show that the ancestral Indians had crossed the Bering Sea Land Bridge into Alaska by 10,000 B.C., near the end of the last great glacial period. With deglaciation these people moved east and south through the Yukon Territory and interior British Columbia and on into the present state of Washington.

Though the area occupied by the ancestral Athapaskans initially consisted of treeless tundra, by 8000 to 6000 B.C. most of central Alaska was covered with spruce forests. The faunal population of this area included moose, caribou, black and grizzly bears, sheep, and a variety of small game and fish.

Unlike the coastal Indians, the Athapaskans had no tribal organizations and only a limited tribal consciousness. Anthropologists, therefore, have described northern Athapaskan culture as continuous, carried on by a series of interlocking groups whose lifestyles differed in only minor details from those of their immediate neighbors.

Athapaskans were exclusively hunters and gatherers who exhibited considerable flexibility in their response to conditions within their environment and to cultural impulses from neighboring peoples. Hunting occupied much of their time. Caribou, abundant at certain times of the year, were driven between two long, converging rows of wooden sticks that led to a large enclosure of branches where the hunters had set up snares of semitanned moose or caribou hide. Once caught, the animals were easily killed with bow and arrows. They also employed water drives, and once the animals had been driven into a lake or stream they were quickly killed with lances or stabbed with knives. The larger moose were tracked down and shot or sometimes caught in deadfall traps.

Athapaskan fishwheel,
Copper River
*(Heath Ives Collection,
Archives, University of Alaska,
Fairbanks)*

Bears, wolverine, and smaller fur-bearing animals were also caught in dead-falls, shot with bow and arrow, or captured in rawhide nets. Snares sufficed for hares and ptarmigans (grouse).

Depending on the area, the Athapaskans fished for salmon with dip nets and basket-shaped traps; they also caught a variety of other fish, such as trout, whitefish, and pike, employing a variety of fishing methods. Ptarmigan and spruce hens, ducks and geese, and roots and berries supplemented their diet. Periods of starvation, however, were not uncommon.

During the aboriginal period, all winter hunting was done on foot, since dogs were not yet used for pulling sledges or toboggans. Snowshoes were important, therefore, and many northern Athapaskans made two types. The hunting snowshoes were long and rounded in front for walking over fresh snow, while the travel snowshoes were shorter with a pointed and sharply upturned front end.

The Tanaina Indians in the Cook Inlet–Susitna River basin were the only Athapaskans to live on the seacoast. Influenced by their Eskimo neighbors, they became skillful sea mammal hunters, borrowing the necessary material culture traits required for coastal life.

The more mobile a particular group, the simpler its dwellings, while sedentary groups employed more complex forms of construction. The shelter reflected the subsistence activities characteristic not only of particular times of the year but also of climatic variations. Generally, they built log or pole houses of various sizes covered with animal hides. There were many differences among the dwellings constructed, but all used the same basic materials. The more sedentary groups, such as the Ingalik in the Yukon and Kuskokwim basins, occupied permanent winter villages and summer fish camps. Living near Eskimos, their winter houses closely resembled the semisubterranean, earth-covered Eskimo houses of southwestern Alaska.

Most aboriginal northern Athapaskans spent at least part of the year in small groups consisting of a few nuclear families. If resources permitted, small groups came together and combined into a regional band, such as for caribou hunting. And although adult males made decisions together, leaders often emerged who attained prestige and influence by demonstrating their superior abilities, particularly as hunters. The northern Athapaskans knew both offen-

Athapaskan woman and child
(*Eva Alvey Richards Collection, Archives, University of Alaska, Fairbanks*)

sive and defensive warfare, often producing a war leader who demonstrated great physical strength. Generally, then, leadership was not hereditary but acquired, and once a leader lost his special abilities he ceased to exert any influence.

As among all other Alaskan groups, the nuclear family constituted the basic unit of social organization. Furthermore, Athapaskan extended kinship was characterized by the matrilineal sib organization. These sibs were held together by reciprocal social obligations. And a member generally had to find a mate outside his own sib.

Among many Athapaskans the potlatch—a ceremony in honor of the dead—constituted an important feature of social organization. Not only did the ceremony aid in assuaging grief, but it was also one of the chief means by which prestige was attained.

The Athapaskan belief in reincarnation in animal form blurred the distinction between animals and humans, and it pointed out the importance of placating animal spirits to enable people to continue using the natural environment. Northern Athapaskan religion also emphasized individual rather than community rites, because the survival of hunters depended largely on individual skills. Their mythology was quite complex and provided answers for most of the questions concerning the origin of the world and man. In addition, they lived in a many-spirited world which they believed influenced every aspect of their lives and destinies. Shamans—the individuals in the culture with the greatest personal power—were the only religious practitioners. They used certain magical-religious rites to control the spirit world, prevent and cure disease, bring game to hunters, predict the weather, and foretell the future.

As with other Native Americans, many of the early beliefs and practices that characterized the life cycle of the northern Athapaskan Indians either are no longer carried out or have changed greatly.[14]

The Aleuts

Like other native groups, the Aleuts adapted themselves superbly to life in the harsh terrestrial and marine environment of the Aleutian Islands. They developed a rich culture and secured a well-balanced livelihood from the rich fauna of the sea. But neither their culture nor livelihood long survived the first European contact with the Russians in the 1740s.

An Eskimoid people, the ancestors of the Aleuts settled on the fog-shrouded and windswept islands thousands of years ago. For roughly 1,000 miles the Aleutian Islands stretch from the Alaska Peninsula in a long, bow-shaped chain of some seventy treeless islands, excluding the numerous islets. The American anthropologist Waldemar Jochelson described the islands well in 1928: "All of the islands are of volcanic origin, and are covered with high mountains, among which are both active and extinct volcanoes. The shore line is irregular, the rocky mountains sloping abruptly to the sea. The bays are shallow, full of reefs, and dangerous for navigation. The vegetation is luxurious though limited to grasses, berry-bearing shrubs, creeping [plants], and varieties of low willows." Alpine mosses and lichens cover the mountain slopes, while "in the narrow valleys between the mountain ridges and on the low isthmuses with insufficient drainage are fresh-water lakes with hummocky shores.... The absence of arboreal vegetation is due not to climate, which is comparatively mild, but to the constant gales, and to the fogs and mists that are encountered in Aleutian waters, and that deprive the plants of much sunlight." The Aleutian weather is the result of the meeting of the cold waters from the Bering Sea on the north side and the warm Japan Current on the south. "There are only two seasons: a long autumn and a short, mild winter. Both the incessant winds and gales cause the slightest cold to be felt and, in summer particularly, the constant fogs hide the sun."[15] On the eastern Bering Sea side lies the relatively shallow continental shelf, while the extremely deep Aleutian trench under the Pacific parallels the islands.

Various estimates have been given of the aboriginal population, and they vary anywhere from 15,000 to 30,000. Although these numbers seem high, no exact demographic information exists, and the estimates have to be accepted. In any event, smallpox, measles, tuberculosis, venereal diseases, and pneumonia—as well as Russian guns—drastically reduced the Native population to 2,247 in 1834 and to about 1,400 in 1848. In 1848 a smallpox epidemic struck, further reducing the number of Aleuts to approximately 900. By 1864 intermarriage had increased the population once again to 2,005; but the census in 1890 indicated a decline to 1,702 persons, 968 of whom were Aleuts and 734 of mixed blood.[16] Margaret Lantis, an American anthropologist, has concluded that at least 80 percent of the Aleut population was lost in the first two generations of Russian-Aleutian contact. "A few were taken to southeast Alaska and California; most, however, were not merely lost to their homeland, they were totally lost."[17]

The many explorers who visited the Aleutians have provided an adequate

Inhabitants of Unalaska
(Historical Photograph
Collection, Archives,
University of Alaska, Fairbanks)

picture of Aleut home life but little of the social structure. According to these observers, the typical Aleut house was large and built underground, containing several related nuclear families. Villages were composed of related individuals. Large villages might have as many as seven such dwellings, although evidently only a few houses were occupied at any one time. These were the permanent settlements, usually located on the northern, Bering Sea side of the island because of more abundant fish resources and a larger supply of driftwood. The Aleuts also built seasonal dwellings, and they bathed in the sea to harden themselves against the climate.

Households usually included a man and his wife or wives, older married sons and their families, and sometimes a younger brother and his family. The adolescent sons of the household head were sent to their mother's village to be raised by her elder brother(s). Although anthropologists have been unable to determine the Aleuts' rule of descent, many assume matrilineal descent.

Aleuts generally were permissive regarding sexual relations and marriage, but incest was well defined and prohibited.

At death, the body of a highly honored person was often mummified, and occasionally slaves were killed to show the grief of the principal survivor. Aleut society, according to its eighteenth- and early nineteenth-century observers, was divided into three classes: the honorables, common people, and slaves. Despite the information available, however, the cultural and historical place of the Aleuts among the peoples of their region is still pretty much a mystery. Margaret Lantis concludes that "comparison of Aleut cultures and those cultures both east and west" will find that "over a generalized Yuit base there is an overlay of Pacific Eskimo and, through it, Tlingit culture in such things as wealth and status. . . ." There may also be cultural links with various Siberian groups.[18]

It is clear that Aleuts, over thousands of years, developed a functional society that enabled them to wrest a very adequate living from their difficult environment. The aboriginal culture disappeared very quickly under Russian oppression. However, individuals, as well as parts of the old culture, survived; and with the help of the Russian Orthodox church the Aleuts began to develop a new culture.

The Eskimos

Much has been written about the Eskimos, particularly the Greenlandic and Canadian Eskimos, because of their adaptations to a far-north arctic environment. But Alaskan Eskimos did not face the same rigors. Instead, they inhabited a great diversity of environments that do not fit the popular conception of a bleak, dark, and snow-driven landscape forcing people to live in snow houses (igloos) and eat blubber.

Many experts today agree that the Arctic-Mongoloid peoples first arrived in the Bering Sea area from 15,000 to 10,000 years ago. They were the progenitors of the Eskimos and Aleuts as well as various Paleo-Siberian groups.[19] Eskimo culture developed in western Alaska, and it was also in Alaska that the division into Eskimo and Aleut stocks occurred. In time, the Eskimos developed

Eskimo family, Cape
Prince of Wales,
ca. 1910
(*Lomen Collection, Archives,
University of Alaska, Fairbanks*)

techniques that allowed them to exploit the arctic seas. The so-called Arctic small-tool tradition represents the technological base for Eskimo culture. Reaching back to Siberia, it crystallized in Alaska and eventually spread across the Arctic from Alaska to Greenland.

The small-tool tradition, however, did not penetrate the Pacific drainages. When it eventually reached Bristol Bay it had been considerably modified. The tradition was extremely flexible and allowed its bearers to hunt on land or sea. In time, various distinct subcultural forms developed in the coastal zone from the Arctic small-tool tradition. In the north, for example, whale hunting evolved, and economic systems based on salmon fishing developed along Bristol Bay, while the small inland groups became caribou hunters.[20]

The Eskimo language stock eventually separated to form the Inupiaq and Yupik languages during the first Christian millennium. The latter subdivided again into Sugpiaq Aleut and Central and Siberian Yupik.[21] Throughout prehistoric times there were many population shifts within the area. For example, Eskimos were extending their control inland along rivers flowing into the Bering Sea and the western Arctic Ocean, and, in the process, acculturated and assimilated other Indians. On the southern fringe, however, the Aleuts successfully encroached upon the peninsular Eskimos from the west.

Eskimo social life centered around the nuclear family as the primary unit. But in a culture with an overwhelming emphasis on subsistence activities, men were obligated not only to their households and kindred but also to voluntary associations such as organized whale-hunting crews. Among the Yupik, the ceremonial house for men was very important in the individual lives of all males. Consequently, these so-called *kashgees* were patricentric, while the households were matricentric. Most marriages took place within the community. Adult males taught traditional skills to the boys in the *kashgee*, while mothers taught their daughters in the home.

Physical survival depended on the hunters' ability to take game and fish. These animals, therefore, occupied an important place in tribal religions, and Eskimo supernaturalism was based, to a great extent, on charms that aided individuals. More complex, but still individually based, were the family charms passed down a patrilineal line among some groups, or the knowledge required among Pacific Eskimos before hunting the whales. There were also many taboos, such as the prohibition against combining land and sea products. The Bering Sea Eskimos, the oldest group, had developed an intense involvement with the species taken. The so-called bladder feast, for example, was the most complex of the various cults and focused primarily on the seals. The arctic hunters and fishermen, on the other hand, did not develop rituals as complex as those of the Bering Sea peoples or the whalers. In short, Eskimos shared many traits that were found among other peoples. The term ''Eskimo,'' therefore, stands for much subcultural diversity. Like other aboriginal inhabitants of Alaska, they evolved ingenious and highly flexible techniques and lifestyles which enabled them to live in a rugged arctic and subarctic environment.

Little is known about the early migrants who traveled eastward across the Bering Sea Land Bridge from Asia between 10,000 and 40,000 years ago or more. Evidence of human occupation in Alaska is not as ancient as elsewhere on the American continent and dates back to about 11,000 years ago. More than 2,700 archaeological sites have been identified in Alaska, but the age of only a few of them has been determined because of the high cost involved in field work and analysis.

What is clear is that Alaska's Eskimos, Indians, and Aleuts developed widely varying lifestyles that were superbly adapted to their respective envi-

Eskimo hunters in Umiak, ca. 1908
(Lusk Album, Archives, University of Alaska, Fairbanks)

ronments. Living in harmony with the land and seas, they flourished until they encountered the industrial and technological culture of the Caucasians. A long decline ensued, and today only fragments of their once rich cultures remain.

·2·
The Russian Period

The Discovery of Alaska

ALASKA appeared on the world scene rather late. Vitus Bering, a Danish sea captain in the Russian navy, discovered Alaska in 1741. For the next 126 years, Russian influence was felt in varying degrees. But at no time was there ever more than a fraction of the native population or the land under Russian control. Those Russians who came were mainly private individuals interested in the fur trade, and few settled permanently. They, more than the Russian government, which was frequently plagued by instability, gave Russian America its unique character.

Bering's voyage was the culmination of a great Russian eastward expansion. With little government assistance, Russian fur hunters, the *promyshlenniki*, had gradually penetrated Siberia and brought a massive territory under control. Since Russia had been the first European state to establish itself on the Pacific, it is not surprising that its crews and not those of the more advanced powers—England or France—were the first to come to Alaska. At the time of Bering's historic expedition Russia was still feeling the effects of changes initiated by Bering's original sponsor, Peter the Great.

When Peter and his brother, Ivan V, came to the throne of Russia in 1682, Europeans scorned Russia as a backwater of civilization inhabited by a people more Asiatic than European, a people for whom human life had little value. Prejudice aside, the country was retarded politically, economically, and socially. Its ruler was absolute, the administration and system of justice was haphazard and chaotic, and the armed forces not much better than an undisciplined horde. Over half the population was in a state of bondage, in contrast to the West where serfdom had almost died out. Travelers to Russia brought back tales of gross ignorance, immorality, and drunkenness among the people. That Russia was different from the West was generally acknowledged and has several explanations. Russia had not experienced the Renaissance or the Reformation. Her heritage was Byzantine, not Roman; civilization and Christianity had been brought into the country from Constantinople. The Tartar invasion and conquest had shut Russia off from the West for two centuries and had stunted her development.

Yet even before Peter the Great, Russia had come under Western influence. Peter's interest in the West had been stimulated through contact with foreigners in what the Russians called the German quarter of Moscow, since to them all foreigners were Germans. From them he learned that Europeans looked upon Russia as inferior in its development and that Russians were regarded almost as barbarians. After assuming personal rule Peter traveled to the West to see for himself. His journeys took him to England, Holland, Prussia, and the Hapsburg empire. Much impressed, Peter was convinced that Russia must modernize and that change was essential if she were to survive as an independent state, let alone become a great power.

Throughout his reign Peter kept Russia in a state of turmoil. With the exception of a single year, from 1719 to 1720, the country was always at war. In his haste to reform Russia, Peter had resorted to a number of what today are called "crash programs." These were frequently in conflict with each other. Although his personal inclinations were not directed toward cultural affairs, he nevertheless became a patron of the arts and literature because he believed that Russians had to first learn to think and act like Westerners before they could succeed in mastering the superior political, technological, and military skills of the West. He ordered the people to wear Western clothing even though the indigenous long coats were better suited to provide protection against the severe Russian winters than were the shorter ones used in milder climates. Westerners were brought in not only to train Russian soldiers but to teach etiquette and table manners to the nobility.

Peter did not care a bit if his edicts violated the most sacred of Russian traditions and beliefs. He abolished the office of patriarch and placed the Orthodox Church under control of a civil official. Russian men were told they must shave, though to the devout this was tantamount to committing sacrilege: all their icons showed the deity wearing a beard. Peter's role and influence in Russia has aroused bitter controversy. To his admirers he is the founder of modern Russia and the builder of Russian greatness. His critics point out that his reforms were not well planned, that they bore most heavily upon the poor, and that Russia was more divided than ever by the end of his reign.

Peter's scientific interests set the stage for the Bering voyage. He had brought together at his new capital, St. Petersburg, the symbol of the new Russia, a nucleus of scholars to form the Academy of Sciences. From them he learned that the North Pacific which touched upon his realm was the least-known area of the world. He readily accepted the suggestion that he outfit an expedition to determine the relationship of America to Asia, to see whether they were separated from each other or joined together. Peter, who was not unaware of the prestige that would come to himself and his regime following the successful completion of such an enterprise, gave the order to Bering to go to Kamchatka, and there or in some other place to build one or two ships and sail north until he found the American coast. In characteristic fashion the tsar did not mention how this was to be done or the obstacles involved. He died soon after, in January of 1725. But his widow and successor, Catherine I, gave her blessings and support to her husband's project.

Kamchatka, the great Siberian peninsula on the Pacific, had been discovered only recently—in 1697—and was largely unexplored. To reach Kamchatka the men had to travel across Siberia to Okhotsk, and from there across the Sea of Okhotsk. Okhotsk, their immediate goal, was a mere hamlet five thousand miles from St. Petersburg. Neither this village nor any place in Siberia had facilities for shipbuilding. Bering had to bring with him the skilled workers, equipment, and supplies for the job. They were literally trailblazers, driving their horses over existing roads, building others as needed. In winter, dog sleds provided the main source of transportation. Wherever it was possible, waterways were used, with the men making their own boats. More than a year elapsed before the men, who had been divided into three groups and who endured great hardships on the journey, finally arrived at Okhotsk. There they set to work to build a craft that would carry them across the sea to Bolsheretsk, a tiny port on the west coast of Kamchatka. Kamchadals, as the natives of Kamchatka were called, were pressed into service to carry the supplies and equipment 500 miles to a site on the Pacific near the mouth of the Kamchatka River. There their sailing vessel, the *Gabriel*, was built to take them on their Pacific voyage.

Bering's Two Expeditions

In July 1728 the *Gabriel* started on its northward course, staying close to the shore. After sighting St. Lawrence Island, the ship passed through the strait which now bears Bering's name, but because of the dense fog the ex-

Kamchatka Village, Siberia, 1898
(Samuel Call Collection, Archives, University of Alaska, Fairbanks)

plorers could not see the American coastline. After reaching a latitude of 67° 18'N, Bering decided to turn back, fearing that the ship would be trapped by ice if it advanced further. They had already passed the point where the Asiatic coast could be seen disappearing from view to the west, while to the east there was not a glimpse of land. Bering concluded from these observations that America and Asia were not joined. On the return voyage, poor weather conditions in the strait again limited visibility and prevented confirmation of Bering's observations. On September 2 they were back in Kamchatka. The following spring the *Gabriel* was blown off course during another attempt to reach the coast of North America. On June 8, 1729, Bering turned back, rounded Kamchatka, and sailed to Okhotsk.

When Bering returned to St. Petersburg on March 1, 1730, he did not receive a hero's welcome. His expeditions were termed a failure, and his conclusions became the subject of derision. Had anyone really seen that America and Asia were not joined? it was asked. Conditions in Russia at the time did not appear at all conducive to government support for further exploration. For the third time in five years a new ruler was on the throne of Russia, now the Empress Anna, daughter of Ivan V. Her position was precarious: as the widow of the German duke of Courland she was accused of being partial to foreigners and was forced by the nobility to accept severe limitations on her authority. Within two years, however, after her position became more secure, she was persuaded by some of the German scientists in her entourage to give support to the advancement of knowledge.

Bering was called upon in 1732 to head a very large expedition that would coordinate the activities of scientists, explorers, and government officials engaged in work with a wide range of objectives. One group was to explore and map the Arctic coast; another, under the leadership of the scientists Gerhard Muller and Johann Gore, was to undertake a thorough reconnaissance of Siberia, studying its plant and animal life as well as the customs, language, and folklore of the people. Martin Spanberg was directed to sail to Japan and there to establish trade relations. Bering's special assignment was to explore the American coast.

Almost a year was spent in assembling the men and securing the necessary supplies; several more years were to elapse before the various groups could get underway. Bering had to devote almost his entire attention to housing and feeding his men and their camp followers, soothing ruffled feelings, and mediating quarrels. The costs of the expedition had been grossly underestimated. Each request for additional funds brought angry retorts that money was being squandered recklessly with no visible results. Finally, after Spanberg's departure for Japan, Bering and his men were able to leave for Ohkotsk in 1737 to begin the work of building oceangoing vessels. This was completed in the summer of 1740. After wintering in Kamchatka at Avacha Bay, the two ships and their crews, including several scientists, headed out into the Pacific in June 1741. Bering himself commanded the *St. Peter,* and Aleksei Chirikov commanded the *St. Paul.* On June 20 the two vessels became separated despite the efforts of their captains to remain in contact with each other.

The honor of the discovery of Alaska properly belongs to Chirikov and his men, who sighted land on the 15th of July at what is believed to be Prince of Wales Island of the Alexander Archipelago. Bering's ship, which had sailed in a more northerly direction, came upon Kayak Island the next day. Because his crew was suffering greatly from scurvy, Chirikov sent one of his two small boats ashore to procure water in an effort to bring some relief to his men. When the crew did not return, the remaining small boat was sent in search of it; that boat also disappeared. After waiting several days in the hope that his men would return, Chirikov reluctantly gave the command to return to Kamchatka, which they finally reached on October 8.

Meanwhile, the surgeon on board the *St. Peter*, Georg Wilhelm Steller, persuaded Bering to allow him to go ashore on Kayak Island to look for antiscorbutic plants to help alleviate the misery of his men, who were also suffering from scurvy. A noted German scientist, Steller was able to gather some native artifacts and a number of specimens of plants, and to capture a few birds. After a few hours Bering, a nonscientist who looked upon such activities as time-consuming, ordered him to return immediately to the ship or be left behind. Before the harbor at Avacha Bay could be reached, the *St. Peter* was wrecked on one of the Commander Islands, which today bears Bering's name. There he and several of his men died and were buried. In the spring of 1742, survivors of the original crew of seventy-five built a ship out of the wreckage of the *St. Peter* and made their way back to Kamchatka.

When the survivors of the *St. Peter* and the *St. Paul* drifted back to St. Petersburg in the next few years they found a new ruler on the throne of Russia. Elizabeth, the daughter of Peter the Great, had become empress as a result of a palace revolution. She did much to make St. Petersburg a modern city, but unlike her father she tended to be indolent and much less concerned with matters of state than with her personal appearance (she was said to possess 15,000 dresses). Neither she nor her advisors were interested in the American discoveries. They regarded Russia as primarily a European state whose energies were to be concentrated upon the power struggle on the continent. Since the country had a small population and possessed the vast and even less populated territory of Siberia, overseas colonies were hardly necessary. Except for issuing a directive that the natives pay a tax called the *yasak*, and that they be well treated, Elizabeth's government ignored Alaska.

After Bering's second expedition the Russian government gave virtually no support to enterprises concerning Alaska. Those Russians who came were private individuals lured there by the fur trade. When Bering's survivors returned to Russia they brought with them pelts of a number of animals, notably the sea otter, one of the finest of fur-bearing animals. A ready market for their skins developed, particularly in China. Russian fur merchants sent ships to the Aleutian Islands to procure the animals. These islands are almost treeless and have a mild climate with an average rainfall of 100 inches a year. Their inhabitants, the Aleuts, a people closely akin to the Eskimos, lived in underground dwellings and were among the most skilled hunters of the sea. When the *promyshlenniki* (Russian fur hunters) came, they quickly made themselves masters of the islands. A rough, hard-drinking, mostly illiterate lot, they became almost a law to themselves and made virtual slaves of the Aleuts,

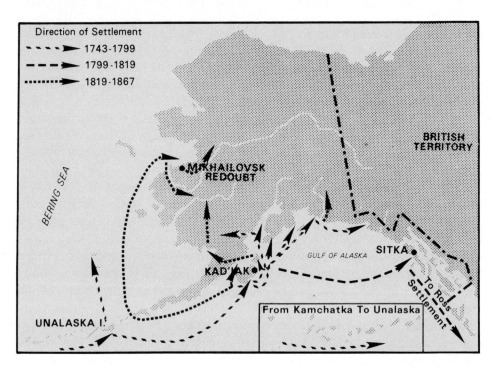

Routes and times of
settlement of Alaska by
the Russians
*(from Svetlana G. Fedorova, The
Russian Population in Alaska and
California, © 1973 by
Richard A. Pierce)*

forcing the men to do the hunting while they dallied with the women. On
several occasions the Aleuts attempted to revolt; the greatest fighting took
place on Umnak and Unalaska islands in the years from 1762 to 1766. After the
entire crew of a vessel commanded by Denis Medvedev was killed, their deaths
were avenged by Ivan Soloviev, a Russian mariner. According to Father Ioann
Veniaminov's account, Soloviev bound together a dozen Aleut youths and fired
a carbine or rifle into the group. It is said that the bullet lodged in the ninth
man. After that the Aleutians were at peace.

International Rivalries in the North

Russian penetration of the Aleutians roughly followed a pattern of exploiting one group of islands of the chain until the fur supply became exhausted and
then moving eastward to the next, eventually reaching the mainland. As the
distance from Kamchatka increased, the cost of the operations went up correspondingly, making it more difficult for smaller companies to survive. By 1770
a few merchants—Gregory Shelikhov, Lebedev-Lastochkin, and the Panov
brothers—dominated the Aleutian fur trade.

These changes in the nature of business enterprise were accompanied by
increasing government awareness of the area. Elizabeth had died on Christmas
day of 1762. She was succeeded by her nephew, Peter III, whose reign was
brief. Within a year of his accession, his wife Catherine, a member of a
German noble family, succeeded in engineering his overthrow and gaining
acceptance as ruler. Far more enterprising than Elizabeth, Catherine was well
steeped in the writings of the Enlightenment and corresponded with some of its
leaders—Voltaire, Diderot, and d'Alembert. She devoted much of her time to
government business and proclaimed her intention to be an enlightened ruler.

She issued directives demanding better care and treatment of the Aleuts, and terminated the *yasak,* the tax of furs which the natives had never understood. Nothing was done, however, to enforce her decrees. She sent several exploring parties to America, but two of these never came near Alaska, while the third merely went into previously visited regions.

Russian movements in the north did not pass unnoticed. Fear of Russian expansion southward brought about a resurgence of Spanish activity in the Pacific. Charles III, the reigning monarch of Spain, commissioned José de Galvez to begin the colonization of California. He founded San Diego and San Francisco. Several expeditions were sent north by the viceroy of Mexico in 1774, 1777, 1778, and again in 1790 to take possession of Alaska for Spain. Except for making some claims and leaving a few markers, there were no serious attempts at occupation of the territory. Spain's power had been declining for more than a century. In a controversy that developed with England at Nootka Sound near Vancouver Island, Spain gave way. Aside from a few names that have been given to places and waters in Alaska—Bucareli, Valdez, Cordova, Revillagigedo, and Malaspina—Spain left no trace.

After the Spaniards came the English, French, and Americans, none of whom expressed territorial ambitions. Captain James Cook, one of England's greatest navigators, came north in 1776 intent on finding a passage from the Pacific to the Atlantic. His mapping of the Alaska coast became the standard guide for over a century, and it was he who proved that America and Asia were not joined. Like the Spaniards, the British contributed to the naming of places in Alaska: Cook Inlet, Prince William Sound, and Cape Prince of Wales, among others. Although Cook was killed in the Hawaiian Islands after leaving Alaska, his men, under the leadership of Captain Charles Clerke, continued on to Canton. There they sold at fabulous prices the sea otter pelts they had obtained from the natives. From then on, British fur traders were active in Alaska despite the efforts of the Russians to keep them out. The French sent only one expedition, that under the ill-fated Jean La Perouse, who perished on the way home. French energies were directed elsewhere after the outbreak of the great revolution in 1789. Americans, who were to rival the British in the competition for the Alaska fur trade, made their initial voyage in 1789.

The increasing foreign competition was a cause of concern to the Russian companies. They especially feared the British, who could offer the natives better and cheaper goods than they. As a means of restricting their movements, the Siberian fur merchant Gregory Shelikhov and his partner Ivan Golikov established on Kodiak Island the first permanent Russian settlement. Shortly thereafter, Shelikhov appealed to the empress to be given a monopoly of the fur trade, arguing that only a single powerful Russian company could resist the inroads of the British and the Americans. Catherine was not convinced. She saw little value in the American colonies and feared that a single strong company such as Shelikhov desired, intent on combating the foreigners, would bring Russia excessive involvement in Pacific affairs. She explained in a letter to him that she was philosophically opposed to monopolies. She was not impressed by his assertion that his primary concern was in converting the natives to Christianity and thus bringing prestige to the Russian Empire. She did give

Gregory Shelikhov
*(Historical Photograph
Collection, Archives,
University of Alaska, Fairbanks)*

him a medal, but neither the money nor the monopoly he desired.

By 1790 the initial phase of the Russian era was coming to an end in Alaska. The era of unrestricted private enterprise was ending, and Russian activities were increasingly more organized and widespread. The Aleutians had been conquered but were no longer the center of the Russian efforts. A permanent settlement had been made at Kodiak, the Pribilofs had been discovered, and a few posts had been established on the mainland. Where there had once been many companies, now there were but a few. And somewhat unwillingly the Russian government was concerning itself more with Alaskan affairs.

The Baranov Era and the Founding of the Russian-American Company

By 1786 Gregory Shelikhov could point with pride to his accomplishments in America. He had become the leading fur merchant in America, holding shares in the rival Lebedev-Lastochkin Company as well as the controlling interest in his own organization. A poet's allusion to him as a Russian Columbus has something of a hollow sound since he was no seaman and not much of an explorer; but with the settlement of Kodiak the Russian occupation of America had taken on an air of permanency. When he came to Kodiak in 1784 he had brought with him a party of 192 men and his wife Natalie, the first white woman to come to Alaska. Their settlement on the northeast end of the island at Three Saints Bay was for a time left undisturbed, but as the Kodiak islanders—an Eskimo people more warlike than the Aleuts—became increasingly apprehensive of the objectives of the newcomers, they decided to attack. Upon being informed, Shelikhov struck the first blow: he ordered a bombardment of the rock where the hostile natives had gathered and frightened them into submission. In May of 1786, Shelikhov left a pacified Kodiak, entrusting the management of the enterprise first to Konstantin Samoilof, then to the Greek Eystrate Delarov, before finally finding the man he wanted, Aleksandr Baranov.

Baranov's Arrival in America

Baranov was the outstanding personality of Russian America. His long tenure, first as manager of the Shelikhov enterprises and later as head of the Russian-American Company, has been fittingly called the "Baranov era." He had little formal education and was neither by training or inclination an administrator. He had no ambition to be an explorer or a colonizer, though he did a little of both. He was first and foremost a businessman whose main objective was to make a profit for his employer.

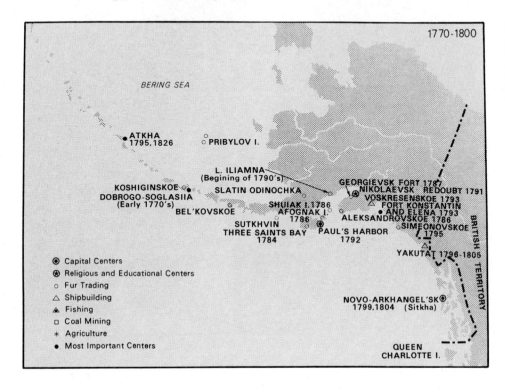

Russian settlements in Alaska and their economic functions, 1770-1800 *(from Svetlana G. Fedorova, The Russian Population in Alaska and California,* © *1973 by Richard A. Pierce)*

A Siberian fur merchant, Baranov had been invited several times by Shelikhov to manage his affairs in America, but each time he found reasons why he could not come. Only in 1790, after he had suffered serious financial reverses, did he agree to accept the post in America. He left behind in Russia a wife and daughter whom he never saw again. Enroute to America he became ill, and was later shipwrecked on Unalaska, an island of the Aleutian chain, before finally arriving in Kodiak in 1791.

Russian America was at that time very vaguely defined. The settlements were scattered and isolated one from another. Kodiak, the largest, was an unprepossessing village. Its owner Shelikhov had not yet achieved the position of undisputed supremacy in America which he coveted. The Lebedev-Lastochkin Company had agents on Cook Inlet and controlled the Pribilof Islands, with their valuable seal rookeries, while other Russians were operating

Aleksandr Baranov
(Historical Photograph Collection, Archives, University of Alaska, Fairbanks)

in the Aleutians. Disputes were frequent, and with no existing government agency to resolve controversies, they often ended in violence. On one thing all Russians were in agreement: foreign competition had to be curtailed. Not only did the Americans and the British have better and cheaper goods to sell to the natives in exchange for furs, but they were not burdened with the expense of maintaining costly settlements. And far worse, they sold arms to the natives, which the Russian residents feared would be used against themselves.

Not long after his arrival, a tidal wave destroyed the colony. Rather than rebuild, the new manager recognized the desirability of removing the principal settlement of the company from Three Saints Bay to Pavlovsk harbor, on the north side of Kodiak Island. The reasons lay partly in the better harbor and also in the abundance of forests at the latter place, facilitating the construction of the necessary buildings and fortifications.[1] Baranov soon found that he was very much on his own and could not depend on Shelikhov for aid. Supply was always a problem; the colony imported almost all of its finished goods and much of its food. Not only did Russia produce little in this respect, but Russian ships coming to America were few and far between.

Baranov, always resourceful, violated orders against doing business with foreigners and began trading with American and English sea captains who furnished him with the goods he needed in exchange for furs. He made friends with James Shields, an English naval officer experienced in shipbuilding, and engaged him to construct a vessel. Most of the work was done at Resurrection Bay, where the quality of timber was better. Since many necessary materials were unavailable in America, substitutions—not always of the highest quality—were made. When it was finished the ship was christened the *Phoenix*. It was used in American waters and made two voyages to Siberia; but its chief value may have been symbolic, a demonstration of what the colony could accomplish.

Labor was a key problem in Russian America. With more than half the Russian population in bondage, few were eligible to emigrate. Most of those who came to America were illiterate, a few were convicts who had been promised freedom, and more than one worker crossed the sea under compulsion. Agents of the company frequented the taverns of Okhotsk; men who had too much to drink might awake the next morning bound for the New World.

Life in America had its drawbacks. The men's quarters were rudimentary, and their diet was mainly dried fish, supplemented by garden vegetables in summer and occasionally fresh meat when the hunters were lucky. Tea and sugar were luxuries dependent on the arrival of ships. Each worker signed a contract for seven years and was given a share of the company's stock, with his income depending on the profits realized. The cost of living was high. At the end of the year, when accounts were settled, many of the *promyshlenniki* discovered that they had spent more than they had earned. Those still in debt when their seven-year contracts had expired had no alternative but to sign up for another seven years.

Almost as soon as he stepped off the boat, Baranov sensed that he was very much on trial. His predecessor Delarov had left him a complement of fifty men, and they were rough by any standard. Any weakness on his part could prove

Kodiak, with Russian blockhouse built under the direction of Aleksandr Baranov
(*Historical Photograph Collection, Archives, University of Alaska, Fairbanks*)

his undoing. To win the men's respect he joined in their most dangerous activities. And as the company's chief officer responsible for law and order, he drew up a code of conduct and rigidly enforced discipline. Each Sunday he lined up the men for parade. Punishments varied with the alleged crime: it was the lash for stealing, while those accused of murder had to be sent to Siberia for judgment by a government court.

To get the men to work and to keep them from destroying one another while suffering the hardships and monotony of life in America, Baranov realized that he needed something more than discipline. Their pleasures became his pleasures. Baranov personally took charge of brewing a drink in which crab apples, rye meal, and cranberries were basic ingredients. He invited each man to drink as much as he could hold but forbade drinking during working hours. Since facilities for amusement were virtually nonexistent, any occasion—saints days, of which there were many, birthdays, the arrival of a ship—all furnished excuses for a party. Baranov usually took the lead in the singing. Every so often he became overpowered by the combination of food and drink and lost control of himself, striking out with his fists at whomever he could reach; the next day he would attempt to make amends by presenting his victims with gifts.

The Russians, who were not race-conscious, invited natives to these festivities. Baranov very much appreciated the role played by native women in helping many Russians adjust to life in the New World, and he himself took a mistress, the daughter of a Kenai chief. While encouraging these liaisons, he set down regulations governing the relations of the two races. Prostitution was forbidden. Once a Russian took a native woman to live with him, he was obligated to provide for her even after they had lost interest in each other. Children of these unions were recognized as belonging to the mother, but many a Russian decided to remain in America after his contract had expired rather than be parted from his offspring and perhaps from their mother.[2]

Natives made up much of the work force. Like his predecessors, Baranov used the superior skills of the Aleuts in hunting sea animals, while the *promyshlenniki* were employed in trapping, curing skins, guard duty, and a variety of chores. He learned to converse in some of the native dialects. The Aleuts, already a conquered people, were frequently sent on long expeditions far from home, despite their protests. Yet Baranov was fond of telling visitors that these were his children whom he protected and cared for in their old age. With the Indians who resisted Russian encroachments it was a different story. And Baranov had to be constantly on the alert for an attack.

Baranov sought to impress upon the natives that he had been sent by the tsar, the great father across the waters, to be their overlord and protector. He soon found himself put to the test. Complaints began to come in from residents of Cook Inlet accusing employees of the Lebedev-Lastochkin Company of raping women, robbing men of their furs, and burning dwelling places. Baranov appealed to Shelikhov, still a stockholder in the offending organization, to use his influence to bring these outrages to a halt; but he received no replies to his entreaties. When Baranov tried to explain to the natives that he had no jurisdiction over the Lebedev-Lastochkin Company, his aboriginal audience reminded him of his previous assertions of supremacy. Knowing that he could no longer avoid the challenge, Baranov led a party of men to Cook Inlet and there confronted Grigor Konovalev, the leader of the alleged wrongdoers.

Konovalev jeered at Baranov, reminding him that he was simply a lackey of the Shelikhov Company without any government authority and defying him to do his worst. Baranov responded by ordering Konovalev and seven of his followers seized and placed in irons. They were sent to Siberia, where a court acquitted them of all charges. Fortunately for Baranov, the Lebedev-Lastochkin Company retired from business in America soon afterward and made no further trouble.

New Settlements and the Founding of the Russian-American Company

In 1794, not long after the Cook Inlet affair, eight monks arrived in Kodiak. Though not a practicing Christian himself, Baranov believed that religion had a salutary influence and had requested that Shelikhov send him a village priest, a man with a good understanding of human nature and experienced in working with people. Instead, Shelikhov, intent on impressing the empress, had gone to the cloisters of the Valaam Monastery in Finland to recruit monks who would concentrate on converting the natives to the Russian Orthodox faith. Once in America, these priests, members of the superior white clergy, refused to take part in the work of the colony and constantly challenged Baranov's authority. They accused him of harshly exploiting the natives and *promyshlenniki* and advised them not to take orders from him. They also condemned him as a drunkard and as a sinner living with one woman while married to another, and they wrote to some Russian officials requesting that he be removed from his position. The clergy claimed great success in converting natives, but though many of their congregation professed to become Christians, they continued to practice their ancient rites and adamantly refused to abandon polygamy. One of the monks was killed by natives at Lake Iliamna, where he had gone to preach.

Baranov made no attempt to avenge his death; furthermore, he could see no reason for sending men to the Lake Iliamna region, in which he had no interest. When the furs on Kodiak Island began to decline, he moved in a different direction in his quest for new sources of supply. The most ambitious of his undertakings was Yakutat, designed to serve the fur trade and also to provide Russian America with food. Its founding represents the single Russian effort to bring permanent settlers to the New World. Shelikhov had obtained permission to take serfs out of Russia, and with them he sent some ex-convicts to Yakutat. But Yakutat, located in a glacial area unsuitable for farming, was a failure from the very beginning. The serfs, accustomed as they were to taking orders almost from birth, made poor pioneers. They lived in constant dread of the fierce Tlingits (called the Kolosh by the Russians), who destroyed the village in 1804.

Far more important in the history of Russian America was the founding of Mikhailovsk, after St. Michael the Archangel, six miles north of the present city of Sitka. Baranov had first visited the island which today bears his name in 1795. There he observed foreigners in what he regarded as Russian territory, exploiting a very lucrative trade with the natives. Intent on driving out the interlopers and having this profitable business for his company, he paid the Tlingits a small sum for rights to the land. Then in 1799 he returned, bringing with him about a thousand Aleuts and a hundred Russians with their native wives, although about thirty canoes were destroyed by storm on the way. After seeing much of the new post completed, Baranov returned to Kodiak with most of the Aleuts and some of the Russians.

Meanwhile in St. Petersburg, unknown to Baranov, decisions had been made that would affect Russian activities in America. When Shelikhov died in 1795, his dreams of exclusive privileges in America had not been fulfilled. His son-in-law and successor as head of the company, Nikolai Rezanov, had reached an agreement in 1797 with its leading rival after the demise of the Lebedev-Lastochkin enterprise, the Mylnikov Company, to amalgamate into a new organization—the United Russian Company. Rezanov, a member of the nobility, had much easier access to the royal court than did the merchant Shelikhov. He perceived that the new emperor, Paul, who succeeded Catherine in 1796, was no slavish admirer of his late mother's policies and was far less unyielding on the subject of monopoly than she. Rezanov had little difficulty in obtaining a charter in 1799 granting the newly established Russian-American Company sole rights in America for twenty years. The Shelikhov-Mylnikov group held the majority of shares, with the rest being divided among members of the imperial family, to whom some were given as a means of currying favor,

and among several small companies as compensation for having been forced out of business in America.

The Russian-American Company patterned itself on the model of the British East India Company, a private business firm possessing limited powers of government. The advantages of this type of organization and of having a single strong company in America were pointed out to Emperor Paul. The Russian position in America could be strengthened with a minimum involvement of his regime. Foreign competition could be brought under control, while the government could always repudiate any action of the Russian-American Company as having been unauthorized if challenged by a foreign power. In accepting the charter the company promised to support an expanded program of colonization, to establish schools, and to concern itself with making the natives loyal subjects of the Russian state and members of the Orthodox Church. In return the government gave the company permission to cut timber from state forests and to buy arms and ammunition at cost from the official arsenals.[3]

The directors of the company named Baranov their chief manager in America, an honor which he first heard about some three years later when he was brought news of the forming of the new organization and of Emperor Paul's assassination. This change affected his position slightly. The government advanced him to the rank of collegiate councillor, equivalent in the Russian system to a title of nobility; this enabled him to deal more effectively with naval officers who in the past had resented taking orders from a mere

Government store-house, New Archangel (Sitka)
(Historical Photograph Collection, Archives, University of Alaska, Fairbanks)

merchant. The title of governor was never formally bestowed on him, though he has been referred to as such. He and his successors bore the title of chief manager. Otherwise, the Russian-American Company, which had received its charter in 1799, the year Napoleon came to power in France, gave him no greater support than had the Shelikhov Company.

For the following fifteen years, Russia alternately engaged in wars with the French, the Persians, and the Turks, and could spare little for its struggling colony. The company's directors continued to insist that Baranov not deal with foreigners, claiming that every pelt traded represented a loss of profit to the Russians. Survival, however, was dependent on trade, illicit as it might have been. In 1803 the American sea captain Joseph O'Cain, after selling his cargo to Baranov, urged the Russians to allow him to take Aleuts to California to hunt sea otters. This arrangement, in which profits of the voyage were divided equally between O'Cain and Baranov acting for the Russian-American Company, became the model for future transactions between the two and continued with other Americans after O'Cain's death.

While Baranov was in Kodiak in June of 1802, the Tlingits attacked and destroyed St. Michael's, killing or taking captive most of the Russians and natives employed there. A few managed to escape to a British vessel anchored in the harbor. Its commander, Captain Henry M. Barber, who has been accused of conspiring with the Indians against the Russians, brought them to Kodiak, where he demanded a huge ransom from Baranov as his price for having saved the refugees. After some haggling, the two compromised and settled on 10,000 rubles, about one-fifth of the original request.

Baranov had no intention of capitulating to the Tlingits. In 1804 he re-

New Archangel (Sitka)
(Historical Photograph Collection, Archives, University of Alaska, Fairbanks)

turned to the Sitka area with a large contingent of Aleuts and Russians. There, aided by the Russian warship *Neva,* then in America on an around-the-world voyage, Baranov prevailed. The ship destroyed the native village, and its occupants fled. Baranov banished the natives from the island as punishment for their uprising and set to work immediately to build the settlement of New Archangel on the site of the recent habitat of the natives and of the present city of Sitka. New Archangel became the largest town of Russian America, and after Baranov's retirement the governors of Russian America used it as their capital.

During the following summer, the company's director, Nikolai Rezanov, who had recently lost his wife, visited America. Rezanov, an imperialist who was as much concerned with advancing Russian interests in the Pacific as in making a profit for the Russian-American Company, differed with Baranov's views on colonization. He wanted to build up the population of the area and make it an outpost for further Russian expansion. He recommended that more attention be given to recruitment and to the improvement of living conditions in America in order to attract permanent settlers. The system of payment of shares was to be abolished and replaced by salaries so that each man would know exactly how much he would earn in a year. Schools were to be established for the colonists' children. Rezanov warned that unless a conservation program was instituted and the reckless hunting of animals stopped, the depletion of furs was inevitable.

As his stay progressed and he became more aware of the problems facing the colony, he recognized the wisdom of some of Baranov's policies. He realized the hopelessness of waiting for supplies to arrive, and in order to avert famine he too purchased the cargo of an American ship. When even that seemed inadequate, he sailed for California to purchase foodstuffs from the Spaniards. Upon his arrival, Spanish government officials entertained him most lavishly but claimed that their instructions also forbade any business with foreigners. But Rezanov did not return empty-handed. While in San Francisco he met and wooed the lovely Señorita Dona Maria de la Concepcion Arguello, the daughter of the port's commander. They became engaged, the trade barriers were suddenly lifted, and Rezanov sailed with his cargo for the north. By the time he reached New Archangel, the supply crisis was over; Baranov had negotiated an agreement with an American sea captain for what he needed. Rezanov then departed for St. Petersburg to secure permission from the Emperor to marry Dona Concepcion, a Catholic and member of a different faith. After reaching Okhotsk he started out on the long overland journey to the Russian capital, but he had not gone far when he was thrown from his horse and killed. And many of his far-reaching plans for the colonies in America died with him.

With Rezanov's departure Baranov resumed his position as the undisputed head of the colony. A serious threat to his authority arose when several of the *promyshlenniki,* led by Vasilli Naplavkov, a Pole, organized a conspiracy in New Archangel to kill him. An informer revealed the details of the plot to Baranov, and he ordered the men arrested; they were sent to Siberia for trial and received long prison sentences.

Nikolai Rezanov
*(Historical Photograph
Collection, Archives,
University of Alaska, Fairbanks)*

A much greater challenge to Baranov's leadership came with the increasing involvement of Russia in European affairs, culminating in Napoleon's invasion of Russia in 1812. This made the isolation of the colonies complete, and their survival depended on Baranov's maneuverings and dealings. He entered into a very profitable relationship with the famous American fur merchant John Jacob Astor; not wishing to be tied to a single supply source, however, he refused the latter's proposal to completely supply the Russians with goods in return for sole rights to purchase their furs.

Baranov took advantage of the Anglo-American war that broke out in 1812, resulting in the British seizure of Astor's holdings on the Columbia River and the idling of American ships in the Pacific because of their fear of capture by English men-of-war. He purchased or leased several of the ships. These were registered under the flag of the Russians, who had become the allies of the English and thus were protected from seizure. The company's profits for the next two years were enormous. A thriving commerce developed, with these ships bringing goods from the north, Hawaii, the Orient, and California.

Baranov had taken advantage of Spain's troubles to install a base in California, an area highly coveted by the Russians, who believed that it was the only place on the Pacific where wheat could be grown. As early as 1790, Shelikhov had looked to the day when California would be Russian. Rezanov, just before his death, had written to his fellow directors of the Russian-American Company urging the occupation of California, and they in turn demanded action from Baranov. By 1808 the fortunes of Spain were at the lowest. Napoleon had invaded the country, forcing Charles IV and his son Ferdinand to give up all claims to the throne and installing his brother Joseph Bonaparte as king. Although the Spanish resisted bravely and were eventually able to expel the French from the peninsula with the aid of England, they were in no position to resist even the limited actions of the Russians in California. Baranov had sent his trusted lieutenant Ivan Kuskov southward several times before the latter decided on a piece of land on Bodega Bay, north of San Francisco. Kuskov paid the natives a small sum for rights to the territory but ignored the protests of the Spaniards.

The Russians remained at the Ross settlement (now known as Fort Ross) until 1841, despite the demands of the Mexicans who had succeeded the Spanish in California, before they finally sold it to John Sutter, a Swiss entrepreneur. Ross never fulfilled its promises of furnishing the Russian colonies with food supplies, since it was unsuitable for agriculture and provided little in furs.

Even more of a failure was the Russian attempt to intervene in Hawaii. In 1815, Baranov sent a German adventurer, Doctor Anton Schaffer, to the islands to retrieve the fur cargo of a company vessel which had been wrecked on the island of Kauai. Schaffer, who had been told that he must not under any circumstance involve the Russian government, became entangled in the politics of the islands. He tried to bring the islands into the Russian fold by backing the losing candidate in a conflict between the chieftains, and he was forced to leave. Both adventures, in California and in Hawaii, received little support from the Russian government and could hardly be regarded as serious evidence of Russian expansion in the Pacific. They had been forced upon Baranov, requiring much of his attention and causing him to divert men and supplies which could have been used to much greater advantage in the northern area he called home.

Baranov's Dismissal and Death

As early as 1809, following the attempt on his life, Baranov had asked to be replaced, pointing out that he was growing old and that it was time for a younger man to take over. But each time the company found a successor, the man would die before reaching America. Although he was criticized in an 1813 report by Captain V. M. Golovnin of the navy for certain aspects of his rule in America, Baranov felt that the directors of the company were well satisfied with his administration, particularly after the highly profitable years from 1812 to 1814. He was thus very surprised and taken aback when Captain Leonti A. Hagemeister of the Russian Navy appeared in New Archangel in late 1817, demanded to see his books, and informed him that he was no longer chief manager of the company. Hagemeister took over but soon turned the actual administration of the colony over to Lieutenant Semen I. Yanovski, who had married Baranov's daughter. Like many men who have devoted their lives to business, Baranov did not know what to do with himself following this forced retirement. Captain Hagemeister persuaded him to return to Russia, where he could be of use to the directors of the Russian-American Company. Enroute, Baranov contracted a fever in the South Seas and died; his body was lowered into the ocean in Sunda Strait.

More than any other man, Baranov was responsible for establishing the Russian-American Company as a viable commercial institution. Despite a lack of support from home he had been able not only to survive, but because of his resourcefulness to enable the company to pay handsome dividends in the later years. He had been able to give some permanence to the Russian presence and had founded a number of new settlements, greatly extending the area of the company's holdings. He could not, however, be called a great empire-builder. He sent men to California only because he had been ordered to do so. The Russian-American colonies continued to be primarily trading posts, and since the objective of the company was to profit from the fur trade, it could hardly be otherwise. Baranov did little to extend Russian civilization to the New World and was probably as much affected by the natives' culture and life as they were by his. But had it not been for him and his devotion to his employers, the Russian occupation would have ended much sooner than it did.

Russian America After Baranov

Baranov's retirement and death, coming as they did in the closing years of the charter, ushered in a new phase in the rule and development of Russian America. His successors were naval men, and the charter, when it was renewed in 1821, two years after its expiration date, made it mandatory that the chief managers, or governors, be officers of the navy. Compared to Baranov these men had much less interest in business affairs. Their greater emphasis on the improvement of the administration resulted in an enlargement of the bureaucracy. Some of the governors, who usually served terms of five years, were noted explorers; others concerned themselves more with the welfare of the natives. None had any experience in the fur trade. In the words of the Soviet historian S. B. Okun, there was "more order and less peltry" in the new regime.[4]

The announcement of the second charter came at a time when the imperial regime had become more active in international affairs. Alexander I, the ruler of Russia following the assassination of his father Paul in 1801, had played a leading role in the defeat of Napoleon as well as at the peace conference of the Congress of Vienna. In his early years as monarch, Alexander had acquired the reputation of being somewhat liberal, inclined toward reform; but as he grew older he became increasingly more conservative. He was the chief architect of the Holy Alliance and was pledged along with the rulers of Austria and Prussia to intervene and put down by force, if necessary, liberal innovations in the governmental systems of European states. Rumors circulated that the members of the Holy Alliance had promised Spain aid in recovering her recently lost colonies in America.

Otto von Kotzebue's prestigious scientific expedition to the Arctic coast in 1815 appeared to portend heightened Russian interest in the New World. When the imperial regime issued the new charter, it also extended the authority of the Russian-American Company to the 51st parallel, while prohibiting foreign ships from coming within 100 Italian miles* of the coast. Both the Americans and the English took alarm at that. They protested vigorously against exclusion of their nationals from the northern fur trade. Each reminded the Russian government that territory south of the 55th parallel formed part of the Oregon country already claimed and jointly occupied by the United States and Great Britain under the terms of the Rush-Bagot Agreement. George Canning, the British foreign secretary, proposed that the United States and his country act together in warning the Holy Alliance, Russia in particular, against further provocations. But on the advice of the American secretary of state, John Quincy Adams, who was confident of British help in the event of trouble, the United States issued the Monroe Doctrine, which stated that the New World was not open for further colonization.

Russia, already overextended in the play of European power politics, was now eager to compromise and signed a treaty with the United States in 1824, confirmed by England the following year, accepting 54° 40′ as the southern boundary of Russian America. The negotiations between Britain and Russia were more complex, affecting claims to jurisdiction over a much larger area. After some haggling, the Russians and the British agreed on the 141st meridian as the eastern limit of Russian ownership of territory extending from the Arctic to the 56th parallel and south of that line including a narrow strip of land along the coast,[5] thereby conceding to the Russians control over much land that had not even been explored. Far more important from the British viewpoint were the commercial sections of the treaty, guaranteeing to their ships the same rights as those given to Americans in trading freely along the coast for a period of ten years, and, in addition, allowing them entry to the interior on all rivers emptying into the Pacific. Neither treaty mentioned Fort Ross.

The ratification of these treaties ended Russian expansion in America. Trade and trading rights, however, continued to be a major issue. After amalgamating with the Northwest Fur Company in 1821, the Hudson's Bay Company, a British chartered organization, began the construction of a chain of trading stations at 200-mile intervals to the southern limits of Russian America. More efficient than the Russians, the Hudson's Bay Company

---

*An Italian mile is slightly longer than the American mile.

utilized the services of highly trained and educated men and had better and cheaper goods to sell. By employing tactics of underselling its wares and paying more for furs, the "Honorable Company," as it was called, had driven out smaller American firms from the coastal trade.

When Baron Ferdinand P. Wrangell, the most aggressive of the later governors, learned that the Hudson's Bay Company was planning to erect a station on the Stikine River just within British territory, he decided that he must act or else allow the British to capture the interior fur trade by purchasing skins directly from the natives, who in the past had brought them to the coast for sale to the Russians. He ordered the building of Redoubt St. Dionysius at Point Highfield near the mouth of the Stikine, seeking to take advantage of a section of the treaty in 1825 requiring that all English ships stop at existing Russian stations before sailing up the river. When the *Dryad*, under the command of Peter Skene Odgen of the Hudson's Bay Company, approached Point Highfield, it was halted by Russian gunfire. The British sued for damages. Although the foreign offices of both states took part in the negotiation, the two companies settled their differences amicably by themselves. The Russian-American Company agreed to lease the mainland south of Cape Spencer for a period of ten years on an annual payment of 2,000 land otter skins harvested on the western slope of the Rockies. The Hudson's Bay Company further promised to make available each year for sale to the Russians an additional 5,000 skins taken from both the eastern and western side of the mountains, at prices ranging from 23 to 32 shillings for each pelt, and also to furnish foodstuffs and manufactured goods from England at stipulated prices. The benefits to the Russians from the accord were substantial. A nagging dispute had been resolved peacefully, income would be derived from an unoccupied area, and stocks of furs and provisions were readily guaranteed.[6]

A second European power had now come into Alaska. For the next thirty years, until the sale of Russian America to the United States, the Hudson's Bay Company occupied a portion of Alaska, twice renewing the lease of the southern area, though with some modification in terms, and also illegally establishing a post at Fort Yukon, well within Russian territory. Instructions had been given to the manager to feign ignorance of being on Russian land and to move if challenged. But either the Russian-American Company did not know that a violation had taken place, or if it did, preferred to remain quiet. In the leased area, John McLoughlin, the chief factor of the Hudson's Bay Company on the Pacific, established the posts of Fort Durham, usually referred to as Fort Taku because of its location at Taku Harbor, and Fort Stikine, replacing the Russian Redoubt St. Dionysius. He asserted that their existence was necessary for a firm foundation of British power and authority. His views were challenged by Sir George Simpson, the economy-minded governor of the Hudson's Bay Company in America, who questioned their value in terms of the cost of maintenance and men needed for defense. He ordered Fort Taku closed in 1842 and Fort Stikine in 1847, following a series of incidents involving natives. McLoughlin's son, the commandant at Fort Stikine, was killed and the British were saved from disaster only by the timely arrival of the Russians.

For the remainder of their stay in the south, the men of the Hudson's Bay

Company conducted their trade using a boat patrolling the rivers. When given the opportunity in the sixties to convert their lease into a permanent possession, the Hudson's Bay Company refused an offer to purchase territory of "so little value" because the decline of the fur trade had been so great.[7]

The Russian government's interest in America following the Napoleonic Wars was short-lived. Governors of the colonies found themselves more burdened with directives than Baranov had been, and while support from St. Petersburg had improved, Russian America was still very much on its own and far from being the center of attention in the capital. However, a strong governor such as Wrangell was able to advance the company's position. He reorganized the administration of the colonies and improved the efficiency of its operation. As an economy measure, he closed all the shipyards in Russian America except the one at New Archangel, and he built a sawmill at Ozerskoi Redoubt. He sought to stabilize the fur trade by instituting a conservation program. Wrangell was an experienced explorer, and he and his fellow governors gave much support to scientific studies and expeditions using naval officers and navigators of the merchant marine. Their accurate observations and maps supplanted the crude information obtained by Baranov from hunters and natives.

According to the geologist Alfred Brooks, Mikhail Tebenkov, first as explorer and later as governor, "did more than anyone else to bring about a better knowledge of Alaska's coast," by compiling all available cartographic information and publishing a series of charts based on these. The exploration of the interior was the work mainly of creoles, as the children of Russians born in the

Early Fort Yukon
(*Historical Photograph Collection, Archives, University of Alaska, Fairbanks*)

colonies were called. Some were almost illiterate, others had been educated in the school at New Archangel, and a few in St. Petersburg. Alexander Kolmakov, aided by Ivan Lukin, who had been sent by Wrangell to explore the Kuskokwim following its discovery by Lieutenant Vasili Malakov, navigated the river as far as the Koyukuk. The most extensive of these expeditions, undertaken by Lieutenant Lavretti Zagoskin, went up the Yukon as far as the Tanana River.

Life in Russian America took on some refinements after the Baranov era. Baroness Elizabeth Wrangell was the first of the wives of the Russian governors to live in America. Thanks to her, New Archangel acquired a more orderly social life. The governors and their ladies sponsored balls. Visitors to America expressed pleasure at the attention they received and how well they were entertained. But some, like George Simpson, the governor of Hudson's Bay Company, pointed out how great was the disparity in living conditions between the company officials and the common folk in their hovels. Simpson paints a dismal picture of the town's smells and lack of sanitation, calling it the most miserable place he had ever visited. New Archangel did possess a few more imposing structures, among them the cathedral, rebuilt by Wrangell, and the governor's mansion, known as Baranov's Castle after the original structure on the site. The capital had several schools: one, intended for the training of boys in the rudiments of mathematics and navigation, had been greatly improved when Lieutenant Adolph K. Etholen, later governor of the colony, became its director in 1833; another, a finishing school for girls, was founded by Mrs.

Russian church and trading store, Sitka, ca. 1898
(Historical Photograph Collection, Archives, University of Alaska, Fairbanks)

Margaretha Etholen. The church assumed responsibility for the education of the natives, setting up schools at New Archangel, Kodiak, Unalaska, and several other places; but most members of the clergy tended to look upon learning as secondary to their principal mission, the saving of souls.

A notable exception was Ioann Veniaminov, a man of great intellectual gifts who rose eventually to the position of metropolitan of Moscow. He arrived in the Aleutians in 1824 and was brought to New Archangel by Wrangell. There he established an ecclesiastical school which was later converted into a seminary for training natives as priests able to conduct services in their own languages. Named as the first bishop for America and Kamchatka, Veniaminov remained in New Archangel until 1858, when the seat of the diocese was transferred to Siberia. While in America he recorded his observations on the activities of volcanoes and made detailed notes pertaining to meteorology. He devised an alphabet and grammar for the Aleut language, and later scholars acknowledged their indebtedness to him for his studies in Aleut culture. He worked hard to improve the living conditions of the native people and won their respect and admiration.

The governors after Baranov instituted new policies in their dealings with the natives and improved the relationship between Russians and natives, which, however, still retained aspects of a truce. Matvei Muraviev, the governor from 1820 to 1825, invited the Tlingits to return to the island from which they had been banished by Baranov, but restricted them to living in a village just outside New Archangel where they could be readily observed. They were permitted to enter the Russian settlement only during certain hours and had to leave by sundown. Spies in the village regularly reported on their activities. In 1855 the Tlingits attacked New Archangel and were beaten off. The Aleut population, heavily decimated by disease and harsh treatment in the early years of the Russian occupation, increased slightly during this period.

Far more impressive was the growth in numbers of the creoles, who became a significant factor in the life of the colonies, furnishing much of the needed labor supply, especially as skilled workers. Some of the creoles rose to responsible positions, such as the explorers Andrei Glazunov, P. V. Malakhov, and Alexandr Kashevarov, several navigators of company vessels, and priests. The company made an effort to aid those seeking to learn a trade or acquire the rudiments of science and navigation, and it even sent some to Russia for further education. Once he accepted such benefits, a person was required to remain in the company's service for ten to fifteen years. The creoles constituted a separate element in Russian America, never fully accepted by the Russians or the natives. They themselves tended to look down on the natives and frequently refused to join in hunting parties with them even though that might mean a loss of income. Creole women almost never married natives, but creole men usually selected their mates from among native women.[8]

While the colonies underwent a social transformation, the character of the Russian American fur trade changed significantly. Over-hunting in the earlier eras substantially reduced the animal population, so that the once lucrative sea otter nearly became extinct. The market for furs declined. China, the Russian American Company's best customer in the past, was severely weakened by

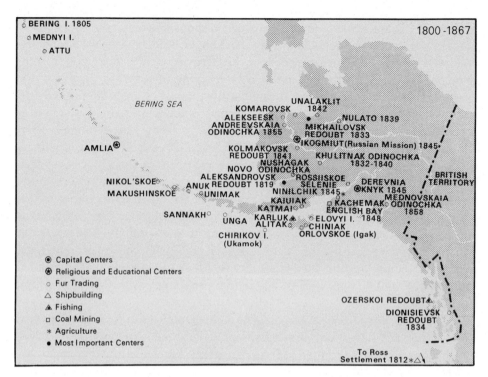

Russian settlements in Alaska and their economic functions, 1800-1867
(from Svetlana Fedorova, The Russian Population in Alaska and California, © 1973 by Richard A. Pierce)

conflicts with Western powers and curtailed its purchases. The Russians, who had never cultivated the art of processing, found themselves—despite the high quality of their skins—at a marked disadvantage in competing with the Americans, British, and Canadians, all of whom made greater efforts to satisfy their patrons.

When the Second Charter expired in 1841, Nicholas I, who insisted on personally reviewing all matters pertaining to the administration, delayed its renewal for three years before extending the company's authority for another twenty years. An extreme conservative, Nicholas I never disguised his antipathy for an organization some of whose directors had been implicated in the ill-fated Decembrist revolt at the beginning of his reign in 1825. But the real issue for him and his government centered on the question of the company's very existence and the role it should play. The new charter stressed the governmental aspects of administration and colonization, slighting the company's commercial character. It also ordered its employees to wear uniforms. To avert the threat of bankruptcy to the company, the government granted it special privileges in the Russian tea trade. By 1845 the income from tea far exceeded that from furs. According to the Soviet historian Okun, the imperial regime decided to subsidize the ailing company so that it could put it to use in acquiring the Amur River region. Company ships explored the river; its agents traveled overland, ostensibly on business but actually to learn more about the area and to win support of the natives preparatory to a Russian takeover. When this had been accomplished, Okun says, the Russian government had no further use for the company.[9]

Meanwhile, concerned officials endeavoring to keep the company afloat initiated several new business ventures. Peter Doroshin, a mining engineer

First Russian coal mine,
Kenai Peninsula
*(Historical Photograph
Collection, Archives,
University of Alaska, Fairbanks)*

who was sent to the colonies in 1848, spent four years prospecting in places where lignitic coal occurs; but he did not find high-grade ore. The company hired Enoch Jhalmar Furuhjelm, a Finnish mining engineer, to open a mine at Port Graham, using machinery purchased in Boston. At the time of its greatest activity, this mine employed 131 men and produced thirty-five tons a day, more than enough to meet the colonies' needs; but efforts to develop an export trade failed when the coal shipped to San Francisco sold at a loss. Governor Nikolai Y. Rosenberg became equally discouraged when he discovered that company employees could not compete with the more efficient Americans in the whaling industry nor dislodge these poachers from Russian waters. Of all the enterprises, the ice trade prospered the most, but not enough to justify the company's continued existence.

As the company's financial problems increased, its critics mounted a new offensive, calling into question Russia's ability to defend the colonies from attack. In a memorandum written in 1853, Nikolai Muraviev, the governor-general of Siberia, predicted that the Americans, who already possessed California, would inevitably master the entire North American continent. He recommended selling the colonies to the United States, thereby assuring Russia of a friend in case of a conflict with England, as well as a source of payment for something irretrievably lost. The outbreak of the Crimean War did not affect the colonies, because the Hudson's Bay Company and the Russian-American Company had agreed beforehand to keep their respective territories neutral, a pledge honored by their governments. But it was obvious that England, a great naval power whose ships had shelled the harbors of Petropavlovsk on the

Kamchatka Peninsula, could easily have taken over the Russian holdings. Company officials also expressed apprehension of the effect of an influx of private groups into the area, as might occur in a gold rush which they could not contain. Rumors of an impending migration northward of the Mormons, whose views on polygamy had made them unpopular in the United States, caused some anxiety and stirred the Russian ambassador in Washington to make inquiries.[10]

Even before the close of the Crimean War in 1856, Russia's new ruler, Alexander II, broached an exchange of talks concerning the sale of its possessions in the New World to the United States; but these had been suspended with the outbreak of the Civil War in America. Grand Duke Constantine, brother of the emperor, recommended cession to the United States with or without compensation. Prince Alexandr Gorchakov, the Russian foreign minister, agreed on withdrawal from America, but he wanted at least $5 million for the colonies. The government of Alexander II, desperately in need of money for its program of social reform featuring emancipation of the serfs, looked on continued occupation as a luxury that would draw away support from worthier causes and projects and weaken the Russian position abroad. Like other European states, Russia had embarked on a program of expansion. In the Far East it had annexed the Amur River territory, begun work on the construction of the port of Vladivostok, and was active in Central Asia. The message seemed clear: in pursuing more worthwhile aims elsewhere, Russia would have to release its American possessions.[11]

Russia Sells Its Colony

At a meeting in 1866, Emperor Alexander II, Grand Duke Constantine, and Gorchakov decided to sell the American territories, and they instructed Baron Eduard de Stoeckel, the ambassador to Washington then on a visit to America, to begin negotiations immediately. Stoeckel knew that the American secretary of state, William H. Seward, was interested, and after landing in New York he succeeded through a mutual friend in getting in touch with Seward. The two men met several times in Washington, and in the course of their conversations Seward requested special privileges for American fishermen and fur traders in Russian America. Stoeckel rejected that but proposed instead that the United States buy the territory. Seward strongly urged President Andrew Johnson to accept the offer. Johnson informed the secretary that he had no thoughts one way or another about the matter and that he would follow the recommendations of the cabinet, which then voted support for Seward. For the next week or so the Russian and the American discussed details of the agreement.

According to the story as it is told by Seward's son Frederick, Stoeckel then appeared on the evening of March 20 at the secretary's home and announced that the emperor had consented to accept $7,200,000 for the territory, and that he would come himself the next day to the State Department offices to work on the account. Seward, impatient to conclude the business, asked why they had to wait until the next day. Sometime before midnight the two men

and their staffs finished their work and sent the treaty to their governments for ratification. On October 18, 1867, the United States took possession of Alaska.

Russian Influence in Alaska

The Russian phase of Alaskan history lasted 126 years. Russian activities were limited primarily to the coastal areas; there was little attempt to explore or settle the interior. And at no time were there more than 700 Russians in the colonies. Russians did not come to Alaska to make it their home, and considering that the economic base of the Russian colonies was the fur trade, there was no reason that it should have been otherwise. The initiative for Russian expansion and settlement in the New World came from private individuals and groups, not from the government. Russian America and Russian American interests were a low priority among the imperial regime's objectives. And when

Interior of Russian
church, Unalaska
(*Bunnell Collection,
Archives, University of Alaska,
Fairbanks*)

the Russian-American Company ceased to be profitable, the government ordered it sold.

A critic, Ernest Gruening, devotes only a few pages of his history of
Alaska to the Russian experience, declaring that it was of little significance. But
limited as the Russian influence may have been, the governors after Baranov
were able to introduce into the colonies a semblance of European civilization.
They established settlements and missions, charted the coasts, made the first
scientific investigations of the region's natural history, resources, and ethnog-
raphy, and through the fur trade and shipping drew the region into the world
economy. They converted the Aleuts and some of the Tlingits and Eskimos to
Christianity, introduced the first educational and medical facilities, and strove
to curtail native warfare and slavery. Compared with the policies of neglect
followed by the British Hudson's Bay Company during its presence in southeastern Alaska and with the early years of the American occupation, the Russian record of achievement, accomplished with limited means and scant personnel, was noteworthy and in many ways had a lasting effect.

·3·
The Americanization of Alaska

W HEN THE United States took possession of Alaska in 1867, Americans were not much better prepared to administer and govern the territory than the Russians had been in the 1780s. Nothing in the American background provided the wisdom and experience needed to guide the destinies of a land so distant and so remote. The Civil War had just ended, and the minds of the people and their leaders were focused on the resolution of problems emanating from that conflict. Americans generally were far too excited about the great economic prospects opening at home both in industry and agriculture to concern themselves very much with Alaska.

The acquisition of Alaska aroused some controversy and heated debate. Several newspapers demanded that the Senate reject the treaty, claiming that Alaska was merely a land of ice and snow and deriding its purchase as "Seward's Folly," "Seward's Iceberg," or "Walrussia." Horace Greeley, the acerbic editor of *The New York Herald,* sneeringly advised European potentates with worthless territory to discard Alaska: they would find in Secretary Seward a ready buyer. Seward, while he was not unaware of Alaska's great wealth, was an ardent imperialist primarily interested in the new possession as the first step in building America's Pacific empire. He sought to counteract this adverse criticism by making available to friendly newspapers and persons of influence information concerning Alaska gathered from a variety of sources—visitors to the territory, businessmen, whalers, and fur buyers, among others.[1] Seward presented Charles Sumner with a study made not long before by a group of scientists and explorers sent out by the Smithsonian Institution to investigate the interior and coastal regions of Alaska. The expedition was made in conjunction with the Western Union Company's project of building a telegraph line from the United States to Europe via Alaska and Siberia. In a speech before the Senate, Sumner utilized the reports of the expedition's first leader, Robert Kennicott, and Lieutenant Henry M. Bannister, who combined their own observations with the writings of Englishmen and Russians. Sumner's support was decisive, and the treaty was ratified with only two dissenting votes.

Difficulties arose, however, when the House of Representatives delayed action in appropriating the money to pay the Russian government, claiming that in transactions involving millions of dollars the House should have been consulted. Seward found it necessary to commission an expedition under the leadership of George Davidson to go to Alaska and make another study to convince the recalcitrant House members. Baron Stoeckel, the Russian ambassador, was so fearful that the United States would renege on the agreement that he is said to have spent $30,000 in securing the support of a few influential newspapers and lobbyists to obtain a favorable response from the congressmen. He even suggested that the emperor might shame the Americans into meeting their obligation by offering them the territory without charge, a gesture which his majesty refused to consider, apparently fearing that it might be accepted. On July 18, 1868, nine months after the American occupation had begun, the House approved the appropriation bill. Some congressmen admitted that they voted for the measure only after having been persuaded that to do otherwise would offend an old friend, the Russian government.

For map of Sitka, 1867, see pages 336-337.

In a ceremony at Sitka, General Lowell Rousseau, as the official representative of the president, formally took possession of Alaska for the United States. The treaty of purchase guaranteed Russians and creoles the privileges of citizenship in the United States and gave them the option of deciding within a three-year period whether they wished to become American citizens. A few remained in Alaska, many returned to Russia, and some made their way to California and the Pacific Northwest, where they believed the economic opportunities would be better. For the natives, most of whom had never been under Russian rule, the change of regime appeared to be of little consequence. An American businessman, H. M. Hutchinson of Hutchinson, Kohl & Company of San Francisco, purchased the buildings, ships, equipment, and other movable properties of the Russian-American Company from its last governor, Prince Dmitri Maksoutov. The American government sent a few hundred soldiers, under the command of General Jefferson C. Davis, to posts at Sitka, Fort Wrangell, Fort Kodiak, Fort Tongass, and Fort Kenai, but soon closed the last three. The Alaskan interior was entirely unpatrolled.

General Davis became virtually the ruler of Alaska. Soon after the ratification of the treaty, President Andrew Johnson recommended that Congress act to provide "for the occupation and government of the territory as part of the dominion of the United States." Unfortunately, Johnson—a Democrat heavily under attack from a Republican-dominated Congress for his Reconstruction policies, soon to be impeached in the House of Representatives, and missing removal from the presidency by a single vote in the Senate—had no influence with the legislators, and his pleas fell on deaf ears. Congress devoted little more time to Alaska than it took to extend to the territory American laws governing commerce and navigation while prohibiting within its borders the importation, manufacture, and sale of liquor. Nothing was done to establish civil government, and for the next seventeen years Alaska remained under military rule.

Sitka, the old Russian capital, now became the military headquarters of General Davis. It immediately experienced a land boom and seemed sure to continue as the center of American life. A number of enterprising Americans

Brevet-General
Jefferson C. Davis
(*Historical Photograph
Collection, Archives,
University of Alaska, Fairbanks*)

arrived almost simultaneously with the army, hoping to be first on the scene to exploit the region's reputed wealth. "Eager promoters," according to historian Ted C. Hinckley, "squatted over the whole vicinity of Sitka—preempted the Governor's house and one godless individual even recorded a claim for the church and church lands." These claims were, of course, illegal, but the optimists were confident that Congress would enact laws confirming title to land. The town's residents, with the blessings of General Davis, drew up a charter, elected a governing council, and named William S. Dodge, the collector of customs, mayor. Thomas Murphy started a newspaper which he called *The Sitka Times.* A teacher was even engaged at $75 a month. But Sitka's prosperity soon evaporated. The port's commerce steadily declined. Neither the soldiers nor the natives provided enough business to sustain the merchants. People began to move out, and in the summer of 1873 the Sitka Council held its last meeting.

Many of those who came and departed blamed the federal government for Sitka's decline and Alaska's misfortunes. Congress had failed to provide needed services: there was no regular mail delivery, no lighthouses to guide navigators in the tricky waters of Alaska, and no survey of the land. People had left because they could not get title to land and hence had no assurance that their work would not be in vain. The army had even been used to drive out people who had attempted to preëmpt some land for themselves. In its first edition *The Sitka Times* condemned military rule. Editor Murphy wrote that not until Alaska had a civil government could one "expect to hear of rich minerals having been fully developed by our latent industry but not before."[2]

When Seward, soon after his retirement as secretary of state, visited Sitka, he told his audience that civil government must come "because our political system rejects alike anarchy and executive absolutism"; but he cautioned that since fewer than 2,000 whites lived among 25,000 natives "a display of military force" was necessary. But how necessary? Alaska never experienced the wars between the races that marked much of early American history. Relations between whites and natives in Alaska were characterized more by personal incidents than by unending conflict. William S. Dodge, the collector of customs and erstwhile mayor of Sitka, regretted the lack of discipline among the troops and complained that he had been called out many a night by men and women, Russians and natives alike, requesting protection from drunken soldiers. And misunderstandings were frequent.

Furthermore, Americans had no appreciation of the native culture, while the natives found it difficult to comprehend the rules and regulations of the new masters of Alaska. One evening a native chief, somewhat the worse from

Sitka from steamer, 1890, showing Russian warehouse in foreground, Baranov Castle in back
(Bunnell Collection, Archives, University of Alaska, Fairbanks)

excessive drink, wobbled out of the house of General Davis and entered the parade ground reserved for officers. He failed to stop when ordered to do so by the sentry on duty. A second sentry took direct action when the chief, despite a second challenge, continued across the forbidden area; he kicked him forcibly in the rear. Several followers came to their chief's defense. A scuffle ensued, and one of the Indians wrested a rifle from a soldier and then retreated to his village with the prize. Davis, who was no Indian hater, insisted that the natives be taught to respect the authority of the United States, and he sent a detachment of soldiers to arrest the offending warrior and his chief. On another occasion, after two white men had been killed at Kake, the general sailed to the island to demand the surrender of the murderers. Informed of his coming, most of the inhabitants fled. Davis then ordered their homes burned as a warning to all that lawbreakers must be punished.

The army never relished its Alaska assignment; both enlisted men and officers disliked it, probably suffering more from boredom than from attack by the aborigines. Officials of the army in their annual reports invariably recommended that the troops be withdrawn, since the army possessed neither the authority nor the trained men to carry out functions of civil government. They proposed that in view of Alaska's large area, long coastline, and interior rivers, a revenue vessel be sent to perform the necessary police duties. In 1877 the War Department recalled its men from Alaska, stating that they were needed to suppress an uprising of the Nez Perce Indians in Idaho.

After the army's departure, Mottrom D. Ball of the Treasury Department was the only government official in the territory. A later governor of Alaska, Ernest Gruening, has jocularly referred to this as the era when Alaska was ruled by a customs collector. When fighting between natives and whites erupted in February 1879, some Sitkans, fearful of an impending massacre, called on the navy to send a vessel for their protection. Since no immediate reply was forthcoming, they appealed to the British, who sent a warship, the *H.M.S. Osprey*, from Victoria to Sitka. Then with the arrival of an American warship, the *U.S.S. Alaska*, in April 1879, the rule of the navy in Alaska began.

Economic Activity and Formation of Civil Government

In the minds of many Alaskans in these early years, the real power in Alaskan affairs was not the military but the Alaska Commercial Company. An outgrowth of Hutchinson, Kohl & Co., the Alaska Commercial Company in 1870 bid for and acquired a twenty-year lease from the government giving it exclusive rights to catch seals on their breeding grounds, the Pribilof Islands. Within a short time the company extended its commercial empire to the Aleutians, Kodiak, and the Yukon River Valley, having taken over the Hudson's Bay Company's post at Fort Yukon after the British had been ordered to leave American territory. A most efficient organization, it alone possessed the capital to build and maintain the ships needed to bring people and supplies to the different parts of the vast territory.

As the company's economic power grew, so did its role in the political and social affairs of Alaska, providing schools and medical services in some communities and even taking on the responsibility of maintaining law and order—what there was of it—especially in the interior. Largely owing to the efforts of its agents Napoleon Jack McQuesten, Arthur Harper, and Al Mayo, the Yukon was opened up to mining. These men, though primarily interested in the fur trade, did some prospecting on their own, furnished supplies needed by the gold seekers, and even grubstaked a few of the prospectors.

The Alaska Commercial Company's critics are legion, blaming it for Alaska's backwardness and its failure to obtain self-government. The naturalist William H. Dall, writing in 1868, accused its officers of seeking to crush all opposition and that to attain these ends it "had not hesitated at force, fraud and corruption. . . ." However, a congressional committee called upon to investigate these and other charges absolved the company of abusing its authority, conducting unethical practices against its competitors, showing a lack of concern for the natives, and using its political connections to obtain favors.[3]

When Ivan Petroff was commissioned to take a census of Alaska in 1880, he reported after two years of work that there were only 430 whites in the territory. His calculation, which has been challenged, showed a significant decline from the Russian period. Although the fur trade still was Alaska's leading industry, the fisheries—especially the salmon—and mining were becoming increasingly more important in the Alaskan economy. The first canneries were started in 1878 at Klawock and the Sitka area. By the turn of the century there were almost fifty in operation, most of them owned by members of the Alaska Packers Association. Since the cannery managers brought their own crews, few Alaskan residents were employed. Until 1886, mining in the Yukon had been confined almost entirely to the Canadian side of the river. In that year discoveries of gold made near one of the Yukon's tributaries, the Forty Mile River in American territory, triggered a new rush, followed by that of Birch Creek, which became the most important mining camp and resulted in the establishment of Circle City as the supply center. A few small strikes had been made previously at Wrangell and in the vicinity of Sitka, but most significant was that which led to the founding of the first American town, Juneau.

In 1880, George Pilz, a German-born mining school graduate living in Sitka, grubstaked his employee Joe Juneau and another man, Richard Harris. The two men went prospecting in the vicinity of Gastineau Channel. Harris and Juneau named the creek where they found placer gold, Gold Creek, and they named Silver Bow Basin at the head of the creek. Since only shovels and other relatively inexpensive equipment were needed for this type of mining, the area attracted hundreds of gold seekers. A mining district was established and called Harrisburg, and soon a town, first named Harrisburg, then Rockwell, and finally Juneau began to flourish at a shallow bay called Miners Cove. The area would probably have gone the way of most mining districts after the placers had been worked out if lode, or hard-rock deposits, had not been discovered. Soon, several men established lode mines on the Juneau side of the channel. Eventually John Treadwell, a promoter, obtained a claim from a prospector known as French Pete for a sum ranging from $5 to $400, depending

Early street scene in
Juneau, 1896
(*Mrs. Rufus E. Rose Collection,
Archives, University of Alaska,
Fairbanks*)

upon one's source of information. The claim was located on Douglas Island.
According to geologist Alfred Brooks, the site contained very low-grade ore
and was worthless to French Pete, who did not possess the capital to develop
it. Treadwell recognized its potential and by taking advantage of cheap ocean
freight, water power sites, the abundance of timber, and a favorable climate
succeeded in developing a very profitable enterprise. It provided the year-
round employment which gave the town its economic base. Treadwell sold
out his interests in 1889. There were eventually four mines there—the Treadwell, the 700, the Mexican, and the Ready Bullion—as well as five stamp
mills. By 1890, the Treadwell group had yielded more than $3 million in gold;
other companies were established on the mainland, and the population of
Juneau increased to 1,200.[4]

For map of mining district,
see pages 338-339.

In the absence of a formal government structure, the miners of Juneau and
the interior, like their counterparts in western America, drafted their own form
of frontier democracy known as the ''miners' code.'' In their initial meetings
they decided on the boundaries for their mining district, drew up the rules for
the staking of claims, and elected an official known as the recorder to register
the site staked out by each man. They then prescribed the rules of conduct for
the community, ranging from fines for minor offenses to banishment for
stealing and hanging for murder. A court composed of the miners themselves
would sit in judgment and mete out the penalties.

Although the navy was more popular than the army had been, the clamor
for civil government became more articulate as the white population of Alaska
increased. In 1881 the miners of southeastern Alaska met and elected as their
''delegate to the Congress'' Mottrom D. Ball, the collector of customs. Ball
never was given official recognition, though the House of Representatives
voted to pay his expenses. While in Washington he condemned the American
neglect of Alaska and warned the congressmen that Alaska would not advance
in civilization or population until they passed laws to protect the rights of

The great Treadwell
gold mine, largest
in the world
(*Thomas Gibson Collection,
Archives,University of Alaska,
Fairbanks*)

persons and property. Ball's views were contradicted by Henry Elliott, who had been a member of the Western Union Company's scientific project and was considered an authority on Alaska by many congressmen. Elliott, a fervent champion of the natives and of the conservation of the seals, saw no need for territorial government and its attendant services. He asserted in an article written for *Harper's Weekly* that agriculture would never thrive in Alaska and that the population would always remain small. His colleague on the expedition, William H. Dall, while enthusiastically extolling the potential riches of Alaska's mineral wealth, also remained dubious of the advisability of immediate territorial government.

Most influential of all the spokesmen on Alaskan affairs was the Reverend Sheldon Jackson. Jackson, a Presbyterian minister, made the first of his voyages to Alaska in 1877 (he never became a resident) when he helped organize the Wrangell mission, the first of his endeavors to bring Christianity to the Alaskan natives. He quickly established himself as the authority on Alaska and Alaskan affairs, speaking to hundreds of groups primarily in the northeastern part of the United States, appealing for their aid in his crusade against the evil influence of those whites who corrupted the native men with drink and ravaged the women. And in Washington he was well known among members of the Congress, was the intimate friend and fellow churchman of Benjamin Harrison, later president of the United States and author of the First Organic Act establishing civilian government in Alaska.[5]

Jackson was mainly interested in securing federal support for educating the natives, while Harrison was interested in government organization and administration. Together they were able to achieve Alaska's first civil government and obtain money for an Alaskan school system. Harrison, the chairman of the Senate Committee on Territories, had no illusions about the First Organic Act, and no one has ever suggested that his sponsorship of the measure gained him the presidency. He had introduced bills in previous sessions to no avail, but in the closing days of its first session in 1884, Congress and President Arthur apparently had been persuaded that military rule should end in Alaska.

Aside from agreeing that government should be simple and inexpensive, there was no clear concept of the form it should take. The result was a compromise, a hodgepodge of conflicting ideas and principles, a measure recognized as temporary until Congress could give more thought to establishing permanent institutions. Alaska was designated a "district," the term "territory" deliberately omitted from its title because this implied certain constitutional forms and guarantees. The organic act expressly forbade a legislature, and since Alaskans did not possess the right to vote for their representative, they were not subject to taxation. Laws being necessary for a civilized community, Alaska was given the code of Oregon, then the nearest state to Alaska (Washington was still a territory). These were to be "declared to be law in said district Alaska so far as . . . may be applicable, and not in conflict with the . . . laws of the United States."

The act gave the president authority to appoint the officials of the Alaskan government subject to the approval of the Senate. Of these the most important by far was the judge who had the onerous task of interpreting the Oregon code in Alaska. He also presided over major civil and criminal cases, holding court alternately at Sitka and Wrangell, and was assisted by commissioners sitting in Juneau, Wrangell, Unalaska, and Sitka. The commissioner in Sitka served as ex-officio register of the Alaskan land office. A district attorney, a marshall and four assistants, and the clerk of the court comprised the staff engaged in law enforcement. Aside from writing an annual report, the governor had no real function, and some of the early incumbents merely made a yearly visit to the district.

Many Alaskans protested that the act gave them no rights of self-government and dealt only superficially with their problems. No provision had been made for law enforcement in the interior. The act acknowledged that Alaska constituted a land district and should be governed by the mining laws of the United States but categorically denied that the American land laws extended to the region. It made no provisions for private ownership of property except for allowing the mission stations to retain up to 640 acres of land. The natives were not to be disturbed in their occupancy or use of land, but Congress reserved for itself the ultimate settlement of claims to title. Prohibition was retained. Congress did appropriate $25,000 for the education of all children, native and white, but this was not enough to erect school buildings or pay the salaries of more than a few instructors.

President Arthur, a Republican, appointed John Kinkhead of Nevada, a former resident of Alaska, governor, and he named Ward McAllister of California and E. W. Haskett of Iowa judge and district attorney respectively. Almost immediately a conflict broke out involving the officeholders and Dr. Jackson, who had been appointed general agent for Alaska to administer its educational program. Jackson and the missionaries who sided with him championed the cause of the natives, who, they declared, were being exploited and corrupted by the whites. Kinkhead, though he was a Republican and a Presbyterian like Jackson, was an enemy of the natives; but he strongly supported the whites in their determination to develop Alaska, which he believed should have priority. He aroused Jackson by his opposition to prohibition, which the newcomers resented. Jackson denounced him and the other presidential appointees as high-living, hard-drinking men whose interest in the natives was minimal. Jackson's political enemies in turn accused him of using the money entrusted to him as the general agent for Alaska solely for the benefit of the natives and his church. Haskett, the district attorney, ordered Jackson's arrest on charges of attempting to convert a public road into the private property of the Sitka Industrial School, of which he was a sponsor; but soon the case was dropped.

When Grover Cleveland was inaugurated president, Jackson persuaded him to replace the Alaskan officeholders. This Cleveland did, naming Democrat Alfred Swineford governor. Swineford, a vigorous protagonist of self-government, became the inveterate foe of the Alaska Commercial Company, which he accused of seeking to control the territory; but like Kinkhead, he also drew the enmity of Sheldon Jackson.

The controversy between Jackson, who represented the missionary group, and the governors was essentially a struggle for influence in the nation's capital regarding who should be consulted on Alaskan legislation and political appointments. They were specifically at odds over the question of liquor and its control. Moreover, Swineford was a confirmed racist who boasted how he had had the top of a native shaman's head shaved and then painted red when the old man became recalcitrant. On the other hand, he was concerned about the steady decline of the native population.

The coming of the Americans affected the native peoples more than the Russian occupation had. The Americans not only penetrated the interior but went into the arctic regions as well. And their aggressive exploitation of Alaskan resources threatened the native food supply in some areas.

Whalers who had been present even during the Russian days began hunting walruses after they had decimated the whale population. Walruses were valued chiefly for their ivory tusks, and when these were cut out their bodies were usually left to rot. Eskimos soon took part in this reckless destruction also. Some had become enchanted with the goods that could be obtained from a commercial economy, and they discarded their age-old practice of killing only enough animals for food. Their efficiency in the slaughter was enhanced by the guns they had obtained from the whites. Whole villages were threatened with starvation. In the southeast complaints were also being made that the white men were taking over the salmon runs and endangering the Indian economy.

Missionaries, Reindeer, and Fur Seals

While some missionaries believed that conversion to Christianity was the answer to the native problem, the Reverend William Duncan sought to lead the

Father Duncan's church, called Metlakatla Christian Church, on Annette Island
(*Charles Parr Collection, Archives, University of Alaska, Fairbanks*)

way by creating a model community. He brought 1,000 Tsimshian followers from Metlakatla in British Columbia, where his views on theology had been condemned by his superiors in the Church of England, to Annette Island. On land obtained through a congressional grant he built a new Metlakatla, designed to make the natives self-sufficient. They were taught trades such as carpentry, seamanship, and boat-building, built their own sawmills and a cannery, and engaged in other enterprises. They lived in neat and orderly homes. But despite their prosperity, the younger Tsimshians in particular became restless under Duncan's authoritarian rule, and in 1912 they were able to successfully petition the government for a school, which he had opposed.

Dr. Jackson also threw his great energy into finding an answer to the natives' economic problems, something that would not keep them dependent on the charity of public assistance. His friend Captain Michael Healy of the Revenue Cutter Service suggested that the Eskimos be taught the cultivation of the reindeer, which was the basis of livelihood for the natives of the nearby Chukotsk Peninsula just across the Bering Strait. Jackson, very much taken with the idea, immediately began a campaign of public subscription and obtained enough money to acquire a small herd and hire instructors to train the Eskimos in the care of reindeer. Subsequently, he secured a congressional appropriation to further the work. Thus began a new enterprise in Alaska; it prospered, according to geologist Brooks, despite Jackson's mismanagement.[6]

American concern over another industry, the seal fisheries, and the attempt to prevent hunting of seals on the high seas brought about a diplomatic controversy with Great Britain. Each spring the seals make their way from southern waters to the Pribilof Islands, where the mating process takes place.

Clubbing fur seals in
the Pribilof Islands
*(Barrett Willoughby Collection,
University of Alaska, Fairbanks)*

There the Alaska Commercial Company, which held the islands by lease, designed a conservation program to keep the seal population stable. Since each adult bull has his own harem and keeps the younger males away from the females, the company killed only the "bachelors." But in the water no distinction between male or female, young or old, can be made, and many seals drowned after being shot. To stop this wanton slaughter the United States declared the Bering Sea an American waterway and prohibited all hunting of seals. American warships seized Canadian vessels and crews who refused to heed this edict. Great Britain protested on behalf of its Canadian subjects. An arbitration tribunal meeting in Paris awarded damages of slightly less than a half-million dollars to the Canadians, while the two governments agreed to limit the number of seals taken in a single year.[7]

Alaska on the Eve of the Great Gold Rush

By 1896, the year of the great Klondike discoveries, Alaska was clearly American. Russian civilization had not been destroyed by the coming of the Americans, for the Russian influence had been slight and there was little in the way of civilization to destroy. The decline of Sitka and the small part of Alaska that could be called Russian America had begun long before the purchase of

Juneau City, 1887
(*Historical Photograph Collection, Archives, University of Alaska, Fairbanks*)

Alaska. Alaska and Alaskan affairs were no longer under the domination of a single company. Even the Alaska Commercial Company, which had been accused of dominating Alaskan life, had lost its monopoly in the Pribilof Islands by 1890. Americans were coming and leaving the region as they saw fit without having to obtain permission from an outside agency or government. Juneau was a typically American town, with its variety of privately owned mercantile establishments, schools, and a hospital supported almost entirely by private subscription. It was governed by the miners' code, and possessed, despite the edict of prohibition, nine saloons and two breweries. Alaskans were very much aware of the rudiments of American politics, since they sent delegates to Washington and even participated in national party conventions in 1888. Alaskans complained of neglect with some justification; but in the United States of the nineteenth century federal government action was much more limited than it was to become in a later era.

·4·
Alaska: 1890-1920

The Great Gold Rush

WITH THE discovery of gold in the Klondike came a new discovery of Alaska, America's lost province. Men flocked from all parts of the world to one of the greatest of gold rushes; eventually more than $300 million worth of the metal was taken from the Yukon. Unaware that the Klondike is in Canada, Americans clamored for information concerning Alaska and the North. The trials and tribulations of the prospectors, most of whom were fellow countrymen, became front-page news stories for the "yellow press," then in its infancy. As the gateway to the Klondike, Alaska prospered: new towns and businesses sprang up to meet the needs of those going to the "great diggings." Alfred H. Brooks, the noted authority on Alaskan geology, credits the pushing out of miners from the Klondike in search of new sources of supply with advancing by many years the opening of Alaska's gold fields. Businessmen became intrigued with opportunities for investment in Alaska. Congress responded by making the first significant amendments to the organic act of 1884.

Although it was possible to journey entirely through Canadian territory, most of the gold seekers preferred the more accessible routes from Alaskan ports to the Klondike. Some went entirely by water, departing by ship from San Francisco or Seattle to St. Michael on Norton Sound, an arm of the Bering Sea, and from there transferring to a river craft going up the Yukon to Dawson, the metropolis of the Klondike. This was the easiest but also the longest and most expensive mode of travel, and it was fraught with the threat that a freeze of the river could leave passengers stranded until the spring thaws.

The most celebrated of the routes in legend and verse was the trail of 1898 from Lynn Canal in the Alaska Panhandle across the White or Chilkoot Passes. The Chilkoot route from Dyea, now a ghost town, is shorter but steeper. But the White Pass out of Skagway had the advantage that animals could be used for transporting supplies. Hundreds of horses subsequently slid to their deaths

Men and dogs pull sleds
on their way to the
Yukon gold fields
(Wahte Collection, Archives,
University of Alaska, Fairbanks)

on the ice, frequently overloaded by incompetent or brutal masters. After making the crossing, the thousands of gold seekers proceeded, usually with the aid of a homemade craft, via Lake Bennett and the Yukon River to their destination. For many the most difficult part of the journey was the climb to the summit of the passes. The Canadian government required that each man have at least one year's supply of food. This together with other necessities might weigh as much as several tons. It was common for two men to form a team, pushing part of their cargo on sleds, while carrying as much as 150 pounds on their backs. After reaching the summit one might go back for another load while the other stood guard, and so on, alternately, until all their possessions had been brought up. On April 3, 1898, a great snowslide took the lives of forty-three persons near Chilkoot Pass.

Almost overnight Skagway, the supply center for the Yukon, burgeoned into Alaska's largest town. For those finding employment this was the end of the journey, while others often remained in the town for months on end waiting for favorable weather to leave for Dawson or for the ship to take them home. The town achieved a great deal of notoriety, largely as a result of the activities of Jefferson C. Smith and his gang. "Soapy," as he was called, had been able to make himself master of Skagway and to terrorize its inhabitants because of the virtual nonexistence of any formal government authority. Smith's men, stationed along the Seattle waterfront, advised travelers where to go and whom to see in Skagway. Upon arrival there, they would be met by other members of the gang, taken under "Soapy's" protection, and very often fleeced of their money either at gunpoint or through crooked gambling games. Returnees from Dawson might be treated in similar fashion. Newcomers to Skagway were encouraged to send telegrams to their loved ones announcing their safe arrival. Not long after, they would be asked to pay an additional five dollars for return telegram messages which had been sent "collect." No telegraph line existed in Skagway.

Like a modern Mafia godfather, Smith was regarded by some as a great public benefactor, for as the head of the local welfare agency he was most generous to those in Skagway who found themselves destitute. A patriot, he offered to organize volunteers for service in the war against Spain. But the secretary of war politely declined his help. Smith's rule, however, soon came to an end. In July 1898, under the leadership of Frank Reid, a surveyor, a vigilante group was formed to rid Skagway of the outlaws. At the head of a posse Reid challenged Smith; they exchanged shots, Smith dying instantly. Reid died a few hours later, a martyr in defense of law and order.

Gold Strikes at Nome and in the Tanana Valley

Alaska soon experienced its own gold rush on the Seward Peninsula, the tip of which is only sixty miles from Siberia. Daniel Libby claimed to have found gold as a member of the Western Union Telegraph expedition in 1866. But it was not until 1897 that he returned to the area. With the backing of several men from San Francisco and accompanied by H. L. Blake, L. S. Leising, and A. P. Mordaunt, all of whom had been with him in the Klondike, they organized the first mining district on the peninsula. On September 22, 1898, Jafet Lindenberg, Jon Bryntesen, and Eric Lindblom, known as the "three lucky Swedes" (though Lindenberg had been born in Norway), made their great strike at Anvil Creek, and the Nome mining district came into existence. No great stampede followed immediately, because prospectors had become leery of talk of new El Dorados. Of the newcomers some came from Kotzebue, where they had pursued riches in vain, while others were returning from the Klondike via the Yukon River. They decided after their arrival at St. Michael that they had little to lose in making the 100-mile crossing over to Nome to try their luck once again. After the ice went out in the spring of 1899, confirmation was made of the great discoveries when ships arrived in Seattle laden with treasure from the peninsula, and the rush was on. By October more than 3,000 prospectors were working at Nome.

Life at Nome was much different from life in the Klondike. Although it was more readily accessible, living conditions were far more difficult. The Seward Peninsula is barren of trees. Aside from driftwood, all lumber had to be imported, making it well-nigh impossible for miners to build cabins for themselves or to secure any fuel for heating. In the winter, when temperatures were low and winds were high, a person unable to obtain lodging at Nome or its vicinity had no choice but to leave. There is little game on the Seward Peninsula, and climatic conditions make the growing of vegetables impossible.

Nome, in the words of Alfred H. Brooks, "was anything but a contented community"; its problems were complicated by a general air of lawlessness combined with numerous claim-jumping incidents. A number of professional claim-takers, armed with powers of attorney, had been busy filing claims for themselves and others even though no gold had been found at the time they made their applications, which was contrary to American law. Their claims, as well as those held by foreigners, were challenged by newcomers, who were incensed to find that all the gold-bearing areas apparently had already been

Beach scene at Cape
Nome, 1900
*(Mulligan Album, Archives,
University of Alaska, Fairbanks)*

staked out. By the fall of 1900 mining had come to a virtual standstill, and Nome appeared to be on the verge of civil war. Brooks believes that bloodshed was averted only by the prompt action of Lieutenant Oliver Spaulding, the commander of the small detachment of troops on the Seward Peninsula, in disbanding a meeting called by malcontents for the purpose of taking over the disputed claims. The discovery that the Nome beaches contained gold pushed these controversies to the background. Beach mining is easier than mining in the creeks; there is no frozen material to thaw, and the equipment needed is minimal. Access to the beaches was apparently open to all, although a mining company with adjacent claims attempted to collect royalties. When the miners refused to pay, the company attempted to evict them from the beaches; but the opposition was too great. By the summer of 1900 Nome was a tent city with more than 20,000 men working its "golden sands."[1]

Nome was wide open, condemned by moralists as comparable only to Skagway in its flouting of the law and disregard of convention. "Shootouts, muggings and saloon brawls," according to historian William R. Hunt, "made life insecure." Brooks reports that in all his years of travel throughout Alaska and the Yukon, Nome was the only place he carried a gun or felt any apprehension of being robbed. In 1900 the town was filled with pimps, prostitutes, con men, and gamblers; it had fifty saloons, and that figure soon doubled.[2]

Respect for law and government authority in Nome was further undermined by the appointment of Arthur Noyes as the first judge for the newly created judicial district of northern Alaska. Noyes is remembered today as one

Nome street scene,
ca. 1900
(*Bunnell Collection, Archives,
University of Alaska, Fairbanks*)

of those whom novelist Rex Beach designated as "the spoilers" of Nome. Upon his arrival the judge ordered all disputed claims placed in a state of receivership and named Alexander McKenzie, a former sheriff from North Dakota with a reputation for being the fastest draw in the West, as their administrator. McKenzie hired men to work the mines, dividing the profits with the judge, the district attorney, and a few other cronies. In the meantime, one of the original owners, Charles D. Lane of the Wild Goose Company, made two trips to San Francisco in an effort to have the circuit court of appeals reverse Noyes's decision. Judge William Morrow, speaking for the higher court, directed that the claims be restored, and upon the refusal of McKenzie and Noyes to comply, marshals were sent to enforce the order. McKenzie was brought to San Francisco for trial and sentenced to a year in jail, which was subsequently commuted to three months by President McKinley. Noyes continued as judge until the summer of 1901, when he was removed and fined $1,000 for having been in contempt of court. Joseph K. Wood, the district attorney, and C. A. S. Frost, an agent of the Department of Justice, received sentences of four months and twelve months respectively for their roles in the affair.

Nome's boom was accompanied and followed by strikes in different parts of Alaska: the Kenai Peninsula, Wiseman, Iditarod, and the Tanana Valley, the last resulting in the founding of Fairbanks, destined to become the largest town in the interior. Felix Pedro, an Italian immigrant and former coal miner, is credited with having made the initial discovery of gold in the valley in the creek which today bears his name.

There are several versions surrounding the beginnings of Fairbanks in which Pedro and the merchant E. T. Barnette, later accused of embezzling from the banks of which he was president, played a leading role. Barnette, who had

Felix Pedro, discoverer
of Fairbanks gold fields
(*Historical Photograph
Collection, Archives,
University of Alaska, Fairbanks*)

been a trader for several years in Circle, came down the Tanana River in 1901. Whether by choice or necessity, he anchored the ship that he had chartered, the *Lavelle Young,* on the Chena River, a tributary of the Tanana, in August of 1901. Persuaded by Pedro of the area's potential, he established his store there. From this center grew a town that was named after the vice president of the United States at that time, Charles Fairbanks. Most of the miners who came to the Tanana Valley were experienced men who had come from other diggings. Since expensive machinery and equipment were needed to thaw and extract the metal from the ground, the individual prospector soon became a rarity, and the valley became dotted with a number of small companies. For years Fairbanks and Chena, which lay at the head of navigation on the Tanana River, competed with each other to be the leading town of the district in supplying the neighboring mining camps connected to them by the narrow-gauge Tanana Valley Railroad. Fairbanks won out after Judge James Wickersham moved the headquarters of the judicial district of the interior there from Eagle. Today only a marker indicates where Chena once was, the river having washed away most of the townsite.

By 1905 men were bringing their families to settle in Fairbanks, and the population had increased to 5,000. The town had schools and a hospital; and it also had its seamy side, with saloons open twenty-four hours a day, gambling houses, and "the line," where the prostitutes conducted their business. Its most notorious character was the "Blue Parka Bandit," a highwayman who plied his trade in the valley and was a frequent visitor to Judge Wickersham's court. His gallantry was proverbial. On one occasion, after robbing the Episcopalian bishop he returned the loot, explaining that he was one of the cleric's parishioners. Fairbanks proudly called itself "the largest log cabin city in the world." In 1906 a fire destroyed much of the town, but it was soon rebuilt.

Congressional Response to the Gold Rush

Congressional interest in Alaska grew with the gold rush. On occasion the response of the legislators was most generous but misdirected. In the winter of 1897/98, when the Klondike boom was at its height, the secretary of war acknowledged, in response to some inquiries of congressmen, that prospectors in the Yukon faced starvation. Two hundred thousand dollars was immediately appropriated for relief. Someone connected with the rescue mission, his vision of the North fashioned by scenes of the Christmas season, ordered the purchase of reindeer in Norway to transport supplies to the stricken miners. These "government pets," as critics of the expedition called the reindeer, were shipped to New York, then overland to Seattle, and from there barged to Haines. Most of the animals died before reaching their destination, the long voyages by sea and land having taken their toll. Others died on their way over the Dalton Trail, which is heavily wooded and not suitable for reindeer, which are native to tundra and feed on lichens. The relief expedition should not have been organized in the first place; tales of starvation in the Yukon had been much exaggerated. Besides, the well-organized Canadian government had the situation well in hand: food had been provided almost as soon as cries for help had been made, and nobody went hungry.

Fairbanks, 1904
(Robert Jones Collection, Archives, University of Alaska, Fairbanks)

Lapp reindeer herders
(H. Levy Collection, Archives, University of Alaska, Fairbanks)

Undeterred by the reindeer fiasco, Congress went on to deal seriously with the Alaska problem and enacted more legislation in the next three years than it had in the entire previous era of American rule. They appropriated money that enabled the geological survey to begin its work of exploration and survey. The mining laws of the United States were extended to the district. Army posts were established at Eagle, Valdez, Nome, Haines, and at the junction of the Yukon and Tanana rivers. The Department of Agriculture was instructed to examine the potential of farming in Alaska.

However, far more important in their consequences for Alaska were three measures dealing with the economy and political system. The first, passed in 1898, enabled prospective railroad builders to obtain the necessary right of way and extended the Homestead Act to Alaska, giving settlers their first opportunity to receive title to land. Alaskans, however, were restricted to 80 acres instead of the 160 that had become customary in other parts of the United States. In 1899 the criminal code was amended. In the same year the district received its first system of taxation. Canneries were assessed 4¢ for each case packed. Railroads were taxed $100 for every mile in operation even though the line need not have been completed. Companies had to obtain licenses for the privilege of doing business, the amount of the fee varying with the nature of the enterprise, liquor being the highest of all. Thus—despite the objections of Sheldon Jackson, the district's foremost politician—prohibition, which had been a dead letter almost since its inception, was repealed. By this time Jackson's protégé and a staunch temperance advocate, the Reverend John Brady, who was governor of Alaska at that time, recognized that the government's liquor policy had been a failure and admitted that effective regulation could be achieved only by a high license fee that would limit the number of establishments able to engage in the trade.

In 1900, Congress made substantial revisions in the civil code and directed its attention to the government of Alaska. As a result of the population growth, the number of judicial districts was increased to three. The judge in the southeast held sessions alternately in Skagway and Juneau; St. Michael and then Nome served as the headquarters for the newly created northern division; and in the interior Judge Wickersham, as has been noted above, moved the seat of his court from Eagle to Fairbanks. In 1905, Juneau replaced Sitka, in decline since the Russian period, as the capital of Alaska. This act, in providing for the setting up of towns, gave Alaskans their initial taste of self-government. After fulfilling the requirements of incorporation, a community could then proceed to the election of a council of seven, one of whom acted as mayor. The council was empowered to furnish various services, such as street improvements, police and fire protection, and the establishment of a school system, but it was limited in its sources of revenue. Taxes on real and personal property were restricted to 1 percent of the assessed valuation, while any borrowing was expressly forbidden. Towns were permitted to impose license fees on businesses; and half the money collected was to be used for support of education. Shortly thereafter the federal government removed its system of licenses within the municipalities as an unnecessary duplication, enabling the towns to raise fees and increase income.

The Alaskan Boundary Dispute with Canada

The era of the gold rush brought to a head the Alaskan boundary dispute with Canada that had long been festering. It was generally agreed that the portion of the treaty of 1825 that had sought to define the limits of Russian and British possessions south of the 60th parallel was very much clouded in ambiguity. On several occasions after the United States took possession of Alaska, disputes arose and suggestions were made, chiefly by the Canadians, to settle the controversy, but neither side was willing to undertake the cost and bother of a survey. By 1898 the Canadian case extended to claims of ownership of Skagway and Dyea, which—if they were recognized—would give Canadians direct access to the Yukon without passing through American territory.

Theodore Roosevelt, who became president following William McKinley's assassination in 1901, condemned the demands as totally without merit and refused to allow the matter to be decided by a board of arbitration; in his opinion, such bodies invariably settled disagreements of this kind by dividing the disputed area equally between the rival contestants. Roosevelt instead proposed that a tribunal of six impartial jurists be constituted, three from each side, to examine the merits of the controversy. He named to the American delegation Henry Cabot Lodge, the ultranationalistic senator from Massachusetts; Elihu Root, Roosevelt's secretary of war; and Senator George Turner of Washington, because the trade of that state's chief city, Seattle, would be most affected if the Canadian claims to Skagway and Dyea were upheld. The British-Canadian delegation included Lord Alverstone, chief justice of England, Sir Louis Jette, a former member of the Canadian Supreme Court, and Allen Aylesworth, a distinguished member of the Canadian bar. None of the Americans could be called "impartial jurists." By a vote of four to two the tribunal, with Lord Chief Justice Alverstone siding with the Americans, rejected the Canadian claims except for two small islands in the Portland Canal. Alverstone was accused by the Canadians of having sold out their interests in behalf of British-American relations. And although the Alaskan boundary was now clearly defined, relations between the United States and Canada were long embittered by this dispute and its settlement.

The gold rush played a prominent role in the history of Alaska, marking for some the beginnings of the modern era. It was indeed a time of great excitement. Thousands from all occupations and backgrounds came for adventure. With the new towns that sprang up came the first semblances of self-government, and Alaskans felt they were beginning to receive the recognition that was their due. But essentially the gold rush remains an episode in Alaskan life and development that acted more as a stimulant than as an instrument of change. While it brought more people into the territory and resulted in a population figure that was to remain stable until the great increase following World War II, those who came usually remained only a few years. But interest had been kindled, and there was optimism concerning Alaska and its potential as the twentieth century opened.

Development of Resources

In the mood of optimism generated by the gold rush, schemes were afoot to exploit the riches of Alaska and to make the territory self-supporting. While

The Fairbanks Exploration Company, a subsidiary of the United States Smelting, Refining and Mining Company, ran many gold dredges around Fairbanks. This one worked on Gold Stream Valley near Fairbanks
(*Charles Bunnell Collection, Archives, University of Alaska, Fairbanks*)

investors were attracted by gold and other minerals said to be in great abundance, companies vied for railway franchises and other concessions. The relationship with the federal government, however, remained ambivalent. More help had been coming from Washington, but still more was needed to unlock this treasure house. Even so, some Alaskans believed that federal intrusions in Alaskan affairs had at times been harmful. In addition, Alaskans were beginning to ask for the right to have more of a voice in decisions concerning their destinies.

Even in the Russian days inhabitants of Alaska had been seeking ways to make themselves less dependent on the outside. The possibilities of farming had been examined, and some vegetable gardens had been planted. Travelers to the Yukon River valley during the American era had come back with tales of the tremendous cabbages grown there. But it was not until the gold rushes and the expectations of increased population that "agriculture in Alaska" could no longer be considered a curious "oddity," writes historian Orlando Miller.

In 1897 the Department of Agriculture sent three special agents to southeastern Alaska, the south-central region, Kodiak, the Alaska Peninsula, and the Yukon Valley. After mentioning the difficulties involved in farming in Alaska, they indicated that a "variety of crops" could be grown and that cattle raising and vegetable gardening were already being undertaken. One of the investigators recommended that men be encouraged to settle on small plots and to "engage in mixed fishing, lumbering and farming. All this would be for the purpose of settling the country with a hardy race of fishermen and others used to the water; from which we may secure seamen for the merchant marine and navy, and at the same time . . . develop other resources," and thus establish in Alaska "a great civilization."[3] Based on their recommendations, several agricultural experiment stations were established, the first at Sitka in 1898, followed by others at Kenai, Kodiak, Rampart, Copper Center, Fairbanks, and last, Matanuska in 1917. Danish-born C. G. Georgeson, appointed to head the station at Sitka, was a most ardent promoter of Alaskan agriculture. His constant refrain was that "the hope for the natives and the development of the territory" lay in a prosperous agriculture, for "it stands to reason that if the means to support life exist within the boundaries of the Territory all other resources will become more valuable."[4]

But even more immediate to the pressing needs of Alaska was a good system of transportation. The use of the inland waterways had been considerably improved in the Klondike era with the increase in the number of steamboats traveling the Yukon and later the Tanana. Dog sleds were of importance in some areas, but as yet little progress had been made with the reindeer. The absence of good roads and trails was the greatest problem. Congress in 1898 had authorized individuals to build and collect tolls on roads and bridges, but few indeed had ventured to take advantage of those opportunities. In 1904 another measure placed the burden of road building on the inhabitants of the territory. Each man was made liable to labor two days a year on the roads or to pay a tax of $8 in lieu of that. The U.S. commissioners appointed a supervisor in each district who was to receive $4 a day for his efforts at a time when the prevailing wage was from $6 to $8 daily. But it was not until the passage of the

Dog team at Point
Barrow, 1960s
(Claus-M. Naske)

Nelson Act in 1905 and the establishment of the Alaska Road Commission the following year that road building in Alaska became a reality. The Nelson Act created the Alaska Fund, under the terms of which 70 percent of all moneys collected from license fees outside incorporated towns were to be used for road building, 25 percent for education, and 5 percent for the care of the insane. Major Wills Richardson was appointed to head the commission. Additional revenues were appropriated from time to time by Congress. By 1930, some 4,890 miles of roads and trails, of which 1,031 miles were wagon roads, had been built; the most notable was the Richardson Road connecting Valdez and Fairbanks.

Whereas private companies had little interest in building Alaska roads, the lure of adventure of constructing lines in the far north and the prospects of fabulous profits attracted railway men to Alaska. In the brief time span from September 1897 to March 1898, eleven companies reportedly petitioned for rights of way over 673 miles of land, with several more making application, until the panic of 1907 brought speculation to a halt. In 1903 the Alaska Central Railroad began construction to the interior, went bankrupt in 1908, reor-

Ambulances headed for Valdez with men wounded by Northwestern Railroad marshals in Keystone Canyon, Sept. 25, 1907 (*Whalen Collection, Archives, University of Alaska, Fairbanks*)

ganized as the Alaskan Northern Railroad, and had completed seventy-one miles of track to its destination, Fairbanks, when it ceased operation. Rivalry was most acute over a site for a railroad with its beginning at Valdez. Workmen from the rival Alaska Home Railroad and the Valdez-Yukon lines met and fought what has been called the Battle of Keystone Canyon, a conflict which left several dead. But not long after the encounter both companies gave up the venture. While several small narrow-gauge railroads served the needs of local inhabitants on the Seward Peninsula and in the Tanana Valley, only two of the larger lines prospered: the White Pass and Yukon Railroad built by the Close Brothers of London, thirty miles of which is in American territory; and the 195-mile Copper River and Northwestern Railroad completed by the Alaska Syndicate primarily to carry copper ore from its mines at Kennicott to the port of Cordova.

Varying explanations have been offered concerning the reasons for the failure of railroad building in Alaska. Interest in Alaskan railroads came at a time when railroads were no longer popular in the United States. The railroads had obtained large tracts of land, money at low interest rates, and other subsidies from the federal, state, and local governments, while at the same time they had abused their privileges, charged exorbitant rates, corrupted politics, and offered poor service. The struggling companies in Alaska, beset by the tremendous problems of building in the rugged Alaska terrain, had not only been refused government aid but had been further penalized by having to pay a tax of $100 annually for each mile in operation even before the completion of the line. Further, the railroads had been deprived of a cheap source of fuel by

President Roosevelt's action in closing the coal fields.

Theodore Roosevelt, the first American president to become vitally interested in the conservation of America's resources, issued an executive order in 1906 closing the coal lands of Alaska to further entry, claiming that the existing laws limiting investors to 160 acres were unworkable and conducive to fraud. He asked Congress to enact legislation that would enable prospective coal mine operators to obtain enough land to make mining profitable yet prevent any individual or group from securing a monopoly. But Congress failed to act, and it was not until 1914 that a law was passed making the coal lands once again available for entry.

Among those who had attempted to obtain coal lands in Alaska prior to the Roosevelt withdrawals were thirty-two persons who had given Clarence Cunningham the power of attorney to make selections for them. Acting on their behalf, Cunningham took an option on 5,280 acres of land in the Bering River area, which subsequently were incorporated into the newly established Chugach National Forest by Roosevelt in 1908. Cunningham's efforts to obtain patents for the land suffered repeated delays. Almost as soon as the necessary forms had been filed, rumors began to circulate that the group had never intended to mine coal themselves, as the law required, but had formed their association precisely for the purpose of transferring their claims to the Alaska Syndicate, a consortium of the Guggenheim Brothers and the great New York banking house of J. P. Morgan and Company—the owners of the Kennicott Copper Company, the Copper River and Northwestern Railroad, and several mining, canning, and steamship concerns. The identification of the Cunningham group with the syndicate was to lead to an investigation culminating in the Ballinger-Pinchot Affair, the great national political issue of 1910 which brought about a split in the Republican party and helped elect Woodrow Wilson president in 1912.

For map of coal land claims, see pages 340-341.

Richard Ballinger was a Seattle attorney whose connection with the Cunningham group preceded his appointment as secretary of the interior by President William H. Taft in 1909. He had been the commissioner of the General Land Office when Cunningham first applied for patents on behalf of his clients. As a private attorney, following his resignation from government service, he had advised the Cunningham group of the procedures to be followed in processing their claims. Louis Glavis, an agent of the Department of the Interior sent to Alaska to examine the Cunningham claims, became convinced as a result of his investigations that Ballinger was preparing to validate their transfer to the syndicate. He consulted Gifford Pinchot, the head of the Bureau of Forestry, an ardent conservationist and friend of Roosevelt, who advised him to submit his findings to President Taft, which he did. After reading Glavis' report, Taft ordered Ballinger to dismiss Glavis "for filing a disingenuous statement unjustly impeaching the integrity of his superior officers."

Pinchot himself was later fired on charges of insubordination for having written a letter highly critical of Taft's handling of the affair and of Taft's support of Ballinger. The letter had been sent to Senator J. P. Dolliver, who read it on the floor of the Senate. A joint congressional committee was formed to investigate the Department of the Interior for its handling of the Cunningham claims and to examine the accusations made by Ballinger against some officials of the Bureau of Forestry who, he complained, "had inspired the charges against his Department." Voting on strictly party lines, the majority, composed of stalwart Republicans, exonerated Ballinger of any wrongdoing, while the Democrats and one progressive Republican found him guilty of violating his trust. Ballinger resigned in the summer of 1911. His successor as secretary of the interior, Walter Fisher, the vice president of the National Conservation Association, invalidated the Cunningham claims soon afterward.[5]

Critics of the Alaskan system of government delighted in the publicity given the territory by the Ballinger-Pinchot Affair. Its revelations confirmed what they had been saying all along—that federal control had frustrated the development of Alaska and that only Alaskans sitting in a legislature of their own could deal effectively with the problems of Alaska. The drive for a territorial legislature had its real beginnings in the gold rush days when Alaska was officially called a district. Its supporters especially resented the total exclusion of Alaskans from affairs of concern to them and were scarcely mollified by the changes to the First Organic Act giving Alaska two additional judges and allowing municipalities limited rights of self-government.

But other Alaskans, notably those connected with the fishing and mining industries, saw little need for change. In opposition to the territorialists, as the supporters of a territory for Alaska were called, they argued that Alaska's population was unstable and too small to afford a legislature, and that such a body once constituted would undoubtedly destroy existing Alaskan industry by excessive taxation. They usually were willing to concede that the interests of Alaska might be served if the territory were allowed to have a delegate to Congress with a seat in the House of Representatives. A delegate well informed on Alaskan affairs could advise on matters relating to the territory. He would be able to introduce legislation of concern to Alaska and to take part in the debate. His influence therefore would be greater and far more valuable than a territorial legislature whose authority was apt to be very much restricted. But the territorialists were not impressed by these arguments. A delegate, while useful, was hardly a substitute for an Alaska legislature. He would be only one among many in a body that had little interest in Alaskan affairs. And though he might introduce bills, he could do little to affect the course of legislation in the House. As a voteless member he could not bargain with congressmen to gain their support for legislation of concern to Alaska in return for favors done them.

A chain of circumstances enabled Alaska to secure a delegate. In a series of decisions known as the Insular Cases, the Supreme Court ruled that islands recently acquired as a result of the war with Spain were unincorporated territories belonging to, but not part of, the United States; its residents therefore were not protected by the federal Constitution. Alaska, by contrast, had been incorporated as part of the Union. In a case involving a Fairbanks woman who had been convicted by a six-man jury of running a house of prostitution, the Court held that in the treaty of purchase of Alaska from Russia the United States had guaranteed to the white inhabitants and persons of mixed blood the rights, privileges, and immunities of citizens of the United States. As an Alaska inhabitant the lady was a resident of an incorporated territory; her conviction by a six-man jury in violation of the Sixth Amendment was void. Congress reacted quickly to the Court's views enhancing the status of Alaska, changing its official designation from "district" to "territory," and enacted into law the measure previously recommended without success by President Roosevelt, giving Alaska a delegate to Congress.

In the summer of 1906, Alaska held its first territorial election, asking the voters to choose one delegate for the remainder of the congressional term ending March 4, 1907, and another to sit in the new Congress. Both Republicans and Democrats nominated candidates, but two men without party affiliation—Frank Waskey of Nome and Thomas Cale of the Tanana Valley— won easily, largely because of support of miners of the interior and the Seward Peninsula. Waskey was elected to the short term and Cale to the regular session of Congress. President Roosevelt was advised by Waskey and Governor Wilford B. Hoggatt, a mine owner, that Alaskans did not desire territorial government at this time; consequently, they made no recommendations for any changes in the political system.

In 1909, Roosevelt was followed as president by the man whom he recommended as his successor—William Howard Taft. That same year Taft attended the Alaska-Yukon Exposition in Seattle. There he was warmly greeted by the Alaskans and made a member of the Arctic Brotherhood, and there he outlined his plans for the appointment of a legislative commission to deal with the problems of Alaska. This was a system he had observed firsthand when he had been governor-general of the Philippines. It had worked well there and would, he thought, be most suitable for Alaska, which lacked the population and resources for a legislature. A bill embodying these proposals in a somewhat revised form was introduced into the Senate by the chairman of the Committee on Territories, Albert Beveridge of Indiana. It gave to the president the power to select a council consisting of a governor, an attorney general, commissioners of the interior, mines, and education and health, as well as a representative from each of the four judicial districts to legislate for Alaska.

Wickersham and Home Rule for Alaska

James Wickersham, newly elected as Alaska's delegate in 1908, branded the Beveridge bill a measure fit only for Oriental coolies. A man of magnetic personality, in contrast to his colorless predecessors Waskey and Cale, "the Judge," as he was usually called, described himself in his election campaign as the enemy of the trusts, particularly the "Guggs," whom he accused time and again of seeking to deny the Alaskans any rights of self-government and of wanting to bring the resources of Alaska under their control. On the other side, Wickersham's enemies made much of a letter that came to light shortly before, showing the self-professed "trust buster" as having applied for a position with the syndicate and having been turned down. His opposition to the syndicate thus was termed personal pique and his recent conversion to home rule equally opportunistic and insincere.

Judge James
Wickersham feeding
a moose
(*Lulu Fairbanks Collection,
Archives, University of Alaska,
Fairbanks*)

Once converted to home rule, Wickersham assumed the championship of the movement and introduced several bills for self-government, but without success. By 1911 the drive to obtain a legislature for Alaska was in the ascendancy. President Taft, an adamant opponent, had lost control of Congress in the midterm elections; the Democrats had gained the House, while Senator Beveridge lost his seat in the Senate, and progressives of both parties ousted Republican stalwarts from control. Wickersham, however, was very much aware that home rule still faced great opposition and that substantial concessions would have to be made to different interests in order to get congressional approval and to avoid a presidential veto. Progressives were ideologically committed to self-government, but conservationists among them feared that a territorial legislature would be dominated by developers. Business groups, particularly the fisheries, opposed regulation by the territory and were apprehensive of high taxes. Crusaders for moral reform, hearing Wickersham branded by his foes as the tool of the liquor and gambling interests, questioned whether Alaskans were ready to undertake any responsibilities associated with self-rule.

The Second Organic Act

On August 14, 1912, President Taft signed the bill passed by Congress creating a territorial government, and the Second Organic Act became law. Wickersham's critics—and they were many, including some of those who had been in opposition to home rule—now complained bitterly that he had sold Alaska out. Control of the resources of Alaskan land, minerals, and fisheries all remained in federal hands, the Alaska legislature being expressly forbidden "to alter, amend, modify, and repeal measures relating to fish and game, or to interfere with the primary disposal of the soil." Matters relating to divorce, gambling, the sale of liquor, and incorporation of towns were exclusively the province of Congress, whose permission was needed before any form of county government could come into being. The territory was not permitted to borrow any money; its taxing authority was restricted to 1 percent of the assessed value of property, except for towns, which were allowed 2 percent. The governor appointed by the president had the power of veto extending to items in appropriation bills, which could be overridden only by a two-thirds vote of each house. The legislature as constituted under the act was to consist of two houses: four persons from each judicial district were to be members of the house, and two from each in the senate. Alaska was unique among territories in having no judiciary of its own; the president appointed the four judges, whose authority included both federal and territorial affairs. Congress agreed to pay the salaries of the legislators and officials of government as well as expenses pertaining to administration.

Early Territorial Legislatures: Woodrow Wilson and Alaska

Alaskans, though obviously disappointed by the limitations of the Second Organic Act, proceeded to hold elections and organize a legislature. There was little formal party organization; most of the legislators regarded themselves as independents. Their activities covered a wide variety of subjects. Substantial changes in the criminal and civil codes were made so as to conform more to conditions in Alaska. Labor legislation detailed conditions of employment in the mines, established an eight-hour day, and set up a system of old-age pensions. Women received the right to vote, and this was even before the Nineteenth Amendment had been passed. Native villages in southeastern Alaska were given some rights of self-government, while provisions were made to extend to Indians living a civilized life the rights of citizens. Education received much attention. A territorial board was formed to coordinate the school system and extend aid for schools throughout Alaska, but these were not schools for native children. Segregation, which had first received official sanction from the federal government with the passage of the Nelson Act of 1905, was now being perpetuated by the territory. The Nelson Act had designated part of the revenues received from the sale of business licenses outside incorporated towns to be used to support separate schools for white children and those of mixed blood. Apologists for the dual system argued that native children had poorer backgrounds and that having them in the same schools as whites would not only put them at a serious disadvantage but would result in lower educational standards.

Woodrow Wilson, assuming the presidency in 1913 after a split in the Republican party between Taft and Roosevelt in which the Alaska issue played a significant part, promised that the problems of Alaska would receive the utmost consideration in his administration. An activist, he resumed the practice that had been dormant since the days of Thomas Jefferson of delivering the annual presidential message to Congress in person. His legislative program contemplated substantial reform in the United States. On the subject of Alaska he was very explicit. In his address to Congress he emphasized that "a duty faces us with regard to Alaska," a duty he found "very pressing and very imperative" and which was in effect a "double duty," for it concerned "both the political and material development of the Territory." He urged that Alaska be given "full territorial government," and although he did not elaborate, he undoubtedly was calling attention to the deficiencies in the Alaskan system, where unlike other territories its people did not have the right to elect their governor and choose their judges. He wanted the resources of Alaska unlocked and made available for use, but he counseled that these should not be "destroyed or wasted." He declared that the "abiding interests of communities" must be placed above any "narrow idea of individual rights" that could bring about monopoly. A railroad for Alaska should be built and administered by the government "for the service and development of the country and its people."[6]

Although Congress refused to make changes in the Alaskan system of government, it passed the Mondell Act, reopening the Alaskan coal lands to entry. In line with Wilson's suggestion, a method of leasing was adopted, rather than outright ownership that could lead to monopoly. Prospective coal mine operators were given the opportunity to obtain up to 2,560 acres of land, for which they paid a rental fee ranging from 25¢ per acre for the first year of operation to $1 after the fifth year. For each ton of coal mined, a royalty of 2¢ had to be paid. Alaskan coal thus could be available for use by the railroad whose building Congress had recently authorized.

Even before Wilson took office as president the groundwork had been laid for the federal government's sponsorship of a railroad in Alaska. So staunch a conservative as President Taft reluctantly admitted that the obstacles in Alaska had been too great for private enterprise, but while he agreed to the government's construction of the railroad, he nevertheless insisted that it should be operated by a private company. In the debates that followed concerning the railroad, a few congressmen repeated the old canard that any expenditure in Alaska was a waste of money, while others were disturbed by the contemplation of any government involvement in railroad building. But as historian Edward Fitch points out in his book on the Alaska Railroad, "a faith in railroads combined with a lack of faith in railroad personalities led Congress finally to adopt a program of government ownership and operation for a railroad in Alaska even though Congress disbelieved strongly in government ownership and operation."[7]

Largely owing to the influence of Wickersham, who was regarded as an authority on Alaskan affairs, his advice that the president be given the authority to choose the route of the railroad was followed. Surveys of alternate sites had already been made by the Alaska Engineering Commission established during the preceding administration. After some study and discussion, Wilson directed that the line should run from Seward to Fairbanks in the interior. Thirty-five million dollars was appropriated for the project. Construction began in April 1915, but the road was not finished until 1923. The difficulties in construction were formidable. Work was carried on sporadically and was marked by innumerable delays. Congress followed the practice of making an-

Arrival in Fairbanks of the
Midnight Sun Limited over
the Alaska Railroad
*(Reuel Griffin Collection,
Archives,University of Alaska,
Fairbanks)*

nual appropriations, allotting only so much money for each year's operation;
when funds ran out, work stopped. During the war years the use of men and
materials was drastically curtailed.

Alaska as a "Colony" of the United States

The immediate effect of the building of the railroad was a boom in Alaska.
More than 2,000 men were employed in construction in 1914, with their
numbers rising to a high of 4,500. Although the pay was only 37.5¢ an hour in
early years, the number of applicants for jobs far exceeded demand. Anchorage, now Alaska's largest city, owes its beginnings to the railroad. Begun as a
construction site, it won out in competition with Seward to become the headquarters of the Alaska Engineering Commission. The commission literally built
Anchorage by installing water, electrical, sewage, and telephone facilities, put-
ting in streets, and by providing fire-fighting services as well as a hospital and a
school for the children of its employees. An official of the railway was named as
the townsite manager.[8]

While the government was building a railroad in Alaska, another law
passed by Congress, the U.S. Maritime Act—commonly called the Jones
Act—was placing restrictions on Alaskan commerce. The purpose of the Jones
Act was to build up the American merchant marine. All ships engaged in
commerce between American ports had to be carried on American-owned and

American-built ships. A clause of the act gave shippers the option of using either American- or Canadian-owned forms of transportation in carrying goods from a point of origin in the United States out to any destination on the Atlantic or the Pacific, with the single exception of Alaska. Merchandise entering or leaving the territory had to be transported by American carriers. The Jones Act was clearly discriminatory; but as the Supreme Court noted in *Alaska v. Troy*, a suit initiated by the territory in protest, the Constitution of the United States makes clear "that no preference shall be given any regulation of commerce or revenue to the ports of one state over those of another."[9] Since Alaska was not a state, Congress was free to regulate its commerce as it saw fit. That the provisions of the Maritime Act might most benefit Seattle, Senator Wesley Jones's home city, was not for the Court to decide.

Alaska was very definitely a colony of the United States. Her government, it is said, resembled that of a British crown colony. A limited form of home rule had been achieved, but control of Alaska's resources was in the hands of Congress. Alaska's economy was colonial, since the territory was primarily a supplier of raw materials to the mother country, from whom she obtained most of her finished goods. But circumstances and natural conditions, not governmental decree, had been responsible for giving Alaska a colonial economy. Capital had always been in short supply in Alaska. During the Russian period the fur trade had been the mainstay of the economy. With the coming of the Americans the fisheries, minerals, gold, and, for a short time after 1911, copper had been of primary importance. These involved masculine trades usually limited in employment to a few months of the year, and carried on in remote areas not conducive to permanent settlement and the growth of a permanent population.

Territorial representatives in session in Juneau — first territorial legislature, 1913
(Historical Photograph Collection, Archives, University of Alaska, Fairbanks)

Federal policies were not always helpful. The Jones Act did not allow Alaska to take advantage of cheaper Canadian transportation facilities; how much it harmed Alaska is difficult to tell. The delay in opening the coal fields was inexcusable and definitely hampered Alaskan development; but the failure of a coal-mining industry to attract more users had other causes. Alaskan coal could not find a ready market outside the territory, and in 1914 the navy, which in early years might have wanted the coal, converted its ships to oil. The government ordered the building of a railroad, but this was not finished until 1923. Alaskan agriculture did not become a great and profitable enterprise, but for this the government was hardly to blame. In 1923 in the Fairbanks and Anchorage-Matanuska districts, advertised as the chief agricultural regions, there were only ninety farmers with 22,127 acres of land, only 1,421 of which were cultivated.

America's entrance into World War I had varying consequences for Alaska. The conflict was remote. Alaska was neither a site for training camps nor a center of war production. The population of the territory declined as people went elsewhere to work in war industries and men enlisted or were drafted into military service.

·5·
Normalcy, the Depression, and the New Deal

WARREN G. HARDING succeeded Wilson as president of the United States in 1921. An exponent of the contemporary reaction, he repudiated the idealism of his predecessor, denouncing the League of Nations and declaring in his inaugural address that it was a time for "normalcy and not nostrums." His administration was plagued with scandals. He referred to the presidency as "this damned job," complained about the multiplicity of problems that he so little understood, and confessed his inability to choose from conflicting advice, especially from the economists.

But on the subject of Alaska he was much more positive. The first president to visit the territory, he came to Nenana in 1923 to drive in the golden spike that symbolized the completion of the Alaska Railroad. Harding spoke with feeling about Alaska; he once remarked that "if the Finns owned Alaska they would in three generations make it one of the foremost states of the Union." He urged that Alaska's resources be used to benefit its settlers and to make homes for people in the territory—not to serve outside speculators. He promised that his administration would work to the utmost to help develop Alaska. On his return trip to Washington he became ill in San Francisco and died shortly thereafter. With his death, wrote Ernest Gruening, governor of Alaska during the New Deal era and later U.S. Senator from the newly formed state, Alaska "lost a great friend at court."[1]

It was during Harding's administration that the federal government made its only serious attempt to deal with the problem of the Alaska salmon fisheries. The abundance of salmon in Alaska waters and the ease of catching them had enabled the Indians of southeastern Alaska, in whose diet salmon was the mainstay, to devote their talents to other pursuits and to develop a high culture. The Russians also depended a great deal on the salmon for food; but the commercial era of the fisheries did not begin until the American period, and because of Alaskan conditions the industry was early dominated by outside groups. Alaska lacked capital, and its population was small and scattered. Alaskan natives had little interest in working in the canneries. The great salmon

Fishermen working
with nets around the
turn of the century
*(Wetherbee Collection,
Archives, University of Alaska,
Fairbanks)*

packers, whose headquarters were in Seattle and San Francisco, brought their own crews to Alaska, some to fish and others, mainly Orientals, to work in the canneries they built.

Warnings that overfishing and reckless exploitation were endangering the salmon supply had been forthcoming before the turn of the century. Government regulation, however, was sporadic and ineffective. A law passed in 1889 forbade the damming of streams to catch salmon on their way to the spawning beds, but it was not until three years later that Congress finally appropriated the salary of two inspectors to see that the law was being enforced. But because of the lack of a regular commercial line of transportation, the inspectors were forced to rely on the packers whose activities they sought to observe to take them where they wanted to go. An act of 1896 prohibited fishing in any streams or creeks less than 500 feet in width, and restrictions were placed on the use of gear in the larger rivers. Provisions were made for weekly closing of some fishing grounds, but specific exclusions were made for the Bristol Bay, Cook Inlet, and Prince William Sound areas. Several bills were introduced in succeeding years, but nothing much was accomplished. One exception was a bill placing the control of Alaska salmon in the Bureau of Fisheries of the newly formed Department of Commerce and Labor in 1903, followed by a measure giving the secretary of commerce (whose agency, however, was more interested in the promotion of the sale of salmon than in its regulation) authority to limit fishing within 500 yards of the mouths of rivers and streams.

After 1900 many of the new settlers in Alaska took to fishing as a means of supplementing their income, selling most of their fish to the packers. Bargaining over prices to be paid was most spirited, and occasionally strikes resulted.

Brailing the fish trap —
the salmon will soon be
on the way to the
cannery, 1937
(*Lulu Fairbanks Collection,
Archives, University of Alaska,
Fairbanks*)

To free themselves from dependence on this source of supply, more of the packers began to set up fish traps, "huge permanent installations of log piles and netting" extending "out from the shore for about a half mile across the paths fish travel" on their way to spawning grounds in rivers and streams. Traps were dismantled in the fall and had to be built anew each fishing season. The cost of trap construction was high, but they were easy to maintain; frequently only a single watchman was employed to remove the fish from the trap and to guard them against theft. Traps were the most efficient kind of gear for catching fish, but their employment touched off a great political struggle, which ended only after Alaska had achieved statehood and the legislature made their use illegal.

Although traps were alleged to have brought about the depletion of the salmon, the controversy over their use, according to economist Richard Cooley, was one between labor and capital, resident and nonresident interests, involving the question of who should benefit from the exploitation of Alaska's salmon. Alaskans wanted the fisheries used primarily to encourage settlement by offering more people the opportunity of a livelihood. They feared that unless the use of the traps was prohibited the packers would gain complete control of the salmon fisheries and drive the independent fishermen out of business. In an article in their trade journal, *The Pacific Fisherman*, the packers defended the use of the trap as ". . . the best and only friend the canners have in Alaska" and went on to say: "If this method of catching fish is prohibited it will mean almost the entire dissolution of the industry." The social aspects of this conflict were lost on the Bureau of Fisheries, which considered them none of its affair. Any attempt to restrict the use of the trap was condemned by the chief of the bureau's Alaska division as inimical to the competitive system on which the nation's economy was based. Since traps, unlike other fishing gear, were stationary, they could be inspected regularly and much more easily.[2] During the war years, when the price of fish was high and the supply low, robberies of traps became quite prevalent. Vessels from several government agencies, including the navy, were sent to Alaska to help suppress what were regarded as acts of piracy.

The packers were high in their praise of the Bureau of Fisheries and much preferred federal to local regulation, at least in Alaska. Hearings on the fisheries were usually held in Washington. Small fishermen rarely came since few could afford the trip. But the representatives of the packers never missed a meeting. Their testimony was highly regarded since they presumably knew more about the problems of the fisheries than anyone else, and it was unthinkable that they would give advice not in the best interests of the industry. When the bureau established a Pacific branch in Seattle, the office was conveniently housed in a building where twenty of the major salmon companies were located. *The Pacific Fisherman*, the publishing organ of the packers, very pleased by the continuance of federal control of the fisheries following the passage of the Second Organic Act, openly gloated that Alaskans had been given "a toy legislature to play with."

Both the Bureau of Fisheries and the Department of Commerce strongly resisted any suggestions that the territory be given a voice in the management of the salmon fisheries. William C. Redfield, the secretary of commerce in Wilson's cabinet, expressed fears that the territory could readily destroy the industry by the imposition of high taxes and license fees and wrote that "not

Fish traps at Sunny Point near Ketchikan
(*Lulu Fairbanks Collection, Archives, University of Alaska, Fairbanks*)

even the possibility of such a situation, much less the situation itself, should be allowed to exist." E. Lester Jones, the deputy commissioner of the fisheries, lauded the "unusual training and experience" of the scientists in the Bureau of Fisheries and insisted that "any idea of transferring jurisdiction to the Territory or any other agency should be completely dismissed."[3]

Dr. Hugh Smith, a scientist, became commissioner of the fisheries in 1915. He consistently rejected the notion that there was any cause for alarm concerning the depletion of the Alaska fisheries. He believed that by expanding the program of artificial propagation through the maintenance of the fish hatcheries, "the perpetuation of the Alaska salmon fisheries" could "be achieved . . . without any general or material curtailment of fishing operations or reduction of output."[4] This was something the packers "wanted to hear," and Dr. Smith was hailed for his intelligence and practical wisdom. Artificial propagation was accepted on faith, for no studies were carried out to see if the optimism of Smith, the scientist, had validity. The government made more money available for the hatchery program than was given to carry out other aspects of the bureau's work; only a pittance was made available for its scientific studies and regulatory functions. Warnings from Alaskan fishermen and territorial officials that salmon were declining in great numbers went unheeded so long as the demand, accelerated by government orders during the war, continued.

But at the conclusion of World War I, not only were fish no longer needed in large quantities, but because the great armies and navies were rapidly being demobilized, governments were selling their surplus salmon stocks on the open market. Prices for salmon declined drastically. Spokesmen for the packers then

Cutting blubber from whale at sea, ca. 1917
(*Barrett Willoughby Collection, Archives, University of Alaska, Fairbanks*)

admitted that overfishing had been taking place and that the need for conservation was manifest. "Even before Dr. Smith took office," an editorial writer in *The Pacific Fisherman* stated, "the approaching danger to the salmon fishery and the need of accurate knowledge were apparent to anyone interested in its future."[5] Dr. Smith resigned under a cloud of suspicion in 1921, and three years later his successor as commissioner of the fisheries, Henry O'Malley, informed a congressional committee that artificial propagation was not the solution to the problem of the conservation of Alaska salmon.

In view of the emergency, Herbert Hoover, the secretary of commerce in the new Harding administration, took personal charge and held lengthy hearings on the plight of the salmon industry. When he was unable to secure the legislation from Congress that he felt was necessary to restore the health of the salmon fisheries, Hoover recommended that the president issue an executive order temporarily establishing the Alaska Peninsula Reserve, in which fishing was to be by permit only. President Harding did that on February 17, 1922. This was followed several months later by the Southwestern Fishery Reservation, which included the Kodiak and Bristol Bay areas, after the secretary warned that he would take such action if Congress failed to provide for the relief of the fisheries. Supporters of the reservations maintained that the only way to halt overfishing was to limit the number of people allowed to fish. This restriction by the Harding administration was indeed a revolutionary development, marking as it did—with the exception of a few areas open only to certain Indian tribes—a break in the American tradition of a fishery free and open to all.[6]

Opposition to the reservations came quickly. Dan Sutherland, the Alaska delegate to Congress, claimed that only employees of the large companies—not Alaskans themselves—were able to secure fishing places. He accused the administration of hypocrisy, claiming that the government had never really shown any interest in conservation, as it now claimed, but was really interested only in establishing a monopoly for the salmon packers. His cry was taken up by various newspapers, some of whom predicted that a new Teapot Dome Scandal was in the offing—this time the subject being salmon, not oil. The administration, stung by the force of criticism, now sought to involve Congress, whose support it wanted in finding a solution to the problem of the salmon fisheries. Secretary Hoover accompanied President Harding on his trip to Alaska for the ceremonies marking the completion of the Alaska Railroad. While there he held hearings in several towns to "secure first hand information in regard to fishery conditions in Alaska." Bills based largely on his recommendations were introduced into the House by Wallace H. White of Maine and into the Senate by Wesley Jones of Washington. After considerable debate, the two houses of Congress came to an agreement, and the measure known as the White Act was signed by President Calvin Coolidge in 1924.

Preserving Salmon and Operating the Railroad

The White Act was very much the product of compromise. Two controversial items were deleted before the measure obtained final form: reservations as desired by the packers, and the outlawry of the use of fish traps as sought by the delegate from Alaska. The act gave the secretary of commerce authority "to limit or prohibit fishing in all territorial waters of Alaska" and allowed him to fix the size and character, but not the amount, of fishing gear. As a means of achieving the desired goals in the conservation of salmon fisheries, Congress directed that there should be an escapement of at least 50 percent of the fish to their spawning bed. Steady attempts were made to see that the desired results were being achieved. Secretary Hoover spoke with pride of his efforts in getting the Congress to approve the measure which he believed had achieved the preservation of the Alaska salmon. Shortly after the act was signed, he claimed that the fish were already so plentiful that foreign fishing vessels were invading the Alaskan fishing grounds. By 1925 demand for salmon increased significantly, and as the price rose the salmon catch increased correspondingly. As far as the packers were concerned, Hoover was the savior of the industry, and they considered the government's conservation program successful as long as total output continued to increase year after year.

Whatever may have been its shortcomings—and they were many—the enactment of the White Act was indeed testimony to the efforts of Congress and Secretary Hoover, in particular, to deal with a matter of significance to Alaska. But salmon were primarily of interest only to inhabitants of coastal areas. For Alaskans in the interior the event of greatest import was the opening of the government-built railroad, which was hailed as the advent of a new era of prosperity and settlement.

Completed in 1923, the Alaska Railroad, as it was called, cost $65 million,

President Warren G. Harding driving the golden spike that marked the completion of the Alaska Railroad, Nenana, 1923
(*Lulu Fairbanks Collection, Archives, University of Alaska, Fairbanks*)

almost twice the amount earmarked for construction. Like the construction of the oil pipeline more than fifty years later, inflation and delays in construction accounted for the added expenditures. Successive managers of the Alaska Railroad blamed the poor state of the roadbed and the low quality of the line's equipment for sending the costs of operations unusually high. Seventeen million dollars was appropriated soon after the line began service for improvements, and more was needed to make the road efficient. The railroad was plagued by continuous deficits. Expense of maintenance remained high, the population of the railbelt was small, and passengers were few. The failure to develop an export trade in coal as had been anticipated meant that the area's mines would not provide the freight loads needed to make the railroad a successful enterprise. Blame was attached to the railroad for taking enough business away from the steamboats to cause their decline while failing to achieve much for itself. In Congress the talk of abandoning the line seemed to be ever present.

Calvin Coolidge, who succeeded Harding as president, never exhibited his predecessor's concern for the welfare and development of Alaska. A firm believer in the dogma "the business of America is business," Coolidge's chief worry was that money spent in Alaska appeared to be "... far out of proportion to the number of inhabitants and the amount of production...."[7] He whittled away at appropriations for the territory. In 1925 the agricultural experiment station at Rampart and the mine experiment station at Fairbanks were both closed.

With the exception of agriculture, the 1920s was a period of prosperity for the United States. Not really in the mainstream of American life, Alaska was little affected. The segments of the American economy that prospered were

Noel Wien lands at Circle Springs, one of the first airports in the northern bush. It was built by Frank Leach using a team of horses
(E. L. Bartlett Aviation Collection, Archives, University of Alaska, Fairbanks)

manufacturing, commerce, and related industries and services. Salmon and gold were Alaska's chief exports, while a substantial number of Alaskans provided much of what they needed for themselves. But the twenties witnessed the beginnings of the air age, a development that was to have the most profound effect on Alaska. The airplane became the Alaskan mode of transportation, making it at last possible to travel easily the vast distances from one section to another. In the twenties bush pilots were already beginning to make runs to places previously regarded as inaccessible. The territory began to build landing fields. And today communities which normally would be almost completely isolated because of their remoteness or, as in the case of Nome, icebound for long periods of the year, are able to maintain regular contact with the outside world because of the airplane.

The Great Depression in Alaska

As the twenties drew to a close Herbert Hoover, who had spent much time in Alaska attempting to find a solution to the problem of the salmon fisheries, became president of the United States. It was his misfortune to be in office when the Great Depression struck. Just as Alaska had not shared in the American prosperity of the twenties, it also suffered less from the trauma of the thirties, although it was not entirely unaffected by the Depression. Employment in the mines declined. The value of the fish catch fell with the general drop in commodity prices. The Alaska Railroad, because of its perennial deficits, came under renewed attack. A committee chaired by Senator Robert B. Howell demanded that services be cut and that passenger rates be raised 10¢ a

Matanuska and
Chickaloon train
leaving Anchorage
(*Lulu Fairbanks Collection,
Archives, University of Alaska,
Fairbanks*)

mile and freight rates as much as 50 percent to make the railroad self-supporting. When put into effect, its recommendations resulted only in a further drop in the railroad's income, and after a few years a new and more realistic schedule of rates was adopted. During the thirties, as the Depression deepened in the United States, more Americans began looking to Alaska as a place to come to escape their ills. After all, there were plenty of moose, caribou, and salmon; and land, it was thought, could be had for the asking.

In the heart of the Depression the American people turned to Franklin Delano Roosevelt as their new leader. When Roosevelt took over as president, more than thirteen million people were unemployed, and those with jobs were sometimes not much better off. Wages ranged from 20 to 30 cents an hour in a number of basic industries. It was not uncommon for men and women to receive less than $2 for a ten-hour day of labor. Although he had been much opposed to an extensive public works program, Roosevelt reluctantly came to the conclusion that increased intervention of the federal government was necessary, that more had to be done to keep people from starving even if it meant making the direct relief grants that Hoover had so vigorously opposed. The New Deal was essentially a composite of relief and reform programs that at times seemed to be working at cross purposes with each other. Alaskans shared in the New Deal, but because Alaska was a territory and not a state its share was often small or nonexistent.

However, several actions of the Roosevelt administration were helpful to the territory. The president's decision to devalue the dollar by raising the price of gold to thirty-five dollars an ounce stimulated the industry that had once played a leading role in Alaska's development, resulting in an increase of employment in the gold mines. Direct relief payments, besides aiding their recipients, were of some help in stimulating the economy. The Works Projects Administration gave employment to people on the relief rolls, paying them at a rate slightly higher than the welfare grants they had been receiving but below the prevailing wage scale; the Public Works Administration, under the direction of Secretary of the Interior Harold Ickes, sponsored a variety of projects in which private contractors employed men and women at the prevailing wage in the community. As a result of their efforts a number of public buildings and bridges were constructed, a guidebook to Alaska was published, improvements were made to harbors, totem poles were restored, and a hotel was established at Mt. McKinley National Park. Youths enrolled in the Civilian Conservation Corps; they received $1 a day plus board and room, built roads and trails in the national forests, planted trees, and worked on other reforestation projects. The National Youth Administration helped young people remain in school by making jobs available to them for a few hours a week.

The Matanuska Valley Colony

Of all the New Deal activities in Alaska, the Matanuska Valley Colony excited the greatest interest, an interest extending far beyond the boundaries of the territory. As originally conceived, Matanuska was one of the many projects associated with the resettlement program of the Roosevelt administration designed to take people away from rural districts in which poverty had been prevalent long before the Depression and move them to places where they might lead more productive lives. No other settlement approached Matanuska in the amount of publicity it received, and in none were the expectations so high. The idea of creating a community in the wilderness stirred imaginations. Sponsors of the Alaskan colony included many who were not merely interested in relief and resettlement. Officials of the Alaska Railroad, who had long sponsored movement of people to Alaska, were delighted, for this meant more passengers and freight which would help make the line self-supporting. Roosevelt himself was said to have expressed the view that the establishment of the colony would be of aid to the military. For Alaskans, Matanuska—the first and only occasion in which the United States sponsored colonization—meant that the government was doing something for Alaska. And not the least was the feeling that the colony would clearly demonstrate that farming was feasible in Alaska and that a successful agriculture would do much to make Alaska free from dependence on the outside for sources of supply.[8]

The Matanuska Valley is in the railbelt area of southwestern Alaska; its leading settlement, Palmer, is about forty miles from Anchorage. Prior to the establishment of the colony there had been homesteading in the valley, but few made farming their principal means of livelihood. The climate of the valley is much milder than the latitude might indicate: during winter it is warmer than many areas in the northern part of the United States, though much cooler in summer. Rainfall averages about sixteen inches a year, and the quality of the soils of the valley varies considerably. The way was opened for the new settle-

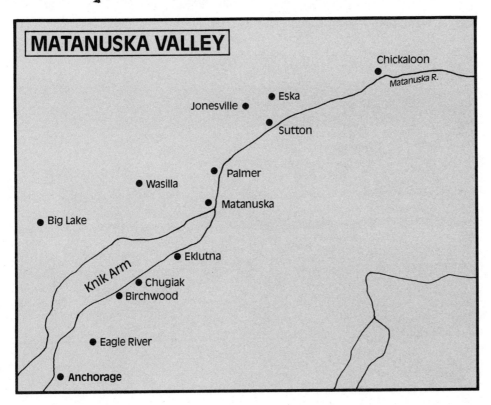

ment when President Roosevelt issued an executive order on February 4, 1935, banning further homesteading in the valley and reserving all remaining land for the colonists.

The Alaska Relief and Rehabilitation Corporation—then a part of the Federal Emergency Relief Administration and later of the Works Projects Administration—was formed to manage the colony. Surveys were made and the land was divided into 208 plots ranging from forty acres to eighty acres, depending on the quality of the soil. Prices ranged from $5 an acre for uncleared land to an unspecified amount in those places where it had been improved. Settlers were to make payment over a thirty-year period at an annual rate of 3 percent interest. The government agreed to build the homes and barns and to pay the costs of transporting families and up to 2,000 pounds of their household goods to Alaska. Farm machinery, equipment, livestock, and supplies were made available by the corporation to the colonists for purchase, lease, or other payment for use. Necessary supplies could be obtained at cost until colonists became self-supporting. Educational, cultural, recreational, and health services were to be provided by the corporation, while the colonists as their part of the contract agreed to observe the directives issued by the corporation relating to farm management and other matters pertaining to the colony.

Two hundred and one families, all residents of northern counties in Michigan, Minnesota, and Wisconsin, were selected from among the applicants for a place in the colony. As descendants of people of northern European stock and coming from areas whose climatic conditions presumably most resembled those of the Matanuska Valley, it was believed they would make the best colonists. The locale from which they came, known as the "cutover region," was once the scene of prosperous lumbering and mining industries. But with

Matanuska Valley colonists drawing farm plots, 1936
(*Lulu Fairbanks Collection, Archives, University of Alaska, Fairbanks*)

the decline of lumbering as a result of excessive cutting and with the copper mines' inability to compete any longer in the national market, employment had become irregular, and the agriculture of the area was very definitely submarginal. Relief workers were given the task of selecting the colonists. Most of them worked hard to find suitable persons for the colony and did not, as was alleged, deliberately foist their most difficult cases on the Matanuska project. Successful farmers were not interested in going to Alaska, where the prospects were at best limited, and many could not go if they wanted. Choices of settlers were limited to persons receiving welfare payments. Lengthy questionnaires had been devised with some care to obtain information on the background of the applicants. But the replies to these inquiries were not always accurate or objective. Friends and neighbors tended to show the candidates in their best light and frequently exaggerated their qualifications. Of those who came to Matanuska, most had had little farm experience.[9]

Great fanfare attended the departure and movement of the colonists. They traveled by train across the country accompanied by newspapermen who interviewed them and reported on their activity. In San Francisco they were entertained at dinners and regaled by speeches. Upon their arrival in Alaska they were greeted at the port of Seward, and at Anchorage a half holiday was declared in their honor. But they had been warned by Don Irwin, the manager of the Matanuska Agricultural Experiment Station, of the difficulties that lay ahead, and their introduction to the valley was not a happy one. It was raining when they arrived in May, and the rainfall for the next few weeks was greater than usual for that time of the year. Because their homes were not ready, they had to live in tents, often surrounded by a sea of mud, some for several months while waiting for workmen to complete the houses.

Discontent was high. Some colonists charged that the promises made to them had not been kept. Letters and telegrams were sent to members of Con-

Matanuska Valley farm
(*Lulu Fairbanks Collection, Archives, University of Alaska, Fairbanks*)

gress and the newspapers voicing the complaints. Nine of the families left in July, soon to be followed by others. The government paid their transportation back to Seattle, and replacements were found, some already living in Seattle. Foes of the New Deal pointed to the colony as just another example of bureaucratic foolishness. Senator Arthur Vandenberg accused the Roosevelt administration of having planted "... in net essence a complete commune under the American flag at Palmer, Alaska," and he spoke of those "people... left stranded 5,000 miles from home in the face of a threatening calamity." Almost simultaneously, the directors of the corporation were being condemned for both running the colony too loosely and for having installed a dictatorship. Plans to establish cooperative marketing resulted in the colony's being termed "Uncle Sam's first collective farm."[10]

The colony had its defenders. Senator Homer Bone of Washington spoke glowingly of the rich farmlands of the Matanuska Valley and contrasted the opportunities afforded the colonists with the dismal life led by those on relief in their home states. Some of the settlers who had been among the severest critics in the very early days of the colony changed their minds after a few months, one declaring that she was now "having the time of [her] life." When rumors appeared that the colony might be disbanded, none of those who had remained seemed to be very happy with the prospect of being sent back home.[11]

The Matanuska Colony was by far the most expensive of all the resettlement projects. Labor costs in Alaska were high. Almost everything needed in the way of equipment and other supplies had to be brought in at great cost. "Above all," writes historian Orlando Miller, "the Matanuska project had to provide almost every facility or service that a new community would need," building and equipping "a general store or trading post, warehouses, shops, garage, community hall, dormitory, offices, staff houses, power plant, cannery, creamery, hatchery, hospital and school." It is estimated that if expenditures related to the colony are taken into account—the transporting of families and goods, providing facilities, construction of roads and bridges in the area of Palmer, the building and maintenance of a school and hospital, loans made to colonists that were never repaid, etc.—the costs would be over $5 million.[12]

Matanuska has been considered a qualified success. With the advent of the war and the building of military facilities in the Anchorage area, the colony found a ready market for its produce. According to Miller, about 31 percent of the original settlers as well as 43 percent of the replacements were still in the colony in 1948. Many who left the colony found jobs or established businesses for themselves elsewhere in Alaska. Palmer benefited substantially from the founding of Matanuska, for people who were not members of the colony moved in to avail themselves of the opportunities afforded by the establishment of a new community. The support given by the government undoubtedly was the most important factor in the Matanuska story.

The New Deal in Alaska

While attention was centered on the newest settlers at Matanuska, Alaska's native peoples were not entirely ignored. The Roosevelt administration promised a "New Deal" for the Indian people. Its chief advisers on Indian affairs rejected the policy of forcible assimilation and recommended that the Indians' cultural heritage be preserved and that they be given more land on reservations as a means of furthering their welfare. Their proposal, enacted into law as the Indian Reorganization Act of 1934, was extended to Alaska two years later and included Eskimos and Aleuts as well as Indian peoples.

Although Alaska never experienced the extensive warfare that had marked relations between the two races in the United States, the coming of the white man had seriously disrupted and in some cases destroyed the native economy. Their standard of living was much lower, they were subjected to social discrimination, and a separate school system had been established for their children.

Alaska's inclusion within the provisions of the Indian Reorganization Act, more commonly known as the Wheeler-Howard Act, enabled several native communities to incorporate and to draw up constitutions for self-government. Loans extended to a number of villages allowed them to set up canneries. Individual fishermen used the borrowed money to purchase boats and gear for themselves, while two of the native canneries established business on a statewide basis. In 1938 the secretary of the interior was authorized to withdraw up to 640 acres of land for the use of the territory's schools and hospitals and for other purposes he might deem advisable. The most controversial aspect of the program was that which contemplated the setting up of reservations and a system of communal land tenure. This was regarded by its sponsors as the means of implementing the provisions of the First Organic Act of 1885: that "the Indians or other persons in the said District shall not be disturbed in the possession of any lands actually in their use or occupation or now claimed by them. . . ." Opposition to the reservations was most vehement. Both natives and whites called the reservations alien to the native way of life, a step backward; and they maintained that what the natives needed was equality and not wardship. The very word "reservation," indicating a restriction on the use of land, has always aroused strong feelings in Alaska. Land given to the natives, it was feared, would be taken from the whites, and any large withdrawals for reservations would thwart the development of Alaska. In the forties, following numerous protests, the plan for reservations was withdrawn and not until 1971, more than a quarter of a century after the era of the New Deal, was a solution of the land claims of Alaska's natives finally resolved.[13]

The effect of the New Deal on Alaska could hardly be called profound. The Roosevelt administration had shown a greater interest in the territory than had any of its predecessors, with the possible exception of Harding's; yet it was Harding's secretary of commerce, Herbert Hoover, who had succeeded in pushing through Congress what, with all its faults, was the most comprehensive measure ever enacted by the federal government for the preservation of Alaska's fisheries. The New Deal had spent more money, though not very much, and had even provided Alaska with a new settlement, but Alaska had never been central to the New Deal or in the minds of its planners. The long-awaited study on Alaska issued in 1937, prepared at the request of Congress, concluded that "an appraisal of the national interests indicates that there is no clear need to speed the development of Alaska."[14] Harold Ickes, Roosevelt's secretary of the interior, whose department was most concerned with Alaska, while more optimistic concerning farming in Alaska than was the author of the committee's report, felt that "Alaska ought to do more for itself instead of running to Washington for everything."[15] Ernest Gruening recalls in his memoirs that just before he left Washington to take up his duties as governor of Alaska in 1939, Roosevelt told him that Alaska had "lost touch with the federal government" and that "a lot of the New Deal . . . hasn't come to Alaska."[16] But in January, only a few months before, Roosevelt had announced that in view of the threatening world situation the reform program of the New Deal was over. "Dr. New Deal" was giving way to "Dr. Win-the-War." It was not the New Deal but the war which broke out in September of 1939 that was to profoundly change Alaska.

·6·
Guardian of the North

World War II

THE 1930s was a troubled period for the United States as well as for Europe. On October 24 and 29, 1929, Wall Street stock market prices plummeted, and by November 13 of that year about $30 billion in the market value of listed stocks had been obliterated. The "great crash" triggered the worldwide "Great Depression." By the middle of 1932 market losses had mounted to approximately $75 billion. By 1933 some 15 million Americans had lost their jobs. America found itself in a desperate situation.

Europe and Asia did not fare well either; in Germany, Adolph Hitler had taken power, while in Italy, fascist dictator Benito Mussolini was riding high. After a bloody and bitterly fought civil war that lasted three years, the fascist dictatorship of General Francisco Franco replaced Spain's republican government. Russia boasted of a "dictatorship of the proletariat" which made the tyranny of the tsars seem benevolent by comparison. Since 1931 economic penetration and military intervention had enabled the Japanese to bring a widening area of China under their control, and in September of 1940 Japanese forces occupied Indochina.

By 1939 war clouds rose ominously across the Atlantic and Pacific, and on September 1 of that year Hitler's armies, led by dive-bombers and tanks, invaded Poland. Shortly thereafter Europe's major powers were embroiled in war.

In 1939 Alaska's only military establishment consisted of the old Fort Seward, renamed Chilkoot Barracks in 1922. An infantry post dating back to the gold rush days, it was located at the upper end of the inside passage at Haines, from where it could observe traffic bound inland over the Dalton Trail or over three historic trails—the Chilkoot, Chilkat, and White passes. Eleven officers and approximately 300 men armed with Springfield rifles manned the post. The installation did not have even a single antiaircraft gun. The troops were immobilized because their only means of transportation consisted of the

Stampeders struggling
over the historic
Chilkoot Pass in 1898
(*Charles Bunnell Collection,
Archives, University of Alaska,
Fairbanks*)

venerable tug *Fornance*. Its engines were so feeble that while returning from
Juneau in December 1939 with the commanding officer on board and encoun-
tering a thirty-knot headwind, it was unable to advance to Haines and had to be
rescued by the Coast Guard.[1] In essence, the territory was indefensible.

However, there had been voices reminding the United States of Alaska's
strategic importance. As early as 1931 the territorial governor, George A.
Parks, reminded the secretary of the interior of Alaska's strategic position as
the most feasible air route to Asia. Air traffic had increased considerably within
the territory, and navigational facilities were badly needed. The governor recommended that the army air corps station planes in Alaska if only to train
pilots in flying conditions as they existed in northern latitudes. The pleas fell
on deaf ears.[2]

In December 1934, Japan denounced the five-power naval treaty of February 6, 1922. Under its terms the United States had agreed—among other
things—not to fortify the Aleutians. Japan's action prompted Alaska's delegate
to Congress, Anthony J. Dimond, to plead for bases at Anchorage or Fairbanks,
and also in the Aleutians: "I say to you, defend the United States by defending

Alaska." The delegate pointed out that the shortest distance between the United States and the Orient crossed the Great Circle Route, located 2,000 miles north of fortified Hawaii but only 276 miles south of the Aleutians. The distance from San Francisco to Yokohama over the Great Circle Route amounted to 5,223 miles, whereas the distance from Yokohama via Hawaii to the nearest point on the west coast of the United States was 6,316 miles. Delegate Dimond reminded his colleagues that these geographical factors would invite an enemy of the United States, moving across the Pacific, to invade Alaska first. Dimond's measures to provide $10 million for an air base and another $10 million for a naval base died quietly in the House military committee and the naval affairs committee respectively.[3]

Early in 1935, however, Congress named six strategic areas in which there would be an army air corps base. Alaska was one of the six areas. In subsequent congressional testimony, military witnesses unfailingly supported such an Alaskan base both for defensive-offensive purposes and for providing training in cold-weather aviation. Brigadier General William Mitchell, an advocate of airpower, highlighted the various hearings with his testimony on February 13, 1935, in which he dramatically declared that Japan was America's most dangerous enemy in the Pacific. "They will come right here to Alaska . . . [which] is the most central place in the world for aircraft, and that is true either of Europe, Asia, or North America. I believe in the future he who holds Alaska will hold the world, and I think it is the most important strategic place in the world."[4] It was to no avail; Congress did not appropriate the necessary funds.

Congressional inaction did not deter Alaska's delegate. Year after year he warned his colleagues of the potential danger from Japan. In 1937 Dimond pointed out that some Japanese, ostensibly fishing off Alaska's coast, were actually disguised military personnel seeking information on the depth, defenses, and landmarks of Alaska's harbors. At the same time he attempted to secure a $2 million appropriation to begin construction of the air base near Fairbanks which had been authorized in 1935. If Hawaii constituted one key to the Pacific, Dimond pleaded, Alaska constituted the other. At the very least, he urged, army air corps pilots should be trained in cold-weather flying. Congress refused the necessary funds. In time Dimond made converts, most importantly General George C. Marshall, the army chief of staff, and Major General Henry H. Arnold, head of the army air force.[5]

In 1940 an appropriation of $4 million allowed construction to begin on a cold-weather testing station for airplanes near Fairbanks. In the meantime, the navy proceeded in a leisurely fashion with its Alaskan construction program. A year earlier, naval air stations at Sitka for $2.9 million and at Kodiak for $8.75 million were authorized. Delegate Dimond apprehensively declared: "We are starting defensive measures too late and proceeding with them too feebly."[6]

Included in the army's budget for fiscal year 1941 was a request for a base near Anchorage for $12,734,000. When the defense budget reached the full Appropriations Committee, however, the entire appropriation for the Anchorage base had been eliminated. Despite testimony asking for a restoration of the funds by General Marshall, Major General Arnold, Delegate Dimond, and others, the House refused the monies on April 4, 1940.[7]

Billy Mitchell by his SE-5, the same type of plane he used in demonstrating the vulnerability of ships to air attack
(*Historical Photograph Collection, Archives, University of Alaska, Fairbanks*)

A few days later, on April 9, Hitler's armies invaded and occupied Norway and Denmark. Now, for the first time, many congressmen realized that the Scandinavian peninsula was just over the top of the earth from Alaska and that bombers able to fly such a distance existed. Both Generals Marshall and Arnold appeared before the Subcommittee on the War Department of the Senate Appropriations Committee on April 30 and once again asked for a restoration of the Anchorage base. Before the Senate subcommittee had finished its hearings on May 17, 1940, the German air force had bombed Rotterdam without provocation or warning, while the German army had seized the Netherlands. The Senate restored the Anchorage base, and the House concurred.[8]

Construction of bases had been underway at various locations, among them bases for seaplanes and submarines on Kodiak Island and at Dutch Harbor at the eastern extremity of the Aleutians. By September 1941, Kodiak and Dutch Harbor had been commissioned as naval air stations and could even handle submarines.

The Civil Aeronautics Authority and the army engineers supplemented naval efforts by building a series of staging fields north from Puget Sound inland, and out to Cold Bay on the Alaska Peninsula.

In the mid-1940s the U.S. Army established the Alaskan Defense Command under Brigadier General Simon Bolivar Buckner. The navy soon followed with the creation of an Alaskan sector under the Thirteenth Naval District headquartered at Seattle and appointed Captain Ralph C. Parker to the command.[9]

Yet, when the Japanese struck Pearl Harbor without warning on December 7, 1941, Alaska was hopelessly unprepared for war. Major General Buckner exclaimed in exasperation, "We're not even the second team up here—we're a sandlot club." There were a few tiny army garrisons, a scattering of airfields guarded by a few bombers and fighters, and a navy fleet of outmoded World War I vintage destroyers and wooden "Yippee" boats which, in the opinion of their commander, "Squeaky" Anderson, "would sink if they got rammed by a barnacle."[10]

Alaska Territorial Guard at Sitka
(Hanna Call Collection, Archives, University of Alaska, Fairbanks)

As early as May 5, 1942, Japanese imperial headquarters ordered that the "Commander-in-Chief combined fleet will, in cooperation with the Army, invade and occupy strategic points in the Western Aleutians and Midway Island."[11]

The Japanese Attack on Dutch Harbor

On the night of June 2, 1942, a Japanese force of two aircraft carriers with eighty-two planes, two heavy cruisers, three destroyers, and an oiler steamed through the foggy North Pacific toward Dutch Harbor. Supporting the task group not far to the west cruised the ships of Vice Admiral Boshiro Hosogaya's northern force, including four cruisers, nine destroyers, and three transports carrying 2,500 Japanese army invasion troops. Submarines screened the fleet. The planes were to strike a paralyzing blow at Dutch Harbor while troops were to land on Adak, Kiska, and Attu and occupy these islands.

The Japanese carrier force had turned into a foggy, cold-weather front earlier in the day after Rear Admiral Kakuji Kakuta, the task force commander, had been alerted by the sighting of a patrol plane in the clouds overhead. The Japanese were uncertain whether it was an American PBY Catalina flying boat or a Russian plane. Not wanting to lose the element of surprise, the task force stayed with the leading edge of the storm.[12] On the morning of June 3, 1942, the carriers *Junyo* and *Rynjo* launched their planes for the attack on Dutch Harbor, less than 170 miles away. Unknown to the Japanese, however, their element of surprise had been lost. The flying boat Admiral Kakuta had seen at noon the previous day had been an American patrol plane.

When the planes of the carrier *Junyo* attacked Dutch Harbor early on the morning of June 3, 1942, they were met by the blazing antiaircraft guns of the alerted American base. The attack planes of the carrier *Rynjo* had lost their bearings in the dense fog and had turned back. From the very beginning both American and Japanese forces realized that despite all human courage and mechanical genius, the forces of nature called the shots in the Aleutians.

Japanese bombs fall harmlessly into the bay during a raid on Dutch Harbor on June 3-4, 1942
(Hanna Call Collection, Archives, University of Alaska, Fairbanks)

The two attacks on Dutch Harbor did not last very long, and the American defenders soon discovered that the base had weathered the opening skirmish of the Aleutian campaign without much physical damage or defense impairment.[13]

Although the attack on Dutch Harbor has been recorded in history as a mere "incident," it nevertheless powerfully influenced the course of the war. The Japanese assault on the Aleutians was designed to divert massive American naval forces north toward Alaska. According to the plan, the main body of Admiral Isoroku Yamamoto's combined imperial fleet was to intercept and destroy the American fleet at Midway Island on June 4, 1942. But because the Dutch Harbor attack diverted Japanese forces needed at the rendezvous, Japan lost the balance of power at Midway, lost a major battle there, and perhaps even the war.[14]

Japanese Forces on Attu and Kiska

After regrouping and some indecisiveness, early on June 5, 1942, Vice Admiral Boshiro Hosogaya ordered Rear Admiral Sentaro Omori, commander of the Adak-Attu Occupation Force, who was then some 225 miles southwest of Adak, to turn back and proceed to Attu. On the morning of June 7, 1942, Omori landed his 1,200 troops on Holtz Bay, from where they marched overland through snow to Chichagof. The main part of the troops got lost and arrived at Massacre Bay by mistake. The remaining troops attacked the little settlement of Chichagof and made prisoners of its entire population of thirty-nine Aleuts and the teachers, Mr. and Mrs. Jones. The Kiska Occupation Force also made its landing on June 7 without opposition from the ten members of the temporary United States weather station.[15]

Subsequently, it has become clear that the Japanese had no intention of capturing anything east of Adak, that they had no plans to invade the Alaskan mainland, Canada, or the United States. Apart from its diversionary aspect, the Aleutian operation was principally defensive, designed to prevent an American invasion of Japan. Having lost at Midway, Kiska essentially had become worthless as the northern anchor of the new defense chain. Nevertheless, the Japanese high command decided to keep the island and develop it as an air base, partly to block a possible invasion and partly for nuisance and morale value.[16]

The Americans did not discover the occupation until June 10, when a Catalina—an amphibious plane—reported four ships in Kiska. This initiated a new phase of the war, with the Japanese attempting to hold what they had and the Americans trying to blast them out. The war for the Aleutians essentially became a contest of air power in which both sides were hampered by the foul weather.[17] The war quickly frustrated both sides. Nobody won fame or fortune, and none of the operations accomplished anything important or had any noticeable effect on the outcome of the conflict. American—and probably Japanese—sailors, soldiers, and aviators regarded stationing in this area of almost perpetual winds, fogs, and snow as little better than punishment. Distance and weather constantly impeded American as well as Japanese operations.

Vice Admiral Hosogaya, commander in chief of the Northern Area Force,

Dutch Harbor
30 years later
(Fairbanks Daily News-Miner)

was responsible for maintaining and defending Attu and Kiska. On the American side, Rear Admiral Robert A. Theobald, commander of the North Pacific Force, had been instructed by Admiral Chester W. Nimitz to keep pounding the two islands until forces could be spared to recover them.

Hosogaya's base at Paramushiro in the Kuril Islands lay 1,200 miles north of Tokyo and 650 miles west of Attu. Ships bound for Kiska had another 378 miles of steaming through reef-infested waters.[18] Admiral Theobald had established his headquarters at Kodiak. Rear Admiral William K. Smith commanded a cruiser task force, while Brigadier General William O. Butler commanded the Eleventh Army Air Force, consisting of medium bombers and fighters, a few Flying Fortresses, and a growing group of PBY's. Major General Simon Bolivar Buckner was the army commander of the Alaskan sector with a token garrison at Fort Morrow on the base of the Alaska Peninsula. Fort Glenn on Umnak Island, 536 miles east of Kiska by air and 660 miles by sea, was the westernmost American airfield. The only American naval and seaplane base in the Aleutians, inadequate and also damaged by the June 4 raid, was Dutch Harbor, about sixty miles eastward on Unalaska Island. Fort Randall at Cold Bay on the Alaska Peninsula possessed a good army airfield but was located another 155 miles eastward by air or 185 miles by sea. Alaska's main advanced military and naval base was on Kodiak Island, some 372 miles east of Cold Bay by air and 505 miles by sea. All needed supplies for the American armed forces had to

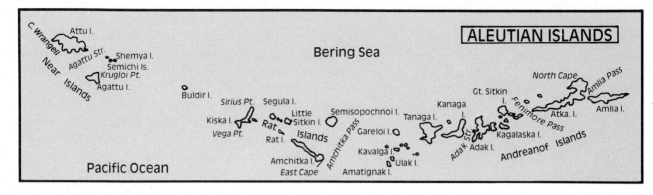

come from Seattle, which meant a flight of 1,742 miles or a sea voyage of 1,957 miles to get reinforcements and material to Umnak.[19]

The Japanese also had a difficult time. On July 7 and 8, 1942, Admiral Yamamoto withdrew four carriers and other capital ships southward. This left Vice Admiral Hosogaya with an insufficient Northern Area Force for offensive operations. He therefore decided to build airstrips on Attu and Kiska from which land-based bombers could defend the Japanese Aleutians. Because of the lack of construction equipment capable of dealing with the spongy muskeg and the underlying frozen volcanic ash, work proceeded very slowly. For all practical purposes, Japanese offensive bombing in the Aleutian campaign ceased after a high altitude attack on the morning of July 20, 1942.[20]

American forces, however, went on the offensive. Admiral Theobald ordered the construction of an airfield on Adak, within fighter-plane distance of Kiska so that bombers could be escorted on the round trip. Construction crews found an almost ready-made airfield in the form of a flooded tidal basin. Army engineers drained and filled it and within ten days finished their job. On September 14, 1942, the first Kiska-bound fighter-bomber strike took off from Adak.[21]

In September 1942, the Japanese abandoned Attu as an economy measure, concentrating their troops at Kiska. By early October of that year, the island, with its massive antiaircraft emplacements and network of underground bunkers, had become virtually impervious. Only Kiska's supply line remained vulnerable. And since the Japanese had decided to abandon the Aleutians at the onset of winter and fall back on the northern Kuriles, they were satisfied with the maintenance of the status quo. Soon, however, the Japanese imperial headquarters changed its North Pacific policy and decided to hold on to the Aleutians.[22]

On October 29, 1942, the Japanese reoccupied Attu, and the American forces soon thereafter landed on Amchitka, only forty miles from Kiska, where they built a forward airbase which became operational in February 1943.[23]

American Defense Efforts

In the meantime, Major General Buckner's Alaska Defense Command had grown to 150,000 troops. With the help of two Army Reserve officers, Captain Carl Schreibner and Major M. R. Marston, Alaska's Governor Ernest Gruening had organized the Territorial Guard, a security force primarily intended to guard the long coastline and pass intelligence on to the armed forces in the absence of the National Guard. Dutch Harbor, the assembly point of the Aleutian theater of war, handled approximately 400,000 tons of shipping a month. Alaskan coal production had increased tenfold in 1942, and the army constructed the four-inch-wide Canol Pipeline to carry crude oil from Norman Wells on the Mackenzie River to a refinery in Whitehorse. From there a three-inch pipeline was to carry the various petroleum products to Alaska. Alaska's population had mushroomed under the stimulus of the military construction boom. And under the protection of the U.S. Navy and Coast Guard, Alaskan fishing fleets made record catches, most for export to the lower forty-eight states.[24]

A road connecting the continental United States with Alaska had been in the talking stage since the 1930s. The opening of the Alaska (Alcan) Highway on November 20, 1942, represented a major engineering achievement. Built to connect many of the landing fields on the air route to Alaska—via Great Falls, Montana; Lethbridge, Calgary, Edmonton, and Grand Prairie, Alberta; Fort St. John and Fort Nelson, British Columbia; Watson Lake and Whitehorse, Yukon Territory; and Northway, Tanacross, Big Delta, Mile 26, and Ladd Field at Fairbanks, Alaska—the 1,420-mile pioneer road wound its way through the wilderness. Seven engineer regiments, aided by forty-seven contractors who were employed by the Public Roads Administration, worked toward each other from various points along the route under often harsh weather conditions and

E. L. "Bob" Bartlett, Secretary of Alaska, opening the Alcan Highway
(E. L. Bartlett Collection, Archives, University of Alaska, Fairbanks)

First convoy to
Fairbanks on the newly
opened Alcan,
Nov. 20, 1942
(*Fairbanks Daily
News-Miner*)

over extremely difficult terrain. They finished the pioneer road exactly nine
months and six days after the start of construction.[25]

Although the road was crude, by December of 1942 army convoys crawled
north to Alaska with supplies and materials for the Alaskan command and for
the Soviet Union as well.

Lend Lease and Intensive Warfare

ALSIB—the Alaska-Siberia Lend Lease route originated on March 11,
1941, when Congress passed H.R. 1776, known as the Lend-Lease Act—was
designed to help hard-pressed Great Britain and any other nation at war with
Nazi Germany. When Germany invaded the Soviet Union on June 22, 1941,
that nation soon became a lend-lease participant.

As early as September 1941, the United States suggested that lend-lease
aircraft be delivered to Siberia via Alaska, using American pilots and crews.
The Russians declined because they considered the route too dangerous.

The exigencies of the war finally made the use of ALSIB imperative, and
from September 1942 until the fall of 1945, some 7,926 combat and transport
aircraft were delivered to the Russians in Fairbanks, who then flew them to
Nome and Siberia.[26] ALSIB cut the travel distance from 13,000 miles via the
Middle East to less than 3,000 miles. In addition, the Russians took over
lend-lease destroyers and other ships at Cold Bay. Cargo shipped by sea from
West Coast ports was escorted by the U.S. and Canadian navies through the

Aleutians and on to Vladivostok, a major Russian seaport.

At the same time, American planes kept bombing the Japanese installations. The winter of 1942/43 turned into the worst one in thirty-four years. Fairbanks temperatures dipped to −67° in December, and in the Aleutians it took crews two hours to get the ice off airplane wings, while blowtorches were used to thaw engines before they would start. Yet despite these handicaps, the bombers dropped more than a half-million pounds of explosives on enemy bases during the last three months of 1942.[27]

Early in January 1943, Rear Admiral Thomas C. Kinkaid, a grizzled naval hero, arrived to replace Rear Admiral Robert A. "Fuzzy" Theobald as commander of the North Pacific Force, and Rear Admiral Charles H. McMorries relieved Rear Admiral W. W. Smith as commander of the cruiser-destroyer group. With the arrival of these two men the Aleutian campaign went into high gear.[28]

On March 26, 1943, Admiral Hosogaya, who had decided to run the American blockade and resupply Attu, encountered a small task group under Rear Admiral McMorries. The subsequent engagement, named the "Battle of the Komandorski Islands," was to have no parallel in the entire Pacific war. Rear Admiral McMorries fought a retiring action against Admiral Hosogaya's forces, twice as large as his own and with double the firepower. The battle lasted continuously for three and one-half hours, and the opponents shot at each other at ranges of eight to twelve miles. No planes or submarines intruded, and neither side did the other great harm. The Japanese finally broke off the battle when Admiral Hosogaya became convinced that he was under air attack. What had happened was that the heavy cruiser *Salt Lake City*, having run out of armor-piercing shells, started shooting high explosives with white phosphor splashes that looked exactly like bombs dropping through the overcast sky.[29] The battle was decisive, because after Hosogaya turned back no further Japanese convoys were to reach the Aleutians.

On May 11, 1943, American troops landed on Attu, a forbidding, mountainous island some thirty-five miles long and fifteen miles wide. Bitter fighting raged for two weeks. On May 28, Colonel Yasuyo Yamasaki took stock of his situation. Of the 2,600 men he had started with on May 11, fewer than 800 fighting men remained. Some 600 were wounded. He estimated American strength at 14,000 men. There would be no evacuation because the fleet of large transport submarines called I-boats had been turned back by the American destroyer screen. The colonel, therefore, decided to attack, in the hope—however remote—of raiding American supplies. That evening he sent his last radio message to Japan, burned his records, and prepared his soldiers for the assault. Lieutenant Nebu Tatsuguchi returned to his post that evening and made his last diary entry:

> At 2000 we assembled in front of headquarters. The last assault is to be carried out. All patients in the hospital are to commit suicide. . . . Gave 400 shots of morphine to severely wounded, and killed them. . . . Finished all the patients with grenades. . . .
>
> Only 33 years of living and I am to die here. I have no regrets. Banzai to the Emperor. . . . Goodbye Tasuko, my beloved wife.[30]

American troops landing at Attu, Aleutian Islands, May 4, 1943 (*Hanna Call Collection, Archives, University of Alaska, Fairbanks*)

On the morning of May 29, Yamasaki made a banzai charge with his remaining men. The Japanese came close to taking back what the Americans had gained in three weeks of bitter and bloody fighting. Individual Japanese soldiers held out in the hills; some were not flushed out until three months later. When finally cornered, every Japanese soldier chose to commit suicide.[31]

It had been an expensive battle. In proportion to the numbers of troops involved, it would rank as the second most costly American battle in the Pacific Theater, second only to Iwo Jima. Landing Force Attu had suffered 3,829 casualties: 549 killed, 1,148 wounded, 1,200 injuries due to the severe cold; 614 disease casualties, including exposure; 318 other casualties, which included self-inflicted wounds, psychiatric breakdowns, drownings, and accidents. The Japanese were practically annihilated. Only twenty-eight prisoners were taken, not one officer among them, and the American burial parties counted 2,351 Japanese bodies; several hundred more dead were presumed to have been buried in the hills by the Japanese during the three weeks of battle.[32]

Kiska — Anticlimax

American attention next turned to Kiska. From June 1 until August 15, army pilots flew 1,454 sorties and dropped 1,255 tons of bombs on Kiska. In addition, the navy bombarded Kiska from its cruisers and destroyers. Unknown to the Americans, however, the Japanese had decided to evacuate the Kiska garrison. At first thirteen big I-boat transport submarines were to be used, but seven of these were lost or crippled in evacuating 820 men. On July 28 and 29 the enemy, under the cover of fog, skillfully brought a surface fleet into Kiska Harbor. Within fifty-five minutes, Rear Admiral Shozo Akiyama, officers, enlisted men, and civilians, numbering 5,183, crowded on board two cruisers carrying 1,200 each and six destroyers averaging 470 passengers each. The ships left undetected and safely reached Paramushiro on August 1, 1943.[33]

Before the evacuation of Kiska, on July 23, the radar of a Catalina had contacted what were believed to be seven vessels some 200 miles southwest of Attu. The American command believed that these ships were a Japanese reinforcement convoy bound for Kiska. American warships rushed to the scene, and on July 26 the American fleet made radar contact and fought what was to become known as "The Battle of the Pips." After expending 1,005 rounds, Rear Admiral R. C. Giffen gave the order to cease firing and at dawn circled back to the scene of the "battle." An observer plane found no debris, no wreckage, nothing but the gray waves of the North Pacific. Apparently return echoes from the mountains of Amchitka and other islands had shown up on radar some 100 to 150 miles distant.[34]

On August 14 the Kiska invasion proceeded on a colossal scale. Two days later the American troops reached the enemy's main camp and discovered all the signs of hasty departure, with food, stores, and weapons only partially destroyed. Yet the Americans suffered casualties. Patrols occasionally shot fellow Americans by mistake. Some twenty-five soldiers died and thirty-one suffered wounds from these errors. In addition, the navy lost seventy men, dead or missing, and forty-seven wounded.[35]

S/Sgt. Edmond Birdsell of San Francisco samples rice left behind when the Japanese fled Kiska
(Hanna Call Collection, Archives, University of Alaska, Fairbanks)

The War's Impact on the North

After the Aleutians had been secured, military activities declined sharply. From 152,000 members of the armed forces in Alaska in 1943, the number declined to 60,000 in 1945 and to a mere 19,000 in 1946. Although military activities decreased rapidly after 1943, the war had a profound and lasting impact on the territory. It irrevocably altered the pace and tenor of Alaskan life. The residual benefits to the civilian economy and the development of Alaska were tremendous. Between 1941 and 1945 the federal government spent well over one billion dollars in Alaska.[36] The modernization of the Alaska Railroad and the expansion of airfields and construction of roads benefited the civilian population as well as the war effort. Many of the docks, wharves, and breakwaters built along the coast for the use of the navy, Coast Guard, and the Army Transport Service were turned over to the territory after the war. Thousands of soldiers and construction workers had come north; and as reflected in population statistics, many decided to make Alaska their home at the end of the hostilities. Between 1940 and 1950 the territory's civilian population increased from approximately 74,000 to 112,000.[37] But this influx put a tremendous strain on Alaska's already inadequate social services, such as schools, hospitals, housing, and local government.

In short, the war was the biggest boom Alaska ever experienced, bigger than any of the gold rushes of the past. Yet, at the end of the war, with the curtailment of defense spending, Alaskans once again were confronted with the problems of a seasonal economy.

The Cold War

The development of tensions between the United States and the Soviet

The 171st Brigade at Fort Wainwright, whose history dates back to General George Custer and beyond, parades on skiis (*Fairbanks Daily News-Miner*)

The C-5 Galaxy, largest airplane ever to fly in Alaska, landed at Eielson Air Force Base in the winter of 1970 *(Fairbanks Daily News-Miner)*

Union after World War II, resulting in the Cold War, rescued Alaska from economic depression and obscurity. The territory's geographical position astride the northern Great Circle Route gave it a strategic importance in the free world, an importance which once again was to bring thousands of troops and the expenditure of millions of dollars.[38]

By 1947 construction had commenced on what was then the largest airfield in the world, Eielson Air Force Base, twenty-six miles south of Fairbanks. Long-range bombers were to use this facility. The rebuilding and expansion of other major defense facilities at Fort Richardson and Elmendorf Air Force Base near Anchorage, Fort Greely near Big Delta, Kodiak, Shemya, Adak, and smaller bases and stations elsewhere got underway as well.

By 1949 military planners had become worried about Russian activities in Siberia and speculated that four-engined aircraft stationed on the Chukotsk Peninsula could theoretically attack the atomic bomb plant at Hanford, Washington, and return to their bases. A limited radar network existed, but much had to be done to upgrade Alaska's defenses effectively. The construction and equipping of the electronic Distant Early Warning Line resulted, soon to be followed by the White Alice system, a tropospheric scatter radio communications network.

The Cold War quickly forced American strategic rethinking, and in the late 1940s military planners decided on the so-called heartland concept of Alaskan defense. This included a virtual abandonment of the Aleutian Islands and a massive strengthening of the military bases in and near Fairbanks and Anchorage. The new concept coincided with a general realignment in the overall strategic emphasis from the Pacific to the Atlantic.[39]

Before the shift in emphasis could be accomplished, however, massive problems had to be overcome in Alaska. As the armed forces had discovered, Alaska was a region of magnificent distances, lethal cold, forbidding terrain, and a still totally inadequate system of communication and transportation. As on previous occasions, the territory challenged American technical imagination and ingenuity. For despite the intensive construction activity during the war, Alaska was still a primitive frontier that lacked housing and possessed no modern economic and social infrastructure to support the defense effort.

Supplies still came mostly by sea from Seattle to the ports of Seward, Whittier, Anchorage, or Valdez, each one insufficient in one way or another. The best was probably Seward, although wood worms had done severe damage to the docks, which required frequent replacements. Whittier, built during the war and located at the head of a fjord in a small glacial ravine, was plagued by high winds and almost continuous rain and snowfall in addition to inadequate docking and unloading facilities. With a glacier behind it, the sea in front of it, and thirty to fifty feet of snow on top of it in the winter, it was isolated, had no recreational facilities, and appeared to be the end of nowhere in Alaska for army personnel unfortunate enough to serve there. Large floating ice cakes and thirty-six-foot tides plagued Anchorage.

The Alaska Railroad, which carried freight from the ports, was antiquated. Completed in 1923 after eight years of construction, the railroad's average daily capacity of some 1,500 tons was insufficient even for normal civilian requirements. It had inadequate rolling stock, grades, and a poor roadbed. In the so-called loop area between Seward and Portage the trains had to traverse a high ravine in an approximately 360-degree circle; the tracks were supported on high, wooden trestles which had been erected many years earlier and which were quite shaky by 1949. In addition, heavy snows and occasional avalanches between Seward and Anchorage often interrupted train service.[40]

The Alcan Highway, a crude gravel road built in 1942/43, connected the territory with the continental United States. Although open the year round, it had a maximum capacity of only 1,000 to 1,500 tons daily. Alaska's 2,500-mile road system was primitive, and not one road from any of the ports was consistently open all winter long.[41]

The territory's communication system was similarly primitive. Only one land line existed, running along the Alaska Railroad. The Alaska Communications System, run by the Army Signal Corps, relied on radio transmission, which was often blocked by atmospheric interference.[42]

Housing was abysmal throughout the territory, particularly for military personnel, thereby severely undercutting morale and causing an almost negligible re-enlistment rate for the territory. Many of the single men among the 20,000-30,000 troops lived in overcrowded barracks and dark quonset huts. Family quarters were scarce and substandard, and rents were exorbitant. Packing-case houses, open walls, and outdoor privies predominated, in addition to severe overcrowding. Construction costs, two and one-half to three times above those in the continental United States, severely limited new housing starts, while exceedingly high prices for food, appliances, and services stretched already modest budgets to their limits. Compounding the problems was the

Dawson Creek, British Columbia — start of the Alcan
(Machetanz Collection, Archives, University of Alaska, Fairbanks)

lack of adequate recreational and social activity.[43]

In order to achieve the "heartland" concept of defense in Alaska, the military realized that vast expenditures would be needed to provide basic facilities. The Defense Department asked Congress for funding, and, though there were delays and cuts in various construction requests, military expenditures approached $100 million in 1949, starting the territory's postwar economic boom.[44]

The Postwar Defense Construction Boom

By June of 1950 it had become apparent that some $250 million worth of construction would be undertaken. All was not rosy, however, because carpenters, electricians, and other craft unions had gone on strike for higher wages. These work stoppages completely halted many projects and considerably slowed others. But workers, undeterred, had been flocking to the territory from the continental United States since early spring. Hoping for quick employment at high wages, their resources were slim, and many suffered hardships because of the prolonged strike.

The influx of defense spending made prices soar. Housing in Fairbanks, always insufficient and mostly substandard, now fetched premium prices. Cabins without electricity or water rented for $150 per month, and rooms in hotels in Anchorage were even worse because rental was anywhere from 10 to 20 percent higher than in Fairbanks—and nothing was available.

Workers earned big money, and they worked a good deal of overtime. Building mechanics, for example, received weekly paychecks that often exceeded $200, in addition to free board and room. The basic daily wage of a waitress amounted to $8.60, that of a cook, $18. Craft unions such as the plumbers and steamfitters, electricians, carpenters, and painters all made over $3.00 per hour. But prices corresponded to wages. Fruits and vegetables, all airborne, were exorbitant. Restaurant meals were high: a plain omelet or a lettuce and tomato salad came to $1.50 or $1.75, and a piece of toast cost 30¢ or 35¢. But despite the prices, business boomed.[45]

Population, like prices, had also skyrocketed. In 1940 the territory boasted 75,000 residents, of whom some 1,000 were military personnel. By 1950 Alaska's population had jumped to 138,000, of whom 26,000 belonged to the military services.[46] Anchorage had been a sleepy railroad town of 3,495 in 1940; in 1950 it had an estimated 11,060 residents—not including several outlying suburbs which would have brought the population to approximately 20,000. Also not included were transients and military personnel stationed at the bases. The population of Fairbanks jumped from approximately 5,600 in 1940 to 11,700 in 1950; and that of Seward, from 949 to 2,063 during the same decade.[47]

While contractors hurried to complete military family quarters, barracks and official quarters, service clubs, warehouses, and power plants, the influx of job-seekers severely taxed Alaska's housing and social services. Transients clogged the cities, and although there was no spectacular increase in major crimes in Fairbanks, Anchorage police reported half a dozen murders during the first half of 1950. Police blamed the increase in robberies in both cities on the boom conditions which had brought thousands of newcomers and transients to Alaska. Gambling flourished in the construction centers, and although it was against territorial laws, officials overlooked the games "so long as these are carried on in an orderly and gentlemanly fashion." The fact was that municipal taxes from these activities had something to do with official leniency. Prostitution flourished despite the fact that red-light districts in both cities had been closed some years earlier. The women now cautiously walked the streets or operated outside the city limits. Cab drivers often acted as steerers, directing customers to prostitutes for a fee.[48]

Despite many problems, Alaskans ultimately stood to profit from the turmoil of the boom. As a result of military construction, the private business sector flourished. In Fairbanks the Community Savings Bank of Rochester, New York, financed the 270-family Fairview Manor development with $3,080,000. In Anchorage the Government Hill Apartments, designed for 696 families, took shape at a cost of $10 million, and the Brady-Smalling Construction Company built two 132-unit housing developments at a cost of $3 million. In both Anchorage and Fairbanks large and small modern houses supported by Federal Housing Authority (FHA) guarantees were built in new subdivisions. The Anchorage suburb of Spenard numbered 3,000 residents, and a modern shopping center was built on a tract that had been part of Alaska's wilderness only five years earlier. In addition, both Anchorage and Fairbanks had new airports under construction. Increased demands stimulated the professional and business communities to expand services.

Considerable sums also went into the expansion of the small highway network and Alaska Railroad extensions and improvements. In short, Alaska coped with its problems.[49] The territory slowly built up a backlog of social overhead. Despite worries within Alaska's business community, the defense boom continued unabated.

A fifty-three-day walkout of the Sailors' Union of the Pacific of the American Federation of Labor (AFL) in the summer of 1952 slowed Alaska's boom somewhat; yet projects planned or already underway continued. Private building expanded significantly, but housing shortages still were critical even though the Alaska Housing Authority built or financed many units during that summer, among them 150 low-rental units in Anchorage and another 75 units in Fairbanks.[50]

Many began to recognize that the territory was quickly becoming a guardian of North American defenses. The massive infusion of military dollars stimulated tertiary growth; modern hotels and office buildings sprang up, and new radio stations gained permission to operate. Air transportation expanded vastly with new commercial airports and connections to most points in Alaska and to many international destinations. Modern subdivisions alternated with unattractive slum areas containing shacks and wanigans, largely the result of slipshod regulations and hurry-up building. In Fairbanks the number of bank deposits doubled between 1949 and 1952, while car registration in Anchorage increased 1,390 percent in a decade, and school attendance increased nearly 1,000 percent within the same period. The population of the greater Anchorage area increased 52.1 percent between April 1, 1950, and December 31, 1951.

But despite the private building boom sparked by defense spending, much remained to be done. Both towns suffered from a shortage of school buildings, and Fairbanks was in dire need of a sewage disposal system. For the first time Alaska offered bright opportunities for young professionals in addition to the

Main Street of
Anchorage, spring 1945
(*Lulu Fairbanks Collection,
Archives, University of Alaska,
Fairbanks*)

Haines-Fairbanks
626-mile military
petroleum pipeline
under construction
in 1954
(*U.S. Army Corps of Engineers*)

customary seasonal employment for floating labor.[51] In short, the territory was in a period of transition from which fewer and fewer people fled as soon as the weather turned cold or a fortune had been made. The accumulating social overhead made living easier and more comfortable.

By 1954 the territory had passed the peak of military construction. Military housing needs had largely been met, and Alaska's defenses were nearly completed with a network of radar defenses and massive military bases. The gains had been great. Within a five-year period from 1949 to 1954 the territory had become habitable on a year-round basis for a vastly increased population. Expenditures for defense and civilian construction combined had been approximately $250 million per year from 1949 to 1954.[52]

When construction for defense installations passed its peak in 1954, much had been accomplished. Alaska's road system had more than doubled, from a prewar mileage of 2,400 miles of dirt and gravel roads to 5,196 miles of high-grade paved highways and gravel roads in 1958. The Alaska Highway and the Haines cut-off had become all-year links. Highway construction received massive funding and was transferred to civilian program direction with the inclusion of Alaska in the federal aid-to-highways program in 1956.

The prewar Alaska Railroad had hauled freight and passengers along a single track 470 miles long from Seward to Fairbanks. Its equipment consisted of coal-burning locomotives and primitive wood-frame cars handed down from the Panama Canal construction project. By 1958 the Alaska Railroad right-of-way had been upgraded, the rolling stock completely modernized, and the coal-burning locomotives replaced by diesel engines.

The ports of Seward and Valdez had been rebuilt and now easily accommodated military and civilian freight, while the new military port of Whittier provided an alternative for landing freight. An eight-inch, 625-mile-long pipeline from Haines pumped oil products to Fairbanks, while surfaced air-fields aided commercial aviation, which successively progressed from single- to multi-engined propeller and then jet aircraft.

But perhaps most important were the people who came to Alaska during and after the war. The majority were members of a mid-twentieth-century American urban industrial society, who expected—and demanded—the same standards of community living and services available in the continental United States. Prosperity induced by defense spending in the far north made it possible to slowly meet these demands. In addition, the expansion and change in the composition of Alaska's population in the postwar period resulted in increasing political agitation for self-government and the eventual attainment of state-hood in June 1958. The culmination of the long statehood struggle came when President Dwight D. Eisenhower signed the official proclamation on January 3, 1959, which admitted Alaska as the forty-ninth state to the Union.[53]

Throughout the 1940s, until at least the mid-1960s, military construction and the maintenance of garrisons and uniformed personnel and their depen-dents made the military the major single element in the economic growth of Alaska. Compared with prewar expenditures of less than one million dollars in the territory, military spending peaked at $512.9 million in 1953 and still amounted to $354 million in 1970. But by the mid-1950s Alaskans were once again looking to their natural resources to help stabilize their economy. By 1954 a $50 million pulp mill was under construction near Ketchikan, and in

Ketchikan pulp mill
(Claus-M. Naske)

1957 the Richfield Oil Company discovered oil at the Swanson River on the Kenai Peninsula. Within a few short years massive oil discoveries elsewhere were to place Alaska in the top ranks of the oil-rich regions of the United States and the Western Hemisphere.

·7·
Alaska's Rocky Road to Statehood

WORLD WAR II had revolutionized Alaska, and along with the influx of new residents came demands once again for the territory's admission as a state into the union.

The idea of self-government had been discussed off and on since 1867, when Sitka residents had made the request: "Territorial government for the Territory [*sic*] of Alaska."[1] While on a world tour at the end of his services in the administration of President Andrew Johnson, William Seward visited Sitka. The former secretary of state and the architect of the purchase of Russian America commiserated with Alaskans in their dissatisfaction with the lack of civil government. "Within the period of my own recollection," he told his audience, "I have seen 20 new states added to the 18 which before that time constituted the American Union, and I now see, besides Alaska, 10 Territories in a forward condition of preparation for entering into the same great political family." Seward confidently expected Congress to furnish Alaskans with a civil government during the coming winter because, he asserted, the American political system rejected "alike anarchy and executive absolutism." Seward concluded that he fully expected "that the political society to be constituted here, first as a Territory, and ultimately as a State or many States, will prove a worthy constituency of the Republic."[2]

Nobody at Sitka on that August day in 1869 realized that it would take a full eighty-nine years for Alaska to achieve statehood. In the meantime, Congress provided Alaska with the rudiments of civil government when it passed the First Organic Act in 1884. Jack E. Eblen, a scholar of territorial government, has concluded that the organic act "provided a crudely modified first-stage government and made no provisions for eventual representative government."[3]

It was not until 1906 that Congress finally passed a measure giving Alaskans a voteless delegate to Congress, in part, perhaps, to meet President Theodore Roosevelt's plea to "give Alaska some person whose business it shall be to speak with authority on her behalf to the Congress." So many different interests—lobbyists of mining, canned salmon, steamship, mercantile interests, as well as the appointive governor and other civil, military, and federal officials—had claimed to represent northern interests that Congress was simply confused.[4]

Despite much effort and the accompanying acrimony, it was not until 1912 that Congress passed the Second Organic Act, which gave Alaska an elected legislature. The territorial legislature had many restrictions imposed on it, among them the inability to regulate Alaska's fish, game, and fur resources, or to assume bonded indebtedness without congressional consent. Despite all its apparent and real defects, the Second Organic Act of 1912 ended Alaska's vague legal and constitutional status. It specifically stated that "the Constitution . . . shall have the same force and effect within the Territory of Alaska as elsewhere in the United States."

Ever since 1868, Alaska had been referred to as both the "District of Alaska" and the "Territory of Alaska." These two terms were also used interchangeably in subsequent debates and committee reports, while the First Organic Act of 1884 had added to the confusion by making Alaska "a civil and judicial district." The distinction between a territory and a district was a crucial one, because the former was thought capable of exercising at least a limited measure of home rule through a locally elected legislature, while the latter was considered incapable of exercising self-government.[5]

Even the term "territory" had been modified in the early twentieth century. As a result of the Spanish-American War of 1898, the United States had acquired Puerto Rico, the Philippines, and other noncontiguous lands. The question soon arose whether or not these new acquisitions should become integral parts of the United States. The Supreme Court decided in the negative in a series of decisions known collectively as the Insular Cases. The Court made a hazy distinction between "incorporated" and "unincorporated" territories. The former were to be subject to the "fundamental" and "formal" parts of the Constitution as well as all public laws applicable to them, while in legislating for "unincorporated" territories Congress was restrained only by the "fundamental" parts of the Constitution.[6] Secretary of War Elihu Root reportedly said of this rather nebulous distinction established by the Court that "as near as I can make out the constitution follows the flag but doesn't quite catch up with it."[7] Under these distinctions Alaska and Hawaii were declared to be "incorporated," whereas the Philippines and Puerto Rico were not.

Historically, statehood had been tied to the territorial classification and, after the Insular Cases, specifically to the incorporated status. The Court also decided that once an area had been incorporated it could not revert to an unincorporated status. Most importantly, the act of incorporation was consistently looked upon as a commitment on the part of Congress to ultimately admit the incorporated territory as a state.[8]

These and other legislative restrictions soon led to demands for additional powers. During the second territorial legislature in 1915, that body passed a joint memorial by Senator Benjamin Millard of Valdez asking that Congress amend the organic act in order to give Alaskans the type of self-government that earlier territories had enjoyed.[9] Republican Senator Oliver P. Hubbard, a Valdez attorney and railroad promoter, introduced a statehood resolution on

March 31, 1915.[10] After much debate, the Senate rejected the Hubbard resolution; undeterred, Hubbard introduced a joint resolution that would enable voters to express themselves on full territorial government or immediate statehood. That also failed.[11]

Delegate Wickersham Introduces the First Statehood Bill in 1916

While the legislature debated the merits of full territorial government and statehood, Delegate James W. Wickersham arrived in Juneau. He had come to Alaska in 1900 from the state of Washington after President William McKinley appointed him as federal judge. By his performance on the bench at Nome and Fairbanks he had established a reputation for fairness, efficiency, and courage. Still, many unsuccessful litigants, some of whom were politically influential, disliked him. He soon became estranged from both the territorial governor, Wilford Hoggatt, and U.S. Senator Knute Nelson of Minnesota for rendering adverse decisions against some of their friends. Nelson successfully blocked his confirmation as judge. After President Roosevelt had kept him in office through five recess appointments, Wickersham resigned in November of 1907.[12] By 1908 he had developed political ambitions, and in November of that year Alaskans elected the former judge to represent them in Washington.

Wickersham landed in Juneau in 1915 on his way to his home in Fairbanks, where he intended to spend the summer. Basically a conservative individual, he had been no friend of home rule, which was reflected in the limited Second Organic Act he had steered through Congress. As a pragmatist, however, he did not intend to jeopardize his political future by adhering to an unpopular position. Home rule had become a powerful emotional symbol. Wickersham therefore announced in Juneau that Alaska was entitled to full home rule and was ready for it. Furthermore, only statehood could achieve that goal. He intended to introduce a measure admitting Alaska into the Union at the next session of Congress. On April 1, 1915, the Juneau *Daily Alaska Dispatch* became the first newspaper in the territory taking a stand for immediate statehood.[13] The territorial legislature debated the issue of full territorial government versus statehood, but most members favored the former.

Delegate Wickersham realized that the incessant demands of John Troy, editor of Juneau's *Alaska Daily Empire*, for "a full territorial form of government" were damaging his political reputation. Action was called for, and on January 4, 1916, the delegate introduced a bill to enlarge the powers of the territorial legislature.[14] The most important feature of this measure proposed transferring management functions over the fishery and wildlife resources to the territory. But the opposition of the commissioner of the United States Bureau of Fisheries killed the bill.[15]

Wickersham had given some thought to statehood as early as 1910, when he wrote an article for *Collier's* with the suggestive title "The Forty-Ninth Star." In it he argued that Alaska was destined to become a state and had, as a matter of fact, "the constitutional right to Statehood." Wickersham also made known his intentions of introducing a statehood bill for Alaska late in 1910.[16] The promised statehood bill never appeared, and one may assume that he may have used the possibility of such a measure as a device to get the organic act through Congress.

The year 1916 was to be different. In late 1916 a newspaper, *The Forty-Ninth Star*, was established in Senator Hubbard's hometown of Valdez. John Frame, a former attorney and newspaperman, became the editor. The express purpose of the paper was the promotion of statehood. Frame admonished his prospective readers: "If you are an Alaskan, then be a Forty-niner. Subscribe for this paper and stand by it until the 49th Star is placed upon that banner of Freedom."[17] The cause received further impetus during the course of a meeting in the Valdez town hall on February 16, 1916, when Statehood Club No. 1 was organized. The fledgling group elected Oliver P. Hubbard its president and authorized him to nominate other officers. The group adopted a twelve-paragraph constitution that committed it to work for statehood and hoped for the establishment of similar committees elsewhere.[18]

In the meantime Wickersham had begun his labors of drafting an enabling act for the proposed state. He patterned his bill after the 1906 measure that had gained admission for Oklahoma. This particular bill, he reasoned, was recent, contained many new ideas, and was liberal in its grants of money and land to the new state. In addition, Oklahoma was a Democratic state, and thus a similar enabling act for Alaska should find favor with the Wilson administration.[19]

On March 30, 1916, the date of the forty-ninth anniversary of the signing of the treaty of cession of Russian America, Delegate Wickersham officially introduced his enabling measure.[20] He had carefully chosen this date to emphasize Alaska's long apprenticeship as a possession of the United States. But it was more of a trial balloon than a serious measure.

The statehood bill, the first in a long line of such measures, was simple and skeletal. It contained the standard provision in enabling acts that the proposed new state be admitted on a basis of equality with the other states. Alaskans were to hold a constitutional convention and write a document acceptable both to the state and to Congress. The projected government was to be republican in form. There were the usual safeguards, such as those for religious toleration and for the franchise without regard to sex, creed, or color. Creditors were to be protected by state assumption of territorial debts. Elementary and higher education was made a state responsibility. The rights of Alaska's Indians, Eskimos, and Aleuts to lands claimed by them were protected in that the future state disclaimed all rights and title to any unappropriated public areas which were claimed by the various indigenous groups until Congress extinguished those rights. The state was prohibited from selling the tidelands or banks or beds of waters within its boundaries, but instead would hold title to these areas in perpetuity for the public benefit.[21]

The land grants to the new state generally followed those made to the public land states. There were land grants for public buildings and for the support of public schools. State universities and charitable, penal, and reformatory institutions also received attention. In addition, the new state was encouraged to develop forests and forest reserves. Various sections dealt with the leasing of mineral and coal lands, including oil and gas, and provided for the disposition of funds derived from the sale and lease of such assets. As a former judge, Wickersham gave special attention to the judicial system and generously allowed four representatives to Congress from Alaska, one from each of the four judicial districts, in addition to the usual two senators.[22]

Congress took no action on Wickersham's bill. In May 1916, Frame moved *The Forty-Ninth Star* to Anchorage. Early in 1917 the newspaper was sold and survived only a few weeks longer as the *Anchorage Weekly Democrat*. Frame himself remained a statehood advocate until his death in 1939.[23] Alaskans reelected Wickersham in 1916 on his own ambiguous platform, in which he favored extended powers for the territorial legislature and statehood "as soon as it can be organized in the interest and to the advantage of the people."[24] The issue of statehood was dead for the present; but it would soon reappear.

One State or Many?

Although statehood had become quiet as an issue, debate over home rule continued, mixed with Alaska's ever-present sectionalism, which soon surfaced concerning the question of partition. Secretary of State William H. Seward had expected the newly acquired territory to ultimately produce one or more states, and James Wickersham had looked forward to four. Senator Knute Nelson of Minnesota, much involved in Alaskan legislation, believed that three states should eventually be created: the first would include the whole southern coast of Alaska, including the Aleutians and the Panhandle; the second, the interior; and the third, the Seward Peninsula.[25] In 1908, journalist W. R. Beers, Jr., expressed his opinion that all the productive country south of the Yukon and Tanana rivers should become the territory of South Alaska; this would exclude the barren tundra to the north.[26] There were other partition proposals from time to time, particularly after the creation of the territorial legislature in 1912.

Most territorial revenues derived from taxes levied on the catching and processing of salmon found primarily off the coast of southeast Alaska and in Bristol Bay. The territory also received 25 percent of national forest receipts from the federal government. Again, the bulk of the productive national forests was located in southeast Alaska. Many residents of that most populous region knew that they generated most of the revenue, and they found it galling that they had to share equal representation in both houses with the three less-populated judicial divisions. Equal representation gave all four subdivisions an equal voice in determining appropriations. Southeastern Alaskans felt that they were not receiving their proper share of the monies, that they were, indeed, supporting the less-developed areas of Alaska.[27] One of the remedies suggested was partition—separating the economically most highly developed Panhandle from the rest of Alaska.

The year 1920 turned out to be a Republican year with the election of Warren G. Harding of Ohio to the presidency. In the race for the delegateship in the north, Dan Sutherland, a Republican, prevailed over his Democratic opponent, George Grigsby. The new president appointed Scott Bone, former editor of the *Seattle Post-Intelligencer* and director of publicity for the Repub-

President Warren G. Harding speaking in Fairbanks in July of 1923
(Mrs. George L. Keys Collection, Archives, University of Alaska, Fairbanks)

lican National Committee, to Alaska's governorship.[28] Upon his arrival in the territory, Governor Bone proved sympathetic to the partition idea. Many such schemes surfaced within the next few years in various sections of Alaska, demonstrating the fierce regionalism of this unwieldy subcontinent. Panhandle newspapers continued to stress the region's distinctiveness from the rest of Alaska, emphasizing the economic prospects for a pulp and paper industry and the continued development of mining and fishing, all of which were expected to substantially increase the population.[29]

Often Panhandle newspapers spoke derisively of the backwardness and remoteness of the west and north. The north repaid in kind; the *Anchorage Daily Times,* for one, expressed the feelings of many in the "backward" areas of the territory that if that "little part of Alaska called 'The Panhandle'" wanted to break off from the rest of Alaska, they would not object.[30]

Residents of the interior also felt that the Panhandle had little in common with the other divisions, but then stressed the fact that Anchorage had little in common with Fairbanks, that "whatever vital we are for here, Anchorage is on record against, just as strong as Juneau is." Only the second division, centered around Nome, saw eye-to-eye with the fourth division, centered around Fairbanks.[31]

Partition had adherents in all the regions for various reasons, and proponents put forth various schemes. One proposed that the territory be divided into West and East Alaska, the former including the areas served by the Alaska Railroad and the latter embracing the Panhandle, Copper River country, and the Upper Yukon Valley in the vicinity of Eagle and the Fortymile district. Still another scheme combined the various regions in the same territory and drew the boundary at the Arctic Circle on the north and the 162nd meridian on the west. This territory would contain approximately 200,000 square miles and perhaps 90 percent of the white population, taxable wealth, and best agricultural lands.[32]

While Alaskans debated partition, President Warren G. Harding decided to visit Alaska. This was the first time a chief executive had visited the territory during his term in office. The visit was of utmost importance to Alaskans, and they looked upon it as an opportunity to present their views to the president on a variety of matters. Harding was interested, among other things, in finding a solution to the administrative tangle which existed in Alaska. Five cabinet officers and twenty-eight bureaus exercised authority over the territory. Many of these agencies were in bitter conflict over how best to develop and use the vast resources of the area. Secretary of the Interior Albert B. Fall, for example, had consistently promoted a plan to concentrate the administration of Alaska into one department (presumably Interior), thus allowing private enterprise to exploit the natural resources as speedily as possible. Secretary of Agriculture Henry C. Wallace, in whose department the conservation-minded Forest Service was located, objected to Fall's plan. President Harding was torn between these conflicting opinions and wanted to investigate on the spot before making any decisions. This was also an opportunity to draw attention to America's neglected territory. The completion of the federal government's Alaska Railroad gave the president the opportunity to drive the official golden spike.

The president and his party, including Secretaries Fall and Wallace as well as Secretary of Commerce Herbert Hoover, traveled on the naval vessel *Henderson*, arriving in Metlakatla, Alaska, on July 8, 1923. There the chief executive was greeted by the town's Indian population and Governor Bone. In all, the presidential party called at eight ports, as well as Anchorage, Nenana, and Fairbanks. Harding was entertained, cheered, admired, greeted, and proudly guided on local tours. At Nenana the president drove the symbolic golden spike, and in Fairbanks he addressed most of the town's 1,500 citizens in the ball park. Then the president and his retinue turned south again and finally sailed for Vancouver and Seattle.

During his visit Harding evidently concluded that few important changes of policy or administration were necessary or desirable. The president delivered his last major speech in the University of Washington stadium on July 27, 1923, a week before his death in San Francisco. He spoke of the future of Alaska and indicated that he opposed radical changes in its administration. He rejected the idea of a sudden exploitation of Alaska's resources such as Secretary Fall had advocated; instead, he endorsed the conservation policies of his predecessors. The president said that he favored a slow, planned evolution that would protect the territory's natural resource endowments yet permit their gradual use. Equally important to Alaskans, Harding declared that the territory was destined for ultimate statehood. "Few similar areas in the world present such natural invitations to make a state of widely varied industries and permanent character," he said. "As a matter of fact, in a very few years we can set off the Panhandle and a large block of the connecting southeastern part as a State."

Alaskan reaction to the president's speech was overwhelmingly favorable. The *Ketchikan Chronicle* asserted that the president's speech "came as a tonic to every Alaskan who has taken off his coat, rolled up his sleeves, and worked for the betterment of the territory." The *Alaska Daily Empire* (Juneau) agreed that there was "nothing the federal government could do that would transform the territory overnight into a populous and wealthy commonwealth."[33]

Secession Movement in Southeastern Alaska

While Harding's Seattle speech and his subsequent death were still being discussed in the nation's press, the inhabitants of southeastern Alaska, the territory's most populous and developed section, were taking steps to secede from the rest of Alaska. Encouraged by the late president's remark that their section would be the first to attain statehood, they wanted to speed that day by establishing a full-fledged territorial government for South Alaska. On November 6, 1923, a referendum was held in all of the large southeastern towns except Sitka, which was not notified in time. Some 1,344 citizens approved the plan; 89 rejected it. With this mandate for partition, twelve delegates assembled in convention in Juneau to prepare for the event. The convention then memorialized Congress for action and included a proposed organic act for South Alaska. To bolster their petition they added a list of their region's impressive material resources and assets.[34]

This move, however, was not merely one designed to bring statehood to South Alaska. The main reason, it appeared, was the old desire to retain tax monies for specific use within that part of the territory. Ralph Robertson, who was the convention president, journeyed to Washington, D.C., to present the memorial and supporting data to the House Committee on the Territories. For three days, March 27–29, 1924, the committee held hearings on a measure introduced by Chairman James Curry of California to reapportion Alaska's legislature. Shortly after the hearings opened, Curry categorically declared that Alaska would not be partitioned nor receive statehood.[35] That effectively ended the separationist movement in southeastern Alaska; the reapportionment bill also died.

The Defeat of Republican Wickersham and the Election of Anthony J. Dimond

On June 15, 1925, after being appointed by President Coolidge, George Parks was inaugurated as governor of Alaska. As an official of the Department of the Interior, Parks had long worked and lived in Alaska. Without political instincts, the new governor conducted a conservative administration for his nearly eight years in office.[36] During his administration the topic of statehood was seldom publicly mentioned.

One exception occurred in 1929. On November 5 of that year, Delegate Sutherland announced his decision not to seek re-election for a sixth term. That very night James Wickersham declared his candidacy, and in January 1930 he issued his platform which, among other items, included support "for a more perfect form of Territorial Government" and territorial control over the fish and game resources. John Rustgard, Alaska's attorney general, opposed Wickersham for the nomination. Rustgard favored an amendment to the organic act giving Alaska as much home rule as earlier territories had known, enabling the territory to gradually assume more governmental functions until "full Statehood is attained...."[37] Wickersham won the nomination and defeated his Democratic opponent George Grigsby in the fall elections. At seventy-four years of age, the veteran again assumed a seat in Congress. He did not, however, repeat his statehood efforts of 1916 during this, his last term in Congress.

The Great Depression spelled disaster for many Republican officeholders, among them James Wickersham. Unopposed in the primary for a second term in 1932, he faced Democrat Anthony J. Dimond, a tall and somber man, in the November election.[38] Dimond had come north from Palatine Bridge on the Mohawk River in New York early in the century. He had taught high school and read some law. While on a prospecting trip in 1911, a shooting accident forced him to abandon gold mining. He resumed his law studies, and not long after leaving the hospital in Cordova he was admitted to the territorial bar and began the practice of law. He served as a commissioner of the Chisana recording district in 1913 and 1914, as mayor of Valdez for ten years, and as territorial senator for two terms.[39]

Although the *New York Times* described him as a man almost entirely lacking in political instinct, a Democrat of long standing who had never voluntarily sought office, he was rated as the most formidable candidate the Democrats had fielded in years. Both Wickersham and Dimond campaigned vigorously, the seventy-five-year-old Wickersham fighting for his political life.

Dimond electioneered by bush plane, and one day while stepping out on the pontoon to get off, he was struck on the shoulder by the plane's propeller. Dimond was thrown into the mud on the bank of the river. Rushed immediately to the hospital in Fairbanks, he was treated for a split shoulder blade, a broken collarbone, and a deep flesh wound. Despite this interruption in his campaign, Dimond won by a substantial margin, and Alaska Democrats gained large majorities in both houses of the territorial legislature. The American public also voted for a national political change, and Dimond began his Washington career in an era of tremendous political ferment.[40]

Dimond quickly made an excellent impression on his colleagues in the House and his acquaintances in the Senate. During his six terms in Congress he worked ceaselessly to expand the powers of the territorial government. In particular, he introduced measures to give Alaska control of the administration of its fish and game resources. In 1938 his efforts were partially rewarded when Congress made a number of reforms that streamlined the administration of the territory's game laws and included many of his suggestions. He also submitted proposals that would have prevented the appointment of a nonresident as governor and that also provided for the election of a territorial chief executive. He introduced measures that would have permitted the appointment of only Alaska residents to positions of district court judges and United States attorneys and marshals. Many of these proposals were designed both to overcome

Anthony J. Dimond
(*Lulu Fairbanks Collection,
Archives, University of Alaska,
Fairbanks*)

carpetbag charges which were often made against federal appointees and to get personnel familiar with the territory and its problems. None of the bills ever passed.

In 1934, Dimond joined forces with Hawaii's delegate and submitted legislation that would have given both territories representation in the Senate comparable to that in the House, but without success. His diligent attempts to persuade Congress to extend the Federal Aid Highway Act of 1916 to Alaska were likewise unsuccessful.[41]

Delegate Dimond and Ernest Gruening

Despite his attempts, the delegate accomplished no more for home rule than had his predecessor, Wickersham. However, changes in the governance of Alaska were made which affected the federal executive. Until 1934, federal relations with the territories had been conducted from the office of the chief clerk of the Interior Department. In that year the function shifted to the newly created Division of Territories and Island Possessions within the Department of the Interior.[42] Ernest Gruening became the first director.

Born in New York City in 1887, Gruening graduated from Harvard College and Harvard Medical School in 1912. Instead of practicing medicine, he pursued a career in journalism and became known for his editorship of a succession of Boston and New York newspapers as well as of the liberal journal *The Nation.* In 1936 the energetic director visited Alaska for the first time and within two weeks had traveled approximately 4,000 miles in order to familiarize himself with the North.[43]

Alaska participated on a modest scale in some of the economic recovery programs of the New Deal. The National Reforestation Act of 1933 provided for the employment of several hundred men. Late in 1933 the federal government raised the price of gold from its fixed price of $20.67 to $35.00 per ounce, once again bringing some prosperity to the industry. Yet, despite benefits from the economic recovery programs of the New Deal, the 1930s brought no basic changes to Alaska. When the National Resources Committee examined territorial conditions in 1937, it found Alaska to be thinly populated and economically primitive.[44]

It was the war that rediscovered Alaska and led to its rapid development, a circumstance neither foreseen nor planned by the federal government. Just a day after the outbreak of war in Europe on September 2, 1939, President Franklin D. Roosevelt announced that John Troy had resigned from the governorship because of ill health and that Ernest Gruening would take his place.[45] Gruening, a strong-willed and combative individual, arrived in Alaska in December of that year. In his inaugural address on December 5, he predicted that Congress would be slow in granting statehood to the first noncontiguous territory but that hurrying the process would be desirable.[46]

Delegate Dimond prodded Alaskans on the statehood issue as early as 1941 and suggested that perhaps territorial legislators should write and adopt a constitution that would give Congress a concrete document to consider, and thus expedite admission.[47] Territorial residents soon read about the pros and cons of statehood in *Alaska Life,* a wide-circulation magazine founded in 1938. In its February 1941 issue the editors committed themselves to work for immediate statehood for Alaska.[48]

In February 1941, William Egan, the freshman representative from Valdez, and John McCormick, a booster from Juneau, introduced a measure to

Territorial Governor
Ernest Gruening in
Barrow, World War II
(*Klerekoper Collection,
Archives, University of Alaska,
Fairbanks*)

hold a statehood referendum. It did not get through the Senate. In 1943, Egan repeated his effort, and it met the same fate.[49]

The Beginning of the Modern Statehood Movement

With the attention the war focused on Alaska, the modern statehood movement began in April 1943 when Senators William L. Langer (Republican,

North Dakota) and Pat McCarran (Democrat, Nevada), at Dimond's request, submitted the first statehood bill since Wickersham's measure in 1916.[50] It was a simple measure dealing with the election of delegates to a constitutional convention and the establishment of a federal district court. It also provided that Alaska "retain all the public property, vacant and unappropriated lands lying within its limits now ceded, transferred, and in the possession of the United States, and may dispose of the same as the said State may direct."[51]

Delegate Dimond followed up with a discussion of the statehood question over radio station WWDC in Washington, D.C., where he asserted that statehood for Alaska was a foregone conclusion. The territory was ready economically and socially and was entitled to it, although the military might prefer to put off any change in the government structure until after the war. Opposition, he predicted, would come from the absentee-owned fishing and mining industries, "who usually cry out in agony at the thought that they may be obliged to pay more taxes." Further economic development and statehood, he concluded, were interdependent.

Reactions to the proposal in Alaska varied. The *Anchorage Daily Times* soon became a supporter, as did the *Ketchikan Alaska Chronicle*; the Wrangell Chamber of Commerce urged passage of the measure, while the Juneau Chamber favored postponement of any action until the end of the war. The Ketchikan and Juneau bar associations unanimously favored statehood.

Secretary of the Interior Harold L. Ickes favored ultimate statehood, but not until Alaska had a sound economy and a stable population. He particularly objected to the section of the bill that proposed to give the future state all vacant and unappropriated public lands. Such action, Ickes asserted, would give to one state the tremendous natural resources that belonged to all Americans.

On December 2, 1943, Dimond crowned his years in Congress when he submitted a companion measure to the Langer-McCarran bill. The political advantages of statehood, he asserted, were immense. Alaska would no longer be a beggar at the nation's capital but instead would become a full member of the union of states.[52] Dimond's measure did not differ fundamentally from the Langer-McCarran bill. It also conveyed "all public property and all vacant and unappropriated lands, including lands reserved or withdrawn from entry" to the new state. Dimond excluded the following: all land and property possessed and actually used by the United States for some government purpose; "all lands with adjacent waters and other property set aside or reserved for the use or benefit of the native Indians, Eskimos, and Aleuts of Alaska"; lands already reserved for or devoted to the support of the common schools and the University of Alaska; Mount McKinley National Park and Glacier Bay National Monument; Naval Petroleum Reserve Number Four; and the Pribilof Islands. Dimond also exempted whatever links in the Aleutian chain west of the 172nd meridian might be required for military purposes. Other federal properties, such as Mount Katmai, Sitka, and Old Kasaan national monuments, wildlife refuges, and reserved petroleum land other than the naval reserve, would pass to the state.[53]

Perhaps Dimond attempted this massive real estate transfer in order to halt the establishment of native reservations. For between April 1942 and May

1944, Secretary Ickes had established five reservations encompassing 1,537,270 acres and inhabited by 921 people, including some whites.[54] Alaskans were virtually united in their opposition to the secretary's reservation policy.

The secretary again responded to the statehood measure. He reaffirmed his position of the ultimate desirability of statehood but again opposed the massive transfer of public lands to state ownership and feared that state management of the fisheries would result in the depletion of the salmon resource. The four executive departments that reported on Dimond's bill did not oppose the principle of statehood, but the Departments of the Interior and Army considered wartime an inopportune time for admission.[55]

Delegate Dimond realized that serious congressional consideration of statehood would not take place until after the war. Although temporarily stymied by the war, the delegate had brought the statehood issue to life. He served six terms and accomplished much. He decided to retire and return to Alaska, particularly with the prospect of appointment to a federal judgeship in the territory.

New Leadership

On taking leave of his colleagues in the House of Representatives late in 1944, Dimond introduced his successor and recommended him highly to the House membership. E. L. "Bob" Bartlett, he told them, felt as strongly about statehood for the territory as he did.[56]

The new delegate, son of Klondike pioneers, was born in Seattle in 1904 and grew up in Fairbanks. He attended the University of Washington, the University of California at Los Angeles, and the University of Alaska. In 1927 he became a reporter for the *Fairbanks Daily News-Miner*, where he remained until 1933, when Dimond appointed him his secretary. Bartlett returned to Alaska in 1934 after holding a number of government positions; Alaskans elected him in 1944 to succeed Dimond.

Soon Bartlett and Gruening, two very dissimilar personalities—the former quiet and persuasive, the latter aggressive and determined—developed a lasting working relationship, and under their leadership the statehood movement soon developed into a crusade. They gave it a vitality and dynamism it had never before possessed.

Bartlett operated effectively and tenaciously in Congress. He made friends easily and kept Alaska's problems, needs, and promises before the Congress. He appeared before every committee of the Senate and House that had anything to do with the territory. And from 1945 onward, he and his friends bombarded Congress with statehood bills in almost every session.

Gruening promoted statehood on a broad front. When he went on lecture tours in the continental United States, he insisted on advertising the issue. He used his connections with the nation's press to advantage. He clearly defined the devils, the "Outside" interests, including Seattle's monopolistic control of Alaskan shipping. The people of the territory had known all along that their freight rates were high. Gruening explained that this was due to a provision in the Maritime Act of 1920 (sponsored by Washington state's Senator Wesley

Alaska's delegate in Congress, E. L. "Bob" Bartlett
(*Vide Bartlett Collection, Fairbanks, Alaska*)

Jones and thus known in Alaska as the "Jones Act") which foreclosed the alternatives of shipment through the Canadian ports of Vancouver and Prince Rupert, both far more economical, and made Seattle the port through which Alaska's trade had to pass.

The salmon fisheries had been declining for a number of years. The governor maintained that the White Act of 1924, a measure that had been hailed as the Magna Carta of fishery conservation by both federal officials and industry spokesmen, worked to the detriment of the small operator in Alaska and protected the large companies and their fish traps—the real culprits. In short, Gruening set up the targets and called upon Alaskans to join the movement. He helped organize the statehood cause within the territory and barnstormed the United States in the service of it.

World War II ended, at least in Europe, in May of 1945. Alaska had profited enormously from the publicity and development it had received thus far in the war. The territorial house, taking advantage of the prevailing idealistic mood, sent a memorial to Congress in early 1945 in which it pleaded dramatically for the extension to Alaska of the "Four Freedoms" proclaimed in the Atlantic Charter, which supported the right of small nations and minorities to choose their own form of government and to have control over their own destinies. The memorial was soon followed by a request to admit Alaska as the forty-ninth state.

Bartlett suggested that Alaskans conduct a referendum on the statehood issue. In 1945 the governor asked territorial lawmakers to make provisions for such a referendum. The legislature complied, deciding that a vote would be taken in the 1946 general election.

Gruening and others realized that an educational program had to be undertaken to assure a large turnout of voters. Congress could not be expected to act on Alaskan statehood without a loud and positive expression from the territorial citizenry. At Gruening's suggestion, a group of Anchorage statehood enthusiasts, led by Evangeline Atwood, the wife of the editor and publisher of the *Anchorage Daily Times*, organized a nonpartisan, nonprofit, territory-wide Alaska statehood association, and they soon had established chapters in various Alaskan cities. The new organization then hired George Sundborg, an old Gruening friend, to make a study of statehood pros and cons. This study was published in pamphlet form as well as in a tabloid supplement provided free of charge to all Alaskan newspapers, encouraging the widest possible distribution.

By mid-1945 the Department of the Interior announced that statehood was now part of the department's policy for Alaska. While the department had been formulating a policy, two congressional groups traveled to Alaska to investigate conditions and to hold informal statehood hearings. The House Subcommittee on Appropriations reported that although the majority of Alaskans favored statehood, the members seriously doubted the territory's ability to assume the burdens connected with it. The House Committee on Territories heard various opinions on statehood but found no agreement as to how soon Alaska should seek admission.

In his State of the Union message in January 1946, President Harry S. Truman gave Alaskan statehood a boost when he recommended that the territory be promptly admitted as soon as the wishes of its citizens had been determined. Pollster George Gallup reported in September of that year that 64 percent of American voters favored Alaska's admission, 12 percent were opposed, and 24 percent were undecided.

Those Alaskans who went to the polls in the general election obviously had been well educated about the statehood issue. Amid much campaigning and publicity, they approved the statehood referendum by 9,630 to 6,822 votes.

By 1947, Alaska's importance in the cold war had generated some support for statehood among members of Congress and other Americans in the continental United States. Therefore, Bartlett again introduced a statehood bill in January 1947. This measure was substantially similar to previous ones except that he now further enlarged the public land grant by proposing to withdraw from reserve and give to Alaska the Aleutian Islands west of the 172nd meridian, the Pribilof Islands and all the lands with adjacent waters, and other property set aside or reserved for the use or benefits of Alaska's natives.

The House Subcommittee on Territories and Insular Possessions held public hearings on the Bartlett bill between April 16 and 24, 1947. As on previous occasions, the Department of the Interior objected to provisions which, with few exceptions, would have transferred to the new state title to practically all the public lands. This was contrary to the practice that had been followed throughout the American West. Lands had always been granted for schools and internal improvements, while the federal government retained the bulk. The Department of the Interior instead proposed a land grant of approximately twenty-two million acres.

The same subcommittee held hearings in Alaska in the early fall of 1947. Traveling from city to city, committee members heard much pro- and some anti-statehood testimony. In Fairbanks the committee heard the most formidable witness against statehood. He was Winton C. Arnold, managing director of the Alaska Salmon Industry, Inc. (a trade organization) and representative of the economically powerful Alaska fishing interests. Arnold had gained the appellation "Judge" in the 1920s in Hyder, a small silver boom town at the southeastern tip of Alaska. In 1933 the redoubtable "Judge" became the Alaskan attorney for the cannery operators and shortly thereafter moved his offices and residence to Seattle. Although still living in Seattle, Arnold was reputedly the most powerful man in Alaska because of his influence on the territorial legislature. In Juneau, where he scrupulously paid his ten-dollar lobbying fee, he supposedly exerted so much pressure that he was credited with killing basic tax reforms from 1939 until 1949, when the legislature finally enacted a basic property and income tax.

Arnold appeared briefly before the committee at three different locations. In each instance he applauded statehood ambitions but disagreed with those who advertised it as a panacea for all of Alaska's problems. The territory could not pay for it, he maintained. Furthermore, land grants to the new state would overlap aboriginal claims. Whatever the legal complexities, he advised the subcommittee, the native land issue should be settled once and for all by the federal government before any steps were taken on statehood.[57]

The 1947 hearings on the statehood bill were important because they placed the issue squarely before Congress. Most of the arguments for and against statehood were brought out into the open. By 1948 opponents and proponents had drawn battle lines, and within Alaska the movement had assumed increased vigor and had drawn new individuals as well as newspapers into the fold.

In February 1948 the House Committee on Public Lands discussed Bartlett's measure. Opinion within the subcommittee was divided. Some members agreed with the Departments of the Interior and Agriculture that the land grants should be substantially reduced to bring them into line with historical precedent. Other members vowed to see to it that Alaska would receive at least 50 percent of the public lands within her borders. The Bureau of Land Management held out for two sections out of every township, which would have amounted to a total grant of twenty million acres.

At this juncture the subcommittee instructed Bartlett to meet with officials in the Departments of the Interior and Agriculture to work out a compromise. In March, Bartlett presented to the subcommittee the new bill, which would give Alaska the traditional four sections out of every township. The subcommittee approved the new measure on March 4, 1948, and in April the full House Committee on Public Lands unanimously approved the delegate's bill and reported it with amendments. However, though it was reported to the House, the statehood bill was bottled up in the Rules Committee. As a result, Alaska statehood died for that particular session. But there were reasons to be optimistic. Hearings on Alaska statehood had been held for the first time, and a measure had been approved unanimously by a committee of Congress.

Undaunted, Delegate Bartlett and his friends in the House and Senate again submitted statehood bills in early 1949. Perfunctory hearings were held in Washington on March 4 and 8, 1949. Again the subcommittee reported the Bartlett measure favorably, and on March 10 the full House Public Lands Committee recommended House passage. Finally, on March 3, 1950, the bill reached the House floor, where it passed by a vote of 186 to 146.

A New Departure

Senate hearings opened in Washington in April 1950. A planeload of Alaskans testified in favor of it. But again they had to compete with the testimony of the most influential anti-statehood witness, W. C. Arnold. The "Judge" appeared before the Senate committee with an elaborate exhibit of charts, graphs, maps, and tables, all designed to demonstrate the inadequacy of the statehood bill under discussion. His arguments ranged widely, from impairment of international treaties and noncontiguity to questions concerned with federal land policies in Alaska and their relationship to the transfer of public lands to the proposed state. He asserted that less than 1 percent of Alaska's land area had been surveyed between 1867 and 1950. At that rate, he concluded, it would take thousands of years for Alaska to acquire all the lands to which it would be entitled under the statehood bill.[58]

The response to Arnold's thorough presentation varied. Delegate Bartlett, bitterly sardonic, observed that the salmon industry was indeed "bleeding with sympathy" for Alaska's well-being. "Do you think," Bartlett asked the senators, that "the salmon industry, opposed to statehood in any form, cares at all how much land is granted in the bill?" Answering his own question, Bartlett stated that the industry had merely seized upon the land issue because it believed that would distract Alaskans and congressional attention. "I have a suspicion," the delegate continued, "that if the statehood bill granted 50 percent of the land to the state, the salmon industry would be before you protesting the national interest was being violated by such a radical departure from the formula heretofore adopted." Legislation of any kind, he said, is always a matter of compromise. He concluded:

> If I could have my way the statehood bill would lavish upon the new state grants of various kinds hitherto unheard of in statehood bills. But we statehood advocates are realistic. We know there is a formula of [sic] new

western states and that the principal elements of that formula will apply here. If it is desired to tip the scales somewhat on the side of liberality for Alaska, so much the better. But we do not want this bill killed with kindness.[59]

It appears certain that Arnold's thorough testimony did raise questions in the minds of many senators about the adequacy of the statehood bill under discussion and about the applicability of the traditional land grant provisions in the case of Alaska. But by the end of June the Senate Interior and Insular Affairs Committee had completed its revision of the statehood bill and reported it favorably. And although the measure died in that Congress, the Senate report marked a turning point in the land-grant formula. Delegate Bartlett reported to his constituents that the Senate had moved out in a precedent-shattering direction in determining how land should be transferred to the new state. Instead of being automatically awarded sections 2, 15, 32, and 36 in each township, the proposed new state was granted the right to take twenty million acres of vacant, unappropriated, and unreserved lands from the public domain best suited to its particular needs. Once the historical precedent for the traditional land-grant formula—with its small land grants and specific township sections—had been broken, the way was open for increasingly generous land-grant provisions in succeeding statehood bills.[60]

The Politics of Statehood — Territorial and National

In the meantime, the 1949 territorial legislative session, in recognition of the popular demand for statehood, had created the official Alaska Statehood Committee. Consisting of eleven Alaskans, the committee's task was to educate the public on statehood and to publicize the issue both in Alaska and the continental United States, as well as to mobilize expert witnesses for congressional hearings.[61]

A complicating factor in Alaska's struggle was Hawaii's ambition for statehood. That territory's agitation toward statehood went back to 1903, and it was not until 1947 that the House passed a Hawaiian statehood measure. It did so again in 1950, right on the heels of the Alaska bill. From 1947 on, the Hawaii and Alaska struggles were closely intertwined.

Partisanship in the consideration of statehood for both territories had become an issue in 1947, asserted one politician, when House Speaker Joseph W. Martin of Massachusetts decided that Hawaii was likely to send a Republican congressional delegation to Washington upon statehood, whereas Alaska probably would elect Democrats. Hawaii's ambitions, therefore, received the Speaker's blessing; the Alaska measure languished in the House Rules Committee. In subsequent years arguments based on racial diversity, disproportionate senatorial representation, and the precedent that might be set for other noncontiguous possessions were used against both Alaska and Hawaii.

With the outbreak of the Korean War in June 1950, national priorities shifted rapidly, and Alaska statehood took a back seat. The war years were lean ones for Alaska's ambitions, though debate resumed in 1952.

Gearing Up for the Struggle

When Republican Dwight D. Eisenhower assumed the presidency in 1953, it quickly became apparent that statehood was now a strongly partisan issue. The Republican leadership quickly recognized that the admission of Republican-leaning Hawaii would bolster their weak hold on Capitol Hill. If traditionally Democratic Alaska were admitted at the same time, however, Republican gains would be neutralized. In his first State of the Union message on February 2, 1953, President Eisenhower reflected this attitude when he urged that Hawaii be granted statehood "promptly with the first election in 1954" but failed to mention Alaska. The House of Representatives speedily passed a Hawaiian statehood bill on March 3, 1953, while hearings on Alaska resumed once again in April.[62]

The House Subcommittee on Territorial and Insular Possessions of the Committee on Interior and Insular Affairs favorably reported a measure in June 1953. The most important change increased the proposed land grant from 40 million to 100 million acres. After this favorable treatment, the Alaska bill promptly disappeared into the House Rules Committee.[63]

In the fall of 1953, members of the Senate Interior and Insular Affairs Committee journeyed to Alaska, where they held hearings. Senator Hugh Butler (Republican, Nebraska), the committee's new chairman, was hostile to Alaska statehood. His arrival in Anchorage was the catalyst that thrust hundreds of Alaskans in the movement. They formed the "Little Men for Statehood" organization, from which soon evolved another group called "Operation Statehood." The latter quickly mounted extensive lobbying efforts.[64]

Another round of hearings commenced in 1954, and on April 1 the Senate passed a combined Alaska-Hawaii measure, the first time that body had passed the two bills. However, there was no complementary action in the House.

By 1955, Alaskans had become very impatient with the lack of progress on the congressional scene. They decided to hold a constitutional convention,

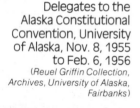

Delegates to the Alaska Constitutional Convention, University of Alaska, Nov. 8, 1955 to Feb. 6, 1956
(*Reuel Griffin Collection, Archives, University of Alaska, Fairbanks*)

partly to impress Congress with the territory's political maturity and partly to win public support. The fifty-five delegates to the convention met at the University of Alaska in Fairbanks on November 8, 1955. On February 5, 1956, seventy-five working days after they had begun their labors, they signed the 14,400-word document, which the National Municipal League termed "one of the best, if not the best, state constitutions ever written." Alaskans went to the polls in April 1956 and overwhelmingly approved their constitution by a vote of 17,447 to 8,180.

The Long, Hard Final Push

Now the final push in Congress could start. Between 1947 and 1956, hearings on Alaska statehood had been conducted on seven different occasions in Washington and three times in Alaska. The printed record totaled approximately 4,000 pages. Statehood bills had been before Congress almost continuously since 1943. Both Democratic and Republican party platforms included promises of statehood for Alaska and Hawaii. In late 1955 a Gallup poll showed that 82 percent of Americans favored the admission of Alaska, while 78 percent supported Hawaii's cause. In addition, some thirty-two national organizations, such as the American Legion and the American Federation of Labor, as well as about 95 percent of the nation's newspapers, endorsed statehood for both territories.[65]

The final push got underway in March of 1957, when the House Sub-

Senator Warren Magnuson (D-Washington), former Alaskan Governor Ernest Gruening, and Alaskan delegate "Bob" Bartlett look at map of new state of Alaska after Senate passage of statehood bill, June 30, 1958
(*Fairbanks Daily News-Miner*)

committee on Territorial and Insular Affairs again held hearings, as did its Senate counterpart. Generally, the two hearings were perfunctory because many members of both committees felt that nothing much that had not already been said could be added to the record. The House committee reported its measure favorably in June. It provided for a land grant of 182 million acres of vacant, unappropriated, and unreserved land to be selected within a period of twenty-five years after admission. It left the aboriginal land claims in status quo, to be dealt with by future legislative or judicial action. The Senate committee reported its Alaska bill favorably in August. It gave Alaska the right to select some 103,350,000 acres from the public domain within a twenty-five-year period after statehood had been achieved.

Although prospects for Alaska statehood appeared bright in 1957, the House leadership delayed action on the final drive until 1958. Finally, in his 1958 budget message, President Eisenhower fully supported Alaska statehood for the first time. The president urged "that the Congress complete action on appropriate legislation admitting Hawaii and Alaska into the Union as States."[66]

After some rough sledding, the House passed the Alaska statehood bill, but only after having reduced the land grant from 182,800,000 to 103,500,000 acres. The House then sent its bill to the Senate, which now had before it the House measure as well as its own version. After some persuasion, the Senate accepted and passed the House bill after extended debate on June 30, 1958. The goal had been achieved, and Alaska joined the Union as the forty-ninth state on January 3, 1959, after President Eisenhower signed the proclamation.

Together with vast changes in its political structure, Alaska received a total

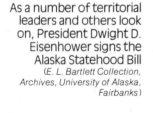

As a number of territorial leaders and others look on, President Dwight D. Eisenhower signs the Alaska Statehood Bill
(E. L. Bartlett Collection, Archives, University of Alaska, Fairbanks)

of 103,500,000 acres to be selected from the vacant, unappropriated public lands within a twenty-five-year period after admission. The magnitude of the federal land grant to the new state can best be understood in a comparison with the acreage turned over to the forty-eight continental states. The total area of the contiguous states consists of approximately 1.9 billion acres, of which 1.4 billion acres at one time were part of the public domain. The federal government disposed of 1 billion acres by various methods over a period of time. Total land grants to the continental states amounted to approximately 225 million acres. The historical record shows that the public land states—those carved out of the public domain—have not been treated uniformly as far as federal land grants are concerned. The midwestern and southern states have received a larger percentage of their total area than have the eleven western states. Florida ranks first with a grant of 24,119,000 acres out of a total state area of 37,478,000 acres—an astounding 64.3 percent; Nevada, with a land grant of 2,723,647 acres out of a total state area of 70,745,000 acres—or 3.8 percent—ranks last. In the overall list of states Alaska ranks seventh, with 27.9 percent of area granted; but it received by far the largest total acreage of any of the public land states. Congress had been generous indeed.

·8·
Transition to Statehood

EVEN THOUGH most residents welcomed Alaska's admission to the Union as the forty-ninth state, a few remained hostile. One of the diehards probably best summed up the sentiments of those remaining opposed by stating, "Wait till the honeymoon is over and the taxes arrive...."[1]

Numerous Alaskans remained uneasy about the impending changes. They feared higher taxes, continuing problems with the fishing industry, the elimination of federal cost-of-living allowances, and the possible suspension of federal welfare payments. Some of these fears may have been quieted by assurances from the United States Civil Service Commission that the statutory authority for paying cost-of-living allowances to federal employees would be unaffected by admission.[2]

Rumors circulated in a number of Eskimo and Athapascan villages that statehood would bring reservations, restrictions of traditional hunting and trapping activities, closure of native hospitals, and the suspension of federal welfare payments. Secretary of the Interior Fred Seaton denounced these rumors and reassured the natives.[3]

Despite these trepidations, statehood was achieved. President Eisenhower, who had been expected to sign the measure no later than July 3, 1958, did not do so until July 7, 1958. And then, instead of signing the admission bill in public, as was customary, he did so in private. Senator James E. Murray (Democrat, Montana) suggested that the president did not want his picture taken together with all the Democrats who had been instrumental in passing the measure: "Lord knows where he's going to find two Republicans who were sufficiently important in bringing about statehood for Alaska to whom to present the two pens he used in signing."[4] If exaggerated, Murray's assessment did at least reflect the tone of the situation correctly, because very few Republicans of national stature had promoted the measure vigorously.

With the president's signature, the statehood bill became the law of the land. It now was up to Alaskans to undertake the necessary steps to get the new state functioning. On July 16, 1958, Governor Mike Stepovich announced that candidates for political office had until July 28 to file. The primary election was to be held at the end of August. Candidates for the U.S. Senate were to run for either the A or B term, neither one identified as to length. Between the governor's proclamation and the primary election, forty-one days elapsed. A seasoned observer characterized the period as one in which an epidemic had been "let loose in the land." George Sundborg, the editor of the *Fairbanks Daily News-Miner*, was amazed and amused that so many were "willing to sacrifice personal gain and give their all for the people of the great state. . . . The same number," he caustically remarked, "feel they very likely deserve it—after all, didn't I write a letter to the editor about statehood back in 1953?"[5] In short, many felt called, filed for candidacy, and campaigned.

At the primary election the voters were also to decide on three propositions which had been inserted into the statehood bill: (1) Shall Alaska immediately be admitted into the Union as a state? (2) Shall the boundaries of the new state be approved? (3) Shall all the boundaries of the statehood act, such as those reserving rights and powers to the United States, as well as those prescribing the terms and conditions of the land grants and other property, be consented to? These were important propositions, and the Alaska Statehood Committee, Operation Statehood, and most candidates for office urged Alaskans to vote affirmatively.[6]

With no preregistration, any Alaskan nineteen years of age or older simply had to appear at the nearest polling place and cast his vote. Officials expected a record turnout of 35,000 people, but instead 48,462 voters streamed to the polling places and overwhelmingly approved the three propositions with votes of 40,452 to 8,010, 40,421 to 7,776, and 40,739 to 7,500, respectively. Many polling stations ran out of ballots and either had fresh supplies flown in or used sample ballots.[7]

There was no primary contest for the U.S. Senate because Democrats E. L. "Bob" Bartlett and Ernest Gruening ran unopposed for seats A and B, respectively; on the Republican side Ralph Robertson and former territorial governor Mike Stepovich also ran unopposed. For Alaska's single seat in the House of Representatives, the Democrat Ralph Rivers, former territorial attorney general, defeated Raymond Plummer, Alaska's former Democratic national committeeman, by a margin of 630 votes in the primary. Henry Benson, the Republican territorial commissioner of labor, would oppose Rivers in November. The field of Democratic hopefuls for the governorship was more crowded; William A. Egan defeated the territorial attorney general, J. Gerald Williams, and the territorial senate president, Victor Rivers.[8]

Alaska's voters had spoken, and the candidates prepared for the November 25, 1958 general election. The two former territorial governors, Ernest Gruening and Mike Stepovich, dominated the thirteen-week campaign. Gruening knew that he had an uphill battle against Stepovich, who had enjoyed much public exposure in recent months and had received 5,721 more votes in the primary than Gruening. Knowing that he would have to work extremely hard to win, Gruening launched a well-organized campaign that blanketed Alaska.[9] Befitting Alaska's new dignity as the forty-ninth state, national political figures journeyed north to help out. Republican Vice President Richard M. Nix-

Alaska's first U.S. Congressman after statehood, Ralph Rivers
(*Fairbanks Daily News-Miner*)

on, Senator John F. Kennedy (Democrat, Massachusetts), Senator Frank Church (Democrat, Idaho), and Secretary of the Interior Fred Seaton all ventured to Alaska to endorse their candidates. Fred Seaton, overanxious to get Mike Stepovich elected, became controversial when, in time-honored fashion, he coupled his campaigning with announcements of projects his department promised to undertake in the new state. In fact, Seaton's approach vastly overshadowed that of his protégé.[10]

On election day, November 25, 1958, a record number of 50,343 out of a possible 65,000 Alaskan voters went to the polls to elect E. L. "Bob" Bartlett by

40,939 votes over 7,299 for Ralph Robertson. Despite the boost Secretary Seaton had attempted to give him, Stepovich polled only 23,464 votes to Gruening's 26,045, while Ralph Rivers comfortably outpolled his rival Henry Benson by a margin of 27,948 to 20,699. In the race for governor, Democrat William A. Egan easily defeated his Republican rival John Butrovich by 29,189 to 19,299 votes. As many Republicans on the national level had sourly predicted, the voters gave Alaska's four top offices to Democrats. Voters favored Democrats just as much in the state legislative races when they chose thirty-three Democratic house members out of forty and seventeen Democratic senators out of twenty.[11]

The election was a disaster for Republicans, probably because their Democratic counterparts were more experienced and better known. However, Republicans had also been badly factionalized for the last couple of decades and had fought as much with each other as with the Democrats.

After the votes were counted, the transition to state government lay ahead, and planning for it had already begun. Here the Alaska Statehood Committee again made substantial contributions, for one of its responsibilities had been to gather information on how to bridge the gap between territorial and state government. The statehood committee had once before engaged the services of the Public Administration Service of Chicago in 1955 to aid in preparing for the constitutional convention. The committee hired PAS again and directed it to start its work in the spring of 1958. During the summer the statehood committee enlarged the scope of the work and increased the initial contract from $25,000 to $35,000. PAS delivered detailed reports outlining the organization of the executive, judiciary, local government, and personnel administration.[12]

While all was getting ready in Alaska, President Eisenhower formally admitted Alaska as the forty-ninth state when he signed the prescribed proclamation on January 3, 1959, together with an executive order creating a new flag for the United States. Soon thereafter U.S. District Court Judge Raymond Kelly administered the oath of office to Governor-elect William A. Egan and Secretary of State–elect Hugh Wade in the governor's office in Juneau, Alaska.[13]

Alaska had finally become a state and, with two U.S. senators and one representative, also acquired modest influence and voting power in Congress. Soon enough the Alaska delegation found occasion to flex its muscles in speeding the passage of the omnibus bill for the new state—an afterthought, as it were, to the statehood bill.

As early as July 1958 the Bureau of the Budget suggested to the president that a study was needed of the fiscal and administrative effects of Alaska's admission on federal legislation and activities. Similar studies had led to measures that had become law after the admission of Oklahoma, New Mexico, and Arizona. Since federal-state relations had been much simpler at that time, the bills reflected that simplicity.[14]

In May 1959 the Bureau of the Budget presented the results of its studies to the House and Senate Interior and Insular Affairs Committees. Basically, the recommendations were designed to put Alaska on an equal footing with the

President Dwight D. Eisenhower signs the Alaska Statehood Bill
(*Fairbanks Daily News-Miner*)

other states. Among other things, the apportionment and matching formulas of various federal grant-in-aid programs had to be revised. Equality of treatment also required that the federal establishment cease developing policies for and conducting governmental functions in Alaska which were exercised by state and local governments elsewhere. The Alaska congressional delegation realized that equality would cost money, as did the Bureau of the Budget, which recommended assistance of $27,500,000 in the form of transitional grants over a five-year period. Under this proposal the state was to receive $10,500,000 for fiscal year 1960, $6,000,000 for fiscal years 1961 and 1962 each, and $2,500,000 for fiscal years 1963 and 1964 each. These monies were to be spent at the discretion of the new state government. The Bureau of the Budget believed that, at the end of the five-year period, enough revenue would be flowing into state coffers from oil and gas leases, monies from the Pribilof fur seal operations, and the sale of state lands for the state to be on its own.[15]

The state faced immediate expenses, such as the operation of the Anchorage and Fairbanks International Airports and seventeen smaller ones. Built by the federal government at a total cost of $41,460,200, the nineteen airports were expected to cost $1,438,000 annually to maintain while earning $1,215,000 annually, leaving a deficit of $223,000 a year. The two international airports were expected to earn the bulk of the revenues, but they were as yet unable to accommodate jet traffic. Major improvements were needed, and the estimated cost was about $9,800,000. By using $3,400,000 of the transitional money, the state could obtain $6,400,000 in matching funds under the Federal Aid Airport Act, enough for the needed construction.[16]

Road construction and maintenance loomed as a large item in Alaska's state budget. The Bureau of the Budget proposed that Congress turn over to Alaska the highways, right-of-ways, and whatever real estate and equipment it owned to build and maintain them. Excluded were roads in Mount McKinley National Park and the national forests and equipment used for their construction and maintenance. To assist Alaska the Bureau of the Budget therefore recommended $4 million for each of the fiscal years from 1960 to 1962 and also asked that the new state be included in the Federal Aid Highway Program. Equality with the other states required that Alaska match 86.09 percent federal monies with 13.91 percent state monies. In other words, if the state could raise $5,940,877 for road-building purposes annually, it would receive some $36,768,519 in federal matching funds. The state was not permitted to use any of the matching monies for maintenance expenses.

State officials foresaw the budgeting strain Alaska surely would experience after the expiration of the transitional grants, and Acting Governor Hugh Wade, representing the desperately ill Bill Egan, pleaded for permission to allow the state to use matching funds for road maintenance. In return, the state was willing to compute only two-thirds of the eligible land area to arrive at the matching formula, knowing full well that this would reduce the maximum yearly grant by approximately $9,500,000.[17]

The Bureau of the Budget, however, insisted that no exception be made in Alaska's case, particularly since other states from time to time had proposed

Through the wilderness along the Alcan
(*U.S. Army Photograph*)

using federal funds for maintenance. All had been denied because the basic purpose of the Federal Aid Highway Program was to speed road construction. In addition, because of the new state's vast land area, it would receive more funds than any other state and initially pay less in matching funds than any other state. The Bureau of the Budget was confident that the new state would be able to collect sufficient revenues within five years to pay for road maintenance itself. Another advantage Alaska had, Bureau of the Budget personnel pointed out, was freedom from bonded indebtedness. And Alaskans paid 3.5 percent of their income in state taxes, as compared with a national average of 4.5 percent.[18]

Some $7,190,000 for mental and general health care, already managed by Alaska, were included in the transitional grant of $27,500,000, and no more monies were to be paid under the old authorization. This was also the case with $200,000 which Congress had authorized the Department of the Interior to spend on the construction of recreational facilities in Alaska during fiscal year 1960/61.[19]

The Eisenhower administration was determined to shorten the transition period from federal to state control and therefore had requested no funds for civilian airports, roads, mental and general health programs, or recreational facilities for fiscal year 1960. Instead, it had asked that Alaska receive the first installment of the $27,500,000 transitional grant. The omnibus bill also provided that the state could ask the president for continued federal operation of various functions until the state's staffing needs had been met and the functions could be transferred to state operation. Transitional monies were to be used for such operations. The state also had the option of contracting with the federal government on a reimbursable basis to provide needed services. In addition, the measure gave the president until July 1, 1964, to lend or transfer outright to the state federal property that had become surplus because of the termination or curtailment of federal activities in Alaska. The new state also was to receive $500,000 in unspent fines and fees collected by the federal district court, monies which would help establish the Alaska court system.[20]

Some statutory inequalities were to remain, justified on the grounds that they did not affect federal-state relationships or confer special benefits to Alaska. One example concerned the general requirement of the Federal Highway Act of 1921 that a state's federal-aid primary highway system not exceed 7 percent of its total highway mileage outside urban areas and federal reserves in 1921. This presented no problem in the continental United States, since the total mileage was nearly the same in 1959 as it had been in 1921. In Alaska, however, there had been less than 2,000 miles of all kinds of roads in 1921, and less than 4,000 miles in 1959. Unless waived, the 7 percent requirement would keep Alaska's primary highway system very short indeed. Precedent for making Alaska an exception existed, because the primary highway systems of Hawaii, Washington, D.C., and Puerto Rico were exempt.[21]

Still another exception concerned the National Housing Act. Because of the drastically higher construction costs in Alaska, Hawaii, and Guam, the federal housing commissioner was permitted to exceed the maximums on the principal obligations of federal insured mortgages by as much as 50 percent.

Street scene,
Seward, 1906
*(Historical Photograph
Collection, Archives,
University of Alaska, Fairbanks)*

Without this permission Alaskans would have been excluded from the program, unable to meet stiff federal standards of design and construction required for obtaining federal mortgage insurance.[22]

The omnibus act also eliminated inappropriate statutory references to the Territory of Alaska and included the state within the "continental United States." And while Congress considered the measure, members added several amendments, among them one by Ralph Rivers (Democrat, Alaska) which increased the transitional funds from $27.5 to $28.5 million.[23]

Another Rivers amendment dealt with the provision of the admission act which temporarily retained federal jurisdiction over Alaska's fish and wildlife resources. Acting Governor Hugh Wade already had signed three pieces of legislation that met the state's responsibility. One of these created the Alaska Board of Fish and Game. Soon thereafter, Secretary of the Interior Fred Seaton reported to Congress that Alaska had met the requirements of the admission act, thereby transferring effective control over its fish and wildlife resources to the state on January 1, 1960.[24]

The omnibus bill, with a minor change, passed the House of Representatives on a voice vote on June 1, 1959, after only an hour of debate, and a few days later passed the Senate in a mere twelve minutes. Senator E. L. "Bob" Bartlett remarked to a friend that during the afternoon before the Senate took up the bill there had been a briefing session with staff members of the Bureau of the Budget. "And that night I studied the whole proposition for over two hours. That makes me madder than anything else," Bartlett jested, "all that waste of time without a single word of opposition or inquiry."[25]

When the president signed the measure on June 25, 1959, Alaska's transition to statehood had been accomplished. The Alaska Statehood Act of 1958 and the clarifying Omnibus Act of 1959 had become a compact between the United States and its people and the state of Alaska and its people transferring sovereign powers and responsibilities and agreeing on certain institutional rearrangements and conditions. Alaska was already in the process of creating its political institutions.

·9·
The State of Alaska

STATEHOOD, contrary to the expectations of many, did not solve all of Alaska's problems. It did not appreciably diminish the federal role in Alaska, it did not result in instant economic growth, and it did cost money—most of which Alaskans now had to raise themselves.

The first problem Alaskans faced was the implementation of the state's constitution. Recognizing that the territorial governor and secretary of Alaska had been presidential appointees, that various other officials were popularly elected, and that many boards and commissions had been created over the years, the framers were determined to end "outside" control and executive fragmentation. The constitution provides for only one elective executive officer, the governor, while the secretary of state, later the lieutenant governor, is determined by being the governor's running mate. The framers limited the number of units within the executive branch to not more than twenty departments, each headed by a single person, appointed by and serving "at the pleasure of the Governor." In case the legislature were to create a board or a commission to head any department, the governor not only would appoint members to such a group subject to legislative confirmation but also would have the power to reject their nominee.

The constitution, following ample precedent, provides for a bicameral (two-chamber) legislature composed of a senate of twenty members elected for four-year terms from sixteen districts, and a house of forty members for two-year terms from twenty-four districts. Subsequent reapportionments have changed the number of districts. In contrast to the biennial meetings of the territorial legislature, limited in length, the state legislature is to convene annually on the second Monday in January and not be limited in length. A ten-member legislative council and a six-member legislative audit committee are permanent interim committees. The governor has the responsibility of reapportionment and redistricting.

The Alaska court system constitutes the third branch of state government. The fifty-four magistrates at the bottom of the pyramid are followed by seventeen district judges and sixteen superior court judges. At the apex is the five-man Alaska supreme court, which has final appellate jurisdiction. The governor appoints all judges from nominations made by the seven-member judicial council, which consists of three attorney members appointed by the governing body of the State Bar Association and three nonattorney members appointed by the governor, subject to confirmation by a majority of the members of the legislature in joint session. The chief justice of the supreme court is ex officio, the seventh member of the council and its chairman. All supreme court justices and superior court judges are subject to voter retention or dismissal at a specified general election held more than three years after appointment. Thereafter, each supreme court justice is subject to approval or rejection every tenth year, and each superior court judge every sixth year. Magistrates are appointed by superior court judges and serve as long as they wish.

Alaska has two forms of local government: boroughs and cities. Framers of the local government article of the constitution were acutely aware of the inadequacies of the traditional pattern of counties, cities, and towns to accommodate the growing needs of an urbanizing country. They believed that Alaska would eventually develop substantial urban areas and that continued growth would create increasing sophistication in local affairs. But the delegates also realized that most of the urban settlements in the Alaska of the 1950s were very small, few in number, and widely separated. So they fashioned a local government organization capable of serving both urban and rural areas, both as they existed then and might develop in the future. As a result, the local government article was designed to provide a simple, flexible system of local self-government, to allow maximum local self-government with a minimum of local government units, and to prevent duplication of tax-levying jurisdictions.[1]

Prior to statehood, cities and school and utility districts provided the only government at the local level. These units exercised only those powers specifically granted to them by the territorial legislature. Only a small portion of Alaska was organized for the performance of local government functions.

The local government article of the constitution mandated a new form of government called the "borough." There were two forms of boroughs, the "organized" and the "unorganized." Standards for creating boroughs included population, geography, economy, transportation, and other factors. In short, each borough was to embrace an area and population with common interests to the maximum degree possible. By 1972, there existed ten organized boroughs. The remainder of the state, not part of any organized borough, was termed the "unorganized borough." Here the state legislature exercised the powers and provided the services normally supplied by local government.[2]

Other articles of the constitution provide for the establishment and maintenance of schools, support for the University of Alaska, and the imposition and collection of taxes.

Ownership and Use of Natural Resources

Another very important consideration occupied the framers of the constitution: natural resources. In an effort to clear away the ambiguities of

Southeastern Alaska
fishing scene,
Hoonah, 1959
(Claus-M. Naske)

federal management policies, which sometimes favored exploitation by nonresidents, the state would "encourage the settlement of its land and the development of its resources by making them available for maximum use consistent with the public interest. The utilization, development, and conservation of all natural resources belonging to the State, including land and waters," were to be "for the maximum benefit of its people." One section provided that "no exclusive right or special privilege of fishery shall be created or authorized in the natural waters of the State," clearly reflecting Alaskans' dislike of the nonresident dominance of Alaska's fishing industry during territorial days.

When Alaskans went to the polls and ratified the constitution by a vote of 17,447 to 7,180 in 1956, they also overwhelmingly accepted an ordinance providing for the abolition of fish traps for the taking of salmon for commercial purposes in the coastal waters of the state. That vote was a lopsided 21,285 to 4,004.[3]

Alaska's fisheries declined even after the abolition of fish traps and the transfer of management from the federal to the state government. Consequently, a 1972 constitutional amendment allowed the state "to limit entry into any fishery for purposes of resource conservation, to prevent economic distress among fishermen and those dependent upon them for a livelihood and to promote the efficient development of the aquaculture in the State."[4] Designed to limit fishing gear in Alaskan waters by an elaborate system of permits, this limited entry amendment soon became embroiled in heated controversy. Kodiak Island fishermen spearheaded an initiative drive in 1976 to repeal limited entry. Voters, however, opted to keep the permit system. Aquaculture, designed to restore depleted salmon runs, has not been controversial among fishermen in general. With state aid, various hatcheries have been built, and the program has gotten off to a promising start.

Spring whale hunting
off Barrow, 1965
(Claus-M. Naske)

The State's First Chief Executive and Secretary of State

Alaskans chose Democrats William A. Egan and Hugh J. Wade as their first governor and secretary of Alaska. These two men faced the rather stupendous task of translating the provisions of the state constitution into working political institutions. Bill Egan was born on October 8, 1914, in the little Prince William Sound community of Valdez. He held a variety of jobs, including truck driver, bartender, goldminer, and fisherman. After service in World War II in the army air corps, Egan returned to Valdez, where he became the proprietor of a general merchandise store. He was a member of the territorial house of representatives between 1941 and 1945, and again from 1947 to 1953. Elected to the territorial senate in 1953, he served one term. In 1955 fellow constitutional convention delegates chose Egan to preside over their deliberations. One observer later reported that "few deliberative assemblies have been so fortunate in their choice of chairmen," because he had "presided with a combination of firmness, fairness, and humor" which helped to weld a group of comparative strangers, "inclined to be suspicious of one another, into a body of friends and co-workers united by their mutual respect and common purpose."[5]

The new administration got off to an inauspicious start when Egan became so ill that he required hospitalization and several operations in Seattle. Wade became acting governor, a difficult position for him to assume because Egan

Left to right — Governor William A. Egan and wife Neva, U.S. Senator Ted Stevens (R-AK), and Congressman Howard Pollock (R-AK)
(*Fairbanks Daily News-Miner*)

had not briefed his running mate. Wade recalled that Egan was essentially "a loner": "When I took over as Governor, on the first day, why, I hadn't talked with him for twenty minutes before or during the campaign. . . ." But Wade performed his duties as acting governor capably for more than three months, using the service of various territorial officials. Egan recuperated from his near-fatal illness and returned to Juneau in April of 1959, during the closing days of the first session of the first legislature of the state of Alaska, where he resumed his duties as chief executive.[6]

The First State Legislature

The first session of the first Alaska state legislature convened on January 26, 1959, amid an atmosphere of confidence as Alaska bravely stepped into a new era. Lawmakers were not greatly concerned with state finances and budgets, because Alaska started as a state with a comfortably large surplus in its treasury acquired during the last prosperous years as a territory, the certainty of five years of generous federal transitional grants, and the prospects of a growing oil and gas boom. Relieved of money worries, the first session turned its attention to organizing the new state government.

In its State Organization Act of 1959 the new legislature created twelve departments: administration, law, revenue, health and welfare, labor, commerce, military affairs, natural resources, public safety, public works, education, and fish and game. Each department was to be headed by a single executive appointed by the governor. The principal executive officers of the departments of education and fish and game were to be appointed by the governor from nominations made by boards affiliated with these departments. The legislature also drafted a variety of land laws and created a division of lands within the department of natural resources. The division was to choose, manage, and dispose of the state's more than 104-million-acre entitlement under the statehood act. The state wished to select the resource-rich lands in order to stimulate economic development and create a year-round local economy; but the process was slow. No adequate inventories of Alaskan lands existed, and the Bureau of Land Management moved at a snail's pace in approving, surveying, and patenting state selections. Another inhibiting factor was awareness that land ownership entailed expensive management responsibilities, such as classification, surveying, and fire control. The money would not last long. The imposition of the land freeze in 1966 and the withdrawal of national interest lands in the wake of the Alaska Native Claims Settlement Act of 1971 have further impeded state land selections. As of March 31, 1971, the state had selected 68,818,500.34 acres, and patented a mere 9,759,136.37 acres of state selections. Obviously, the optimistic expectations Alaskans had shared that statehood would free the new political entity from the constraints of the federal government were misguided.[7]

Alaskans quickly found that the federal government continued to play an important role in the state's government and economy. The Department of Defense, for example, continued to spend hundreds of millions of dollars annually on manning, maintaining, and improving its defense installations in Alaska. It also continued to operate the state's telephone and telegraph communication system until that was sold to private enterprise in 1971. The Department of the Interior loomed large in managing the extensive public domain and providing a range of social and other services found in all of the other states. The Department of Transportation operated the Alaska Railroad, and the U.S. Forest Service of the Department of Agriculture managed the state's two extensive national forests. The list of federal agencies involved in Alaskan affairs seemed endless. A few figures will illustrate the pervasive federal influence. Of a total employed work force of 62,900 in 1959, 16,800 were federal employees. And although federal employment slowed in subsequent years, federal workers still numbered 17,300 in 1971 of a total employed work force of 110,600. By 1971 all government employees made up more than one-third of the total employed work force; that growth was attributable to the expanding needs of local and state government. In 1959 the former employed a modest 3,000 and the latter 2,600. These figures had risen to 9,000 and 11,700, respectively, by 1971.[8]

Statehood No Panacea for Alaskan Needs

Alaskans had desired statehood in part because they believed it would result in fairly rapid and diverse economic development. In fact, in order to survive as a political entity capable of fulfilling the role of a self-supporting state, Alaska desperately needed basic economic development. It possessed a few small lumber operations, a couple of pulp mills, a mining industry consisting of one underground and several relatively minor placer operations, and an ailing and seasonal salmon fishery and fish-processing industry. The only bright prospects were the potential for tourism to expand and oil and gas production to increase.

Patrick O'Donovan, a British newspaper correspondent, perhaps best summed up the dream and reality of Alaska shortly after the statehood bill passed Congress:

> They like to call this the last frontier. It is not; it is the new sort of frontier and there are several of them in the world. A young man cannot come here with his hand and his courage and carve an estate out of the wilderness. You can get a 160-acre homestead from the Government for all but nothing. To develop it properly you are likely to need a capital of $25,000 or three generations of peasant labor. The banks will not be kind. You can work for a great corporation out in the wilderness, without women or drink, live like a Cistercian in a cell, have your cheeks scabbed by cold in winter, be fed each day like a prince hungry from the hunt and draw a salary of a bank manager. You can find temporary, chancy work in the city, but there is also unemployment. Alaska is a longterm, massive operation, conditioned by its inaccessibility, and its ferocious terrain. It is proper meat for the great corporations with capital the size of national debts and machines and helicopters and dedicated graduates from mining schools.[9]

Statehood proponents had been an optimistic lot, but soon after the attainment of their goal many became convinced that they had attained a stage of political development before they had the economic base for its full support. One tenacious opponent of statehood, Juneau lawyer Bert Faulkner, strongly expressed the fears of many: "Well, I felt that Alaska was not ready for statehood, that it could not support it, that it would be much more expensive to have a state than to rely on the federal government for most appropriations to support what government we had." Faulkner also opposed any new taxes to support the new state because "there's always got to be somebody opposing taxes or we'd be taxed out of existence."[10]

Statehood had been a means of accomplishing several goals: the achievement of full self-government accompanied by improved efficiency and responsiveness of local government; an increase of local control over natural resources; and the political means of severing the economic constraints of colonialism. But all of these goals would cost money, and Governor Egan called attention to this fact when he presented the first complete state budget in 1960. The governor explained:

> During the last half of the current fiscal year, we will have assumed full responsibility for the management of our fish and game resources, an excellent start will have been made on a State Land Management Program, the judicial and other purely state and local functions will have been fully assumed. How will we fare beyond June 30, 1961? Most immediately, we are faced with a progressive reduction of the transitional grants available under the Alaska Omnibus Act [a federal aid program] with those grants ending by June 30, 1964. At that time we will have to make up several millions of dollars if we are not to curtail services.[11]

By 1960 numerous Alaskans, as well as outside observers, began to share the doubts expressed for so long by Juneau lawyer Bert Faulkner and others of his persuasion. Journalist Ray J. Schrick reported on "Alaska's Ordeal" in the *Wall Street Journal* in early 1960. Schrick observed that the "job of equipping the huge frozen back country with the political machinery for self-government is less than half-done."

A financial crisis loomed ahead, and Alaska sectionalism had reasserted itself in bitter squabbling among numerous local factions over where highways should be located and how boroughs should be established. One group, centered in Anchorage, wanted to move the state capital from Juneau, while another wanted its region to secede from the new state entirely. Alaska's woes, Schrick continued, would affect American taxpayers because the federal government might well be called upon to foot "as much as 74% of the bill for a proposed $323 million state construction program in the next six years."[12]

Alaska's projected expenditures on highways alone for the next fiscal year amounted to $48 million, some $12 million more than the state general fund budget. Approximately $43 million of these monies would come from the federal government; but the state still had to raise $5 million as a match. The highway department had employed only twelve individuals in 1959; employment skyrocketed to nearly 1,000 when the state took over the functions hitherto performed by the federal Bureau of Public Roads. Every mile of road built added between $800 and $1,500 a year in maintenance expenses, and federal funds could no longer be used for those expenses.

On February 20, 1960, the state officially took over state civil and criminal cases, which meant opening eight superior courts and replacing four former federal district courts, appointing ten district magistrates, and trying to settle "over 3,000 unfinished cases from Uncle Sam." The Nome Chamber of Commerce complained that the administration had assigned only one state trooper and no full-time prosecutor to its area, which is as large as the states of California and New York combined. "We were better off under the federal government," concluded many of Nome's citizens. One state official told Schrick that "economically you can't even justify Alaska's existence but it's here—just like Washington, D.C." Alaskans, however, were determined to make statehood work. Pilot Jim Dodson of Anchorage, a member of the anti-statehood minority, perhaps best expressed this determination: "We created a monster up here. We weren't ready for it [statehood]. But now that we've got it, we're going to make a go of it."[13]

Statehood had put Alaska in the national limelight, however, and some Alaskans were cautiously optimistic about the future. An increasing flow of new settlers, investors, and tourists had arrived in the new state in 1959. New motels, hotels, and resorts were either in the planning or construction phase, and more oil had been found. Alaska now possessed four modestly producing wells, and oil companies intended to undertake substantial exploratory work. This was reflected in the state's first competitive oil and gas lease sale in December 1959, when several companies paid approximately $4 million for a total of 77,000 acres. Japanese investment groups which, together with American capital assistance, built the second pulp mill at Sitka had interested other

Halibut

King crab

Ice fishing near Akiachak

Ketchikan fishing fleet

Ketchikan
old timer

Dog sled on
ice pack near Barrow

Children of Barrow

Couple from Kotzebue

Landing a whale
near Barrow

Woodcarver,
Sitka

Totem poles near
Ketchikan

Eskimo drummers
and dancer

Cook Inlet oil
drilling platform

Gold dredge, Nome

Independence Mine
near Palmer

Sitka Russian dancers

Tlingit canoe, Haines

Alaska state ferry

Fishing boat, Homer

Lumberjack

Ketchikan pulp mill

Fishwheel on
the Tanana River

Drying salmon

Spring whaling
near Barrow

Netting fish,
Juneau

Japanese companies in examining Alaska's coal, iron, and oil potential as a possible source of raw materials for the Orient.[14]

But there were many uncertainties as well. Federal defense spending was tapering off, and the long-ailing salmon industry recorded a record low pack in 1959. The salmon fisheries outlook was obscured by continued fishing of Alaskan-spawned salmon stocks by Japanese fleets in the Bering Sea and the mid-Aleutians area. And although the Japanese were fishing in international waters and west of a 170° longitude demarcation line set up by international treaty, treaty makers subsequently discovered that they had not placed the dividing line far enough toward Kamchatka, because Bristol Bay salmon had been using this mid-ocean area for a place to mature before returning to their home streams to spawn. Adding to the fishery worries was the fact that for the first time big Russian trawlers and factory ships were appearing in the Bering Sea, utilizing fish species such as sole, haddock, flounder, rockfish, and cod. Americans, who generally did not use those species, were afraid that the Russians soon would be dragging the halibut grounds.[15]

Alaska's chief executive drew attention to some of these problems and also to the general causes for the increased financial costs of statehood in his 1960 budget message. The governor also warned that available revenues would fail to meet those costs by several million dollars, but he hoped that monies would be forthcoming "from increased state land revenues, mineral lease receipts, stumpage payments, and other sources."[16]

Thereupon Governor Egan presented a balanced budget to the legislature that included proposed tax increases of two cents per gallon on highway motor

Cutting up a bowhead whale off Barrow, spring 1965
(Claus-M. Naske)

fuel and one cent on marine motor fuel sales, plus the expenditure of approximately $15 million of federal transitional grants and withdrawals from the general fund surplus. Such a combination of monies would normally not be available, and it was the Alaska State Planning Commission that more fully explained just how far beyond its means the state would be living. At current rates of income and expenditures, the committee predicted, Alaska would be some $30 million in debt by the end of the 1966 fiscal year on operating programs and $70 million in debt if the financing of a minimum—and sorely needed—capital improvement program were included.[17]

The 1960 legislature, together with the Alaska State Planning Commission, gave the first accurate assessment of the new state government. Transfer of functions from the federal government to the state had been almost completed. The most dramatic revelation concerned the shift in monetary terms; from a high of $38 million per year during territorial days, the administration would be managing expenditures in excess of $104 million in 1961, and state employment was to increase from 3,900 to approximately 4,600, including University of Alaska and Alaska State Housing Authority employees. Even the most optimistic, looking beyond the year immediately ahead, could not help but be disturbed by the financial crunch that had to be faced soon.

The Economic Realities and Party Politics of the 1960s

When the legislature met in 1961, it realistically considered Alaska's financial predicament and raised tax rates where they would do the least harm to future economic development. This legislature gave Alaskans the chance to do a fair job of managing the new state's financial affairs if spending restraints were used and the state encountered some luck along the way in the form of expansion in crude petroleum and gas production, income from competitive oil and gas lease sales, expansion in the fisheries through diversification, and expansion of the forest product industries. And luck was with the new state. While defense spending, Alaska's major industry since the 1940s, steadily dropped during the 1960s, the value of the major natural resources rose encouragingly. Crude petroleum worth $1,230,000 was extracted in 1960; by 1967 the value had risen to $88,187,000. Gas rose from $30,000 in 1960 to $7,268,000 in 1967. Alaska's income from the oil industry had kept pace with expanding production. In 1960 the state treasury received a modest $3,372,000. By 1967 this had risen to a respectable $35,613,000.

Following the attainment of statehood, the abolition of fish traps, and the transfer of management control from the federal to the state government, significant advances were made. But much had to be learned about management techniques, and fishermen eventually would have to diversify and start using the great bottomfish resources off the coast, which so far only the Russians and Japanese harvested. There was a need to enforce international conservation agreements. For years the Coast Guard had been handicapped in enforcing these agreements because of a lack of equipment. Ever so slowly, however, Congress had been strengthening the Coast Guard. If much needed to be done, a great deal already had been accomplished by 1967, including the creation of a vigorous king crab fishery worth in excess of $10 million per annum. In 1960 the wholesale value of the fish catch had amounted to $96,689,000, and by 1965 had risen to $166,572,000. In 1967, however, it declined to $126,696,000, primarily because of a drastic decline in the salmon runs.

In 1960 the timber industry had an estimated annual payroll of $18.3 million and turned out wood products with an estimated end product value of $47.3 million. By 1967 these figures had risen to $25 million and $77.7 million, respectively.[18]

While many Alaskans worried about the state's economic future, the Alaskan electorate trooped to the polls on November 8, 1960, to participate for the first time in a presidential election. Most observers, except for a few die-hard Republicans, believed the state's three electoral votes to be securely in the Democratic column. There was ample ground for Democratic optimism in the forty-ninth state since the Republicans had been successful only twice since the Second World War, once in 1946 and once in 1952.

Party labels, however, mean little in Alaska because issues important to the state do not fit traditional party molds. Voters from the left to the right on the political spectrum are freely distributed in both political parties, and notions of party loyalty are elusive at best. When Vice President Richard M. Nixon narrowly defeated Senator John F. Kennedy at the Alaska polls, many Alaskan Democrats considered the outcome an upset. Within the state the Republican party made an astounding comeback, reducing the Democratic lead in the state house from thirty-four to twenty-one seats. In the senate the Republicans gained five seats. And although Alaska's congressional delegation was still Democratic and the state legislature boasted a Democratic majority, the 1960 election clearly ended the overwhelming Democratic predominance and, in effect, made Alaska a two-party state.[19]

Actually, statewide elections between 1958 and 1972 showed a substantial drift toward Republican voting, although the Democrats were dominant for most of the period.[20]

Perhaps reflecting the Republican drift, Alaskan voters in 1966 voted out veteran Democrat William A. Egan, who was seeking a third gubernatorial term, and narrowly elected colorful and ambitious Republican Walter J. Hickel, Anchorage real estate developer and hotel owner. The new governor, perhaps best remembered for his decision to authorize a winter haul road from Livengood on the Yukon to Sagwon on the North Slope to improve logistics to the oil fields, quickly abandoned the executive mansion when President-elect Richard M. Nixon nominated him as secretary of the interior.

On that same day, December 11, 1968, the most powerful Alaskan in the history of the territory or the state, Senator E. L. "Bob" Bartlett, died after undergoing major arterial heart surgery in a Cleveland hospital. Before Hickel's successor, Keith H. Miller, took over as governor, Hickel appointed Republican Theodore F. Stevens to fill Bartlett's position. This was an ironic choice, because Stevens had recently lost his bid in the primary for the U.S. Senate when he was defeated by Elmer Rasmuson, president of the National Bank of Alaska and one of the state's wealthiest men. Stevens thus gained the coveted

President Richard M. Nixon and his former secretary of the interior, Walter Hickel, 1971
(*Fairbanks Daily News-Miner*)

Senate seat by appointment after he had failed to win it by election.

Governor Keith Miller promptly named the winter haul road the Walter J. Hickel Highway. Hickel made a wise choice in appointing Stevens, for he sent to Washington a man who had extensive contacts in the Department of the Interior and was well versed in Washington's folkways. Hickel needed Stevens' help, because prior to his Senate confirmation the rough-hewn and bullheaded Hickel had made reckless statements to the press that aroused the ire of many. The secretary-designate had stated that he opposed placing federal lands "under lock and key" just for the sake of conservation and that it would be wrong to set water pollution standards so high that "we might even hinder industrial development." Senate foes held up Hickel's confirmation for weeks, but they eventually approved the new secretary. Soon, however, fate dealt unkindly with the secretary. First, the Hickel Highway turned into a canal in the spring of 1969 as the underlying permafrost began to melt and erode away. One observer called the highway, built to accommodate the trucking industry, "the biggest screwup in the history of mankind in the arctic." And then, to add insult to injury, President Nixon fired his secretary of the interior in 1970.[21]

Natural Disasters

In retrospect, the first decade of Alaska statehood was an exciting and trying time for its citizens and leaders alike. First there was the continuing struggle to attempt to provide for an ever-growing array of badly needed state services in the face of strictly limited monetary resources. The Egan, Hickel, and Miller administrations limped from one oil and gas lease sale to another.

Then, suddenly, on Friday, March 27, 1964, one of the greatest recorded earthquakes of all times, measuring from 8.4 to 8.7 on the Richter scale, struck south-central Alaska and in a few minutes caused damage almost beyond description. Fortunately, the loss of life was relatively low; but property damage was estimated at approximately $380 million at a minimum and almost $500 million at the maximum.[22]

On March 30 the *Washington Daily News* reported that "pioneer-spirited Alaskans, undaunted by still another damaging earthquake, today began rebuilding shattered towns and cities, searched for more victims . . . and braced for more shocks to come." In the meantime, technicians and mechanics arrived to restore essential services, and medical teams and rescue units "fanned out through the 900-mile coastal arc ripped by more than 10 million times the force of an atomic bomb to minister to the injured and prevent typhoid epidemics." Space was made available for the 2,000 homeless in Anchorage alone, while Abe Romick, the state's commissioner of commerce, predicted that many Alaskans would never recover economically from the disaster. Kodiak's famous crab

Earthquake 1964 — bluff area at 9th and N Streets, Anchorage
(*U.S. Army Photograph*)

Earthquake 1964 —
Turnagain house
wreckage
(*U.S. Army Photograph*)

Earthquake 1964 —
Turnagain damage area
(*U.S. Army Photograph*)

and salmon canneries were shattered, buildings from the towns had floated as far as two miles out to sea, and Seward's shoreline looked as if it had been bombed. In Valdez the waterfront looked "as though it was sawed off"; docks had been shattered, and homes "snapped from foundations and shredded into kindling." Most of the office buildings in the center of Anchorage had been destroyed or severely damaged, and one store had sunk so far into a fissure that only its roof showed on the buckled street level.[23]

The massive Good Friday earthquake was not confined to Alaska; huge tidal waves, called *tsunamis*, battered the Pacific coast. Crescent City, California, experienced four such *tsunamis*, which severely damaged the town and killed ten (another fifteen were reported missing). And at Depoe Bay, Oregon, a *tsunami* killed four.[24] The eyewitness report of twelve-year-old Freddie Christofferson from Valdez illustrates the enormity of the earthquake. Freddie had gone to the town's dock to watch the unloading of the freighter *Chena*, which hailed from Seattle. The boy had just left the dock when "the earth started shaking." His companion hollered "earthquake," and they took off running. "When I looked back, I saw the ship up in the air. The water was up on the dock. The ship hit the dock. Then it blew the whistle and pushed off. The dock went up in the air after the ship left. It just exploded in a lot of planks. I never did see any of the people on it when it happened."[25]

Industry as well as government responded swiftly and generously. Commercial airlines and the military dramatically displayed their airlift capabilities by lifting hundreds of tons of emergency supplies, including drugs, food, water, electrical insulators, oxygen, blankets, flashlight batteries, heaters, and even sterile baby bottles to the disaster areas. They also airlifted engineers and architects to inspect and restore damaged buildings, and electricians and natural gas workers to restore utilities. The example of one airline suffices to show the tonnages transported: the company reported that it flew 145,000 pounds to Alaska in a three-day period. Because of this swift response of the airlines and other industries, Alaska quickly returned to normal conditions.[26]

Upon the urging of Senator Bartlett, President Lyndon B. Johnson established the Federal Reconstruction and Development Planning Commission for Alaska, headed by Senator Clinton P. Anderson (Democrat, New Mexico). A month later, a careful assessment showed that earthquake damage had amounted to $205,811,771 rather than the expected $400,000,000, and on August 14, 1964, President Johnson signed into law legislation that generously aided Alaskan reconstruction.[27] Various debts owed to the federal government by individuals or the state were adjusted or forgiven; provisions were made for the repair of the transportation network; and numerous urban renewal projects were designed to aid stricken communities.

South-central Alaska quickly recovered, but a few years later, in August 1967, the Chena River, which bisects the town of Fairbanks, overflowed its banks and put much of the city under some eight feet of water. Although confined to that one city, property damage was heavy; but once again the federal government lent a helping hand. The Small Business Administration, as in the earthquake disaster, extended necessary long-term loans at favorable rates of interest to put Fairbanks back on its feet.

Earthquake 1964 —
collapsed Alaska
Railroad dock at Seward
(*U.S. Army Photograph*)

Earthquake 1964 —
Fourth Avenue between
B and C Streets,
Anchorage
(*U.S. Army Photograph*)

The Euphoria of Oil

Not all was disaster in Alaska. Early in 1968 the Atlantic-Richfield Company struck the ten-billion-barrel Prudhoe Bay oilfield on Alaska's North Slope. In the subsequent oil lease sale in 1969, the twenty-third since statehood, oil companies bid in excess of $900 million. Euphoria reigned, and there was hope that Alaska's perpetually rocky economy would now stabilize and diversify.

With over $900 million dollars in the bank, many citizens believed that Alaska's financial problems had been solved. The question clearly was, What do we do with all the money? The legislative council of the state of Alaska in association with the Brookings Institution scheduled a series of conferences in late 1969 with leading citizens to discuss directions for the future. In four successive meetings a broad cross section of Alaskans examined and discussed the financial foundations for future Alaska, the use of human resources, the quality of the natural environment, and alternative futures for the state.

Throughout the sessions, participants called for preserving the "unique" Alaskan lifestyle, defining it as one which "affords the conveniences of technological innovation combined with the opportunity and values of living as close to nature as possible." Most agreed that a compatibility between the oil industry and the Alaskan lifestyle could be achieved with "well enforced, proper regulation."[28]

In the seminar dealing with Alaska's future financial foundations, the participating citizens listed priorities. While cautioning the state government to "take it easy" in spending the bonus money, they urged that the funds be used to solve urgent social and economic needs. They called for the expansion and upgrading of educational facilities throughout the state, particularly in rural areas; for safe water supplies and adequate waste disposal plants; for improvement in mental health care, and for effective alcohol rehabilitation.[29]

Some urged the establishment of a special trust fund and the use of only the interest for funding various programs, such as research institutes whose work would set the pace for the resource development of the North; others suggested that a portion of the money be used for private land development, such as the building of homes and businesses. Generally, participants wanted Alaska to change very little, maintain its open spaces and its game, its clear streams and air, and remain a land of opportunity.[30]

Discussions of the use of human resources focused on education, welfare, and concern for the aged. Participants urged that regional high schools with boarding facilities be established so that native children would no longer need to be sent outside for schooling. The need for bilingual education was stressed, as was the provision of curriculum materials relevant to the cultures from which the students came. High on the priority list were specific courses to help students meet the identity crises facing them upon leaving home and entering an alien cultural environment: courses in Alaska native history, culture for rural and urban students to create pride in native children, and respect for other cultures among urban students; more vocational education; a more effective cultural-orientation program for new teachers; and encouragement of natives to enter the teaching profession.[31]

The last of the series of four seminars was entitled "Alternative Futures for the State of Alaska." All participants agreed that Alaska's future was to be one in which harmony would reign between man and the natural environment, with strict controls on pollution and environmental degradation; in which the emphasis would be on living and not just making a living; in which technology and material development would be used in the service of man; in which ethnic, racial, and cultural diversity would be proud accomplishments, discrimination would be eliminated, and all people would feel a common kinship; in which good health would be assumed as a right and people would not have to compete to achieve it; in which the arts, the contemplative life, and other cultural pursuits would receive equal attention with material activity; and finally, one in which the political process would achieve respect through the participation of an alert and active citizenry.[32]

Members of the Brookings Institution team and outside experts in social-economic planning tried to warn the "representative" group of approximately 150 Alaskans that they probably could not eat their cake and have it too. But many seminar participants rejected such cautions. One speaker pointed out that 80 percent of Alaskans already were members of the urban-technological society and that the rapidly approaching changes would destroy rural lifestyles, values, and perhaps the natural environment itself. Another argued that Alaskans had no choice because technological change possessed its own dynamics. No one had been able to determine the pattern of urban-technological life. What made Alaskans think they could do better? Would Alaskans succeed in establishing their own priorities and translate those into policies? Participants thought they could, but many contradictory statements were made. One group characteristically observed that "we don't need many people in Alaska for resource development but we will probably get them anyway and they will create overpopulation in places here as in the lower 48." That same group then went ahead and overwhelmingly recommended that the Alaska Highway be paved.[33]

The seminars certainly served to educate and inform the participants and the public, and the recommendations that were made were to serve as guidelines for legislators. The seminars also enabled conservatives and liberals, Republicans and Democrats, to sit down and reason together and to realize that they shared common values and goals—an essential for the coordinated functioning of any group. The policy statements provided by the groups varied in their quality and level of generality. A call for a base level or minimum standard of living could easily be translated into substantive measures, while a statement that society should place technology and material development in the service of man, not vice versa, was merely noble-sounding rhetoric that could not easily be given force in any specific instance. Perhaps most notable was the progressive, humanistic tenor of the policy statements. All participants stressed the importance of upgrading the educational services in the state, particularly in the rural areas, guaranteeing a minimum standard of living, basic sound health for all, and the need for preserving the quality of the natural environment.

Planning Attempts by the Governor's Office

Not to be outdone by the legislative council, the office of the governor of Alaska contracted with the Stanford Research Institute to prepare planning guidelines for the state based on identified or projected physical, economic, and social needs of the state and the resources available to meet those over the next few years.

The institute recommended substantial upgrading of urban services, such as water, sewer, and solid waste disposal, and improvements in education, manpower development, public welfare, and health. The consultants warned, however, that far from transforming Alaska into an embarrassingly rich state, the North Slope oil discoveries at best would help to place the state on a more comparable basis with its fellow states in terms of financial position and the availability of adequate public services. The high living costs and other disadvantages of a relatively remote and sparsely populated land would persist. In fact, the consultants warned, the oil boom might accentuate these factors unless the bonus money and other state revenues were used wisely and in the public interest.[34]

The Question of Moving the Capital

Whether or not all the public monies will be used wisely is still pretty much up in the air. One example will suffice to illustrate the ever-present urge to spend tax dollars foolishly. Soon after Alaska achieved statehood, Robert B. Atwood, the wealthy, powerful, and influential publisher of Alaska's largest newspaper, the *Anchorage Daily Times*, began campaigning to move the state capital from Juneau in southeastern Alaska, considered fairly inaccessible, to some place closer to the state's population center. State voters decisively rejected capital move initiatives in 1960 and again in 1962 because of competing needs and scarcity of money.

In 1974, however, the move proposal was approved, though it provided that the new capital could not be within a thirty-mile radius of either Anchorage or Fairbanks. This provision was included because politicians and business people in the two cities did not trust each other's intentions and had lobbied hard to make certain that the other city would not get the new capital.[35]

The new capital was to be located in an undeveloped area, but no specific sites had been listed on the referendum ballot, and no cost estimates were available. In short, citizens had voted for a concept without considering the ultimate costs or benefits. When asked why they desired to move the capital, Alaskans most often stated that they wanted to have the capital in a central and accessible location. Perhaps the post-Watergate distrust of government and the desire to have an open and visible government played a role in the vote as well.

Alaska's newly elected Republican governor, Jay S. Hammond, no friend of the move, acceded to the will of the voters and appointed a Capital Site Selection Committee headed by Willie Hensley, an Eskimo former legislator from Kotzebue who had run for Alaska's lone seat in the U.S. House of Representatives in 1974. During his unsuccessful campaign the capital move

Jay S. Hammond takes
the oath of office for
governor of Alaska, 1975
(*Fairbanks Daily
News-Miner*)

initiative had been on the primary ballot, and Hensley had spoken against it
wherever he went. He felt that Alaska had many urgent needs to be met before
the capital should be moved; moving the capital ranked at the very bottom. The
committee was charged with proposing and evaluating possible capital site
locations. With a handsome budget and many consultants, and after much
travel across the state, the committee came up with three possible sites:
Willow, approximately thirty-five air miles north of Anchorage, with an estimated price tag of $2.46 billion; Larson Lake, about eighty air miles north of
Anchorage, some $2.56 billion; and Mount Yenlo, approximately seventy air
miles northwest of Anchorage, with a price tag of $2.7 billion. Consultants
pointed out that in each case the state would have to assume only about
one-fifth of the estimated costs. They expected private developers to supply the
difference.[36]

Some state legislators attempted to give voters a fourth choice by adding
"none of the above" but failed in their efforts. In 1976 voters chose Willow,
the least expensive of the three proposed sites. The selected site is located less
than a mile east of the settlement of Willow and covers about 100 square miles
of state-owned land. Even before the Willow site was selected by the voters,
private land in the Matanuska–Susitna Valley, particularly that near Willow,
rose enormously in paper value in anticipation of the move.[37]

After voters had selected the site, the Hammond administration had to
decide how the move was to be financed. There were two possibilities: use
revenues accruing to the state from the Prudhoe Bay oilfield, which had begun
flowing in June 1977; or put the method of payment to the voters in the form
of a bond proposition. Opponents of the move hoped for the latter course,

assuming that a massive bond issue would force a rethinking of the issue. Opponents of the move therefore launched a petition drive in April 1977 to get on the 1978 ballot an initiative requiring Alaska voters to approve a bond issue before the capital could be moved. In that same year a group calling itself FRANK (Frustrated Responsible Alaskans Needing Knowledge) launched a petition drive seeking to put the true cost of the move on the ballot. The petition drive closed on December 15, 1977, and Alaskans had a chance to do some rethinking in light of the costs involved.

In the meantime, however, a new committee had been established to plan for the capital. Like its predecessor, it had a handsome budget, and its members traveled widely throughout Alaska in attempts to solicit public thinking on how the new capital city should look.

Capital move opponents took heart in early 1977. Results of a survey conducted by the Anchorage-based Rowan Group, which was hired as part of the governor's Alaska Public Forum program, revealed that Alaskans still preferred Juneau, which has the most spectacular natural setting of any state capital, over any other site for their capital. A representative sample of urban and rural Alaskans, when asked where the state capital should be, preferred Juneau by 41 percent; Anchorage received 15 percent, Willow 13 percent, and Wasilla 7 percent. The remainder were undecided or preferred other locations in the state.[38]

When Alaskan voters trooped to the polls in the November 1978 general election, they decisively rejected a bond issue in excess of $900 million for moving the capital. Voters obviously determined that spending many millions for a new capital is a waste of money. Clearly, modern means of electronic communication can accomplish the goals of the move—easy accessibility and communication—at a fraction of the cost. Perhaps Alaskans decided that there are far more important priorities needing attention, such as providing adequate educational opportunities for Alaska's bush residents. At the end of 1978, then, the voters had given conflicting directions to their legislators and the governor. Still on the books was the 1974 approved capital move—yet in 1978 they had voted down the necessary funds to get the move underway. It is clear that more will be heard in the future about the pros and cons of relocating the capital.

The Upset Victory of Jay S. Hammond, Self-styled Bush Rat

The capital move issue is just one of many major developments affecting the future of Alaska. One of the most interesting of these developments was the election of Jay S. Hammond to the governorship in 1974. Born in Troy, New York, on July 21, 1922, the son of a Methodist minister, Hammond attended Pennsylvania State University and the University of Alaska, where he received a baccalaureate degree in biological sciences in 1948. Hammond had been a U.S. Marine Corps fighter pilot between 1942 and 1946 in the South Pacific. In 1952 he married Bella Gardiner, a part Eskimo woman, in Palmer, Alaska. He was an apprentice guide, fisherman, hunter, and trapper in Rainy Pass in the Alaska Range between 1946 and 1949 and served with the U.S. Fish and Wildlife Service from 1949 to 1956 as pilot-agent. Hammond established

Jay S. Hammond — from
bush rat to governor
(*Fairbanks Daily
News-Miner*)

his own air taxi service, became a registered guide, and built a sportsmen's lodge on Lake Clark and a fishing lodge on Wood River Lakes. First elected to the state house in 1959 as an Independent, Hammond switched to the Republican party two years later. He served for six years in the house, becoming minority and majority whip. He became mayor of Bristol Bay Borough in 1965, and was elected to the state senate in 1966, where he served for the next six years, becoming majority party whip, majority leader, chairman of the rules and resources committee, and finally, senate president. Because his district was drastically reapportioned in 1972, Hammond chose not to run again, but once again was elected mayor of Bristol Bay Borough. He held that position until his election to the governorship in 1974.

Hammond's campaign for the governorship was a formidable undertaking because he had to defeat two former governors in the Republican primary— Walter J. Hickel and Keith H. Miller—and then incumbent Democratic governor William A. Egan in the general election. Hammond and his supporters started pounding the pavement, literally ringing thousands of door bells. Hammond asked Lowell Thomas, Jr., son of the famous broadcaster and himself a member of the Alaska legislature, to run as his lieutenant governor. This was a smart move, because Thomas had a far better name recognition than did Hammond at that point. A simple campaign brochure proclaimed, "It takes teamwork . . . they will work together for Alaska . . . we have only one special interest . . . the Alaskan people."[39]

Hickel, Nixon's former secretary of the interior, was heavily favored in the Republican primary because of his name and substantial financial backing from development interests. Hickel underestimated Hammond's candidacy, saving his money for his anticipated battle with Egan. To the chagrin of many Republicans, Hammond dumped Hickel decisively in the primaries. Then, after a hard-fought campaign, Hammond defeated Egan by the margin of 287 votes in the November general election.

Hammond readily admitted that he was an environmentalist, which is considered a political liability in Alaska because most important environmental lobbying efforts are identified with "outside" interests, particularly the California-based Sierra Club. These groups are accused by many Alaskans of desiring to "lock up" the state forever from economic development. Hammond offered a middle course between those "who would develop for the sake of development" and those "who would conserve for the sake of conservation." Hammond believed that each particular development project should be weighed individually and the question be asked: "Will the people of Alaska really profit from this?" Hammond proposed to formulate basic policy guidelines with the help of Alaska's voting public. These guidelines were to determine the "use of our resources which will insure that our nonrenewable resources are developed when they can offer long-term benefits to all Alaskans, and that our renewable resources be maintained so there is a continual base for Alaska's economy."[40]

Hammond soon created the eleven-member Alaska Growth Policy Council, which in turn created the Alaska Public Forum, designed to assemble citizens around the state to discuss major state issues and make recommendations to the governor, the legislators, and other state leaders. The Alaska Public Forum took six issues of immediate concern to the people of Alaska and also listened to a seventh issue area, chosen by the participants, which provided a regional perspective. The public makes recommendations on these seven issues through regional workshops, local community meetings, and mail-in questionnaires. The comments then are turned over to the decision makers. The six questions asked are as follows:

1. How should the state use its new oil and gas money in the future?
2. What human needs do you think are most important?
3. How should public school construction be financed in both organized and unorganized boroughs?
4. What should be the primary objective for managing Alaska's lands?
5. What should be the state's policy on future oil and gas lease sales?
6. What is the best use of Alaska's royalty oil and gas?

It is clear that the Alaska Public Forum has helped open communications between the voters and state leaders by broadening people's participation in developing major state policies, particularly those having the most important implications for Alaska's future.[41]

Although Hammond is intensely disliked by the development forces, particularly the *Anchorage Times*, his rapport with the average voter seems to be good. In a state that is unimpressed by formality, the governor fits well. By and large, he has not isolated himself from the public with numerous aides and

Governor Jay S.
Hammond cruising on
new bike trails in
Fairbanks, 1976
(*Fairbanks Daily
News-Miner*)

press spokesmen; he has remained very accessible, as are his top adminis-
trators. Bearded, casually dressed, and a colorful speaker, he projects an image
of the typical Alaskan. Hammond has insisted that development pay its own
way. He is a fiscal conservative and has emphasized that Alaskans should not
rely on oil and gas revenues for operating the state government, but rather rely
on income from renewable resources and general taxation. The governor has
repeatedly reminded Alaskans that of the $900 million the state received in the
1969 Prudhoe Bay lease sale, only $504 million was left by January 1975, and
that was going fast.

The state had been spending more than it had taken in, using the bonus money to make up the deficit. But this is not to say that the bonus money had been wasted; the monies had been used to increase spending for badly needed education, housing, welfare, and transportation. In fiscal year 1970 the state's general fund budget had grown to $160 million; and by 1975 the total budget had increased to about $725 million.[42] Despite the approximately $1 billion per year that will accrue to the state in the 1980s, Hammond emphasized that Alaska had to plan ahead and develop a sustaining economic structure not solely based on the extraction of nonrenewable resources. It was no surprise, therefore, when Hammond announced that he wished to run for a second term to complete his program. But even before 1978 began, Anchorage state senator Chancy Croft had announced his candidacy for the Democratic gubernatorial nomination. He established a campaign organization and began to collect funds. It soon became clear that Croft and Hammond would be challenged for the nomination. Early in the fall, Anchorage hotelman Bill Sheffield announced his intention to run, but he soon dropped out of the contest when his wife became ill. Early in 1978, two other Democrats, former Fairbanks state senator Ed Merdes and state representative Nels Anderson, entered the race. The latter dropped out, only to be replaced by Palmer state senator Jay Kerttula. The field had become crowded.

On the Republican side, former state house speaker Tom Fink entered the race, and supporters of former governor and Secretary of the Interior Walter J. Hickel formed an organization called the "Spirit of Alaska," attempting to gain 10,000 signatures on a petition asking him to run. As expected, the organization quickly gathered more signatures than it had announced as its goal. Persuaded by that support, Hickel, too, plunged into the contest.

By this time, former state commissioner of natural resources Tom Kelly of Anchorage and state senator Kay Poland of Kodiak had filed as independent candidates for governor and lieutenant governor, while Don Wright and Joe Vogler from Fairbanks entered the race on the Alaska Independence Party ticket. And while the independent candidates did not appear on the primary election ballot, they participated in debates and meetings along with the other gubernatorial hopefuls.

On primary election night, Hickel led Hammond by about 9,000 votes, while Merdes was ahead of Croft by about a hundred votes. On the next day, however, Croft had overtaken Merdes and Hickel's lead dwindled rapidly as votes poured in from outlying areas. Soon charges of widespread election irregularities were raised and a recount requested. After the dust had settled, Hammond held a 98-vote edge over Hickel, and Croft led Merdes.

On September 20 Hickel and Merdes filed an election challenge suit, and in October Superior Court Judge Ralph Moody overturned the August 22 primary and ordered a new one with Hammond, Hickel, Merdes, and Croft on the ballot. About a week later, however, the state supreme court overturned Moody's decision and ordered the election to proceed with Hammond and Croft on the ballot. With less than a week before the November 7 general election, Hickel launched a quick write-in campaign. Hammond, however, reclaimed the governor's chair with 49,580 votes; Hickel received an astounding 33,555 votes, while Croft came in third with 25,656 votes. Independent Kelly received some 15,656 votes, and Wright a mere 2,463 votes (*All-Alaska Weekly*, December 22, 1978).

The contest had been a confusing one. It pointed out the general difficulties of conducting elections in such a far-flung state, and as a result of the legal challenge procedures have already been significantly tightened. The state supreme court acted wisely in overruling Judge Moody. It would have been unfortunate to set such a precedent, enabling disappointed candidates to seek a new election.

What to Do with Alaska's Public Lands?

There are other major developments under way in the forty-ninth state. One of the most momentous involves the disposition of millions of acres of so-called D-2, or public interest, lands. Named after section 17(d)(2) of the Alaska Native Claims Settlement Act, it directed the secretary of the interior to designate eighty million acres of Alaska's federally owned lands for national parks, wildlife refuges, national monuments, national forests, and wild and scenic rivers. The act barred development of the federal domain until the acreage would be withdrawn.

In 1973 Secretary of the Interior Rogers C. B. Morton recommended the withdrawal of 83.3 million acres for permanent protection. Congress had until December 1978 to act on the secretary's recommendation but was not bound by the size; it could set aside less or more acreage. If Congress did not act, the lands would once again open up for leasing and development.

Perhaps some background is essential to understanding. At the time of the Alaska Native Claims Settlement Act in 1971, the state had not even come close to selecting its statehood grant of 104 million acres. Since the 1966 land freeze, no selections had been made. Now natives had priority rights in selecting their acreage of some forty-four million acres. Congress had created the Joint Federal-State Land Use Planning Commission for Alaska as part of the Alaska Native Claims Settlement Act of December 18, 1971. The state legislature enacted complementary legislation, which helped to get the planning commission off the ground. Since 1972 the commission has attempted to implement its responsibility to seek ways of avoiding conflicts among state and federal governments and to recommend changes in laws, policies, and programs affecting land use and management in Alaska.[43]

While the Joint Federal-State Land Use Planning Commission studied the land and made its recommendation, Congress in 1977 considered a number of proposals. There was the Interior Department measure covering 83.3 million acres, while the environmentalists proposed to withdraw 144 million acres in bills introduced by Representative Morris K. Udall (Democrat, Arizona) and Senator Henry M. Jackson (Democrat, Washington). At the other extreme were various Alaskan developers and politicians who favored a sufficiently flexible policy that would not permanently lock up any land. Somewhere in between were various schemes, such as one favored by Governor Hammond, Senator Ted Stevens (Republican, Alaska), and Representative Don Young (Republican, Alaska) which favored some type of co-managerial system by the federal and state governments, including natives and private landowners, allowing comprehensive land use planning for the entire state.

Development forces denounced both the Interior Department's bill for 83.3 million acres and Udall's measure for 144 million acres as totally unacceptable, while environmentalists also labeled the Interior Department's bill as totally inadequate. Congressional committees held hearings on the measures in the continental United States and Alaska in the summer of 1977.

In the summer of 1978, the House overwhelmingly passed the Udall land bill. This measure proposed to set aside 124 million acres of Alaska's land; some 43 million acres were included for new national park lands, 76.4 million acres for refuges, and 2.7 million acres as wild and scenic rivers.[44]

On June 30, 1978, Senator Stevens introduced a land measure of his own. Stevens proposed to add 10,450,000 acres to national parks, monuments, and preserves, 8,040,000 acres to national wildlife refuges, 5,720,000 acres to national forests, and 1,000,000 acres to national wild and scenic rivers—a total of 25,210,000 acres. In addition, the senator proposed that 56,890,000 acres be established as federal cooperative lands to be managed by federal agencies after the state government had committed substantial amounts of its own lands to the cooperative management scheme.[45]

By mid-October of that year, the Carter administration and congressional leaders had produced a compromise Alaska land bill. The measure contained the following major provisions: (1) at least 51 million acres of national parks and wildlife refuges, a designation which precluded most forms of development; (2) approximately 11 million acres in the Arctic National Wildlife Range designated as wilderness, excepting an area along the coast which was to remain open for oil and gas exploration; (3) major mineral discoveries already made, such as the U.S. Borax claim in Misty Fjords near Ketchikan, to be excluded from federal conservation units; (4) hunting to be permitted in national park preserves with the exception of the Gates of the Arctic National Park in the Brooks Range (the House bill had closed about 65 million acres to hunting, the compromise measure approximately 27 million acres); (5) the creation of a small national recreation area in the Wrangell National Park to allow mineral entry; (6) the courts to decide the location of transportation corridors across federal conservation units after needs had been determined by the state and the Interior Department; and (7) subsistence management, calling for minimal federal oversight and the courts to mediate conflicts between sport and subsistence hunters. After Senator Mike Gravel (Democrat, Alaska) requested and failed to receive guarantees for seven transportation corridors across federal lands, he killed the compromise bill through the use of a parliamentary maneuver.[46]

Secretary of the Interior Cecil Andrus acted swiftly after the failure of the compromise measure. On November 16 he withdrew 110 million acres under section 204-E of the Bureau of Land Management Organic Act, and on December 1 President Carter signed an executive order under the provisions of the Antiquities Act of 1906 creating seventeen national monuments containing 56 million acres.[47]

Conservationists were elated, while many residents were outraged. In demonstrations in major Alaskan towns, dissatisfied citizens burned or drowned, depending on the location, effigies of the president. The state government filed suit against the federal government contending that the Draft Supplemental Environmental Impact Statement submitted by the Interior Department was inadequate and that the statehood act had been breached. In the great confusion prevailing at the end of 1978, there was one hopeful sign—Congress has promised to make land legislation a top priority in 1979.

As of this writing, an excessive amount of acreage has been closed to any kind of development. On the other hand, Alaska has some of the last wilderness lands of the United States—and a good portion of these lands merit permanent protection.

What about Alaska's future? Will history repeat itself to the extent that Alaska will merely be a supplier of raw material for various colonial nations? The Russians came for the furs, and ever since the 1740s the Great Land has experienced various booms and busts. Americans exploited the fisheries and mined for gold and copper in the nineteenth and twentieth centuries. In the twentieth century Alaska once again became important because of its strategic position in the Arctic. The oil boom emphasized Alaska's importance as a resource storehouse, and not only American corporations, but also the Japanese, the British, the Canadians, and the West Germans lust after Alaska's wealth in oil, fisheries, timber, and minerals.

Unfortunately, Alaska has little control over world resource demands. It seems clear that most decisions affecting the life of the average Alaskan will continue to be made in Washington, D.C., and in corporate boardrooms from Tokyo to London and from Ottawa to Bonn.

·10·
Native Land Claims

The Threat to Native Lands

THE 1968 discovery of the 9.6-billion-barrel Prudhoe Bay oilfield on Alaska's North Slope and the subsequent decision to build the 48-inch-diameter, 789-mile-long pipeline from the Arctic to the ice-free port of Valdez on Prince William Sound captured public attention. Billed as the largest construction project in American history at a cost of nearly $8 billion dollars, it has provided newspaper headlines for years. This will be discussed in the following chapter.

Of perhaps greater long-range importance for Alaska, however, is the Alaska Native Claims Settlement Act of 1971, known as ANCSA. The provisions of this legislation embrace two basically unrelated causes: namely, the fight of native Alaskans for a greater share and role in Alaska's development, and a national concern that the course of this development not endanger lands of special conservation value.

There can be no doubt that the descendants of Alaska's aboriginal inhabitants historically have participated but little in Alaska's economic development and its attending social benefits. As a consequence, they have suffered loss of lands and resources essential to their traditional ways of life.[1] Organized protest has been weak, sporadic, and divided along ethnic and geographic lines. Actually, there was little reason for protest in southeastern and interior Alaska during the first decade of American rule because there was little interference with traditional uses of the lands and waters.

It was a different story along the Arctic coast, where Yankee whalemen had moved into the Bering Sea by 1848 either by way of the Okhotsk Sea or by passage through the Aleutian Islands. Soon as many as 250 vessels cruised along the edge of the ice pack in pursuit of the bowhead whale. In 1848 the first American ship, the *Superior* of Sag Harbor, New York, passed through Bering Strait and entered the Arctic Ocean. Others soon followed, and when whalemen found the bowhead in short supply, they often hunted walrus for their oil and tusks.

The whalers *Jeanie*, *Newport*, and *Fearless* in Arctic shore ice in 1897
(Call Collection, Archives, University of Alaska, Fairbanks)

The whalemen had a devastating effect on the natives who lived along the shores they frequented. Drunkenness and diseases soon ravaged the population. Ivan Petroff, Alaska's first census taker, reported the decimation of St. Lawrence Island Eskimos that occurred in 1874, when 400 or more people succumbed to famine and disease. Petroff observed that "living directly in the track of vessels bound for the Arctic for the purpose of whaling and trading, this situation has been a curse to them; for as long as the rum lasts they do nothing but drink and fight among themselves." John Murdock, an American scientist, and Captain John Healy of the Revenue Service called attention to yet another problem stemming from whaling activities. In the course of trade with whalers, natives acquired modern firearms, which immensely increased their hunting efficiency and probably helped deplete the vast caribou herds. In addition, whalers and Eskimos competed for the bowhead and walrus, soon resulting in reduced numbers and famine for the Eskimos. It has been estimated that approximately 200,000 walrus were killed between 1860 and 1880.[2]

By 1878 the Tlingits and Haidas were experiencing the encroachment of white commercial fishermen on their traditional fishing grounds. The various Pacific salmon species, one of the most important food resources for various native groups, were soon harvested commercially. In 1878 canneries were established at Klawock and Old Sitka. The salmon canning industry spread rapidly northward and westward into central and western Alaska between 1882 and 1884, affecting Eskimos and Aleuts as well. From an initial pack of 8,159 cases of forty-eight one-pound cans, annual production quickly rose to approximately 2,500,000 cases at the turn of the century and averaged 4,800,000 cases during the 1920s. Between the years 1934 and 1938 the salmon pack rose to an average of 6,905,843 cases, but over-exploitation dropped the average annual yield between 1954 and 1958 to 2,787,600. Since then, although still fluctuating, the production trend has been downward.[3]

Whereas natives had always caught salmon based on their immediate and winter needs as well as for some trade, commercial packers caught as many as could be processed and sold. Using a variety of deadly efficient gear, such as the stationary fish trap and mobile seines, they soon overfished the salmon stocks. In short, the story was the same as with Alaska's other natural resources. Intense and often wasteful exploitation of the sea mammal, fish, and fur resources of Alaska soon resulted in severe damage to the economic base of the North's varied native cultures.

The Rush for Alaska's Natural Resources

At first white exploitation was confined to the seas. In time, however, intrusions into native lands inevitably occurred. Chilkat Indians had always jealously guarded their trade monopoly with the interior Indians. In the spring of 1880 an Alaskan navy commander sent a steam launch to escort a party of nineteen prospectors led by Edmund Bean to the Chilkat country. There the commander's emissary, Chief Sitka Jack, aided by a barrel of molasses, persuaded the Chilkats to open the Chilkoot Pass to the Bean party. The prospectors climbed the pass to the Yukon River but failed to find gold in sufficient quantities.[4] But once the doors had been opened, they could no longer be closed. White penetration had begun and would become increasingly disruptive to the aboriginal way of life.

Despite the paper assurances of both the Treaty of Cession of Russian America and the First Organic Act of 1884, which promised the continued use and occupancy of lands to holders of aboriginal rights, there was little actual regard for the act, which declared that "the Indians or other persons in said district shall not be disturbed in the possession of any lands actually in their use or occupation or now claimed by them, but the terms under which such persons may acquire title to such lands is reserved for future legislation by Congress. . . ."[5]

The non-native population of Alaska grew slowly, and American citizens and others, in their quest for profits from the natural resources of the Great Land, readily ignored whatever aboriginal land rights existed. It was the discovery of gold in sizable quantities in Alaska and in Canada's neighboring Yukon, however, that led to the first large-scale migration to Alaska. Population figures illustrate the changes that occurred. When in the early part of October 1880, Joe Juneau and Richard Harris discovered gold in Silver Bow Basin near what later became Juneau, Alaska's population consisted of an estimated 430 non-natives and some 32,996 natives. By 1880 the number of non-natives had grown to 4,298, while that of the natives had declined to 25,354. In 1900 non-natives outnumbered natives for the first time, 30,450 for the former and 29,542 for the latter.[6]

The flood of argonauts spread from Dawson in the Yukon Territory along the Yukon River, and by 1900 the beaches of Nome swarmed with nearly 20,000 adventurers; thousands of others were scattered along rivers and creeks. In 1902, Felix Pedro discovered gold near what was to become the city of Fairbanks in Alaska's interior. Other prospectors went to Cook Inlet, the Kenai

Spring whaling off
Barrow, 1965
(*Claus-M. Naske*)

Peninsula, the Copper River area, and elsewhere. Soon the Eskimos of western Alaska and the Athapaskans of the interior experienced the impact of white fortune seekers. Prompted by the gold rush, Congress in 1898 extended the homestead laws to Alaska which, among other things, reserved suitable tracts of land along the shores for "landing places for canoes and other craft used by such Natives."[7]

In 1906 the passage of the Native Allotment Act enabled Alaskan natives to obtain legal title to 160-acre homesteads to be selected from the unappropriated and unreserved public domain.[8] Although enabling natives to gain title to land, it was a regressive piece of legislation since it endeavored to turn hunters and food-gatherers into homesteaders. Alaskan lands, for the most part, were not suitable for agricultural pursuits. Only eighty allotments, and most of these in southeastern Alaska, were issued under the act between 1906 and 1960.

Between 1914 and 1917 the president of the United States made ten withdrawals for Alaskan natives amounting to some 490,368 acres.[9] The primary goal of the first native organization to be formed on a more than local basis was the winning of citizenship. The Alaska Native Brotherhood, founded by nine Tlingits and one Tsimshian in Sitka in 1912, was followed in 1915 by a woman's organization, the Alaska Native Sisterhood, and within a decade chapters—called camps—existed in most towns and villages of southeastern Alaska.[10]

Natives and Territorial Politics

Along with the intention of winning citizenship, the ANB also concerned itself with Indian education and the abandonment of aboriginal customs considered "uncivilized" by whites. The latter concern was prompted by one of the provisions of the General Allotment Act of 1887, which provided for acquisition of citizenship by Indians who had "severed tribal relationship and adopted the habits of civilization."[11]

In part through ANB efforts, the 1915 Alaska territorial legislature passed several acts relating to Indians. One enabled them to become citizens; in order to do so they had to demonstrate that they had given up their tribal ways and adopted the habits of civilized life instead. The other provided self-government for native villages where the inhabitants were members or descendants of Tlingit, Tsimshian, or Haida Indian tribes and where there were forty or more adults.[12] In 1924 Congress followed suit when it made citizens of all American Indians.[13]

In the meantime, on July 5 and 6, 1915, a number of Athapaskan chiefs and headmen met at the Thomas Memorial Library in Fairbanks with Delegate James Wickersham and various officials, among them C. W. Richie and H. J. Atwell, the acting register and the receiver of the United States Land Office at Fairbanks, and the Reverend Guy H. Madara, Episcopal minister in charge of all Episcopal missions in the Tanana Valley. Rev. Madara stated that the Athapascan leaders represented some 1,500 of their followers and had come to discuss land questions and educational needs. Since none of the Athapaskan leaders spoke English, Paul Williams of Fort Gibbon acted as interpreter. Dele-

Founders of Alaska Native Brotherhood, 1912. Left to right: Paul Libertz, James Watson, Ralph Young, Eli Katinvok, Peter Simpson, Frank Mercer, James C. Johnson, Chester Worthington, George Field, William Hobson, and Frank Price
(Walter Soboleff Collection, Archives, University of Alaska, Fairbanks)

Tanana chiefs,
Fairbanks, 1915
(Charles Bunnell Collection,
Archives, University of Alaska,
Fairbanks)

gate Wickersham told the assembled leaders that he expected increasing home-steading activity which would soon take up all the good land, and "when all the good land is gone . . . the Indians are going to have to move over." The delegate offered two alternatives—160-acre homesteads or reservations.

Homesteads, the Indians argued, were incompatible with their semi-nomadic lifestyle. And Chief Ivan of Crossjacket probably best expressed Indian opposition to reservations by stating, "[We] wish to stay perfectly free just as we are now and go about just the same as now. . . . We feel as if we had always gone as we pleased and the way they all feel is the same." Chief Joe of Salchaket said: "We want to be left alone. As the whole continent was made for you, God made Alaska for the Indian people, and all we hope is to be able to live here all the time. . . ." Paul Williams, the interpreter, eloquently summarized their plight.

> Just as soon as you take us from the wild country and put us on reser-vations . . . we would soon all die off like rabbits. In times past our people did not wear cotton clothes and clothes like the white man wears, but we wore skins from the caribou. We lived on fish, the wild game, moose and caribou, and blueberries and roots. That is what we are made to live on—not vegetables, cattle and things like the white people eat. As soon as we are made to leave our customs and wild life, we will all get sick and soon die. We have moved into cabins. There is no such thing now as the underground living and as soon as we have done this the natives begin to catch cold. You used to never hear anything of consumption or tuber-culosis. The majority of people say that whiskey brings tuberculosis to the Indians, but this is not true. It is because we have changed our mode of living and are trying to live like the white man does.[14]

Delegate Wickersham promised to report the chief's opposition to reservations to Washington, though he himself disagreed with them: "I think that a reservation is excellent and the best thing that can be done for the Indians...."[15] The meeting adjourned with the delegate admonishing the Indians that "as soon as ... [you] have established homes and live like the white men and assume the habits of civilization ... [you] can have a vote."[16]

Wickersham no doubt did report the sentiments of the Athapaskans to the secretary of the interior. That is where the matter rested. A few years later, in 1926, Congress amended the Townsite Act which enabled Alaska natives to receive restricted deeds to surveyed town lots. The legislation also exempted Indians and Eskimos of full or mixed blood from all forms of taxation on lots occupied and claimed by them. Between 1926 and 1971 the federal government surveyed only 28 of more than 175 native villages and issued restricted deeds to their inhabitants.[17]

The New Deal Embraces Alaska's Natives

On June 18, 1934, Congress passed far-reaching legislation known as the Indian Reorganization Act, or the Howard-Wheeler Act. Its intent was to improve the lot of native Americans in keeping with the spirit of the New Deal.[18] In 1936, Congress extended the Indian Reorganization Act to Alaska, including the authority to create reservations if approved by a majority vote of not less than 30 percent of the natives involved.[19] Both Secretary of the Interior Harold L. Ickes and his commissioner of Indian affairs, John Collier, firmly believed that the revival and preservation of American Indian culture required the establishment of reservations.[20]

The act soon became embroiled in territory-wide controversy because of its reservation provisions. Both natives and whites objected to that particular feature, the latter fearful that even more land would be closed to utilization, preventing the development of resources and therefore hampering economic growth. Natives feared that the reservations would repeat the miserable pattern of the "lower 48." What especially startled Alaskans was the announcement that there would be approximately 100 reservations from which all but local native residents would be excluded. This announcement was coupled with the creation of the large Venetie reservation just north of the Arctic Circle. If 1.4 million acres were to be withdrawn for the benefit of some twenty-five Athapaskan families, many reasoned, then perhaps as much as one-third to one-half of Alaska would eventually be enclosed within the 100 reserves. Many natives feared that they might be confined to small areas with limited resources.

Despite the controversy, however, by 1946 the secretary of the interior had included seven villages in six reservations. The Venetie reservation, the largest, included the villages of Venetie, Arctic Village, Kachik, and Christian Village, while Unalakleet, the smallest, contained a mere 870 acres. The secretary established the other reservations at Akutan, Little Diomede, Hydaburg, Karluk, and Wales.[21] Numerous other villages prepared petitions for reservations, and three villages voted against them. After 1946 no others were

Athapaskan man
constructing birch
bark canoe
(*Eva Alvey Richards Collection,
Archives, University of Alaska,
Fairbanks*)

created under the act. Later on, a court held that the Hydaburg reservation had not been legally established. Native villages, however, continued to submit petitions to the secretary of the interior requesting reservations. By 1950 some eight villages had submitted such petitions embracing approximately 100 million acres. The Department of the Interior, however, did not act on any of them, probably because by then public opinion seemed opposed to the reservation system because it represented racial segregation and discrimination.[22]

Reservations were not the only avenue for safeguarding native land rights. After years of efforts by various of its members, Congress enacted the Tlingit and Haida Jurisdictional Act of June 15, 1935, which had been introduced by Alaska's delegate, Anthony J. Dimond. The measure authorized the Tlingit and Haida Indians of southeastern Alaska to bring suit in the United States Court of Claims for any claims they might have against the United States. The Tlingits filed a suit against the United States demanding $35 million "for the value of the land, hunting and fishing rights taken without compensation." The court of claims, however, dismissed the case in 1944 because the Tlingit-selected attorneys had not been approved by the secretary of the interior as the act required. Several times the deadline for filing claims expired, only to be extended by Congress.[23]

After two such extensions, the Tlingits and Haidas filed a claim for compensation for tribal property rights in southeastern Alaska expropriated by the United States. In a 1959 decision, the court of claims decided that the Tlingits and Haidas had established aboriginal Indian title to six designated areas in southeastern Alaska. After dragging through the courts for another nine years, the court of claims awarded $7,546,053.80 to the Tlingits and Haidas on January 9, 1969. The court also found that, except for eight small parcels for which patents were granted, Indian title to an area of 2,634,744 acres had not been extinguished.[24]

In 1946, Congress passed the Indian Claims Commission Act, which permitted Indian tribes to sue the United States for certain claims not previously allowed. Most of the claims involved compensation for loss of lands held by Indian title. But not until 1951, shortly before the time for filing expired, did twelve Alaskan native groups file their claims, some of which were for compensation for loss and damages apart from the loss of Indian title lands.[25]

Natives, Resources, and Alaskan Politics

While natives asserted their claims to the federal government, they also were determined to make political gains in Alaska. As early as 1924, Tlingit attorney William L. Paul won election to the territorial house of representatives. Twenty years later, in 1944, Frank Peratrovich of Klawok and Andrew Hope of Sitka won house seats; Frank G. Johnson of Kake was elected to the house and Peratrovich to the senate in 1946. In the legislative session beginning in 1952, seven natives held seats.[26] From then on, native political gains were slow but steady.

The 1950s also witnessed a fundamental change in Alaska's economy. By the mid-fifties the military, long a mainstay of the economy, was losing interest in the territory. At the same time, however, Alaska began to re-establish an economy based upon natural resources. In 1957 the Richfield Oil Company discovered oil at Swanson River on the Kenai Peninsula, and by 1959 there were high production wells on the Kenai Peninsula. Exploration and development extended to offshore Cook Inlet, where additional oil and gas fields soon were brought into production. The influx of people into Alaska, a post-World War II phenomenon, and the change in Alaska's economy were accompanied by efforts to obtain statehood for the territory.

The First Organic Act of 1884 and the second one in 1912 had both contained disclaimers for lands used and occupied by natives. The statehood act of 1958 renewed this pledge, specifically stating that the new state and its people disclaimed all rights or title to lands "the right or title to which may be held by Eskimos, Indians, or Aleuts" or held in trust for them. It did not,

Native Alaska forest fire
fighter for the Bureau
of Land Management,
summer 1958
(Claus-M. Naske)

however, define the "right or title" which natives might have, correctly leaving this for future action by Congress or the courts. More importantly, Congress granted the new state the right to select 102.5 million acres from the "vacant, unappropriated, and unreserved" public lands of the United States, another 400,000 acres from the national forests, and 400,000 acres from other public lands for community expansion. Congress intended Alaska "... to achieve full equality with existing states not only in a technical, judicial sense, but on political, economic terms as well ... by making the new state master in fact of most of the natural resources within its boundaries."[27]

Among the first legislature's early actions in 1959, which included a variety of laws making possible the transition from territoriality to statehood, was the creation of a Department of Natural Resources. Through its Division of

Lands the department would choose, manage, and dispose of the state's 102.5 million acres from the public domain. While the legislature provided general guidelines for the Division of Lands to follow, it was up to this agency to determine state criteria in its land selection program and to decide which among the many possible uses of the land was in the public interest. Ever so slowly and carefully, under the able direction of its first director, Roscoe Bell, the agency began to select tracts of land here and there. No one really knew what most of the land in Alaska contained, and furthermore, the director was acutely aware of the state's limited financial resources and the strains on those resources that land management would impose.

In the meantime Alaska natives, who made up about one-fifth of the state's population in 1960, continued to live mostly where they constituted a majority—in the approximately 200 villages and settlements widely scattered across rural Alaska. They confidently expected to continue using the land as their ancestors had done for thousands of years.

Soon, however, threats to native land rights emerged, to which natives responded by forming local and regional organizations, eventually uniting statewide. The fear of losing their land aroused the natives and radicalized them. An identity revolution occurred in villages across Alaska during the 1960s, and by 1968 even inhabitants of the most remote settlements understood what was at stake. A number of factors had contributed to that revolution: one was the establishment on October 1, 1962, of the *Tundra Times*, the first statewide native newspaper, under the capable editorship of Point Hope Eskimo Howard Rock; another was the emergence of several energetic and able young native leaders who were able to think simultaneously as U.S. citizens and as natives.

Project Chariot

The first governmental threat to native lands occurred as early as 1958. A year earlier the Atomic Energy Commission had established the Plowshare Program for employing peaceful uses of atomic energy by attempting to blast out an artificial harbor at Cape Thompson near the Eskimo village of Point Hope on the shores of the Chukchi Sea. This undertaking was called Project Chariot.

Archaeological records indicated a continued existence for at least 5,000 years of that village on a spit of land projecting into the Chukchi Sea, and for that same period of time the inhabitants had depended on the fish, seals, and whales of the sea and the game animals, chiefly caribou, of the immediate hinterland. As early as 1959 the Point Hope Village Council had objected to Project Chariot. On March 3, 1961, the Village Health Council wrote President John F. Kennedy in opposition to the proposed chain explosion of five atomic bombs. The blast, they objected, would be

> too close to our hunting and fishing areas. We read about the cumulative and retained isotope burden in man that must be considered. We also know about strontium 90, how it might harm people if too much of it gets

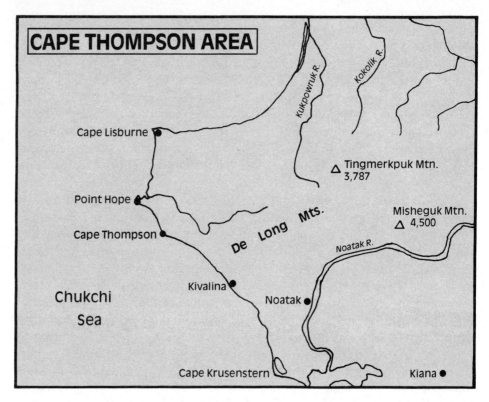

CAPE THOMPSON AREA

Cape Lisburne

Kukpowruk R.

Kokolik R.

Tingmerkpuk Mtn.
3,787

Point Hope

Misheguk Mtn.
4,500

Cape Thompson

De Long Mts.

Noatak R.

Chukchi
Sea

Kivalina

Noatak

Cape Krusenstern

Kiana

in our body. We have seen the Summary Reports of 1960, National Academy of Sciences, on "The Biological Effects of Atomic Radiation." We are deeply concerned about the health of our people now and for the future that is coming.[28]

In the meantime, the Atomic Energy Commission (AEC) asked the United States Geological Survey (USGS) for a study of the geological and oceanographic factors relevant to excavating a harbor on the Alaskan coast between Nome and Point Barrow. They later requested a detailed report on a twenty-mile coastal strip south from Cape Thompson; and the Lawrence Radiation Laboratory at the University of California contracted with the E. J. Longyear Company for studying the economical mineral potential of the coast. No travel money was authorized for either study.[29]

Soon both reports came back. The USGS found "the northwest coast of Alaska . . . relatively unknown geologically," while the Cape Thompson area was "largely unexplored" and ice-blocked nine months of the year. Longyear reported optimistically that within twenty-five years a port at Cape Thompson would handle the "substantial" amounts of oil and coal believed to be abundant near the cape. Both reports had been based on literature searches for relevant data rather than on investigations at the spot. On June 5, 1958, Chairman Lewis Strauss of the AEC requested a 1,600-square-mile withdrawal of land and water from the public domain in the Cape Thompson area. The explosion was scheduled for 1960.[30]

Dr. Edward Teller, the famous Hungarian-born physicist and father of the H-bomb, led a group of scientists and AEC officials to Alaska in July of 1958 to sell Project Chariot. Teller assured his Alaskan audiences that two-thirds of the projected $5 million targeted for the project would be spent in Alaska. The Alaska press wholeheartedly supported the blast in that it would funnel needed federal funds into the new state and put Alaska on the map; but business leaders were skeptical of the alleged mineral deposits and the need for a harbor. A few members of the science faculty at the University of Alaska, a handful of citizens, and a few key government officials questioned the alleged safety of the proposed blast.[31]

Alaskan dissenters demanded that the AEC establish a scientific basis for its assertion that Project Chariot would harm neither human life nor livelihood. Faced with this task, the AEC lost faith in Chariot and announced that the project would have to be dropped for lack of support in the state. Lawrence Laboratory physicists quickly recognized that a crisis existed. The project had to be sold properly. Two of them toured the state warning that Project Chariot's fate depended on endorsement by chambers of commerce and the state legislature. By mid-March 1959, the Fairbanks Chamber of Commerce backed the project and others were falling into line while the legislature gave its official blessing. Preparations resumed, but by now the AEC announced that the project would be only an excavation experiment because the harbor likely would not be commercially useful.[32]

The AEC did finance biological studies which showed rich and varied flora and fauna. These were the first pre-explosion surveys ever undertaken by the AEC, and their assessment triggered bitter disagreement. One botanist quit the project, maintaining that the environmental committee uncritically went along with the predetermined policy of the AEC, since the official press release stated that no biological reasons existed for stopping the project.[33]

Not until the spring of 1960 did AEC officials visit the villages. The village council members of Point Hope listened politely and then voted unanimously to oppose Project Chariot. In addition to the Point Hope–Project Chariot controversy, another—concerning hunting rights—was brewing in Barrow, the northernmost settlement. State representative John Nusinginya was arrested for shooting ducks outside the hunting season established by an international migratory bird treaty. Two days later, 138 other men shot ducks and presented themselves to federal game wardens for arrest; but they were merely cited for their violations. By 1961 the charges against all of them had been dropped. Finally, in November 1961, representatives from all along the coast met at Point Barrow for a conference on native rights, which was sponsored by the American Association on American Indian Affairs, a private charitable organization based in New York City.

They discussed many of their mutual concerns. The native representatives claimed that the proposed site for Project Chariot belonged to them and asked the Department of the Interior to revoke the research license the Bureau of Land Management had granted to the AEC. The representatives opened their report by stating:

We the Inupiat have come together for the first time ever in all the years of our history. We had to come together in meeting from our far villages

Eskimo school children
at lunch recess,
Barrow, 1965
(Claus-M. Naske)

from Lower Kuskokwim to Point Barrow. We had to come from so far together for this reason. We always thought our Inupiat Paitot [the people's heritage] was safe to be passed down to our future generations as our fathers passed down to us. Our Inupiat Paitot is our land around the whole Arctic world where the Inupiat live.[34]

Eskimos and public opposition eventually forced the government to abandon Project Chariot at Cape Thompson. Furthermore, the conference did win the attention of high officials of the Department of the Interior and also led to the development of the first regional native organization to be established since the founding of the Alaska Native Brotherhood nearly half a century earlier. The new organization adopted the name Inupiat Paitot ("the people's heritage") and chose Guy Okakok of Barrow as president.

Other Dangers to Native Lands — Minto Lakes and Rampart Dam

Project Chariot had been aborted, but there were other dangers to native land rights. The Alaska Statehood Act constituted the greatest threat, because while it recognized the right of natives to lands which they used and occupied, it did not and could not provide any means of assuring such use and occupancy. State land selections of the 102.5 million acres from the public domain proceeded cautiously but steadily, thereby endangering the continued use of lands by natives.

It was in the Minto Lakes region of interior Alaska where state land selections first conflicted with native hunting, fishing, and trapping activities.

Eskimo school child,
Barrow, 1965
(Claus-M. Naske)

In 1961 the state wanted to establish a recreation area near the Athapaskan village of Minto and to construct a road into the area to make it accessible to Fairbanks residents. State officials also had an eye on the future development of oil and other resources in the area.[35] Learning of these state plans, the village of Minto asked the Department of the Interior to protect their rights and reject the state's application for the land. In response, the Bureau of Indian Affairs late in 1961 began filing protests on behalf of the natives of Minto, Northway, Tanacross, and Lake Alegnagik over land totaling approximately 5,860,000 acres and conflicting with some 1,750,000 acres of state selection.[36]

As early as December 1961 the Department of the Interior reacted by ordering the state director of the Bureau of Land Management (BLM) for Alaska to dismiss protests unless the claims clearly fell within the regulation that "lands occupied by Indians, Aleuts, and Eskimos in good faith are not subject to entry or appropriation by others." On February 20, 1962, the regional solicitor for the Department of the Interior issued an opinion in which he asserted that "Indian title" was involved in the protest and that therefore a determination of the facts had to be made.

Subsequently, BLM managers were told not to accept protests of this type. The solicitor suggested that protests be dismissed on jurisdictional grounds because the only occupancy recognized in BLM regulations was that which led to the issuance of allotments under the Alaska Native Allotment Act. Following instructions, BLM personnel dismissed a number of native protests in 1962 which the claimants appealed to the director of the BLM. In early 1963 the director advised Alaska BLM offices to make no more decisions at the local level and instead to forward case records to Washington for consideration.[37]

While the natives filed protests and the BLM weighed what steps to take next, the Alaska Conservation Society met in Fairbanks in February 1963 to discuss the proposed Minto Lakes recreation area. Attending the meeting were some 150 local sportsmen and conservationists, as well as Richard Frank, chief of the Minto Flats people, who hunted and fished and found some seasonal employment with the river barge companies and as fire fighters. Most of the people also used more than a million acres of land, including the lakes where the state planned its recreation area, in their search for food. Frank told his listeners that the lakes belonged to his people, that this was their traditional hunting ground, and that without the use of the area his people would go hungry. Frank also told how the Bureau of Indian Affairs had asked his people in 1937 if they wanted to go on a reservation. The village had rejected the idea, but Frank's father, then the chief, had made a map showing the area where they hunted and fished. In 1951 the Minto Flats people had filed a land claim with the Fairbanks office of the BLM. The chief at that time had simply taken a map and indicated with a circle the approximate area his people used. In the wake of oil exploration around nearby Nenana in 1961, Frank took his father's map to the BLM office and indicated what lands his people claimed. Frank resented the fact that the state planned to build a road across village-claimed lands without consultation.[38]

Roscoe Bell, head of the State Division of Lands, suggested that the state and the Minto people resolve their differences. He proposed that the state select and patent the land and then sell parcels of it back to the Indians. Frank flatly refused to go along with that scheme: "As long as I'm chief, we won't give up our land. We have the same idea the state has. The state wants to develop this land and that's our aim, too." Thereupon the Minto people hired attorney Ted Stevens, who had just spent a number of years in the solicitor's office at the Department of the Interior. Stevens offered his services free.[39]

The *Tundra Times* spread Frank's fighting words to every native community in the northern part of Alaska. Editor Howard Rock, commenting on what was happening in Minto, wrote: "We Natives should realize that we will not be able to compete fully with big business for a long time yet. Since we cannot do that now, we should try to hold on to our lands because that is the greatest insurance we can have. . . . Without land, we can become the poorest people in the world."[40]

Between 1962 and 1966 threats to native-claimed lands multiplied, and the story of Minto was repeated over and over again. The most spectacular involved the proposal for building a dam 530 feet high and 4,700 feet long at the Rampart Canyon on the Yukon River. At a cost of several billion dollars, the dam would generate five million kilowatts and would put the entire Yukon Flats—a vast network of sloughs, marshes, and potholes that is one of the greatest wildfowl breeding grounds in North America—under several hundred feet of water. The proponents of the scheme, the U.S. Army Corps of Engineers, intended to create a lake with a surface area greater than Lake Erie or the state of New Jersey; it would take approximately twenty years to fill.

An organization named Yukon Power for America, armed with an initial budget of $100,000, intended to lobby the Rampart project through Congress. Businessmen, newspaper publishers, chambers of commerce, and mayors of Alaska's principal cities belonged to Yukon Power for America. Yukon Power for America published a colorful brochure entitled "The Rampart Story," which extolled the benefits of cheap electrical power, namely, three mills per kilowatt-hour. This power would in turn attract industry, it was said, notably the aluminum industry. Alaska's junior U.S. senator, Ernest Gruening, wholeheartedly supported the project. So did his administrative assistant, George Sundborg, the author of a book on Grand Coulee Dam entitled *Hail Columbia*. Sundborg dismissed the entire area to be flooded, which contained seven villages, as worthless since it contained "not more than ten flush toilets. Search the whole world and it would be difficult to find an equivalent area with so little to be lost through flooding."[41]

The U.S. Fish and Wildlife Service, on the other hand, reported to the Army Corps of Engineers that "nowhere in the history of water development in North America have the fish and wildlife losses anticipated to result from a single project been so overwhelming." The authors of the report strongly opposed authorization of the Rampart Canyon Dam and Reservoir project.[42] Paul Brooks, a conservation writer, estimated that some 1,200 natives would have to be relocated elsewhere; that the livelihood of 5,000 to 6,000 more in Alaska and approximately 3,500 in Canada's Yukon Territory would be affected by the reduction in the salmon run; and that the moose range with an estimated eventual carrying capacity of 12,000 animals would disappear, together with wildfowl breeding grounds and the smaller furbearers.[43]

Rampart Dam eventually died a quiet death for a variety of reasons, including adverse ecological and economic reports backed by the opposition of Alaska's natives and an increasingly well-informed public.

Various Alternatives for Settling Native Claims

During these controversies the state had continued to claim its allotted lands, and by 1968 it had selected 19.6 million acres, of which some 8.5 million acres had been tentatively approved and over 6 million acres had been patented.

In that same year Alaska natives had legal ownership of fewer than 500 acres and held in restricted title only 15,000 acres. Some 900 native families lived on twenty-three reserves administered by the Bureau of Indian Affairs. These reserves, which included 1.25 million acres of reindeer lands, totaled 4 million acres. An estimated 270 million acres of land remained in the public domain. Some 37,400 rural Alaska natives lived on that land and the twenty-three native reserves, while another 15,600 of their kin lived in Alaska's urban areas.[44]

The only recourse open to natives consisted of filing protest to the state land selections, and between 1961 and April 1, 1968, native protest filings covered some 296 million acres; by the middle of 1968 the filings covered almost 337 million acres.[45]

Early in 1963 the Alaska Task Force on Native Affairs established by the Department of the Interior issued a report that stated that a resolution of native land rights was long overdue. The report cited the failure of the First Organic Act to provide the means by which natives might obtain title to land and noted that in the following seventy-eight years Congress had "largely sidestepped the issue of aboriginal claims." If Congress ever was going to define native rights, the report concluded, it should do so promptly. The Alaska Task Force also included specific recommendations for solving the native land problem. It called for the prompt grant of up to 160 acres to individuals for homes, fish camps, and hunting sites; withdrawal of "small acreages" for village growth; and designation of areas for native use—but not ownership—in traditional food-gathering activities.[46]

With the help of the Association on American Indian Affairs and its executive director, William Byler, natives successfully opposed the implementation of the Alaska Task Force recommendations. Part of the opposition was based on the fact that there were no provisions for cash payment for land lost or for mineral rights for lands they would receive. Alaska's congressional delegation offered differing approaches as well. Senator Ernest Gruening favored settlement through the U.S. Court of Claims, while Representative Ralph Rivers felt that that would take too long. He favored congressional extinguishment of native claims coupled with cash compensation. Senator Bob Bartlett urged that state land selections be allowed to proceed before a land settlement was reached. One million acres for villages would be sufficient, he suggested, while cash payments should be made for other lands natives claimed.[47]

At that point four basic courses of action seemed plausible: natives might seek the establishment of reserves under existing laws; resolve their claims in the federal court of claims; obtain legislation at the state level to protect their land rights; or attempt a congressional settlement. Reserves would be held in trust for natives by the federal government, and thus that option did not hold great appeal. The Tlingit-Haida experience with the courts made the judicial alternative unattractive. Congress had allowed the Tlingit-Haida to sue in 1935, but not until 1959 had the court of claims supported the case and decreed that their claims were compensable. Later the compensation was fixed at $7.5 million. State action was rejected because most state legislators agreed that native land rights could be resolved only by Congress.[48]

Paul Tuckfield —
baseball player,
Barrow, 1965
(*Claus-M. Naske*)

Native leaders briefly considered state legislation that would protect their rights. One proposal would have created reservations surrounding villages, each twenty square miles in area. Natives rejected the proposal as inadequate, and most state legislators thought that only Congress could resolve the issue. But most native leaders also realized that congressional settlement was enormously uncertain since, because it was sovereign, it could extinguish or recognize rights, grant little or no land, or decide to give compensation only for lands given up.

While the various alternatives were being examined and discussed, none was pursued. This would have to await the formation of a statewide native organization with sufficient financial resources to pursue a settlement.

The First Outlines of a Land Settlement Take Shape

What made the organization of a statewide group difficult was the deeply rooted mistrust that many natives harbored for people outside their own geographical regions. Throughout the 1960s various native groups organized themselves, and in October 1966 representatives of all the native organizations and numerous individual villages met in Anchorage to form the organization that was to become the Alaska Federation of Natives. In the preamble to its constitution, adopted the following year, the AFN made its purpose clear. It was to secure the rights and benefits to which natives were entitled under the laws of the United States and Alaska; enlighten the general public about natives; preserve cultural values and seek an equitable solution to native claims; promote the common welfare of Alaskan natives; and foster continued loyalty and allegiance to Alaska and the United States.[49]

In the spring of 1967 a small group of natives who had attended the Anchorage meeting the previous fall met again and formally established the AFN. Despite some disagreements with the Eskimos and interior Athapaskans, the AFN began to function in 1967.[50] Before the AFN became a reality, however, Secretary of the Interior Stewart Udall stopped the transfer of lands claimed by the natives until Congress had settled the land claims issue. Udall's action followed native protests against state plans to sell gas and oil leases on the North Slope on lands tentatively approved for patent to the state.[51]

In the meantime, Governor William A. Egan had lost to Republican Walter J. Hickel, an Anchorage contractor and motel owner, in the 1966 elections, while Republican Howard Pollock had defeated Representative Ralph Rivers, who had not favored a settlement. Before the election of Hickel, the Egan administration and the Democratic congressional delegation had maintained that the land claims were a federal problem. During his campaign Hickel had not stressed the claims issue but instead had concentrated on the theme of getting Alaska moving economically.[52]

After he became governor, Hickel promptly overrode a Bureau of Land Management decision not to allow the lease sale, which then proceeded as planned. In the meantime the natives attempted to enlist the governor's support for a settlement. After initial resistance, Hickel proposed the outlines of such a settlement, calling for granting natives full title to some lands around their villages and surface rights to a larger acreage.[53]

In May 1967 the Department of the Interior finally drafted a settlement bill for congressional consideration. In essence the measure proposed a grant of 50,000 acres to each native village and the payment of a small amount of cash to each individual. The Department of the Interior, however, would maintain its paternalistic role and control both the land and the money.[54]

The Alaska Federation of Natives, learning of the proposal, met in Anchorage and voted to oppose it; they requested Senator Ernest Gruening to introduce legislation making possible a court of claims settlement instead. In the late fall the AFN met again, this time to listen to Hickel's attorney general, Edgar Paul Boyko, urge cooperation between the natives and the state against the Department of the Interior, which he characterized as a common enemy. The state wanted to avoid lengthy litigation, afraid that the oil companies with lease holdings in the Arctic would leave. Boyko proposed compensating the natives for lands already taken on the basis of their value at the time of statehood in 1959, and giving full title to other lands as well. A few weeks later Hickel appointed thirty-seven members of a land claims task force which was to write a mutually acceptable bill.[55]

Such action was very desirable because the land area affected by Udall's freeze had rapidly grown as natives had filed additional claims, ranging in size from a 640-acre claim by Chilkoot Village to the 58 million acres claimed by the Arctic Slope Native Association. Because many of the claims were overlapping, the total acreage amounted to 380 million acres, more than the state's land area.[56]

In January 1968 the land claims task force delivered its report, recommending that legal possession of forty million acres be given to native villages; that all lands currently used for hunting and fishing activities be available for such purposes for 100 years; that the Native Allotment Act remain in force; and that 10 percent of the income from the sale or lease of oil rights from certain lands be paid to natives up to a total of at least $65 million. The settlement was to be carried out by business corporations, one of which would be statewide and the rest of which would be organized by villages and regions. The task force also recommended that the state legislature pass companion legislation providing $50 million to natives from mineral revenues from certain lands, but only if the freeze were lifted before the end of 1968.[57]

Senator Gruening introduced a bill recommended by the land claims task force in 1968. The Senate Interior and Insular Affairs Committee promptly held a three-day hearing in Anchorage which opened on February 8, 1968. A large crowd attended the hearing, including many Eskimos, Indians, and Aleuts from across the state. Committee members listened to native leaders explain the proposed settlement and urge prompt action on the measure.

The principal opposition came from the Alaska Sportsmen's Council, which objected to the granting of public lands but approved of cash payments. On the other hand, the Alaska Miners' Association, represented by George Moerlein of its Land Use Committee, claimed that the U.S. government was "neither legally nor morally obligated to grant any of the claims put forth by the various Native groups or by the Native Land Claims Task Force." Quoting the Indian Claims Commission Act of 1946, which required that claims either be presented before 1951 or that they not be presented at all, Moerlein stated that except for claims filed by that deadline, "neither the United States, the State of Alaska, nor any of us here gathered as individuals owes the Natives 1 acre of ground or 1 cent of the taxpayers' money." Phil Holdsworth, the lobbyist of the Alaska Miners' Association, disagreed with Moerlein's assertion, stating rather that there indeed existed a moral responsibility to settle the claims.[58]

Committee members also listened to older village people describe why a settlement was needed. Peter John of Minto described how plentiful game used to be around his home, but how increasing hunting pressure from whites had caused a steep decline. He said that there had been an abundance of furbearing animals, such as muskrats, mink, fox, beaver, and otter. Mining activities, however, had filled many of the lakes and creeks with silt, driven away the furbearing animals, and killed most of the fish. Walter Charley of the Copper River Indians said: "Game, up to a few years ago, was always plentiful. Some of my people still hunt moose as well as caribou. They have to live. We also fish. Two years ago the state put very strict limits on the number of fish that each family could take. We were only allowed 20 sockeye salmon and five king salmon." After much protest, however, this limit had been increased to 200 fish. There were no jobs, and out of a total of 500 people in the Copper River area, only twelve held full-time jobs. "The rest of our people live from hand to mouth and the living they can make from a little bit of trapping, fishing, and firefighting." George King, an Eskimo from Nunivak Island, complained that the federal government had reserved the island as a national wildlife refuge in the 1930s. "The island has apparently been set aside for ducks, musk ox, and reindeer. We have not even been able to get a townsite, and, according to the Executive Order establishing the reservation, we are not even there. It is hard for us to understand why the government reserves all of Nunivak Island for the animals and left none of it for the people." The government, contrary to previous pledges, had completely deprived the Nunivak Islanders of all their land.[59]

Pressures for a Settlement Intensify

The Hickel administration generally supported the proposed settlement but urged speedy lifting of the land freeze because it prevented oil leasing on federal lands. Since the state received 90 percent of the federal revenues from such leases, it was losing money.[60] After the election of Republican Richard M. Nixon to the presidency in 1968, native leaders worried about the continuation of the land freeze which, in Udall's words, had "held everyone's feet to the fire. . . ." Just before giving up his office Udall signed an executive order changing the informal freeze into law.[61]

When President-elect Nixon chose Walter Hickel to replace Udall, Hickel was a vocal critic of the land freeze. Hickel, who had a reputation as a developer, needed all the support he could obtain, including that of the AFN, because powerful conservationist groups objected to his Senate confirmation. In return for AFN support, Hickel promised to extend the land freeze until 1971 or until the claims were settled. He was confirmed by the Senate as Nixon's new secretary of the interior.[62]

In 1968 Senator Henry Jackson, the chairman of the Senate Interior and Insular Affairs Committee, requested the Federal Field Committee for Development Planning in Alaska to carry out a comprehensive study dealing with the social and economic status of the natives, a study of historic patterns of settlement and land use, and an examination of the many elements of land ownership and claims. Headed by Joseph H. Fitzgerald, this small federal

President and Mrs. Richard M. Nixon at the home of former Secretary of the Interior Walter Hickel and his wife Ermalee, Sept. 1971 (*Fairbanks Daily News-Miner*)

agency had been established following the 1964 Good Friday earthquake to bring about coordinated planning among federal and state agencies.[63]

Early in 1969 the Federal Field Committee for Development Planning in Alaska completed its 565-page study of the native land problem. The committee recommended a land grant of between four and seven million acres, the right to use public lands for subsistence, a $100 million compensation for lands taken in the past, and a 10-percent royalty on mineral revenues from public lands in Alaska for ten years.[64]

Congressional hearings on proposed claims legislation were held in 1969, but no bill emerged from the committees. The native cause was strengthened through the continuation of the land freeze, support from the Association on American Indian Affairs, and various national newspapers. Furthermore, former Supreme Court Justice Arthur Goldberg represented the AFN, enhancing its national image. Soon Ramsey Clark, a former U.S. Attorney General, joined Goldberg.[65]

In the meantime the Department of the Interior proposed a settlement differing considerably from that endorsed by Hickel's task force. The department proposed to give natives about 12.5 million instead of 40 million acres of land, and $500 million instead of $20 million, but no royalty or any sort of revenue sharing. Soon the natives presented their own proposal, which included full title to 40 million acres of land, allocated among the villages according to their size; $500 million and a 2-percent royalty in perpetuity on all revenues from all other public and state lands in Alaska; and the creation of a statewide native development corporation and up to twelve regional corporations, coinciding with areas inhabited by various native groups, who were to manage the land and money received in the settlement.[66]

It was a far-reaching proposal, designed to avoid problems that had arisen elsewhere with Indian claims settlements. It avoided a per capita distribution of cash—which could be quickly squandered—and also retained the native concept of communally held land but adapted it to changing times.

The various interest groups responded quickly. The Department of the Interior recommended that all federal reservations be used in settling the claims, including Naval Petroleum Reserve No. 4, which Alaskans and the oil industry had long been trying to open for development. The Forest Service objected to including any portions of the Chugach and Tongass national forests in the settlement. The conservationists wanted the natives to receive as little federal refuge land as possible and also desired guarantees that none of the land would pass out of native hands. The natives strenuously objected to any Department of the Interior trusteeship.

The oil and gas industry worried because the federal field committee had suggested that competitive leasing be required throughout the state, not just in areas known to contain oil. The various independent companies knew that this would mean bonus leasing, requiring large outlays of cash at the time leases were sold, and feared they would be unable to compete with the major oil companies. Ten Canadian independent oil companies had a special problem because they had filed for noncompetitive federal oil and gas leases in Alaska between March 1967 and November 1968. The lease applications covered approximately 20 million acres and had cost $3 million altogether. But because of the natives' protests and the land freeze, the Bureau of Land Management had not processed these applications. They wanted language in the bill protecting their priority rights.[67]

The Western Gas and Oil Association wanted to be sure that existing federal and state mineral leases were not changed, while other oil companies and the state wanted to make sure that tentative approval for patent, as well as actual patenting, would be considered an "existing right." The state had already leased some 2.4 million acres, mostly on the North Slope, which were only tentatively approved for patent by the BLM at the time of the land freeze. Furthermore, the state planned to offer more leases on tentatively approved land at its September 10, 1969 lease sale. While the settlements proposed by the Department of the Interior recognized tentative approval as a valid right, the natives argued that their claims took precedence over the statehood act and that they should be allowed to take tentatively appointed state lands. This cast a shadow over how valid the state oil and gas leases were on these lands.[68]

The state also worried about native claims to tentatively approved lands, and Governor Keith Miller's administration argued that mineral rights to any land given to natives remain under state control since the statehood act had given the state control over all leasable minerals. Giving these rights to individuals or corporations constituted a violation of that compact.[69]

On November 18, 1969, just after the Senate Interior Committee had started to draft one acceptable bill from the three proposals before it, Governor Miller wrote Senator Henry Jackson objecting to the nine townships for each village and suggesting that two, or even fewer, would be appropriate. There would be no mineral rights in the lands given to the natives, and no 2-percent

The famous Prudhoe
Bay field lease sale,
presided over by Tom
Kelly (third from right)
Commissioner of
Natural Resources, State
of Alaska, Sept. 1969
(*Fairbanks Daily
News-Miner*)

royalty provision or any other revenue sharing.[70]

Over much opposition from the *Anchorage Daily Times* and much of the
Alaska business community, Alaska Senators Mike Gravel (Democrat) and Ted
Stevens (Republican) worked out a compromise that would give the natives
$500 million in congressional appropriations; title, including mineral rights, to
between five and ten million acres around the villages; use of another forty
million acres for subsistence purposes; plus a 2-percent royalty for a specified
numbers of years.[71]

Chairman Henry Jackson, angry over the bickering within his committee
and leaks to the press, soon announced that his committee planned to disregard
all previous settlement proposals and start from scratch, writing a totally new
bill. The committee was back where it had been the previous summer, and a
year had passed.[72]

The Proposed Oil Pipeline in Doubt

In the meantime the state held its twenty-third competitive oil lease sale in
Anchorage on September 10, 1969, bringing in over $900 million in bonus
bids. The sale was the psychological high point for Alaskans since the discovery
of the Prudhoe Bay field in 1968.

Soon the Trans-Alaska Pipeline System (TAPS), the incorporated joint
venture of Atlantic-Richfield, British Petroleum, and Humble Oil, applied to
the Department of the Interior to construct a hot-oil pipeline from Prudhoe Bay
in the Arctic to Valdez on Prince William Sound, a distance of 790 miles.
Secretary Hickel was under pressure from opposing interest groups: the oil

Prior to construction of the Yukon River bridge, ice bridges were built across the river in winter to permit trucking operations for the Trans-Alaska Pipeline
(*Alyeska Pipeline Service Company*)

companies and most Alaskans wanted the $900 million project to get under way, while conservationists wanted it delayed because of the innumerable environmental, technical, and economic questions that the project posed.[73]

After much negotiating—and when Secretary Hickel was just about to issue the permit for the construction of the North Slope haul road—five native villages asked the federal district court in Washington on March 9, 1970, to stop Secretary Hickel from issuing the permit. The villages said they were claiming the ground over which the pipeline and the road would pass. Avoiding the native claims issue, Federal Judge George L. Hart enjoined the Interior Department from issuing a construction permit across 19.8 miles of the route over land claimed by sixty-six residents of Stevens Village. A few days later three conservation groups sued the Department of the Interior, asking it to halt the TAPS project because it violated stipulations of the 1920 Mineral Leasing Act and the new National Environmental Policy Act. On April 13, 1970, Judge Hart issued a temporary injunction against the TAPS project.[74]

By now the oil companies realized that there would be no pipeline unless the native land claims were settled first. British Petroleum soon agreed to help lobby for a native claims bill and agreed to persuade its partners to do likewise.

Alaska Natives Finally Compensated

In mid-April of 1970, Senator Jackson outlined the provisions of a bill on which his committee had tentatively agreed. It awarded $1 billion to the natives but authorized revenue-sharing only for a limited number of years. Natives would receive only a little more than forty million acres of land, and instead of the twelve regional corporations which the AFN sought, the measure authorized one for the Arctic Slope and two statewide corporations, one for social services and another for investments. Within five years of enactment, the educational and social programs of the Bureau of Indian Affairs would be terminated. Despite native protests, the full Senate adopted the Jackson measure. The AFN now had to look to the House for a more favorable bill.[75]

But there had been gains. The AFN, strapped for cash, had received a $100,000 loan from the Athapaskan village of Tyonek on Cook Inlet. Tyonek earlier had reached a cash settlement with the federal government over land disputes and therefore had been able to help bankroll the struggle. Still, there was not enough cash, and the AFN appealed for voluntary contributions. At this point the Yakima Indian Nation of the state of Washington extended a $250,000 loan to the hard-pressed AFN, enabling it to continue its congressional lobbying efforts. These apparently bore fruit when soon thereafter the House Subcommittee on Indian Affairs informally agreed that natives should be granted forty million acres.[76]

There were other good omens. The National Congress of American Indians decided to give unqualified support to the AFN's struggle to obtain a congressional claims settlement. This action gave the AFN a significant source of national support. In Alaska, Keith H. Miller was defeated in the gubernatorial election by former governor William A. Egan, who had expressed a willingness to work with the AFN. Nick Begich, a state senator who had stated that ten million acres was an inadequate settlement, was elected to Alaska's lone seat in the House of Representatives. Furthermore, the Arctic Slope Native Association, which had earlier withdrawn from the AFN over a disagreement, rejoined by the end of the year. With the AFN unified once again, its settlement proposal kept the twelve regions and the $500 million initial compensation, plus the 2-percent share in future revenues from public lands. It raised the land provision to sixty million acres and accepted the Arctic Slope argument that the regions with the largest land area should also receive the most land and money.[77]

Soon after Congress convened in 1971, Senators Fred Harris (Democrat, Oklahoma) and Ted Kennedy (Democrat, Massachusetts) introduced the measure in the Senate, while Congressman Lloyd Meeds (Democrat, Washington) submitted the companion measure in the House. Senator Jackson's bill was also reintroduced in the Senate, and Wayne Aspinall, Chairman of the House Committee on Interior and Insular Affairs, submitted still another measure that would grant a mere 100,000 acres.[78]

The final drive now started. Efforts centered on the bill's progress in the House because attempts to have the Jackson measure amended in the Senate had failed during the previous year. Lobbyists descended on Congress, but perhaps the most important factor in moving the White House and Congress toward a settlement was the continuing delay in construction of the Trans-Alaska Pipeline. Oil companies and contractors had made enormous investments and impatiently waited to recover these.

Early in April 1971, the lobbying efforts bore fruit; President Richard M. Nixon, in a special message to Congress, presented a settlement scheme. It provided for forty million acres by absolute legal possession, $500 million compensation from the federal treasury, and an additional $500 million in mineral revenues from lands given up. On the same day the administration bill was introduced, AFN president Donald Wright met with Nixon, who indicated that he would veto any bill with inadequate land provisions.[79]

Events now moved quickly, with Alaska Congressman Nick Begich playing the key role in the House in dealing with balky chairman Wayne Aspinall. On August 3, 1971, the subcommittee reported its recommendations to the full House. It provided for forty million acres of land, with eighteen million available for immediate village selection and twenty-two million to be picked after the state had completed its selections under the statehood act. Some $425 million was to be paid from the federal treasury in compensation over a ten-year period, and $500 million would derive from the state's mineral revenues. Also included was the concept of regional corporations desired by the AFN. The bill, after clearing a strong challenge from conservationists, passed the House.[80]

The Senate also acted swiftly and reported a measure that would provide $500 million from the federal treasury and a like amount from mineral revenue sharing. It would provide fifty million acres of land, but twenty million would be for subsistence use, not ownership; and it established only seven regional corporations. Senator Mike Gravel of Alaska had proposed a land-use planning commission, which was also included. In November the Senate passed the measure with but little opposition.[81]

The conference committee reported its measure in early December, having compromised on several dozen items. There would be title to forty million acres, compensation amounting to $962.5 million, of which $462.5 million was to come from the federal treasury and the rest from mineral revenue sharing. Twelve regional corporations would administer the settlement. The compromise bill passed both houses, and after approval by the AFN, President Nixon signed the measure into law on December 18, 1971.

Implementing the Complex Settlement

The land settlement act was a complex measure, hastily drawn so Congress could pass it quickly before adjourning. The law extinguished native claims based on aboriginal title in Alaska in return for granting the legal title to forty million acres. Except for Annette Island, existing reserves were revoked, as was the Native Allotment Act, which had allowed trust status. The natives were to receive $962.5 million, to be paid over a number of years. All U.S. citizens with one-fourth or more Alaska Indian, Eskimo, or Aleut blood living when the settlement became law were entitled to become beneficiaries, unless they were members of the Metlakatla community on Annette Island. All eligible natives were to become stockholders in the business corporations after registering and proving native ancestry. Based on the region considered home, the native would be enrolled in that particular regional corporation and become the owner of 100 shares of stock. No rights or obligations of natives as citizens, nor rights or obligations of the government toward natives as citizens would be diminished, but federal programs affecting natives were to be studied to determine whether or not changes were called for. Within three years the secretary of the interior was to deliver his recommendations to Congress regarding the future operation of these programs.[82]

The act also authorized the secretary of the interior to withdraw up to eighty million acres of land in Alaska for study and possible inclusion in existing national parks or forests, wildlife refuges, or wild and scenic river systems. Congress then was to decide what areas to include. The ten-member Joint Federal-State Land Use Planning Commission was to recommend how to dispose of Alaskan lands, keeping in mind the interests of various groups, such

The Kignaks of Barrow
(*Claus-M. Naske*)

as natives and other residents of Alaska and the national interest as well.[83]

By the summer of 1972, land distribution began, and in mid-summer twelve regional corporations had been established. On July 2, ten of the corporations received their first federal checks for $500,000 each. Most of this money had to be passed to the villages, which were to incorporate as soon as enrollment of natives had been completed. Most of the money was to be used in making the land selections from the one hundred million acres Secretary Rogers C. B. Morton had set aside. Villages were to pick their lands first, some twenty-two million acres. The acreage each received depended on the enrollment; villages with an enrollment between 25 and 99 would receive 69,120 acres, while those with 100 or more would receive 161,280 acres. Villages would make their selections over a three-year period, and then regional corporations could make theirs over a four-year period.[84]

Regardless of size, villages in southeastern Alaska could choose only a single township, or 23,050 acres, because the Tlingit-Haida had earlier received a cash award from the federal government. In the rest of the state, villages were restricted from selecting land in national forests or wildlife refuges, land chosen by the state but not yet patented, and Naval Petroleum Reserve No. 4 on the North Slope. Instead, selections had to be made elsewhere from available lands.[85]

Villages would own the surface rights to their lands, while regional corporations owned the subsurface or mineral rights. Villages situated on revoked reserves had the choice of acquiring full ownership to surface—and subsurface—rights, but by so doing were excluded from the monetary benefits of the act. The measure provided another two million acres to be distributed to special native corporations organized in once historic native places now largely occupied by white populations—namely, Sitka, Kenai, Kodiak, and Juneau—and for various other special purposes, such as cemeteries and historic sites.[86]

The $462.5 million was to be paid into the Alaska Native Fund over an eleven-year period, while $500 million from mineral revenue sharing went into the same fund. Payments from this fund were to be made to regional corporations only, which in turn retained some monies and paid out others to individuals and village corporations.[87]

Why Did Congress Settle the Claims?

As a result of the settlement act, neither the natives nor Alaska will ever be the same again. Despite much rhetoric, the land claims settlement has ended native subsistence culture, which is the way Alaska natives and their ancestors have lived from time immemorial. Numerous conferences have been held around the state in the last few years in which participants assure each other that they will be able to maintain the traditional ways and also fully partake in modern American life. However, the talk is illusory. Natives have to learn to think like Western whites in order to succeed with their corporations. At best, the claims settlement will make native transition into the white world a bit easier.

The AFN displayed superb organization and exercised sophisticated political judgment in its dealing with the federal courts, bureaucracy, and Congress. It showed the proper amount of strength and yet knew when to compromise. But there is no question that the kind of settlement they achieved was due largely to the Prudhoe Bay oil discovery and the desire of industry to extract the oil and bring it to market. There was the widespread belief that if only Alaskan oil could be brought to market most of America's energy problems would be solved. A quick settlement of native claims was essential because they stood in the way of oil extraction.

In addition to the energy concerns, there also came into play a new consciousness of the environment. Various conservation groups were eager to settle the uncertain Alaskan land question and preserve large areas of pristine wilderness for the benefit of future generations. The civil rights movement undoubtedly played an important part as well. After a long and hard fight, American blacks had succeeded in pressuring Congress into passing a modern civil rights bill, long overdue. In the process they had succeeded in sensitizing American society as a whole to the plight of various minorities.

The Scramble to Divide Alaska

All of these forces happened to come together in 1971, and they helped produce the generous settlement act of that year. But perhaps the problems had just begun, because now the natives, the state, and the various agencies of the federal government scrambled to cut up Alaska.

The Joint Federal-State Land Use Planning Commission, not without dissent among its members, made its first recommendation in August of 1973. Reflecting its largely Alaskan composition, it stressed the "multiple-use" concept for the seventy-eight million acres the secretary had withdrawn in 1972. The commission urged that more than sixty million acres be opened for limited mineral development.[88]

At the same time, conservation groups lobbied vigorously for the creation of parks, wilderness areas, and refuges; and an Alaska task force within the Department of the Interior formulated alternative proposals for the eighty-odd million acres. The task force also was subject to the varying pressures of the industry interests, the conservationists, and the state—all wanting the land for themselves. But it also had to deal with federal agencies: the Forest Service intended to create vast national forests, while the Bureau of Land Management desired to maintain its control.[89]

In December, Secretary Morton asked Congress to add 63.8 million acres to the national park and refuge systems. He proposed three new national parks: the Gates of the Arctic in the Brooks Range, another in the Wrangell Mountains, and a third centered around Lake Clark in southern Alaska. Mt. McKinley National Park was to be enlarged with parcels of land to both the north and south. Morton further proposed nine new or expanded wildlife refuges, encompassing 31.5 million acres, and the creation of three new national forests and expansion of the Chugach National Forest, involving some 18.8 million acres.[90] Congress had until December 1978 to decide precisely which lands were to be put into which categories. In the meantime, the conser-

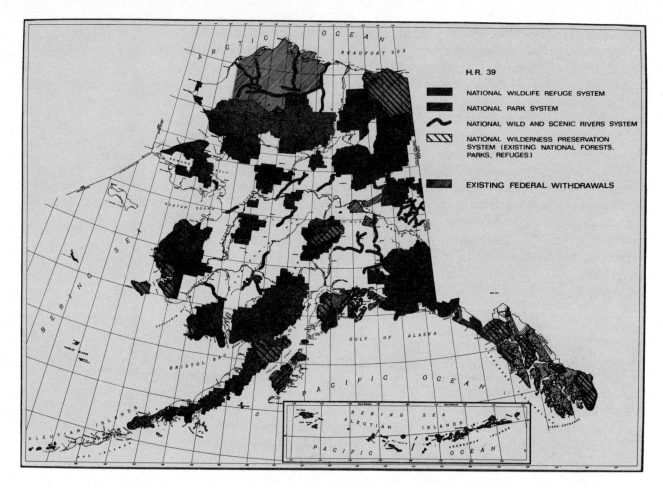

H.R. 39, Udall Land
Conservation Bill, died
in Congress, 1978
*(from Alaska Department
of Fish and Game)*

vationists, the state, and various extractive interests have been lobbying for their pet schemes.

In the meantime, the native regional corporations have rented office space and hired a cadre of professionals, enabling them to begin their corporate existence. By 1975 there was no doubt that native investments had already made a substantial impact on Alaska's economy. And although the cumbersome federal bureaucracy had delayed transfer of most of the approximately forty million acres of land that will eventually belong to the native community, money from the settlement had been flowing steadily into corporate treasuries. By December 1975 the regional corporations had received a total of $270,306,168 of their $962,500,000 monetary settlement.[91]

During 1975 the Bristol Bay Native Corporation, based in Dillingham, made the biggest purchase to date of any corporation by acquiring the Peter Pan Seafoods Company. Included in the multimillion-dollar deal were canneries at Dillingham, King Cove, and Bellingham, Washington; shrimp processing plants at Squaw Harbor and Coos Bay, Oregon; some 60 large and 120 small vessels; four fish camps in Alaska; a five-acre boatyard in Seattle; and 1,000 acres of land in Alaska, Washington, and Oregon.[92] In addition, five regional corporations pooled their resources and founded the United Bank of Alaska. Most regional corporations also explored for oil, gas, and hard rock minerals.[93]

The Activities of the Regional Corporations

A look at the activities of the various corporations provides a view of their diversity, style of operation, opportunities, and difficulties. The Cook Inlet Region, Inc., a corporation with 6,000 stockholders, paid some of the highest legal fees of any of the corporations; it also had difficulties in its land selection process. Most of the Cook Inlet lands have already been pre-empted by the federal government, the state, the borough, and private landowners. Cook Inlet Region, Inc., therefore, had to make many selections to take the place of such lands. Despite these difficulties, the corporation spent considerable monies in 1975. It purchased five hotels and motels in Anchorage, bought one of the largest warehouses in the state and an office building, and formed a joint venture to develop and sell single family houses and townhouses. It also participated in two joint venture contracts on the Trans-Alaska Pipeline project. Perhaps one of the most profitable possibilities may accrue to Cook Inlet Region, Inc., through the development of coal lands. An intricate land swap agreement between the federal government, the state, and the corporation has gone through and been approved by the courts, and the corporation therefore will be able to choose about 321,040 acres in the Beluga Coal Field.[94]

The Calista Corporation, second largest of the regional corporations and centered in the Yukon-Kuskokwim region, spent several million dollars on a variety of projects. These included a first-class hotel in Anchorage, a subdivision near Knik, an earth science consulting firm, a mobile home park in Valdez, and a 108-foot crabber trawler. With fifty-six villages in its region, Calista had received some $47.3 million from the Alaska Native Fund by December 1975.[95]

Ahtna, Inc., has 1,000 stockholders in the Copper River basin. It received the smallest financial endowment of any of the corporations; yet corporate leadership put the money to good use. Since the Trans-Alaska Pipeline crosses the region's landholdings, Ahtna worked out a lease agreement with Alyeska Pipeline Service Co. for the pipeline corridor, and the company also agreed to buy gravel from Ahtna. In early 1974 Ahtna also negotiated one of several joint ventures for pipeline work with the construction firm of Rogers and Babler. Pooling monetary resources, the regional corporation and all eight village corporations formed a company called Ahtna Development Corporation to serve as the economic arm for the nine corporations. Their first joint venture consisted of the construction of a $1.5 million lodge, restaurant, and bar complex in Glennallen that was designed to serve the tourist trade. And pending congressional approval of the Wrangell–St. Elias National Park proposal, Ahtna hopes to become a co-developer of the area in cooperation with the National Park Service.[96]

NANA Regional Corporation, a moderate-sized corporation based in Kotzebue, won a $15 million contract in 1974 for its Security Systems Division to guard the northern pipeline camps. It then acquired NANA Oilfield Services and NANA Environmental Systems, both involved in the North Slope oilfields. The corporation built a $2.6 million hotel in Kotzebue and owns a modern apartment building as well. The corporation acquired jade mining claims in the Brooks Range and also became involved in the reindeer business.[97]

The Aleut Corporation invested some of its funds in two 120-foot crabber draggers and another 222-foot fishing vessel, and in a joint venture exploration for copper.[98]

The Bering Straits Native Corporation invested in transportation, construction, and housing—industries most crucial to its Nome-based shareholders. It bought Pacific Alaska Airlines, a nonscheduled charter company; a trucking firm based in Anchorage and Fairbanks, Alaska Truck Transport; and Coastal Barge Lines. After the purchase of Coastal Barge Lines, Bering Straits formed a corporation named Grand Alaska, Inc., which includes Anchorage Trailer Sales and Fairbanks Mobile Home Sales, both using the barge line to ship their units to Alaska. Also under consideration was the possibility of building mobile homes on the Seward Peninsula, and after two years of joint ventures with Central Construction of Seattle, it bought the company. Although Central Construction had operated almost exclusively in Alaska, corporate management planned to extend operations to Washington, Montana, Oregon, and Idaho. The corporation also bought a large block of stock in Alaska National Bank of the North and acquired half interest in the Alaska branch of the California-based engineering and surveying firm CH2M Hill, called CH2M Hill of Alaska.[99] Unfortunately, many of the investments were hastily made and the corporation lost much money.

The Southeast Alaska Corporation, Sealaska, was the most cautious investor. While waiting for 400,000 acres of timberland to be conveyed by December 1977, the corporation constructed a 30,000-square-foot office building in downtown Juneau.[100]

Koniag, Inc., limited its investment to Kodiak Island: it bought the

Shelikof Net Co. and Kodiak Outboard, a retail marine supplier. It built a combination office-apartment building in downtown Kodiak, and through its Kodiak Kwik Copy offers commercial printing. Still unsettled were the in-lieu land selections of Koniag, Inc., which it hoped to make on North Slope acreage with oil and gas potential.[101]

Doyon Corporation is based in Fairbanks and, with twelve million acres, is the largest regional corporation. The corporation has concentrated on developing the natural resources of the region, such as oil and gas, asbestos, and gold. In 1975, Doyon concluded a contract with the Louisiana Land and Exploration Company for gas and oil exploration in the Kandik area near the Canadian border east of Circle City. In addition, the consortium of BP Alaska Exploration, Inc., Ethyl Corporation, General Crude Oil Co., McIntyre Mines, and Union Carbide explored Doyon lands for gas and oil deposits. So far, however, no gas or oil has been found. Doyon also had a joint venture with Alaska International Construction for maintenance of the pipeline haul road north of the Yukon.[102]

Chugach Natives, Inc., based in Cordova, invested its money around the rim of the Gulf of Alaska in such ventures as the development of deep-water ports to service offshore oil and gas exploration. As one of the largest landowners in Seward, the corporation planned the development of subdivisions and also put money into the pioneer aquaculture efforts by the Cordova Aquatic Marketing Association.[103]

Finally, the Arctic Slope Regional Corporation limited its investments to its own area, often in conjunction with village corporations. It put a great deal of money into such basic village needs as fuel supply systems and grocery stores. It also involved itself in various pipeline-related joint ventures and closed contracts with a number of oil companies for exploration rights and production options on corporation lands.[104]

The preceding sketch briefly outlines the variety of economic activities and investments pursued by the regional corporations. The new corporations organized just in time to take advantage of one of Alaska's greatest boom periods. Pipeline construction enabled the new corporations to gain valuable business experience through contracts which ranged from security to catering, from heavy construction to revegetation along the pipeline right-of-way. Many of these contracts were joint ventures and brought needed profits to the corporations during their early years.

The Regional Corporations Mature

By early 1977 the pipeline was virtually complete, and now the native corporations have to compete in shrinking markets. Mineral exploration continues on corporate lands, but generally the corporations are consolidating their holdings in the post-pipeline period. Doyon Corporation invested a large chunk of money to acquire the historic Pioneer Inn hotel and shopping complex in Lahaina on the island of Maui, Hawaii. Sealaska Corporation, which did not participate in pipeline activities, bought the Alaska Brick Company of Anchor-

Unloading halibut,
Juneau, 1966
(*Claus-M. Naske*)

age. This new acquisition does between $11 and $12 million worth of business a year, and includes a concrete block operation; Pacific Western Lines, a barge operation; and Alaska National Corporation, an import-export branch which imports building products from Japan. Development of the corporations' substantial timber resources is tied up by environmental regulations and the threat of lengthy lawsuits. The Bristol Bay Native Corporation, which previously had made the largest purchase with the acquisition of Peter Pan Seafoods for about $9 million, added to its investment by buying Anchorage Westward Hotel, with twenty-two stories and 546 rooms, Alaska's largest hotel. The estimated purchase price amounted to approximately $18 million.[105]

The native regional corporations have become firmly established in Alaska's economy within the last few years. They have contributed much to diversifying the state's economy. Obviously, problems remain. The settlement act provided a twenty-year tax moratorium on native lands, which has put much pressure on corporate leadership to put lands into production. Village corporation permission is required before the regional corporations are allowed to explore and produce subsurface mineral deposits. It is already apparent to many that regional corporate profit goals are often incompatible with village subsistence goals. Perhaps a congressional extension of the tax moratorium will ease some of the development pressures.

But perhaps, most importantly, most of the native corporations have quickly realized that they are business corporations first and foremost and native corporations second. This has contributed to the split between the village natives and the so-called Brooks Brothers Natives—individuals who have seen and experienced a much wider segment of the world than their village brethren and have assumed leadership in the corporations and in political life. It may be safely assumed that the corporate structure, just like the historic white incursions, will materially contribute to the disappearance of traditional native lifestyles. Before the settlement, Alaskan natives roamed over much of Alaska in search of subsistence; since the settlement they have become landowners, their domain defined by stakes—one in each of four corners. Now natives worry about trespassing and right-of-ways just as their white brothers do.

The 1975 Omnibus Act Clarifies ANCSA Ambiguities

It was to be expected that a complex piece of legislation like ANCSA would be ambiguous in parts and that Congress would soon be asked to more clearly define its intent and rectify some of the apparent injustices. In 1975 Congress passed such an omnibus act, which became law in 1976. A major part of the new law concerns the Cook Inlet region, where not enough lands were available for regional and village corporation selections. The law authorized a complicated exchange of lands between the United States, the Cook Inlet Region, Inc., and the state of Alaska as a means of satisfying the region's entitlement under the Alaska Native Claims Settlement Act of 1971. In order to accomplish this land exchange, the governor and the Alaska legislature, after heated debate, reached some accord. The legislature then enacted the necessary legislation authorizing the exchange, to become effective March 12, 1977. The legislature had acted hurriedly in order to meet a congressionally mandated deadline and recognized that comprehensive legislation was needed for future land exchanges. After much deliberation and helpful guidance from the Joint Federal-State Land Use Planning Commission, the legislature enacted the necessary regulation that clearly spelled out the requirements to be met before land exchanges could be made by the executive branch.[106]

The Omnibus Act clarified many more sections. For example, it extended native enrollment for one more year and provided that monies received under ANCSA not be used in lieu of various federal programs but merely for extinguishing land claims.[107]

By the spring of 1977, a mere 3.5 million acres of land out of some 44 million acres due the native corporations had been conveyed. The federal bureaucracy was working very slowly, indeed.

Remaining Uncertainties and Problems

The problem of land conveyance is a long and cumbersome one and has been complicated by disagreements between the applicants and the Bureau of Land Management over easements. Historically, all conveyances of public lands to private parties have contained a right-of-way reservation to the federal government for power transmission and telephone and telegraph lines, ditches, and railroads. The BLM feels that native lands to be conveyed should contain similar reservations. The bureau is also attempting to protect public access to all the waters of the state in its final easement recommendations.

The native corporations have been bitterly opposed to the easement policy. Their reasoning is that any easements, when and if desired, should be purchased by the interested parties. The easement problem, of course, is a very complicated one, and unless adequate provisions are made once Congress has set aside the so-called D-2 lands, or national interest areas, it will be nearly impossible to develop and transport to market resources from both native and state lands.

The delay in identification and selection of native lands has had an adverse impact on state selection rights under the Alaska Statehood Act of 1958. ANCSA relegated the state to second place behind the natives in land selection rights. To complicate matters even further, natives selected some 102 million acres, whereas their entitlement amounted to approximately 44 million acres. In short, the state still has a long way to go before selecting, and receiving title to, its 103.5-million-acre entitlement. In fact, many observers now doubt whether the state will be able to select its full entitlement in view of federal plans for Alaskan lands and ANCSA selections. There just may not be enough land left.

There is no question but that the Alaska Native Claims Settlement Act of 1971 provided a revolutionary solution to a long-standing problem. One may argue about the long-range effects of the settlement. One school of thought holds that it liberated Alaska's natives and provided them with land and money, the basis of political power. This, in turn, enabled the native community to take its rightful place in Alaskan society. On the other hand, it can be argued that the settlement represented the final irony in white-native relations. In exchange for a certain amount of money and acreage, Alaska's natives are giving up their unique lifestyle and mode of living. They are exchanging the life of the hunter and gatherer for that of the corporation member interested in resource development and stock dividend payments. It is also clear that the inclusion of section 17 (d)(2) in ANCSA created innumerable problems which should not have accompanied the act. Only the future will tell which, if any, of the problems have been solved.

·11·
The Discovery of Oil

NO SINGLE event in Alaska's history has had an impact on the region of intensity comparable to that of Atlantic-Richfield's discovery of the gigantic 9.6-billion-barrel Prudhoe Bay oilfield in 1968. The initial discoveries of oil deposits, however, were made long ago, many decades before phrases like "energy crisis" and "environmental degradation" became household words.

Thomas Simpson, an employee of the Hudson's Bay Company, first observed oil deposits along the Canadian Arctic shore while engaged in his coastal survey of 1836–37. As the first traveler to reach Point Barrow from the east, he certainly could not foresee the later frenzy of oil exploration in North America's Arctic.[1]

Somewhat later in the century, Ensign W. L. Howard, a member of the United States Navy's 1886 exploration expedition headed by Lieutenant George M. Stoney, extensively explored the North Slope of Alaska. Howard found oil near the upper Colville River and brought back a specimen.[2] In 1856 oil seepages were found on the west side of Cook Inlet, and were noted in the Katalla-Yakataga area in 1896.

In more recent times William Vanvalin, a United States Bureau of Education teacher in the Arctic village of Wainwright, heard reports of an oil lake. In 1914, Vanvalin traveled 550 miles to the east side of Smith Bay, one mile from the Arctic shore—now a part of the United States Naval Petroleum Reserve No. 4—where he found two springs of what appeared to be engine oil. Vanvalin quickly staked his claim on the hill from which the streams oozed, as well as on the little lake into which they drained. Since he had but little time on this journey, he hastily put out his stakes and put up a sign naming the place the "Arctic Rim Mineral Oil Claim." Although Vanvalin probably never returned to his claim, he did not forget his discovery, and in later lectures on the North and its wonders he mentioned the oil lake.[3]

In the same year that Vanvalin staked his oil claim, Ernest Leffingwell, an explorer, reported oil seepages approximately fifty miles southeast of Point

Cudahy Oil Company on the shore of Bering Lake ca. 15 miles from Bering River coal field. Katalla oil field.
(Barrett Willoughby Collection, Archives, University of Alaska, Fairbanks)

Barrow. Tests indicated oil of very high quality, and oilmen started to take notice of the region and its potential. There were other reports of similar seepages at various locations on the North Slope, and natives told Alfred H. Brooks, the head of the Alaska division of the United States Geological Survey, that the most extensive oil seepages occurred at a site 300 miles east of Point Barrow, near the Canadian boundary.

Still later, in 1921, representatives of Standard Oil Company of California and General Petroleum Company examined the seepages near Barrow, finding the two flows that encouraged their hopes of finding oil in quantities suitable for commercial production. Favorable geological conditions also existed elsewhere in Alaska. In 1902 the Alaska Oil Company had drilled a wildcat well at Puale Bay, near the mouth of Cook Inlet. At about the same time the Chilkat Oil Company had drilled another well in the Katalla district on the coast east of the mouth of the Copper River. Although both were unsuccessful, the operators had found enough encouragement to continue testing. In 1904 the Alaska Oil Company had drilled two more dry holes at Cold Bay. The Chilkat Oil Company was luckier at the time and found oil in the Katalla district. Between 1902 and 1931 it drilled thirty-six wells, eighteen of which produced oil. Production, however, was small, ranging from just a few to twenty barrels per day. In 1911 the Chilkat Oil Company built a small topping plant which began operating in 1912 and for twenty-one years supplied local demands for gasoline and heating oils. Late in 1933 a fire destroyed the boiler house at the topping plant, and the company abandoned the entire operation.[4]

During the thirty-one years of its production history, the Katalla field produced only a modest 154,000 barrels of oil—not even enough to supply local needs. The Katalla wells had been shallow, most not over 1,000 feet and none more than 2,000 feet deep.

In 1923 the Standard Oil Company of California drilled a 5,000-foot wildcat well at Cold Bay which proved to be dry, and in the same year the Associated Oil Company drilled two wells on the Pearl Creek dome. Although both wells showed signs of oil and gas, they were abandoned in 1924.

Naval Petroleum Reserve No. 4

Despite failures, geologist Alfred H. Brooks maintained his optimism regarding territorial oil. The press quoted him in June of 1922 telling a Seattle group that he was confident "that oil will be found in Alaska, and the probabilities are that there are extensive [oil] areas in the Territory." Perhaps President Harding was influenced by Brooks' optimism when he created Naval Petroleum Reserve No. 4 by executive order on February 27, 1923. The reserved area on the North Slope comprised approximately 37,000 square miles, extending from Icy Cape on the west to the Colville River on the east, and was bounded by the Endicott Mountain Range on the south.[5]

The United States Navy subsequently asked the Geological Survey to conduct a topographic and geological reconnaissance of the entire area to map the petroleum reserves. Brooks submitted a detailed work plan spanning a period of five years, and the Geological Survey accomplished its task. It was not until World War II, however, that the navy was instructed to develop additional oil reserves. In 1944 the navy started an extensive exploration program on Naval Petroleum Reserve No. 4. First Seabees (naval construction battalions) and then—from 1946 until 1953—contractors ranged over the reserve and also explored a similarly large area of public land contiguous to the reserve. Seabees mapped the Umiat area in 1944 and drilled their first wildcat well in 1945. Although the well showed light-gravity oil, it could not be completed as a producer because there was not enough oil. The same was true of the second well.[6]

In 1946, Arctic Contractors, a joint venture of three especially qualified firms, continued to carry out all phases of exploratory work except for geological research, which members of the United States Geological Service performed. The contractors drilled eleven wells in the Umiat area, outlining a field that contained an estimated 100 million barrels of recoverable oil.[7]

Between 1944 and 1953, when the navy suspended its exploration of the reserve, thirty-six wildcat wells had been drilled and forty-four core holes had been sunk, varying in depth from 2,000 to 11,800 feet. Arctic Contractors found two minor oil and three natural gas fields but made no commercially significant discoveries. By 1953, however, the navy's findings suggested that the area north of the Brooks Range might contain extensive reserves of both oil and gas.[8] While the navy could claim some success, in 1936 and 1939 the Havenstrite Oil Company had also found some oil and gas below 4,700 feet on the Fritz Creek anticline; but it could not get production underway.[9]

The Oil Industry Takes an Interest in Alaska

By 1957 more than 100 wells had been drilled in Alaska, financed by private capital. Outside of the few wells in the Katalla field, none had been commercially successful. Still, oilmen dreamed of sudden riches to be wrested from Alaska's promising oil structures. The year 1957 will be remembered for a long time by the industry. Humble Oil and Refining Company drilled the most promising dry hole ever in Alaska, the Bear Creek wildcat. Though it went to 14,900 feet and showed signs of both oil and gas, it was not a commercial find. It was, however, a very expensive well, at a cost of about $6 million.[10]

On July 23, 1957, Richfield Oil Corporation cored into the oil sands of what became the Swanson River field, establishing Alaska's first truly commercial oil production. It was Richfield's first wildcat in the territory, and the company had been lucky indeed, because the drilling rig, situated on the Swanson River oil structure, nearly missed the reservoir. Richfield completed its Swanson River Unit 1 on September 29, 1957, after drilling to a depth of 12,384 feet. Oil flowed from the discovery well at the rate of 900 barrels a day, and it also produced 122,000 cubic feet of gas. A second well was started in the same year and completed in 1958. Eventually, eleven dry wells were drilled in the task of outlining the boundaries of the Swanson River field.[11]

And although that discovery did not trigger an immediate oil rush, it did result in a leasing boom in the territory. By September 28, 1965, Alaska had held its fifteenth competitive lease since the first one, recorded on December 10, 1959. The state offered a total of 3,728,456 acres for lease during those six years, of which 66.9 percent, or 2,494,714 acres, were snapped up by the oil companies. The state had taken a total of $66,134,155 in its fifteen lease sales, which averaged $26.51 for every acre leased.[12]

By 1965 the oil industry had become an important part of Alaska's economy; five oil and eleven gas fields had been developed. Between 1958 and January 1, 1966, the state received a total of $122,223,000 in direct cash payments from the oil industry—approximately $480 per person in Alaska, which compares to the $756,805 the territorial government had received between 1947 and 1957. Most of the money came from bonuses on competitive leases, which provided more than $66 million. In addition, the state received 90 percent of the rentals paid to the federal government for leases on federal lands. It also collected 90 percent of the royalty paid to the federal government for production from the Swanson River field.[13]

By 1966, in the short span of nine years since the first truly commercial discovery in 1957, the oil industry had become an integral part of Alaska's economy. Natural gas heated homes in Anchorage; a refinery on the Kenai Peninsula processed Alaskan crude into heating oils and jet fuels; and Union Oil Company, through its subsidiary Collier Carbon and Chemical Corporation, was spending some $30 million in constructing the biggest ammonia plant on the west coast and another $20 million jointly with Tokyo Gas and Chemical Company in building the world's biggest urea plant—both located on the Kenai Peninsula.[14]

The oil industry and many Alaskans were optimistic about future prospects. Experts believed that the upper Cook Inlet area had not been fully explored and still held much promise; the lower Cook Inlet was virtually untouched; and Geophysical Services, Inc., had sent seismic crews into the Bristol Bay area and the Gulf of Alaska to check these two oil provinces for some twenty oil companies. Although oilmen seemed almost certain that Alaska's North Slope contained sizable reserves, they were put off by the region's inaccessibility and climatic rigors. The industry estimated that it needed to discover between 200 and 500 million barrels of recoverable oil before it could establish an economically viable field on the North Slope. In 1966 industry spokesmen estimated that producing and moving oil to markets even after the discovery of such a big field would "test the ingenuity of the American petroleum industry." They added that "there's nothing to be done with the gas."[15]

While geologists and seismic crews roamed Alaska's wide spaces, annual crude oil production rose from 187,000 barrels in 1959 to 74 million barrels in 1969; and natural gas, from 310 million cubic feet to 149 billion cubic feet. Wellhead value of this production, on which the state levied its taxes, had risen from $1.5 million in 1960 to $219 million in 1969—at which point the oil industry had become Alaska's foremost natural resource extractive industry.[16]

The Prudhoe Bay Discovery

On January 16, 1968, oil became big news when it was announced that a substantial flow of gas had been found in the Arctic. Various companies had been exploring the North Slope for some time, and geologists speculated that the Atlantic-Richfield Company's willingness to make the announcement at that time was an indication that the optimism about oil and gas development prospects on the North Slope was well founded. Two days later Atlantic-Richfield Company's exploration manager, Julius Babisak, described the gas well, known as Prudhoe Bay State No. 1, as "encouraging." He said: "This is a very rank wildcat. We are keeping information on it tight. I think you can understand why."[17]

Judging by subsequent events on Alaska's North Slope, it was indeed understandable that Atlantic-Richfield, in partnership with Humble Oil and Refining Company, wanted to limit its disclosure on the strike. Alaskans speculated that Prudhoe Bay State No. 1 was the first nonmilitary oil discovery ever reported from the Arctic Slope and hoped that it would be but the forerunner of additional discoveries big enough to make commercial production possible. Drilling continued amid growing industry optimism. In February, ARCO reported that it had cased the well at 8,708 feet and found oil-saturated sands in the lower seventy feet.[18]

Early in March, ARCO announced, amid much speculation, that the company had made a major find, that its discovery well flowed oil at the rate of 1,152 barrels a day. On June 25 ARCO announced that a second well, drilled about seven miles southeast of the discovery well, had also found oil. This supported the Prudhoe Bay discovery.[19]

While ARCO cautiously conceded that the discovery was significant, geologists in Fairbanks surmised that Alaska's North Slope might well contain

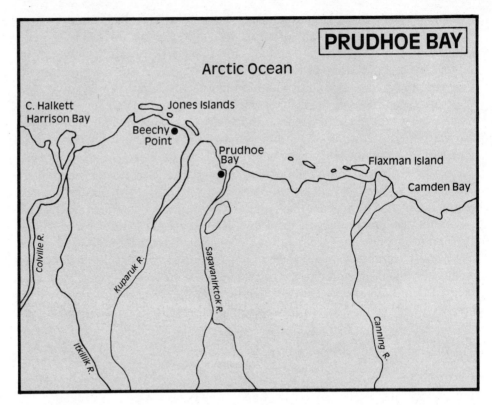

one of the largest oilfields in the world. Expert opinion ranged from "evidently mammoth" to "almost certainly of Middle-Eastern proportions."[20]

ARCO's discovery had been largely a matter of luck, for in 1966 the company had decided to drill a wildcat well on the North Slope leases it had acquired in a state sale. Geologists proposed two drilling sites, one at Prudhoe Bay and the other inland near the Saganavirktok River. ARCO chose the latter, calling it Susie Unit No. 1, spent $4,500,000, and came up with a dry hole. That was an inauspicious beginning. The company decided to give it one more try—this time at Prudhoe Bay, called Prudhoe Bay State No. 1—and this time the oil gushed up and the great Alaska oil rush was on.[21]

The Hickel Highway

In 1967, prior to the rush, Alaska's Governor Walter Hickel requested the state legislature to create a NORTH Commission. This body was to ponder ways to develop Alaska's Arctic. In August of 1968 the NORTH Commission met, no longer to ponder ways to develop the Arctic but rather to devote its attention to planning for an orderly development. Governor Hickel, in private life a real estate developer and contractor, painted a bright picture of the Arctic's future for his NORTH Commission members. "We are going to see villages grow to towns and towns grow to cities and a vigorous, new breed of people working and playing and raising families and building libraries, schools, museums, universities, and theaters where there is nothing now but tundra." While many members of Alaska's business community applauded the governor's remarks, others, concerned with Alaska's unique wilderness and lifestyle, were dismayed. All could see, however, that momentous changes were coming.[22]

Conservationists predicted that development would play havoc with the finely balanced ecology of the Arctic, and they expected the state government to be insensitive to environmental concerns. Governor Hickel did not disappoint these groups. In order to give Alaska's trucking industry an opportunity to participate in the rush, Hickel approved the construction of a road approximately 400 miles long from Livengood, about 60 miles north of Fairbanks, across the frozen tundra to Sagwon, on the North Slope. Shortly after Governor Hickel ordered the construction of the winter road, President Richard M. Nixon appointed him secretary of the interior. Hickel's successor, Governor Keith H. Miller, promptly named the project the "Hickel Highway." From the beginning it was a mess. Instead of compacting the snow on the tundra without disturbing the permafrost under it, state bulldozers scraped off the snow and protective ground covering and gouged a road into the tundra. This made a trench, and much time was lost clearing windblown snow out of the roadway. Open only for about a month—from March to April—the road carried a total of 7,464 tons of freight. About 80 percent of that went to the oilfields. The cost of freight delivered to Sagwon, well short of the Prudhoe Bay exploration area, still amounted to $240 a ton—approximately the same as airfreight. The same tonnage could easily have been carried by three trips of the giant Hercules air transports, which require only a 5,000-foot runway at each end.[23]

The worst was yet to come. During the spring breakup the "Hickel Highway" rapidly turned into a water-filled canal as the exposed permafrost melted and water from surrounding areas drained into the roadbed. But once committed to a particular project, no matter how impractical or expensive, governments tend to forge ahead. Prodding from the trucking companies helped also, and during the winter of 1969/70, the state highway department compounded its mistake and reconstructed the winter road. Since some sections had eroded badly, portions of the road had to be rerouted, resulting in two ditches rather than one.[24]

No matter what the state did or did not do, events moved forward. For weeks potential bidders for the approximately 450,000 acres of North Slope oil lands to be leased by the state of Alaska had been gathering in Anchorage. Texans in big hats and cowboy boots mingled with conservatively dressed New York investors and dapper and shrewd oil experts from London. The influx of outsiders strained accommodations in Anchorage; all hotels, from the Westward to the Captain Cook and Traveler's Inn, as well as every tiny motel and rooming house, were solidly booked. All over the city, oil-company men, executives, geologists, drilling experts, and accountants huddled together to plan strategy. Companies like ARCO, British Petroleum, Sinclair, Colorado Oil and Gas, and Union Oil, already holding leases on the North Slope, were anxious to guard the geological information on which they planned to base their bids for the remaining acreage, while those companies not so fortunate had to assemble every clue and bit of information they could in order to put together sensible bids on the various tracts.

The Spectacular Prudhoe Bay Lease Sale

Prior to the sale date of September 10, 1969, companies without actual lease holdings sent seismic crews to find prime unleased land, and scouts and spies repeatedly flew to the North Slope in an attempt to gain clues by observing equipment, watching the comings and goings of crews and supplies, and trying to estimate the depth of holes being drilled and analyze reports of test burn-offs. Tips were sold across bar counters in Fairbanks, and oil company and state employees were propositioned for information. As the lease sale date approached, widespread publicity built suspense. Articles appeared in the national magazines and newspapers, and television specials were made about the Prudhoe Bay oil strike, the coming sale, and the state of Alaska. Media crews from Japan, Europe, and Britain's BBC, in addition to ABC, CBS, and NBC crews, prepared to cover the bid openings. In addition to seats held by oil company representatives, there were extra ones for the general public. By 6:00 a.m., people lined up halfway around the block from the Sydney Lawrence Auditorium for these spots. Alaska was front-page news across the Western world for one day. Never had there been so much media coverage in Alaska as on that Wednesday morning.[25]

Those in attendance from the East Coast, Europe, and Japan may have been amused by the rather folksy opening ceremonies, but not the Alaskans present. After reciting the Pledge of Allegiance, everyone sang Alaska's state song, "Eight Stars of Gold on a Field of Blue." Commissioner of Natural Resources Tom Kelly, the master of ceremonies, next made some sprightly remarks about Alaska's resources and the widespread interest in both preserving and responsibly developing its wilderness. Next Larry Beck, a local poet and self-proclaimed "Bard of the North," jauntily dressed in parka and mukluks, recited his own poem paying tribute to the oil industry. Governor Keith Miller reminded all to manage Alaska's birthright wisely and concluded that Alaska would never be the same again.[26]

After the opening ceremonies concluded at 10:30 a.m. in the Sydney Lawrence Auditorium, the serious business began. Dozens of oilmen and their bankers, packing briefcases containing several hundred million dollars, quietly filed up and presented state officials with sealed envelopes containing their bid checks for 179 tracts of land. For the next several hours the bids were read off, tract by tract. The Gulf–British Petroleum consortium took the first six tracts at the mouth of the Colville River with bonus bids of $97 million. Each announcement was cheered, and by 5:15 p.m. the state had received a 20-percent down payment on the $900,220,590 in bonus monies. Loaded into bags, the money was taken to the airport and flown by chartered jet to the Bank of America in San Francisco for deposit, so that not a penny of interest would be lost. Amerada Hess was the high bidder of the day with $272 million, followed by Union of California and Pan American Petroleum with $163 million and Gulf and British Petroleum with $97 million. Standard of California, Phillips, and Mobil in consortium were fourth with $96 million.[27]

Since statehood, Alaska had held a total of twenty-two lease sales, which had netted less than $100 million. Then, in one day, the state sold oil leases on less than .001 percent of its total landmass and raised more than $900 million.[28] Those residents who had always claimed that Alaska would be the nation's treasure chest of natural resources finally had their proof. Others, interested in maintaining Alaska's open spaces, its magnificent wilderness, and their own lifestyles, were apprehensive about the vast changes in the making.

What to Do with All the Money

All through that winter Alaskans debated what to do with their money. Many believed that Alaska's financial troubles were at an end, for there was speculation that the Prudhoe Bay discovery represented the mere tip of the iceberg. What other oil provinces, on land and offshore, many asked, awaited exploration? Many had visions of schools, hospitals, community centers, roads, pensions for all, and free scholarships and tuitions for those who wanted them. The legislative council hired the Brookings Institution, and Governor Miller bought advice from a team of twenty-four from Stanford Research Institute and from New York petroleum consultant Walter J. Levy.[29] There was much talk about the best and wisest way to develop Alaska, and many assumed that the state should be developed. The Brookings Institution arranged four successive meetings in Anchorage, where a broad cross section of urban Alaskans examined and discussed the financial foundations for the future of the state, the use of its human resources, the quality of the natural environment, and alternative futures for the state. What distinguished the Brookings sessions were the repeated calls by participants for preserving the "unique" Alaskan lifestyle, defining it as one which "affords the conveniences of technological innovation with the opportunity and values of living as close to nature as possible." Most agreed that a compatibility between the oil industry and the Alaskan lifestyle could be achieved with "well-enforced, proper regulation."[30]

Planning for the Trans-Alaska Pipeline

The lease sale and the subsequent debate over what to do with all the money were the highlights of that season. In the meantime, the Trans-Alaska Pipeline System (TAPS), an unincorporated joint venture of Atlantic-Richfield, British Petroleum, and Humble Oil, applied to the United States Department of the Interior in June 1969 for a permit to construct a hot-oil pipeline across 800 miles of public domain from Prudhoe Bay on the North Slope to tidewater at Valdez on Prince William Sound. TAPS estimated that it would cost approximately $900 million to build the pipeline. Secretary of the Interior Walter J. Hickel, Alaska's former governor, was under great pressure to grant the construction permit promptly. Conservationist groups across the United States also applied pressure not to grant a construction permit. The giant project posed innumerable environmental, technical, and economic questions for which no one had yet furnished any answers.[31]

The oil companies, even without the permit in hand, already had made a number of decisions. The first one was to build a conventional buried pipeline;

Early Valdez
(*Charles Bunnell Collection,
Archives, University of Alaska,
Fairbanks*)

but the companies had not considered what effect oil at 160° F would have on Alaska's permafrost. Secondly, despite a number of feasibility studies investigating various routes for the pipeline, TAPS opted for an Alaskan one and announced in February of 1969 that they planned to build the pipeline from Prudhoe Bay to Valdez. TAPS sought and was given permission from the Department of the Interior to conduct geological and engineering investigations along the proposed route. This permission required that former Secretary Stewart Udall's land freeze order be modified. This the Senate Interior and Insular Affairs Committee approved, and investigations began. Thirdly, the companies had decided that they needed 48-inch-diameter pipe in order to transport two million barrels of crude oil a day once the pipeline was operational. The companies also wanted to have the pipe by September 1969 in order to start construction in July of that year. Since no American company made pipe of that size, the order went to three Japanese firms—Sunimomo Metal Industries, Ltd., Nippon Steel Corporation, and Nippon Kokan Kabushiki Kaisha. This move annoyed Secretary Hickel and other development-minded Alaskans because Kaiser Industries had offered to build a steel mill in Alaska. As it eventually turned out, the 800 miles of steel pipe at $100 million was probably the biggest bargain of the whole project.[32]

In April 1969, Secretary Hickel announced the creation of a departmental task force to oversee North Slope oil development and designated Russel E. Train, an under secretary, to head the new organization. Train, a former head of the Conservation Foundation who later became the first chairman of the Council on Environmental Quality, had been brought into the department to mute conservationist opposition to Hickel's appointment. A month after Hickel set up the task force, President Nixon, under pressure from conservation groups, expanded it to include a conservation-industry ad hoc committee as well as representatives of other government agencies. The expanded task force was to report on plans to protect the arctic environment by September 15, 1969.[33]

On June 6, 1969, TAPS filed a formal application for "an oil pipeline right-of-way together with two additional right-of-way and eleven pumping plant sites for the construction of a 48 inch diameter oil pipeline system." Under Secretary Train immediately sent TAPS chairman R. E. Dulaney a list of questions to which satisfactory answers had to be found before construction could proceed.[34]

Dulaney quickly replied, reiterating that the pipeline should be constructed consistent with wise conservation practice and that a good pipeline dictated design and construction procedures that would cause a minimum of disturbance to the natural environment. Dulaney sent along a twenty-page

The first shipment of 48-inch-diameter pipe for the Trans-Alaska Pipeline arrived in Valdez in Sept. 1969 (*Alyeska Pipeline Service Company*)

document detailing the planning and research done to that date. TAPS planned to bury the hot-oil pipeline beneath the streambed of all the rivers it crossed. A system of block valves would shut off the oil should a break or leak occur. Crews and equipment would clean up the oil that did spill at various intervals. TAPS also had commissioned a number of studies to preserve and revegetate the tundra, and it also was taking core samples along the proposed route to determine what kind of permafrost they would encounter. This was the first of many such exchanges between TAPS and the Department of the Interior.[35]

In the meantime, the department sent its own personnel to Alaska to reconnoiter the route. After the survey, the interior group concluded that the TAPS plan to bury most of the pipeline was not feasible, particularly after talking to specialists at the University of Alaska and to Dr. Max Brewer, an arctic expert and the director of the Naval Arctic Research Laboratory.[36]

Although in June 1969 there was as yet no National Environmental Policy Act, TAPS had to comply with the 1920 Mineral Leasing Act, which provided for the ground necessary for the pipe—four feet in this case—and for twenty-five feet on either side of the pipe, for a total corridor of fifty-four feet. Yet TAPS asked for a 100-foot right-of-way. Additionally, since the land freeze would have to be modified, approval would have to be obtained from the interior committees of Congress in order to adhere to a promise which Senator Jackson and the Alaska Federation of Natives had extracted from Secretary Hickel.[37]

TAPS also planned to build a haul road to the North Slope paralleling the pipeline from Livengood, a ghost town north of Fairbanks. Subsequently, TAPS and the state of Alaska agreed that TAPS should build the road according to state secondary-road specifications and then, when it had completed the pipeline, turn the road over to the state. On July 22, 1969, the state asked for a modification of the land freeze to allow the construction of a state highway from Livengood to the Yukon River, a distance of fifty miles, where TAPS planned to have the oil pipeline cross the river. On July 29, Secretary Hickel asked the Senate Interior Committee to approve such a modification on the land freeze order. The committee complied and the secretary lifted the freeze for that particular purpose. TAPS promptly gave the contract to Burgess Construction Company of Fairbanks, and work commenced on the first part of the Trans-Alaska Pipeline project.[38]

Problems

On September 15, 1969, Under Secretary Train's task force submitted its preliminary report to the president. After reporting on the status of the TAPS application, the task force also listed problems to which no solutions had yet been found. These included the permafrost, the questionable availability of gravel for insulating the pipeline from the ground, the earthquake danger along the route, waste disposal, water pollution from oil spills or tanker discharges, and the effects of so much human activity on wildlife. There were other problems that did not have to do with the environment, such as the native claims and the size of the right-of-way.[39]

In the meantime, conservationist groups began organizing opposition to TAPS, and by the fall of 1969 the Sierra Club and the Wilderness Society were urging members to write their congressional delegations about the project. But conservationists also knew that the only time Congress would have any real control over the decision-making process would be when Secretary Hickel asked the Department of the Interior committees to approve a modification of the land freeze for the right-of-way. He was expected to do so sometime in the fall.[40]

While conservationist groups worried, the Department of the Interior and TAPS methodically removed the legal obstacles to the project one by one. On September 19 the various native villages claiming land over which the pipeline would pass waived their claims to the right-of-way. On September 30 the Department of the Interior published the first of many sets of stipulations for construction of the pipeline, said to be the most rigid governmental controls ever imposed on a private construction project. Implementation of these controls was to be left to Bureau of Land Management (BLM) personnel in the field.[41]

On October 1, 1969, Secretary Hickel asked Congress to approve his lifting of the land freeze for the entire project. The House Interior and Insular Affairs Committee seemed willing to approve his request; however, unable to round up a quorum, it delayed any decision until the last week in October. During the interim, the House Indian Affairs Subcommittee was to tour native villages in Alaska and also take a look at the proposed pipeline corridor. Senator Jackson's Interior Committee was more skeptical than the House's Committee, and Jackson stated that he would have to hold hearings on the proposed modification of the land freeze before making a decision. Nevertheless, Under Secretary Train appeared before Jackson's committee and argued that the freeze should be lifted as a necessary preliminary step.[42]

When Train appeared before the House Interior and Insular Affairs Committee, he was surprised by the displeasure expressed by the two ranking members, who had just returned from their Alaskan tour. They had observed denuded hilltops, a swath cut in the wilderness for miles, and all sorts of drilling activities. The congressmen were particularly upset because this activity had occurred without their permission. Actually, the work the congressmen observed had been approved; Congress had allowed TAPS to build the road to the Yukon River and collect core samples of the soil along the pipeline route.[43]

Hickel and TAPS

On October 23, Senator Jackson sent Secretary Hickel a list of questions that had to be answered before his committee could approve any modification of the land freeze. These questions were exhaustive and dealt with almost every phase of the pipeline, from permafrost to native rights. The House, learning of Jackson's questions, decided to wait until they had been answered.[44]

It took Hickel nearly a month to reply to the questions, and when he did so his answers were ambiguous at best. He did state that TAPS had not solved the engineering problems to his satisfaction. In early December, Hickel told

Senator Jackson that his department would do nothing until TAPS had solved its problems with permafrost, although he was certain that TAPS would find solutions to this problem. Still, Senator Jackson was concerned about the effect on the pipeline environment.

The Senate committee then notified the secretary that it had no objections to lifting the freeze, after pointing out that the National Environmental Policy Act, then in its final form, provided, among other things, for a public statement of the environmental impact of any federally financed project on federal lands, including an evaluation of alternatives to it. A few days later the House Interior and Insular Affairs Committee followed the Senate's lead in notifying Hickel that it did not object to lifting the land freeze for the pipeline. Secretary Hickel did not immediately grant the permit, although he modified the land freeze, allowing him to lift it entirely when called for. The BLM thereupon started to classify some five million acres along the proposed pipeline route as a transportation corridor, while TAPS refiled its permit application, requesting a 54-foot right-of-way and temporary special land-use permits for additional footage up to 146 feet in places along the route.[45]

Secretary Hickel intended to issue a permit for construction of the 390-mile haul road, and in January 1970 TAPS issued letters of intent to contractors for the entire road from the Yukon River to Prudhoe Bay. The companies, anticipating firm contracts, soon hauled heavy equipment up portions of the old "Hickel Highway" and up a new winter road to convenient staging areas along the road's tentative route. The companies wanted to start construction immediately when the final permit was issued. At about the same time, the BLM authorized TAPS to proceed with the centerline survey for the haul road. But when Secretary Hickel was about to issue the haul road permit, natives and conservationists asked a federal district court in Washington, D.C., to prevent him from doing so.[46]

Prior to construction of the Yukon River bridge, two air-cushion transporters were used to ferry supply trucks for the Trans-Alaska Pipeline across the Yukon. The crafts were supported on a cushion of air and were pulled across by cables.
(Alyeska Pipeline Service Company)

Natives Object to the Pipeline

What had occurred was that some of the villages that had signed a waiver of their claims to the pipeline right-of-way the previous fall were now reneging. The villagers wired Hickel and told him that TAPS, contrary to a prior promise, had not chosen any native contractors and furthermore had selected firms unlikely to give jobs to natives. On March 9, before anything had happened in the case, five villages asked the federal district court in Washington, D.C., to stop Secretary Hickel from issuing the construction permit because they claimed the road right-of-way crossed their lands. And on April 1, 1970, Judge George L. Hart, Jr., enjoined the Department of the Interior from issuing a construction permit across 19.8 miles of the route, land claimed by the residents of Stevens Village. Judge Hart stated that he would reconsider the temporary restraining order in ten days.[47]

In the meantime, the Wilderness Society, the Friends of the Earth, and the Environmental Defense Fund sued the Department of the Interior in the same court on March 26, asking that the TAPS project be halted because it violated both the 1920 Mineral Leasing Act and the new National Environmental Policy Act. Judge Hart scheduled a hearing on this case for April 13, 1970.[48]

Alaska's Governor Keith Miller now decided to take matters into his own hands, and based on an 1866 statute that grants states rights-of-way over public lands "not reserved for public use," the governor authorized the haul road himself. TAPS, however, chose to wait for a federal permit. On April 13, Judge Hart, after listening to arguments from the lawyers employed by the various parties, issued a temporary injunction against the TAPS project.[49]

The oil industry suddenly realized that Alaska presented problems that would not easily be overcome. And British Petroleum, after much maneuvering, agreed to help lobby for a native land claims settlement and also agreed to persuade other companies in TAPS to join in that effort. Nothing happened immediately because TAPS was in the throes of reorganization: in the fall of 1970 it became a well-organized Delaware corporation named the Alyeska Pipeline Service Company, Inc. The new corporation included the same oil companies that had started TAPS. By mid-1970 the plans for construction of the Trans-Alaska Pipeline were stymied, and the oil companies realized that the real obstacle consisted of the native land claims, which had to be resolved before any progress could be made (discussed in the preceding chapter).

Alternative Methods for Transporting Oil

While that political drama was played out on the Washington and Alaska stage, several other methods for transporting the oil from the Arctic to commercial markets were considered. As early as 1968, the Humble Oil and Refining Company had committed itself to a $50 million experiment with the 115,000-ton *S. S. Manhattan*, the largest United States flag merchant ship. This supertanker was to navigate the Northwest Passage in an attempt to determine whether or not it would be commercially feasible to transport the oil via this route. To conquer the passage, Humble converted the *S. S. Manhattan*

The experimental oil tanker *Manhattan*, which negotiated the Northwest Passage from east to west with the help of two Canadian ice-breakers, 1969
(Fairbanks Daily News-Miner)

into a powerful icebreaker. The ship's hull was equipped with protective belts of steel plate; the bow was designed to attack the ice at a sharp 18-degree angle rather than at the 30-degree angle of most traditional icebreaker bows. In addition, the bow was sixteen feet wider than the rest of the hull so that the ship's hard nose could break a wide path in the ice. Equipped with a 43,000-horsepower plant, nearly one and one-half times larger than those on most other ships twice her size, the *Manhattan* during the summer of 1969 broke through the 6- to 18-foot-thick pack ice and through pressure ridges as thick as 100 feet. The ship was also equipped with two helicopters which scouted the route ahead, and it contained varied scientific equipment measuring stress and gathering data. The *Manhattan* had the help of a Canadian and an American icebreaker; once, when it became stuck in the ice-choked McClure Strait in the Canadian Arctic Archipelago, it was freed with some difficulty. On the way home it was carrying a single symbolic barrel of North Slope oil when the ice put a hole in one of the oil tanks (which was filled with seawater) "big enough to drive a truck through." In any event, by late 1970, following a second summer excursion by the *Manhattan*, Humble decided that it was impractical to construct larger icebreaking tankers.[50]

Other alternatives to the pipeline were considered during the early and even late planning stages; all were abandoned for reasons of logistics, cost, or safety. In 1972 there was talk of another version of the supertanker, this one a flying Boeing version. The Boeing Company earlier had suggested the possibility of using fleets of conventional jumbo aircraft for lifting the oil out of the Arctic. Boeing now unveiled a giant airplane that would be powered by twelve

747-type engines. With a 478-foot wingspan and an 83-foot tail, the plane would have a gross take-off weight of 3,500,000 pounds. A fleet of such aircraft would have been designed to carry oil, gas, or other natural resources in two wing-mounted removable pods, 150 feet long and 26 feet in diameter. The plane never advanced beyond the drawing board.[51]

In 1973 the idea was advanced of using giant, 900-foot nuclear-powered submarines carrying 170,000 tons of cargo for transporting the oil. These submarines, it was suggested, could be redesigned as 300,000-ton subsea tankers. Made by General Dynamics Corporation and formally presented to the North Slope oil companies, the submarines would be 140 feet at the beam and have a hull depth of 85 feet. Twin screws would provide a cruising speed of eighteen knots. Roger Lewis, the president of General Dynamics, declared that his corporation had already formulated plans to build these submarine tankers at its Quincy, Massachusetts shipyards. The oil companies, however, did not pursue the idea.[52]

There were other plans, such as extending the Alaska Railroad to Prudhoe Bay and carrying the oil to market in tank cars. But this idea did not get beyond the discussion stage either. Finally, Mark Wheeler, a cartoonist from Ketchikan, suggested that the oil companies use a 789-mile-long human bucket brigade to get the oil to tidewater at Valdez.[53]

TAPS Becomes Alyeska Pipeline Service Company, Inc.

By late 1970, TAPS finally completed its metamorphosis and became the tightly organized Alyeska Pipeline Service Company, Inc., headed by Edward Patton, formerly of Humble Oil. At the urging of Hugh Gallagher, a representative of British Petroleum and a former administrative assistant to Senator E. L. "Bob" Bartlett, Patton hired William C. Foster as the company's chief lobbyist. Foster, a young Washington attorney with extensive federal and Alaskan connections, had also been a Bartlett staff member in the 1960s and had helped to modify the new state's laws after it attained statehood in 1959. Foster advised his client to push for a land claims settlement satisfactory to the natives so that there would be no subsequent lawsuits to further delay the pipeline. Such a settlement was achieved when President Richard M. Nixon signed the Alaska Native Claims Settlement Act into law in December 1971.

While the native claims settlement progressed through Congress, the Department of the Interior dealt with the pipeline issue. The land claims settlement cleared only one obstacle for the pipeline. The department still had to comply with the national environmental policy and mineral leasing acts.

After the Department of the Interior released its Draft Environmental Impact Statement on the pipeline in January 1971, subsequent public hearings brought forth some 12,000 pages of testimony. Permafrost was not the only problem. Another question raised was whether the pipeline should go through Canada rather than Alaska. The Department of the Interior was not eager to explore this alternative, insisting that it had to consider only the application for an Alaskan pipeline. The department changed its tune, however, after the appeals court for the District of Columbia ruled in January 1972 that the

National Environmental Policy Act required the broad considerations of alternatives to any proposed federal action.[54]

There were disadvantages and advantages to a Canadian route. A pipeline through the Arctic National Wildlife Range and up the Mackenzie River would be much longer, pose many of the same engineering problems, and, above all, pass through a foreign country. It would also take much longer to complete. On the other hand, it would avoid the numerous earthquake zones in Alaska, a point stressed by the conservationists; and it would not involve tanker traffic on Canada's rugged west coast, which would endanger Canadian and Alaskan fisheries. Most importantly, it would provide a means of delivering Prudhoe Bay's estimated twenty-six trillion cubic feet of natural gas to the American Middle West in an economical fashion.[55]

Conservationists were particularly effective in keeping several additional issues in public view. The above-ground portions of the line might hamper caribou migrations; and timber clearing, gravel excavation, and access-road construction would disrupt natural habitats, silt streams, and fish spawning grounds. Even with a carefully engineered and constructed, trouble-free pipeline, the conservationists contended, there would almost certainly be accidental oil spills from the tankers operating out of Valdez. Furthermore, the oil and construction boom, new access roads and airstrips, and temporary and permanent settlements would, without adequate planning and controls, result in haphazard land development, speculation, inflation, and intensified resource exploitation.[56]

Construction Permit Granted by Congress

As if these issues were not frustrating enough to the oil companies, the Cordova District Fisheries Union filed suit against the proposed Valdez terminal in April 1971, contending that Alyeska had not met the requirements of the National Environmental Policy Act. Furthermore, Rogers C. B. Morton, the new secretary of the interior who assumed office in 1971 after the dismissal of Walter Hickel, was uncomfortable about the pipeline and disapproved of his predecessor's open advocacy of it. The new secretary not only disowned the draft impact statement the department had released before he came into office, but he also refused to be pinned down to any sort of timetable for approving the project.[57]

Throughout the spring of 1971, Secretary Morton was under considerable pressure from the industry to grant the permit, and from conservationists to deny it. In June 1971 the secretary visited and toured Alaska, and on his return to Washington he said that he now understood more about Alaska. Many Alaskans interpreted this remark to mean that the secretary favored the pipeline.[58]

On March 15, 1972, Secretary Morton, acting under the authority of Section 17(d)(1) of the Native Claims Settlement Act, withdrew some eighty million acres to be considered for inclusion in the natural conservation system and another forty-five million acres for public interest lands, including many forests and mineral deposits. He also set aside an additional forty-four million

The Valdez pipe storage yard in 1971. In the center, background, is the then partially cleared site for the pipeline's marine tanker terminal
(*Alyeska Pipeline Service Company*)

acres for native land selections, bringing total native withdrawals to ninety-nine million acres. Natives would eventually gain title to some forty million acres.[59]

On March 20, 1972, the Department of the Interior released its nine-volume environmental impact statement on the Trans-Alaska Pipeline. Packed with detail, the volumes dealt with the possible environmental degradation but argued that Alaskan oil was needed on the U.S. West Coast. Alyeska, however, had indicated that when the line reached its full capacity of 2 million barrels per day, some 1.5 million would go to the West Coast while another 500,000 barrels would go to "Panama," a catchall term for all markets outside the West Coast. Actually, as Alyeska president Patton admitted, some of the oil might be sold to Japan.[60]

In reality, the marketing of the oil was up to individual North Slope companies, and as early as 1970 British Petroleum had signed an agreement with a number of Japanese oil companies that included marketing an undisclosed number of barrels of crude oil there. Phillips Petroleum had proposed an import-export plan under which the companies would trade their excess Alaskan crude for Japanese rights to Middle Eastern oil, which could then be sold on the U.S. East Coast.[61]

Most importantly, perhaps, the impact statement asserted that the United States could not afford to wait two more years before developing the Alaskan reserves; for in the meantime the Arab countries, in an effort to force a change in American policy toward Israel, had cut off oil supplies to the United States. The pressures to develop reliable domestic energy supplies became almost irresistible. By the winter of 1973, Americans debated the energy crisis, and perhaps for the first time most people realized that the era of cheap and plentiful energy had come to an end. As former Secretary of Commerce Peter

Peterson so very aptly put it, "Popeye is running out of cheap spinach."[62]

Amid much pressure from all sides, Secretary Morton announced on May 11, 1972, that it was "in the national interest of the United States to grant a right-of-way permit for the trans-Alaskan pipeline...." Morton assured everyone that his decision was the result of much careful consideration of the nation's interest "in maintaining a secure and adequate supply of vitally needed energy resources."[63]

On August 15, 1972, Federal Judge George L. Hart, Jr., dissolved the temporary injunction against the Trans-Alaska Pipeline. After hearing the case, the appeals court in February of 1973 ruled that the rights-of-way and special land use permits which Secretary Morton proposed for the pipeline violated the mineral leasing law. The court ruled that Alyeska had to petition Congress if it intended to use a right-of-way exceeding fifty-four feet. The Justice Department appealed to the Supreme Court and asked it to expedite the case so construction could start as soon as possible. On April 7, 1973, however, the United States Supreme Court refused to review the lower court's decision. A couple of days later Secretary Morton urged Congress to act immediately on the necessary right-of-way legislation. After much political maneuvering, Congress finally decided to bypass NEPA and authorize the pipeline. President Richard M. Nixon signed the measure into law on November 16, 1973.

Preliminary Construction Begins

On January 23, 1974, the secretary of the interior signed the primary federal right-of-way permit for construction of the Trans-Alaska Pipeline. Edward L. Patton, the president of Alyeska Pipeline Service Company, Inc., welcomed this action and assured the secretary that his company would endeavor to get all other permits and at the same time make all necessary preparations to "assure the earliest possible starting date of construction, so that Alaska oil can reach the U.S. West Coast market during 1977."[64]

But even before the signing of the permit gave Alyeska the green light, the company already had taken preliminary steps to get the construction phase underway. In mid-December 1973 it had announced that contractors were building an ice bridge across the Yukon River as well as opening winter trails and ice airstrips to resupply the seven remote construction camps strung along the pipeline route north from the Yukon to Prudhoe Bay.[65]

A week before the signing of the permit, Alyeska requested bids for site work at Valdez and Prudhoe Bay and for camp housing to be used in construction of the tanker terminal and pump stations along the pipeline, and the company also awarded contracts, after competitive bidding, for the purchase of some $9.2 million worth of heavy construction equipment.[66]

After that Alyeska moved at a fast pace. It named Bechtel, Inc., of San Francisco to manage the roads and pipeline construction for the project, and it named Fluor Alaska, a subsidiary of Fluor Corporation of Los Angeles, to manage construction of the marine tanker terminal at Valdez and of the pumping stations along the pipeline. A host of subcontractors received awards for various phases of the work as well, and in February, Mechanics Research, Inc., of Los Angeles was awarded a federal contract to provide third-party surveillance of pipeline construction. Working under federal coordinating officer Andrew Rollins, the company was authorized to make certain that adequate environmental safeguards were taken in design and construction of the line. Soon after Alyeska had selected the contractors for the haul road, the state gave the company the last necessary permit—a lease covering the 246 miles of state land which the pipeline would cross.[67]

By late summer construction had begun in earnest on the Trans-Alaska Pipeline. Only a short five years before, in August 1969, social and physical scientists had met on the University of Alaska campus for the twentieth Alaska Science Conference to discuss the state's future. Much had happened in those five years, and there had been a great deal of talk about planning for the future and anticipating change. Yet there had been few preparations, and the state government was no more ready for the oil boom than were the several communities about to be affected.

Below-ground sections of the Trans-Alaska Pipeline are buried in trenches 8 to 16 feet deep and compacted with select material before being buried. About half of the pipeline is below the ground. (*Alyeska Pipeline Service Company*)

One of the most strongly affected towns was Valdez. Before the boom it was a small community of about 1,200 residents, located along the shore of the Valdez arm of Prince William Sound, the deep fjord in which the tankers would dock and load Prudhoe Bay oil. The oil would be collected at a tank farm across the bay from the town. Old Valdez had been almost totally destroyed and washed away in Alaska's catastrophic Good Friday earthquake on March 27, 1964. Residents decided to rebuild their town on more stable geological foundations four miles to the west of the old site. The construction of the Trans-Alaska Pipeline terminus across the bay from Valdez brought thousands of new residents to the town, swelling the population to approximately 8,000. Valdez housing, public services, schools, and shopping facilities became totally inadequate. Prices soared, and the shelves at the town's two grocery stores often were all but empty, forcing families to drive 115 miles to Glennallen, a little highway community, or even more than 300 miles to Anchorage to do their shopping. To accommodate the new residents, Valdez began the construction of four trailer courts, new hotel and motel facilities, a new airport terminal building, an $11-million high school, and a United States Coast Guard center to direct the tanker traffic in Prince William Sound.

The Impact of the Boom

Fairbanks, the other community to feel the direct impact of the Trans-Alaska Pipeline, is located in Alaska's interior plateau, in the broad Tanana Valley on the banks of a winding tributary, the Chena River. Alaska's second largest city, with an area population of approximately 64,000 (1976), Fairbanks had its beginnings in the summer of 1901 when Captain E. T. Barnette, heading up the Tanana River with a boatload of trade goods, was sidetracked into the Chena River and decided to make a winter cache near the present site of the town. Stampeders in 1903 and 1904 established the new gold mining community after Felix Pedro made the initial gold discovery in the summer of 1902, twelve miles north of Barnette's trading post on what is now Pedro Creek.

Named after Senator Charles Fairbanks of Indiana, later vice president of the United States under President Theodore Roosevelt, the town became an administrative center in 1903 when the federal judge, James Wickersham, moved his third division court to Fairbanks from Eagle on the Yukon River. This move helped keep the town alive after other gold-mining boom towns had decayed and disappeared. The Fairbanks economy diversified over the years, linked to its role as a service and supply center for interior and arctic industrial activities, military bases, the University of Alaska, government offices, tourism, and, in recent years, construction of the Trans-Alaska Pipeline.

Fairbanks residents had grown cautious after the oil boom of 1969 collapsed. At that time, in anticipation of immediate construction of the Trans-Alaska Pipeline, many local businesses had laid in large inventories and made long-term financial commitments. When the boom did not materialize, there were numerous bankruptcies, and many others underwent drastic financial reorganization. By late summer of 1974, however, Fairbanks was about to experience the oil boom.

The Valdez terminal for
the Trans-Alaska Pipe-
line. It is located on the
ice-free Port of Valdez
across from the city
by the same name, 1976
(*Alyeska Pipeline
Service Company*)

At the end of June 1974 the influx of modern boomers hoping to land a
pipeline job had swelled the population of Fairbanks. There were only twenty-
seven listings under "furnished apartments" in the daily newspaper, with
efficiencies renting for $200 per month and two-bedroom apartments going as
high as $450. Most restaurants had doubled their prices from the fall of 1973; a
cup of soup and a sandwich, for example, at an economical lunch counter cost
$2.25. Everywhere there were lines, and it took fifteen or twenty minutes just
to drive through the ten-block downtown area at rush hour. At certain times of
the day, giant Hercules cargo jet planes roared overhead every ten minutes.

One graphic illustration of the dramatic increase in commerce spurred by
the beginning of construction on the Trans-Alaska Pipeline is the number of
operations at Fairbanks International Airport in 1974 as compared to 1973. In
1973 there were a total of 125,875 landing and take-off operations, of which
60,695 had been logged by the end of June. In 1974 total operations by the end
of June had already reached 77,093, with the heaviest air traffic months still
ahead. Perhaps even more striking is the increase in the number of air taxi

operations and the volume of air cargo handled. Throughout all of 1973, some 24.5 million pounds of freight arrived. Through the end of May 1974, the total volume of landed freight totaled 23.2 million pounds, nearly equal the total volume of 1973. Equally impressive is the number of travelers both originating and terminating in Fairbanks. Through May 1973, 48,592 air travelers had terminated their flight in Fairbanks; 62,322 had arrived in through May of 1974. Likewise, 47,187 air passengers originated their flights in Fairbanks through May 1973; this number sharply increased to 64,655 through May of 1974.[68]

By the summer of 1975, Fairbanks was humming with activity. Money flowed easily, and aggressive hookers populated Second Avenue—dubbed "two street" by the pipeliners—one of the town's main streets. Downtown Fairbanks is architecturally undistinguished, consisting of boxy buildings, many with false fronts, which were constructed more for utility than beauty. Concentrated within two or three blocks of Second Avenue are most of the town's bars,

Double joints of pipe for the northern section of the Trans-Alaska Pipeline were transported on railcars to Fairbanks
(*Alyeska Pipeline Service Company*)

which remain open until 5 a.m. and reopen a few hours later for the early morning drinkers. There are also a few eating establishments, tourist gift shops full of novelties, and the Co-op Drug Store, which offers a large variety of sundry merchandise. It also seems to be the gathering place for many of the town's Eskimos and Athapaskan Indians and their visiting relatives, who may come from such faraway places as Barrow, Point Hope, Fort Yukon, and Allakaket.

For three hectic years Fairbanks experienced all the trauma and excitement of pipeline impact, including increased dollars and debts, increased population and deteriorating public services, increased crime and employment, and increased unemployment. As thousands of workers streamed into the state in quest of high-paying pipeline jobs, the biggest privately financed construction project ever undertaken got underway. On July 27, 1974, Alyeska announced that the first road link south from Prudhoe Bay had been established, and in September of that year the road was officially opened for truck traffic. On March 27, 1975, the first pipe was installed at the Tonsina River.

Construction Boom

By March 1975 the Trans-Alaska Pipeline project, in the preliminary stages until then, was about to launch the main phase of construction all along the 789 miles from Prudhoe Bay to the tanker terminal at Valdez. Alyeska officials hoped to have oil flowing through the line by July 1, 1977. Operating on a tight schedule, Alyeska hoped to have 45 percent of all pipeline work completed at the end of 1975, including the erection of storage tanks and buildings at most pump station sites and the tank and building construction at the Valdez terminal. A total of eighteen oil storage tanks, each having a capacity of 510,000 barrels, were to be built in that particular phase of construction, together with three ballast tanks and several smaller tanks. At the same time, preparations were underway to start offshore work on the pilings at the Valdez terminal. At both Valdez and Fairbanks workers forklifted the forty-foot sections of the 48-inch-diameter pipe, in storage since 1969, from the stacks and cleaned and welded them together into eighty-foot lengths. At other places along the line, crews drilled holes for erecting the 18-inch pipe vertical supports carrying the above-ground sections of the line.[69]

The first construction year ended at the end of April 1975. During that period an estimated fifteen million man-hours had been expended on the effort, and hundreds of thousands of tons of cargo had been shipped north. Furthermore, the first buried and elevated portions of the pipeline were in place about eighty-five miles north of Valdez, and three buried river crossings had been completed. The first installation of pipe and the successful completion of the 360-mile Yukon–Prudhoe Bay highway highlighted the first construction year.[70]

By October 1975 trucks were rolling over the brand new Yukon River bridge connecting with the North Slope haul road. Five piers and two abutments supported the nearly half-mile-long span that had cost $30 million to build. Alyeska assumed one-half of the cost of the bridge, which is owned by

The Sagavanirktok River
crossing of the Trans-
Alaska Pipeline was
carried out at night
about 90 miles south of
Prudhoe Bay
(*Alyeska Pipeline
Service Company*)

the state. The opening of the bridge came just in time: that year's barge fleet of forty-seven vessels, carrying 160,000 tons of oilfield supplies from Puget Sound to Prudhoe Bay, was halted by heavy ice conditions. Only twenty-five of the barges reached their destination. The rest turned back, and most of them offloaded at Seward for shipment by rail north to Fairbanks and then by road to Prudhoe Bay. The bridge was an important link in the transportation chain.[71]

Thousands of workers were battling the climate and the calendar to complete this most costly and controversial of privately financed construction jobs in history. By late 1976 the price tag had escalated from $900 million to $7.7 billion. If nothing were to go wrong, the pipeline was to start up in mid-1977 and carry some 600,000 barrels of oil a day on a 789-mile journey across three mountain ranges, beneath 350 rivers and streams, and through highly active earthquake zones.

Unlike many other construction projects, the Trans-Alaska Pipeline was a cost-plus project in which money was not important at all. At the outset TAPS had no idea of how to build a pipeline in a region where temperatures fluctuated from 60° below zero to 100° above. TAPS was not only going to build a pipeline quickly, but build it exactly as if it were located in Texas. They planned to weld it together, bury it, turn on the taps, and forget it. Vociferous objections from environmentalists and the sharp criticism of federal and state officials eventually forced Alyeska to design and build a line superior to any built before.

The Trans-Alaska Pipeline was also a wasteful project in terms of man-hours and material expended. Whenever there was a question of using more material or using less, invariably more was used. If there was the slightest chance that some machine was needed, it was bought. If management thought it might need additional laborers or craftsmen, they were hired; and pipeline wages were fantastically high—an average of $1,200 per week.

At the height of construction, Fairbanks International Airport hummed with activity. The terminal building and the parking lots were full. Each day the Alaska Airlines Pipeline Express, direct from Houston and Dallas, brought another contingent of "pointy-toes," so called for the cowboy boots many wore. These people were the soldiers of fortune of the oil industry, the professional troubleshooters, drillers, welders, and pipeline layers who have followed their calling from Kuwait to the North Sea, from Africa to Latin America. Motel and hotel rooms in town, if available, cost $50 per night.

Then, as suddenly as the boom had begun, it dropped off. By the summer of 1977 the line had been completed, Alyeska had laid off most of the workers, and the crowds at the airport had thinned considerably. The Fairbanks economy, buoyed by $800,000 a day in wages and purchases during the height of construction, slowed down once again.

Trans-Alaska Pipeline section about to be buried
(*Fairbanks Daily News-Miner*)

Building the Trans-
Alaska Pipeline
(*Fairbanks Daily
News-Miner*)

Oil Flows

At 10:05 a.m. on June 20, 1977, the first oil flowed into the pipeline, nine years after the initial discovery of oil at Prudhoe Bay. After receiving confirmation from the operations control center at Valdez that the pipeline system was ready to receive oil, Alyeska's pump station chief technician directed a station operator to open valves allowing the first barrels of oil to flow into the pipe under producer pressure. Later, a booster pump was activated, bringing crude oil from storage tanks to one of the station's large mainline pumps. Powered by a 13,500-horsepower aircraft-type turbine, the mainline centrifugal pump pushed oil out of the station on its trip to Valdez at an initial rate of 300,000 barrels a day. The only hitch at the beginning of the oil flow was a leak at the flange of a valve at Prudhoe, which was stopped when workers tightened a few bolts.

An above-ground section of the Trans-Alaska Pipeline zigzags south across the North Slope to Pump Station 3 and the Brooks Range mountaintop, above (*Alyeska Pipeline Service Company*)

At the front of the flowing crude oil in the pipeline was a metal device known as a batching pig. Preceding the pig were approximately six million cubic feet of nitrogen gas. The gas purged the line of air, and thus its oxygen, to prevent the danger of an explosion caused by accumulations of crude oil vapor. The pig separated the nitrogen gas from the oil. A wheel attached to the batching pig emitted sounds as it traveled through the pipeline, enabling ground tracking teams to determine precisely where the oil front was located. Personnel equipped with hand-held receivers listened to signals transmitted from a battery-powered radio installed in the pig, checking for leaks, thermal stress, pipe movement, or anything else out of the ordinary.[72]

As the oil started to flow through the pipeline, headline followed headline. First a truck ran into the pipeline and dented it. Since oil had not yet reached that point, workers quickly replaced the damaged section. Then, on June 22, a false earthquake alarm shut down a mainline pump for a brief period. A spokesman for Alyeska explained that the shutdown was triggered by tolerances set too close in the line's earthquake monitoring system. On July 4 a crack in an L-shaped section of the pipe, apparently caused by the accidental injection of nitrogen, again forced the shutdown of the pipeline. Officials halted the oil flow between pipe miles 473 and 474, south of Fairbanks near Pump Station Number Eight.[73]

After the necessary repairs, oil flowed south again until the late afternoon of July 8, when a gigantic explosion destroyed Pump Station Eight, killing one worker and injuring five others.[74] Human error was once again responsible for the mishap. A worker had removed a pump filter and not replaced it before restarting the pump. Oil spraying against hot turbines triggered an explosion that destroyed the pump station. Ten days after the explosion and fire at Pump Station Eight, Alyeska restarted the line, bypassing the destroyed station and bringing Pump Station Nine on line earlier than planned to boost the oil over the mountains.

But the troubles were not over. On July 19 a front end loader damaged the fitting on a check valve about twenty-three miles south of Prudhoe Bay. Some 2,000 barrels of oil flowed onto the tundra before maintenance crews shut down the line for eight hours and repaired the damage. On July 20, the first sabotage attempt ripped a stretch of insulation off the pipeline north of Fairbanks and tore supporting pipe brackets from the line. The line itself was not damaged and the oilflow continued. State troopers soon arrested several individuals, and two men were indicted, tried, and convicted on charges of malicious destruction of property.

The oil finally arrived at the Valdez tanker terminal on July 28, 1977, fulfilling Alyeska's promise three years earlier to deliver oil in Valdez by the first of August. Many Alaskans celebrated the event, particularly Jean Mahoney of Anchorage, who won the Great Alaskan Pipeline Classic lottery of $30,000 for her guess that the oil would reach Valdez in 38 days, 12 hours and 57 minutes, a mere sixty seconds off the actual time. Some 14,000 individuals entered that lottery sponsored by St. Patrick's Catholic Church in Anchorage. The church profited as well.[75]

All went well until February 15, 1978, when a private pilot flying over the line just east of Fairbanks reported seeing a leak. Investigators soon discovered a length of fuse near the site and later concluded that a plastic charge had ripped a hole into the line, spilling 550,000 gallons of oil onto the tundra. Despite intensive efforts, the crime remains unsolved.[76]

But there were bright spots as well. In 1978 oil was flowing through the line at the rate of 1.16 million barrels per day. During the first year of operation 278 million barrels of oil reached Valdez, and with the construction of four additional pump stations along the route and more oil storage and tanker docking facilities at Valdez, the pipeline's capacity can be increased to carry two million barrels per day.

As many expected and feared, however, Alaskan oil has created a glut on the West Coast and necessitated the shipment of some of it through the Panama Canal to the East Coast of the United States; this has resulted in higher

Advertisement
(*Fairbanks Daily News-Miner*)

transportation charges. Since the state of Alaska taxes the sales price of the oil—about $13.50 per barrel—but not the transportation charges, it is generally in the companies' interest to have as high a charge as possible for the use of the pipeline. Before the pipeline opened, the oil industry and the federal government predicted an average wellhead—or state taxable—value of $7.50 per barrel for Prudhoe Bay oil. But when the oil companies began filing their first wellhead prices, they reported a weighted average price of $4.79 per barrel. In April 1978 the average wellhead price per barrel of oil had further declined to $4.39. Even worse, one North Slope producer, Phillips Petroleum Company, shocked state officials with a wellhead price of $1.22 per barrel of oil shipped to the East Coast because of the West Coast surplus.[77]

Understandably, Alaskans and their officials were bitterly disappointed. Robert Le Resche, the state's commissioner of natural resources, most aptly summarized Alaskan disappointments. "Here we are, having endured the negative impacts of construction of the Trans-Alaska Pipeline, and sitting back ready to reap our just rewards, suddenly confronted with a wellhead price far below what anyone ever suggested in the past." In fact, since North Slope oil began flowing through the pipeline in the late summer of 1977, state revenue department officials have been forced to reduce their royalty and severance tax income for the fiscal year 1979 by $308.5 million.

State planners are working on two strategies to stem the erosion of well-head prices. They are seeking federal regulatory decisions to alleviate the West Coast surplus and are fighting court battles over producer-filed pipeline tariffs. Federal responses, however, have been negative on both fronts. One proposal under consideration is an appeal to President Jimmy Carter to allow the shipment of Alaskan crude oil to Japan in exchange for Middle East oil destined for Japan, which would then instead be diverted to the East Coast. If such a decision were made, it would relieve the West Coast surplus and the need for producers to ship Alaskan oil to the Gulf and East Coasts, which results in lower wellhead values.[78]

In the meantime, however, many Alaskans are deeply disillusioned, and some believe that political pressures may develop for a moratorium on oil and gas leasing on millions of acres of state lands. Even more drastic, some state officials predict that the legislature may reduce North Slope production because of "economic waste."

The Future

The pipeline story, however, is far from over, for experts believe that fully a third of the nation's undiscovered recoverable oil and gas may lie under Alaska and on its continental shelf. The Department of the Interior has already sold 409,057 acres of leases in the Gulf of Alaska and is considering 1.6 million acres in the Bering Sea in the near future. Joint federal-state lease sales in the Beaufort Sea are planned for 1979. The government may also open lands to development elsewhere in the state, including Naval Petroleum Reserve No. 4 on the North Slope. The federal government looks to Alaska and its outer continental shelf for the single largest increment of new oil and gas supplies to meet national energy needs in the 1980s and 1990s. Other pipelines will undoubtedly be built.

Alaskans have argued heatedly among themselves and with others whether energy development has been a worthwhile trade-off for the increased economic activity and prosperity. There are those who maintain that the oil boom has irreparably harmed the delicately balanced ecology of the Arctic and has wrought havoc with the independent lifestyle of the state's residents. Those favoring economic growth point to the long-term economic benefits the state will reap, including up to $1 billion in new revenues accruing to the state annually. This contrasts with total state revenues from state sources of about

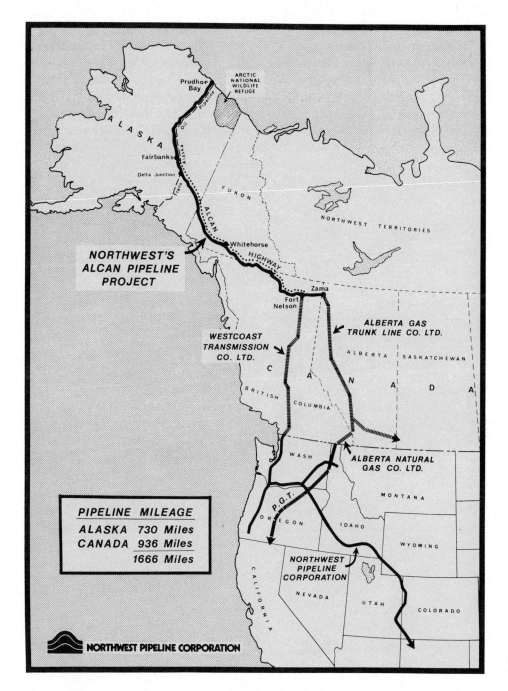

Northwest's Alcan
Pipeline Project
(*Fairbanks Daily
News-Miner*)

$300 million in 1975. In any event, Alaskans themselves have had very little say in the decisions to develop the state's energy resources. The energy crisis of 1973/74, the subsequent price explosion of crude oil, and the national drive toward energy "self-sufficiency" have been the factors that combined to spur Alaskan development.

Oil activities will continue to bring more jobs, money, and people. They will mean additional pipelines, roads, processing and port facilities; and they will put ever greater pressures on the state's land, water, and fish and wildlife resources. Above all, oil development has generated a momentum of its own, and it is largely unaffected by what the state may or may not do. A seasoned observer of Alaska has concluded that the state government, to have any control over the speed of development at all, will have to "rely primarily on policies other than the direct control of petroleum resources—on environmental regulations, tax policies, expenditure programs, and other policy actions that can both mitigate undesirable effects of petroleum development and distribute its benefits more equitably."[79] But perhaps it was an old sourdough who best summed up the momentous changes in Alaska when he said: "They sure have gotta lotta things they never had before, ain't they."[80]

·12·
Looking Back

B ETWEEN approximately 10,000 and 40,000 years ago, Asiatics drifted across the Bering Sea Land Bridge in pursuit of game. They came in small bands, and slowly went as far as the southern tip of North America. The ancestors of today's Indians came first, followed by the progenitors of the Aleuts and Eskimos. For thousands of years, these various groups made Alaska their home. They used the resources of this subcontinent to sustain their lives, and successfully adapted to the varied climates of the North. Then came the white men, who brought modern technology as well as disease. As elsewhere, upon contact with Europeans thousands of Alaskan natives died, most from unfamiliar European maladies.

For more than two centuries since the coming of the white man, Alaska was a remote and neglected province of little concern to either the Russian or, later, the American governments. Russia, very large but sparsely populated, with a poorly developed political and economic system, had little need for new territory. After Peter the Great, who was the energy and vision behind Bering's voyage, its rulers—with the exception of Catherine the Great—were weak and incompetent, and primarily concerned with European affairs. Those Russians who first came to Alaska were private individuals, interested only in the fur trade. With little supervision from the government in St. Petersburg, they reduced the Aleuts, the native people with whom they first came into contact, to virtual slavery. By the end of the century the private traders had been ousted and a government-sponsored monopoly, the Russian-American Company, was given control. By the middle of the nineteenth century, however, the company was in a precarious economic position, subsisting on government favors and subsidies. Because Russian leaders believed that the country could not both defend Alaska and carry out an imperialistic policy in Asia, they sold Alaska to the United States for $7,200,000 in 1867.

Russian influence in Alaska was slight. The few Russians who came limited their stay to the islands and coastal areas, leaving the vast interior almost untouched. Even the Panhandle region, south of what is today Juneau, was leased to the Hudson's Bay Company. Baranov, the outstanding personality of

United States Revenue
Cutter *Bear*, ca. 1900
(*Historical Photograph
Collection, Archives,
University of Alaska, Fairbanks*)

Russian America who came in 1790, was probably more affected by the ways of
the natives than they by the civilization of the Russians. His successors as
governors of Alaska were naval men, who were better educated and among
whom were some explorers of note. They attempted to increase Russian influence among the natives by establishing schools, improving their conditions of
livelihood, and furthering the efforts of the Church to bring Christianity.
Father Ioann Veniaminov, a cleric of the Orthodox Church, devised an alphabet
and gave the Aleuts a written language. The Russians did introduce the natives
to the ways of the white man, and undoubtedly eased the contacts with them
for the Americans. And they did develop Sitka—while by no means a metropolitan center—into the Pacific Coast's largest town for a time. But aside
from a few Russian Orthodox churches and Russian names among the native

population, little remains of the Russian presence in Alaska today.

American rule brought little change to Alaska. The United States in 1867 was not much better prepared than Russia to govern Alaska. The Civil War had just ended; problems of the defeated South were foremost in the nation's mind, while those of Alaska held little interest. With no precedent to guide them in the administration of noncontiguous territories, Congress took the easiest course and turned Alaska over to the military. For the next seventeen years the territory was under the rule of the army and, subsequently, the navy. But even if the quality of American statesmanship had been greater and more thought been given to Alaska, there was little incentive for Americans to trek north.

In an era when the United States was undergoing great industrial expansion, those with money to invest found ample opportunities at home without incurring the risks entailed in a distant land. Employment in the factories was high, and for those wishing to move, land was to be had almost for the asking in the sparsely settled West. When the Russian-American Company left Alaska, the population declined. Most Russians and those persons of mixed blood who had been given the option—under the Treaty of Purchase—to remain in Alaska either returned to their homeland or went to Canada or other parts of the United States where they felt their prospects were much better. A few Americans rushed to preempt land in Sitka, but they soon departed when the hoped-for boom failed to materialize.

Accounts differ concerning the Alaskan natives' preference of the Russians or the Americans. Some altercations between soldiers and the aboriginal population took place, but no great wars such as occurred in the American West ever developed in Alaska.

Alaska's great size, remoteness, and formidable climate seemed to discourage small businesses and favor those possessing large capital. One thriving organization, the Alaska Commercial Company, which apparently had some political influence, was given the monopoly of the seal harvest of the Pribilof Islands. Under the auspices of this company, the Yukon Valley was also opened up for the fur trade. The exploitation of the valuable salmon fisheries began but with virtually no benefit to Alaska or Alaskans. Needed capital for the industry was provided by large packing firms from the outside, who paid few taxes and brought in not only the fishermen but the crews to work in the canneries.

The Gold Rushes

In the 1880s, Alaska was already becoming something of a tourist attraction. The trip to Alaska was long and expensive, however, and tourists did not come in great numbers. It was the lure of gold that began drawing Americans to Alaska. Discoveries of gold in the area of the Gastineau Channel led to the founding of Juneau, the first town established under American rule. Gold was also found on the American side of the Yukon at Fortymile and then Birch Creek. But far more important were the great discoveries on the Canadian side of the great river near the banks of its tributary, the Klondike. Alaska benefitted greatly. Skagway, a port on Lynn Canal, became the gateway to the Klondike, while the Canadian boom stimulated the search for the precious

Charter members of Yukon Order of Pioneers. Standing: Gordon Bettles, Pete McDonald, Jim Bender, Frank Buteau, G. Matlock, Al Mayo, Pete Nelson, Tom Lloyd, Bill Stewart. Sitting: H. H. Hart, Wm. McPhee, (unknown), Jack McQuesten, G. Harrington, (unknown), H. Albert. Center: (unknown) (*Historical Photograph Collection, Archives, University of Alaska, Fairbanks*)

metal in Alaska. Nome, where twenty thousand men worked at one time on its "golden sands," was the scene of Alaska's greatest gold rush, followed by Fairbanks and a host of others, including Iditarod, Chandalar, and Livengood.

The gold rush marked a new discovery of Alaska. Alaska was hailed as Eldorado. Businessmen looked to it as a place for investment. Several government agencies began work in Alaska. A start was made in road building and the surveying of the territory. The people of Alaska for the first time were given political rights of self-government, limited as they were. Towns were permitted to incorporate and elect their own officials. Alaskans were authorized to send a delegate to Congress in 1906. Six years later, Congress granted a legislature to the territory, although it retained for the federal government control over Alaska's land and resources.

By 1910 the main effects of the gold rush had been achieved. The population of Alaska was stabilized at about 60,000, dropping a little during World War I and increasing slightly to a high of 72,000 just before the United States entered World War II. After that war population growth accelerated greatly. For a time the value of the copper mined exceeded that of gold, but minerals began to take second place in Alaska to the fisheries. The number of Alaska fishermen increased, but the control of the resource still remained outside Alaska.

The First Half of the Twentieth Century

Numerous generalizations have been made about the people of Alaska. The population was highly transient, and men outnumbered women five to

Circle City on the
Yukon, 1895
(*Charles Bunnell
Collection, Archives,
University of Alaska, Fairbanks*)

one. Few brought their families with them, and it was said that when they
made their "pile," home they would go. But there were those who loved the
"Great Land," as they called it; and many wrote lovingly about it. Henry W.
Elliott pleaded for the conservation of the seals and for the protection of the
Alaska natives. William Healy Dall was excited by the wealth of its resources
waiting to be developed. John Muir was entranced by Alaska's great beauty.
Sheldon Jackson saw it as a place for the saving of souls, and warned that the
natives be protected from the corruption of the whites.

Alaskans, like residents in other territories, constantly complained that
their interests were being neglected and ignored. But, while neither Congress
nor successive administrations ever made Alaskan affairs an item of priority,
several presidents did give them some attention. Early in the twentieth century, a determined effort was made to keep Canadians from poaching for seals
bound for Alaska in the Bering Sea. Theodore Roosevelt was most adamant in
countering Canadian claims for part of the Alaskan Panhandle, and he closed
the Alaskan coal fields to further entry because he claimed the existing laws
concerning coal mining in the territory were "defective." However, some
Alaskans were highly critical of this action.

Woodrow Wilson, in his first presidential message, demanded that attention be given to Alaska's needs; and Congress, prompted by his urgings, passed
laws allowing the leasing of the coal lands, authorized the building of a railroad
at government expense, but failed to make changes in the Alaskan system of
government which the president felt were most essential. Warren G. Harding,
the first president to visit Alaska, promised much; but the only important piece
of legislation coming from his corruption-ridden and ineffective administration
concerned the Alaska fisheries, a law signed by his successor, Calvin Coolidge.

For the first and only time in the American period, an attempt was made during the New Deal era of Franklin D. Roosevelt to bring people to Alaska for settlement in the Matanuska Valley.

World War II revolutionized Alaska. The territory's strategic location made it a key factor in America's defense program. As thousands of troops were rushed north, navy and army bases were constructed in locations ranging from Unalaska to Kodiak, and from Sitka to Anchorage and Fairbanks. Finally, during the summer of 1942, Japanese forces invaded the Aleutian Chain. America's pride was hurt, and it began intense efforts to oust the enemy. In the spring of 1942 work also began on the Alaska-Canada Military Highway, the Alcan, to link the territory with the continental United States. The 1,671-mile highway was completed with almost incredible speed and opened for military traffic in November of that same year.

By the fall of 1943 the enemy had been expelled from Alaska. Ground forces were reduced from a high of 150,000 men in November 1943 to 50,000 by March 1945. Forts were closed, bases dismantled, and military airfields turned over to the Civil Aeronautics Administration.

The impact of the military activities irrevocably altered the pace and tenor of Alaskan life. The residual benefits to the civilian economy and the development of Alaska were tremendous. In addition to the influx of well over one billion dollars in the territory between 1941 and 1945, Alaskans also benefitted from the modernization of the Alaska Railroad and the expansion of airfields and the construction of roads.

Federal activity declined sharply after 1945, but it was the outbreak of the

Clear Air Force Ballistic Missile Early Warning site
(*U.S. Army Corps of Engineers*)

Cold War in the late 1940s that once again caused the federal government to spend millions of dollars in defense-related activities. Federal projects became the primary source of the Alaskan economy. Within two decades the population of Alaska more than tripled. Anchorage and Fairbanks—especially the former—became the new centers of population. Political demands of the "new" Alaska led to the achievement of statehood in 1958.

Statehood, Oil, and Native Claims

Although the new state stepped boldly into the new era, its finances and budgets soon became major concerns. Alaskans quickly realized that it was very expensive to provide the amenities of modern life to such a sprawling subcontinent. In addition, military expenditures declined in the 1960s. Modest oil discoveries on the Kenai Peninsula in the late 1950s, a growing forest industry, and developments in the fisheries made up for some of the losses in federal spending. But not until the massive Prudhoe Bay oil discovery in 1968 was there reason to believe that Alaska's economy would become more stable.

Alaska Oil & Gas Development Co. Eureka No. 1
(*Fred Machetanz Collection, Archives, University of Alaska, Fairbanks*)

The 1970s witnessed the passage of the Alaska Native Claims Settlement Act, which compensated the state's original inhabitants for losses suffered over many years. With land and money, native Alaskans rapidly became very influential in state politics and business. At the same time, the construction of the Trans-Alaska Pipeline brought a measure of prosperity—and some problems—to the state. Since oil began to flow in the summer of 1977, the state treasury, and with it all Alaskans, has gained some financial stability and security. Americans have continued to flock to the North, settling mostly in the Anchorage area. Alaska's population as of 1978 was estimated at 410,000.

The state also has become a battleground between those who favor the rapid economic development of the state and those who advocate that large areas be set aside in national parks, wild and scenic rivers, wildlife refuges, and national monuments. Congress had until the end of 1978 to make a decision that would strongly affect this conflict. Alaska's sizable natural resources, both renewable and nonrenewable, will undoubtedly be developed and used as national need dictates. And despite many complaints of Alaska's residents, decisions affecting the rate of its development will largely be made on a national and even international level.

·13·
The Sources of Alaska's History

THE SOURCES of Alaska's history are rich and varied. Anthropologists and archaeologists have long been fascinated with the native cultures of Alaska, and bookshelves are heavy with the many studies produced over the years. An excellent early account of the riverine Eskimos of the Yukon and Kuskokwim rivers was written by the Russian Zagoskin in *Lieutenant Zagoskin's Travels in Russian America, 1842–44*, edited and translated from the Russian and published in 1967. Wendell H. Oswalt has ably summarized the state of knowledge about Eskimos in his *Alaskan Eskimos* (1967), and Richard K. Nelson offers a fascinating account of Eskimo hunting methods in *Hunters of the Northern Ice* (1969). Hans-Georg Bandi discusses the various theories dealing with the origin of the Eskimos and the sites, artifacts, and prehistoric cultures in the Eskimo area, extending from Alaska across Canada to Greenland, in *Eskimo Prehistory* (1969).

A standard introduction to the Northwest Coast Indians is Philip Drucker's *Indians of the Northwest Coast* (1963). James Van Stone has summarized existing knowledge about the Athapaskans in *Athapaskan Adaptations* (1974), and Margaret Lantis has done the same for the Aleuts in "The Aleut Social System, 1750 to 1810, from Early Historical Sources," *Ethnohistory in Southwestern Alaska and the Southern Yukon: Method and Content* (1970). Still another study that evaluates most aspects of historical and contemporary native life is the magnificent volume entitled *Alaska Natives and the Land* (1969), written by the Federal Field Committee for Development Planning in Alaska.

Few scholars have dealt with Alaska's Russian period. The few who have, however, have produced some excellent work. Frank Golder's *Russian Expansion to the Pacific, 1641–1850* was reprinted in 1960. Hector Chevigny's *Lord of Alaska* (1942) is a fast-paced account of the colorful and hard-driving Aleksandr Baranov, the third manager and first governor of the Russian-American Company. S. B. Okun, a Soviet scholar, in his *The Russian-American Com-*

pany (1951), furnishes a Marxist interpretation of the formation and activities of that organization.

Recently, Professor Richard A. Pierce of Queens University in Kingston, Ontario, Canada, began a series of translations entitled *Materials for the Study of Alaska History*, published by the Limestone Press (Box 1604, Kingston, Ontario, Canada K7L 508). In this series is V. N. Berkh's *A Chronological History of the Discovery of the Aleutian Islands* (1974), a classic first published in St. Petersburg in 1823. Berkh visited Russian America during the colonial period and talked to veteran seafarers, hunters, and merchants. His account acquainted the public of his day with the exploration and early commercial exploitation of the Aleutian Islands. In this series also is K. T. Khlebnikov's biography of Aleksandr Baranov, entitled *Baranov* (1973). Khlebnikov joined the Russian-American Company as an employee in 1800 and served his first seventeen years in Siberia. Arriving in Sitka in 1817, he helped the retiring Baranov wind up his affairs. For the next sixteen years Khlebnikov served under Baranov's successors. He retired to Russia in 1833, but his connections with the company continued until his death in 1838. A prolific writer, his biography of Baranov—though sketchy in places—provides an essential source for later scholarship. Two modern works by Soviet historians in the Limestone series are Raisa V. Makarova, *Russians on the Pacific, 1743–1799* (1975), first published in Moscow in 1968; and Svetlana G. Fedorova, *The Russian Population in Alaska and California: Late 18th Century–1867* (1973), first published in Moscow in 1971. The former volume supplements V. N. Berkh; Dr. Makarova has used extensive secondary works as well as much new archival material. Dr. Fedorova's work represents the most thorough study to date of Russian activity in this region.

One of the earliest works in English on the Russian activities in North America was that of a young British clergyman, William Coxe, who toured Russia and in 1780 published his *Account of the Russian Discoveries between Asia and America,* reprinted in 1970. Coxe describes the movement of the Russian fur hunters along the Aleutian Islands which commenced during the 1740s. After the publication of Coxe's work, the various explorers who were sent to investigate the Russian efforts wrote accounts of their own. There are the volumes by the famous British explorer Captain J. Cook and his colleagues, G. A. Vancouver, W. R. Broughton, G. Dixon, N. Portlock, and J. Meares.

The members of the Western Union Telegraph expedition, 1865–1867, published some accounts of their labors, among them Frederick Whymper, an English artist, whose *Travel and Adventure in the Territory of Alaska, formerly Russian America—Now Ceded to the United States—and in Various Other Parts of the North Pacific* first appeared in London in 1868. Still an indispensable volume for the Russian as well as early American period is Hubert Howe Bancroft's *History of Alaska, 1730–1885* (1886), reprinted by Arno Press. A wide variety of government publications and documents on the American period fill libraries and archives. They include reports on hearings before various congressional committees and also specific research studies. In short, Alaska has been discussed, debated, agonized over, and studied for a long time.

Congressional hearings have served as a means of investigating conditions in Alaska and provide the forum in which interested groups and individuals were heard. What to do with Alaska's coal lands, as well as questions concerning oil and gas leases on public lands, prompted hearings in 1910, 1912 (two volumes), 1913, 1915, and 1917 (three volumes). The subject of fisheries—their exploitation, conservation, and need for regulation—fills many volumes. Between 1906 and the 1950s and on, hearings on this concern alone filled thousands of pages. Between 1947 and 1956, hearings on Alaska statehood were conducted on seven different occasions in Washington and three times in Alaska. The printed record of these investigations amounted to approximately 4,000 pages. The list could go on, and although congressional concern over Alaska's natural resources has exceeded its interest in health, education, and various other social problems, the latter have also attracted attention.

Hearings provide insights into the views of witnesses and committee members and often expose conflicts between Alaskans and the federal government, between different interest groups, and between competing federal agencies. This is particularly true today, when several federal agencies struggle over the control of land in the wake of the Alaska Native Claims Settlement Act of 1971 and the subsequent need to classify eighty million acres for primary and secondary uses.

The voluminous draft environmental statements concerning the use of these eighty million acres furnish an excellent example. The U.S. Forest Service proposes to put most of the area into national forests; the Bureau of Outdoor Recreation wants to include most areas in the national wild and scenic rivers system; and the National Park Service has expansive plans for numerous national wilderness parks as well as national wildlands. Environmental statements and studies fill whole shelves and are produced by federal, state, and local government bodies, native groups, and private industry. These reports reflect Alaska's growing economic development in the wake of oil discoveries and state and native land selection. These studies employ a small army of consulting firms, university research institutes, environmentalists, planners, anthropologists and archaeologists, engineers, scientists, draftsmen, and writers. And since the history of a region is related to its environment, these bulky studies offer at least sketchy historical assessments. The impact statements also must evaluate the environmental changes that any particular development will produce and offer alternative methods of reducing environmental disruption. The statements are to inform the public and enable governments to act wisely.

The final six-volume environmental impact statement on the then-proposed Trans-Alaska Pipeline furnishes a good example of this fast-accumulating type of study. Prepared by a special interagency task force for the Federal Task Force on Alaskan Oil Development under the auspices of the United States Department of the Interior, it was published in 1972.

The Department of the Interior had received an application from the Alyeska Pipeline Service Company for a 48-inch-wide pipeline right-of-way across federal lands in Alaska between a point south of Prudhoe Bay on the North Slope and the port of Valdez on Prince William Sound. The company intended to design, construct, operate, and maintain the 789-mile pipeline system. Environmental impact would result from such a project, including construction of the accompanying haul road and a gas transportation system of some kind, and from oilfield development and operation of the proposed tanker system. The scale and nature of the project made it inevitable that the project would have an impact on the abiotic, biotic, and socioeconomic components of the human environment far beyond the 940 square miles of Alaska's 572,000 square miles of land area that would be occupied by the pipeline system and oilfield.

The impact could be viewed as beneficial or adverse, depending on the value framework used. Some effects would be unavoidable and could be evaluated with some certainty; others, such as a break in the pipeline or a tanker collision, could not be evaluated with as much certainty.

The principal unavoidable effects associated with the construction, operation, and maintenance of oil production facilities included the disturbance of the terrain—both the fish and wildlife habitat—and the human environment; the discharge of waste materials from the tanker ballast treatment facility into Prince William Sound and of an indeterminable amount of oil into the ocean from tank-cleaning operations at sea; and increased human pressures of all kinds on the environment. Other unavoidable effects would include increased state and native corporation revenues and accelerated cultural change among the native population.

The task force considered alternative routes and transportation systems such as:

1) pipelines from Prudhoe Bay to other ice-free ports in southern Alaska: Redoubt Bay, Whittier, Seward, and Haines;
2) marine transportation systems, including ice-breaking tankers and subsurface tankers;
3) pipelines to terminal ports on the Bering Sea, offshore and overland;
4) trans-Alaska–Canada pipelines such as coastal offshore and onshore routes to the Mackenzie River delta and up the valley to Edmonton; in the Brooks Range to Fort McPherson and up the Mackenzie Valley to Edmonton; and across the central Brooks Range, incorporating a part of the proposed route, to Fairbanks, Big Delta, and east along the Alaska Highway and other corridors to Edmonton;
5) railroads and highways, such as an Alaska Railroad extension from Prudhoe Bay to a southern Alaska port and a new trans-Alaska–Canada railroad route and highway system development;
6) other oil transportation schemes by land, sea, and air.

The task force also considered energy and policy alternatives such as:

1) reduction in demand;
2) increased oil imports;
3) additional production from the Outer Continental Shelf and onshore area;
4) modification of natural gas pricing;
5) nuclear stimulation of natural gas reservoirs;
6) increased use of coal as solid fuel and as a source of synthetic fuels;

7) nuclear power;

8) synthetic sources such as oil shale, tar sands, and coal;

9) geothermal power and hydroelectric power;

10) exotic energy sources and improved efficiency systems.

There were other studies, hearings, and comments, among them two volumes of "Hearings on Proposed Pipeline Legislation, March 6–10, 1972, State of Alaska" and "Comments on the Proposed Trans-Alaska Pipeline" (1971), prepared under the direction of the Alaska Department of Law.

Initially there were two serious contenders, El Paso Gas and Arctic Gas, competing over the right to bring North Slope gas to the energy-starved continental United States. El Paso proposed to run a gas pipeline along the 800-mile oil pipeline to Valdez, liquefy it there, and ship it via refrigerated tankers to Puget Sound and California. Arctic Gas proposed the construction of a gas pipeline through the Arctic Wildlife Range and up Canada's Mackenzie River Valley to the American Midwest. Both companies filed impact statements totaling thousands of pages.

But in a surprise move in the autumn of 1977, Congress awarded Northwest Pipeline Company the right to carry Prudhoe Bay gas through a 5,000-mile pipeline extending from Alaska's North Slope across Canada, with branches to San Francisco and Chicago. It was a political victory for the Salt Lake City-based Northwest Pipeline Company, and executives of the company had reasons to be satisfied, because environmentalists were not expected to protest as they had over the oil pipeline and the routes proposed by the two competing gas firms. Furthermore, construction of the gas line would seem to be simpler than that of the recently completed Trans-Alaska Pipeline. But there are troubles in store; they range from financing the estimated $12 billion needed for the project to the uncertainties about pricing for the expected twenty-six billion cubic feet of gas each year. It may well be that Northwest Pipeline Company will find itself unable to build the pipeline. In that event the scramble over who gets the route would be wide open once again.[1]

The federal government has commissioned scientific studies of Alaska since 1867, the year of the purchase, when the Smithsonian Institution sponsored William Healy Dall's work. Since that time a vast amount of such scientific work has accumulated and represents a valuable source of information for the historian.

Other governmental sources of historical interest include the innumerable annual and special reports and studies by federal executive departments operating in Alaska. It is a long list and a few examples must suffice, such as the national census in which Alaska was included in 1880 for the first time, U.S. Geological Survey bulletins and professional papers, commercial statistics, and weather reports. What is clear is that much of the material is related to the development of some natural resource.

Obviously, there is an abundance of material for political and economic historians; but there are other sources as well. The personal narrative literature about the North is rich and varied. Explorers, missionaries, traders, trappers,

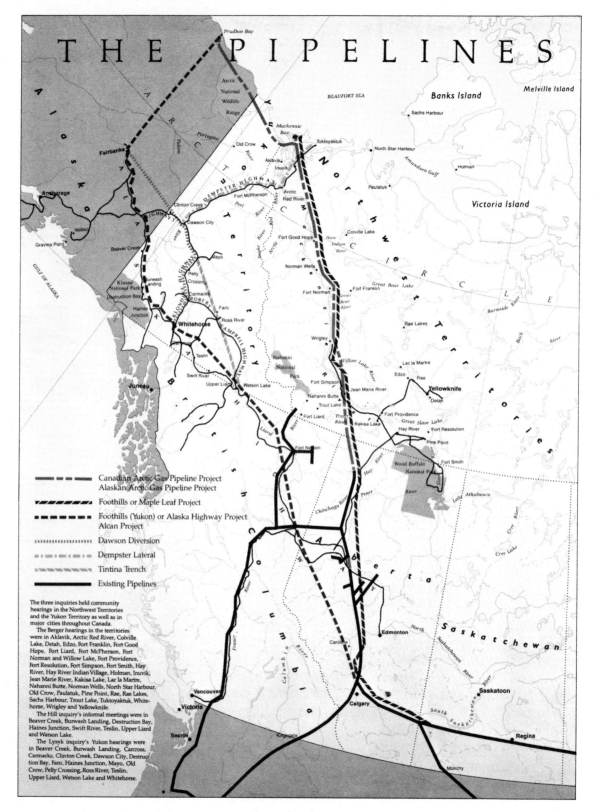

THE PIPELINES

Melville Island

BEAUFORT SEA
Banks Island

Prudhoe Bay

Arctic
National
Wildlife
Range

Sachs Harbour

Victoria Island

Mackenzie
Bay

Tuktoyaktuk

North Star Harbour

Amundsen Gulf

Holman

Old Crow

Aklavik

Inuvik

Paulatuk

Fairbanks

Fort McPherson

Arctic
Red River

Clinton Creek

Dawson City

Fort Good Hope

Colville Lake

Anchorage

Mayo

Norman Wells

Fort Franklin

Great Bear Lake

Burnside River

Valdez

Pelly
Crossing

Fort Norman

Great
Bear
River

Gravina Point

Beaver Creek

Kluane
National Park

Carmacks

Faro

Rae Lakes

Destruction Bay

Ross River

Wrigley

Lac la Martre

Haines
Junction

Whitehorse

Edzo
Rae

Yellowknife

Teslin

Nahanni
National
Park

Willow Lake

Detah

Swift River

Fort Simpson

Jean Marie River

Juneau

Upper Liard

Watson Lake

Nahanni Butte

Trout Lake

Fort Providence

Fort Liard

Kakisa Lake

Great Slave Lake

Hay River

Fort Resolution

Fort Nelson

Pine Point

Fort Smith

Wood Buffalo
National Park

Chinchaga River

Lake Athabasca

Cree River

Cree Lake

--- Canadian Arctic Gas Pipeline Project
     Alaskan Arctic Gas Pipeline Project

--- Foothills or Maple Leaf Project

--- Foothills (Yukon) or Alaska Highway Project
     Alcan Project

····· Dawson Diversion

--- Dempster Lateral

--- Tintina Trench

--- Existing Pipelines

The three inquiries held community
hearings in the Northwest Territories
and the Yukon Territory as well as in
major cities throughout Canada.
   The Berger hearings in the territories
were in Aklavik, Arctic Red River, Colville
Lake, Detah, Edzo, Fort Franklin, Fort Good
Hope, Fort Liard, Fort McPherson, Fort
Norman and Willow Lake, Fort Providence,
Fort Resolution, Fort Simpson, Fort Smith, Hay
River, Hay River Indian Village, Holman, Inuvik,
Jean Marie River, Kakisa Lake, Lac la Martre,
Nahanni Butte, Norman Wells, North Star Harbour,
Old Crow, Paulatuk, Pine Point, Rae, Rae Lakes,
Sachs Harbour, Trout Lake, Tuktoyaktuk, White-
horse, Wrigley and Yellowknife.
   The Hill inquiry's informal meetings were in
Beaver Creek, Burwash Landing, Destruction Bay,
Haines Junction, Swift River, Teslin, Upper Liard
and Watson Lake.
   The Lysyk inquiry's Yukon hearings were
in Beaver Creek, Burwash Landing, Carcross,
Carmacks, Clinton Creek, Dawson City, Destruc-
tion Bay, Faro, Haines Junction, Mayo, Old
Crow, Pelly Crossing, Ross River, Teslin,
Upper Liard, Watson Lake and Whitehorse.

Edmonton

Saskatchewan

Caroline

Vancouver

Victoria

Calgary

Saskatoon

Seattle

Regina

Kingsgate

Monchy

(from Canada Today, 1975)

miners, tourists, and others have felt compelled to describe their experiences. The men and women who rushed north during the gold rushes probably produced a disproportionate share of these narratives, partly because the world at large was fascinated by the northern gold rushes and because adventurous accounts were well received, especially those that promised quick and easy riches.

Since the Klondike in Canada's Yukon Territory drew the largest number of argonauts, many narratives deal with that spectacular strike; but numerous miners also went on to other stampedes in Alaska. One of the best accounts by a journalist and sharp observer is Tappan Adney's *The Klondike Stampede of 1897–98* (1900). Those who participated in the gold rush as teamsters or miners, rather than observers and recorders, gave their narratives a distinctive flavor. A good example of such a book is Arthur T. Walden's *A Dog Puncher on the Yukon* (1928), which fully expresses the excitement and adventure the participants felt.

Many authors, however, exaggerated, boasted, and even told outright lies. This may have been due to forgetfulness or to promptings from ghost writers who wanted to spice up the tale. Edward C. Trelawny-Ansell's *I Followed Gold* (1939) abounds with exaggerated descriptions of actual events at St. Michael, Skagway, and Nome and impossible sled journeys. A colorful fantasy attributed to Jan Welzl, *Thirty Years in the Golden North* (1932), even became a best-seller.

Basil Austin, a stampeder, kept a diary which fully conveys the joys and hardships the stampeders experienced. Published in 1968, it is entitled *The Diary of a Ninety-Eighter*. Herbert L. Heller gathered firsthand accounts of life in Alaska and the Klondike from the men who participated in these events in *Sourdough Sagas: Pioneering and Gold in Alaska, 1883–1923* (1967).

Histories about the gold rushes abound. Pierre Berton, a Canadian, has written the best book about the Klondike, entitled *The Klondike Fever* (1958). As the son of a stampeder, Berton spent his childhood in Dawson. His lively prose and description of individual lives make this a wonderful book. William R. Hunt's *North of 53°: The Wild Days of the Alaska-Yukon Mining Frontier 1870–1914* (1974) is an exciting account of many of the Alaskan gold rushes. Like Berton, Hunt traces the careers of many of the argonauts and paints a colorful picture of their lives against the backdrop of the Klondike, Nome, Fairbanks, the Chandalar, and other locations.

Travel writers have scribbled away for years in their attempts to portray Alaska. The results have been as varied as the people who steamed up the Inland Passage or to St. Michael and up the Yukon River. Many trivia and tall tales have filled notebooks, and Alaskans reading the results have often been pained by the exaggerations and outright falsehoods. It must be remembered, however, that it is a difficult task to encounter the vastness and variety of Alaska and describe it accurately. Yet, some have managed to do so beautifully. T. A. Rickard, a geologist, mining engineer, and editor, visited Alaska's important mining areas in the summer of 1908. His description of Alaska miners and their difficulties in *Through the Yukon and Alaska* (1909) is sympathetic and perceptive; he understood the appeal the country had for the men who wrestled a living from its soil. The charm of the land lay in its vastness, its freedom from restraints, and its uncomplicated life. Judge James Wickersham, Alaska's political giant during the first three decades of the twentieth century and its third delegate to Congress on and off during that period, recorded his impressions in his *Old Yukon: Tales—Trails—and Trials* (1938). The Reverend Hudson Stuck contributed his *Voyages on the Yukon and its Tributaries* (1917), which gives a good picture of travel and life along this great river.

Another good source is the old gold-town newspapers and the back files of a few journals edited by men and women who knew the North and tolerated no nonsense. Among these are *The Alaska Sportsman,* first published in 1935, and *Alaska Weekly.*

There is not much solid historical literature on the North. The explanation, perhaps, lies in the fact that the United States, unlike Canada, is not a northern nation and has not been able to deal adequately with its subarctic possession. There is no lack of research materials or of fresh topics. The National Archives and state and other depositories contain tons of materials concerning important topics, which have been treated very lightly, if at all. There have been no comparisons with other frontiers, and few political biographies. Recently there has been a biography of Judge James Wickersham. Economic, military, administrative, and maritime history have been neglected, to name but a few.

Jeannette Paddock Nichols' *Alaska* (1923) carefully focuses on the first fifty years of American rule. Stuart Ramsay Tompkins' *Alaska: Promyshlennik and Sourdough* (1945) filled a need as a general history. Ernest Gruening's *State of Alaska* (1954) analyzes federal-territorial relationships, and his autobiography, *Many Battles* (1973), deals, among many other events in a rich and crowded life, with his governorship of Alaska between the crucial years 1939 and 1953. Official efforts to map Alaska are ably detailed in Morgan Sherwood's *Army Exploration in Alaska* (1965). Brian Garfield well described the only military campaign fought on American soil during World War II, that in the Aleutian Islands, in *The Thousand Mile War* (1969).

In this decade Ted C. Hinckley has written a lively account entitled *The Americanization of Alaska, 1867–1897* (1973). Orlando Miller has dealt with the Alaskan frontier experience and agriculture in his *The Frontier in Alaska and the Matanuska Colony* (1975). Claus-M. Naske has analyzed and recounted Alaska's struggle for self-determination in *An Interpretative History of Alaskan Statehood* (1973).

There is much more. Let it suffice to state that the oil discoveries have once again moved Alaska into the American consciousness, just as the gold discoveries did in the late nineteenth and early twentieth centuries. Once again national magazines pay attention to the North, and one may expect that national needs for raw materials will keep Alaska at center stage for years to come. Historians also will take note, and when they have waded through the necessary sources, they must interpret their material. If they do their job well, they will discard the persistent romantic notions about Alaska which historian Jeannette P. Nichols has recognized as a barrier in making use of the historical

Anchorage skyline
(*Anchorage Daily News*)

experience as a guide to solve present problems. But not only is history a potentially practical tool in solving problems; it also can, and should, entertain and instruct all of us in numerous ways. Perhaps in the years ahead history will also be used as a basis for fictional creations. Jack London and Rex Beach focused on the gold-rush era. Edna Ferber dealt with present-day Alaska. The material exists, and Alaska's spectacular scenery and varied cultures undoubtedly will challenge writers in the future. On the other hand, it may just be that Americans will respond to Alaska solely in economic terms—as a supplier of needed resources—as they have in the past. Or perhaps they will see Alaska only as a military bastion or respond only to spectacular events as in the past: gold rushes, foreign invasions, or construction of history's largest project, the 789-mile oil pipeline. Only the future will tell.

Notes

Chapter 1

1. Alfred H.Brooks, *The Geography and Geology of Alaska*, U.S. Geological Survey Professional Paper No. 45 (Washington, D.C.: Government Printing Office, 1906), p. 11.
2. Bernard R. Hubbard, S.J., *Mush, You Malemutes* (New York: The American Press, 1943), pp. 70–71.
3. Arthur Grantz et al., *Alaska's Good Friday Earthquake, March 27, 1964*, Geological Survey Circular 491 (Washington, D.C.: U.S. Department of the Interior, 1964), p. 1; Edwin B. Eckel, *The Alaska Earthquake March 27, 1964: Lessons and Conclusions*, Geological Survey Professional Paper 546 (Washington, D.C.: U.S. Government Printing Office, 1970), p. 1.
4. T. Neil Davis and Carol Echols, *A Table of Alaskan Earthquakes, 1788–1961*, Geophysical Research Report No. 8 (College, Alaska: University of Alaska, 1962).
5. Based on information supplied by Dr. Don Triplehorn of the Geology Department of the University of Alaska at Fairbanks and on Clyde Wahrhaftig, *Physiographic Divisions of Alaska*, U.S. Geological Survey Professional Paper 482 (Washington, D.C.: U.S. Government Printing Office, 1965).
6. *Fairbanks Daily News-Miner*, October 11, 1975; *Anchorage Daily News*, October 10, 1975; H. Glenn Richards, "Tectonic Evolution of Alaska," *The American Association of Petroleum Geologists Bulletin*, January 1974, pp. 79–105.
7. Michael Churkin, Jr., *Paleozoic and Precambrian Rocks of Alaska and Their Role in its Structural Evolution*, U.S. Geological Survey Professional Paper 740 (Washington, D.C.: U.S. Government Printing Office, 1973).
8. J. E. Ransom, "Derivation of the Word Alaska," *American Anthropology*, July 1940, p. 551.
9. A. L. Seeman, "Regions and Resources of Alaska," *Economic Geography*, October 1937, p. 334.
10. The discussion of Alaska's geography and climate has been based on U.S. Department of the Interior, Bureau of Reclamation, *Alaska: Reconnaissance Report on the Potential Development of Water Resources in the Territory of Alaska*; House Document 197, 82nd Cong., 1st sess., 1952; U.S. Department of the Interior, Office of Territories, *Mid-Century Alaska* (Washington, D.C.: Government Printing Office, 1958); and National Resources Committee, *Alaska—Its Resources and Development* (Washington, D.C.: Government Printing Office, 1938).
11. Helge Ingstad, *Westward to Finland* (New York: St. Martin's Press, 1969).
12. T. D. Stewart, *The People of America* (New York: Charles Scribner's Sons, 1973), pp. 51–55.
13. Philip Drucker, *Indians of the Northwest Coast* (Garden City, N.Y.: The Natural History Press, 1963), pp. 1–176.

14. James Van Stone, *Athapaskan Adaptations* (Chicago: Aldine Publishing Company, 1974), pp. 1–89.
15. Waldemar Jochelson, "People of the Foggy Seas," *Natural History*, IV (1928), 413.
16. Federal Field Committee for Development Planning in Alaska, *Alaska Natives and the Land* (Washington, D.C.: Government Printing Office, 1968), p. 238.
17. Margaret Lantis, "The Aleut Social System, 1750 to 1810, from Early Historical Sources," in *Ethnohistory in Southwestern Alaska and the Southern Yukon: Method and Content*, ed. Margaret Lantis (Lexington, Ky.: University of Kentucky Press, 1970), p. 179.
18. *Ibid.*, pp. 292–295.
19. Hans-Georg Bandi, *Eskimo Prehistory* (College, Alaska: University of Alaska Press, 1969), p. 176.
20. Wendell H. Oswalt, *Alaskan Eskimos* (New York: Chandler Publishing Co., 1967), pp. 238–240.
21. *Native Peoples and Languages of Alaska*, 1974, a map designed by Michael E. Krauss, director, Alaska Native Language Center, University of Alaska, Fairbanks, AK.

Chapter 2

1. Hubert Howe Bancroft, *History of Alaska, 1730–1885* (San Francisco: A. L. Bancroft & Company, 1886), p. 324.
2. Hector Chevigny, *Russian America* (New York: Viking, 1965), pp. 81–83.
3. S. B. Okun, *The Russian American Company* (Cambridge: University Press, 1951), pp. 44–45.
4. *Ibid.*, p. 225.
5. The boundary south of 56° was imprecisely stated and not finally settled until 1903.
6. John S. Galbraith, *The Hudson's Bay Company as an Imperial Factor* (Berkeley: University of California Press, 1957), p. 154.
7. Ian Jackson, "The Stikine Territory Lease and its Relevance to the Alaska Purchase," *Pacific Historical Review*, XXXVI (1967), 305–306.
8. Svetlana G. Fedorova, *Ethnic Processes in Russian America*, Occasional Paper No. 1, Anchorage Historical and Fine Arts Museum (Anchorage, n.d.), pp. 13–15.
9. Okun, p. 221.
10. Okun, pp. 220–223; Anatole Mazour, "The Prelude to Russia's Departure from America," Morgan Sherwood (ed.), *Alaska and its History* (Seattle: University of Washington Press, 1957), pp. 163–164, 167–170.
11. F. A. Golder, "The Purchase of Alaska," *American Historical Review*, XXV (1919–20), 419, 423.

Chapter 3

1. Thomas A. Bailey, *A Diplomatic History of the American People* (New York: Appleton-Century-Crofts, 1950), pp. 397–404.
2. Ted C. Hinckley, *The Americanization of Alaska, 1867–1897* (Palo Alto, Cal.: Pacific Books, Publishers, 1972), pp. 42, 49–52.
3. Ernest Gruening, *The State of Alaska*, 2nd ed. (New York: Random House, 1968), p. 67; cf. Hinckley, pp. 91, 93.
4. Alfred H. Brooks, *Blazing Alaska's Trails*, 2nd ed. (Fairbanks: University of Alaska Press, 1973), pp. 302–306.
5. Hinckley, pp. 152–156.
6. Brooks, pp. 488–490.
7. Bailey, pp. 446–449.

Chapter 4

1. Alfred H. Brooks, *Blazing Alaska's Trails*, 2nd ed. (Fairbanks: University of Alaska Press, 1973), pp. 376–380, 390–391.

2. William R. Hunt, *North of 53°* (New York: Macmillan, 1974), p. 113; Brooks, pp. 397–398.
3. Orlando Miller, *The Frontier in Alaska and the Matanuska Colony* (New Haven: Yale University Press, 1975), pp. 17–18.
4. *Ibid.*, pp. 18–19.
5. For the story of the Cunningham claims, see Herman E. Slotnick, "The Ballinger-Pinchot Affair in Alaska," *Journal of the West*, X, no. 2 (April 1971), 337–347.
6. U.S. Congress, *Congressional Record*, 51, pt. 1 (December 2, 1913), p. 45.
7. Edward Fitch, *The Alaska Railroad* (New York: Praeger, 1967), p. 43.
8. *Ibid.*, pp. 49–52.
9. *Alaska v. Troy*, 258 U.S. 101 (February 27, 1922).

Chapter 5

1. Ernest Gruening, *The State of Alaska*, 2nd ed. (New York: Random House, 1968), pp. 270, 282.
2. Richard Cooley, *Politics and Conservation: The Decline of the Alaska Salmon* (New York: Harper & Row, 1963), pp. 97–98.
3. *Ibid.*, p. 96.
4. *Ibid.*, p. 88.
5. *Ibid.*, pp. 104–105.
6. *Ibid.*, pp. 106–108.
7. Gruening, p. 271.
8. Orlando Miller, *The Frontier in Alaska and the Matanuska Colony* (New Haven, Conn.: Yale University Press, 1975), pp. 38–45.
9. *Ibid.*, pp. 62, 69–71.
10. *Ibid.*, pp. 83–87, 99.
11. *Ibid.*, pp. 88–89.
12. *Ibid.*, pp. 102–104.
13. Compare George W. Rogers, *Alaska in Transition* (Baltimore: The Johns Hopkins Press, 1960), pp. 248–250 with Gruening, pp. 255–259, 364–368.
14. National Resources Committee, *Alaska: Its Resources and Development* (Washington, D.C.: Government Printing Office, 1938).
15. Harold Ickes, *The Secret Diary of Harold Ickes*, vol. 2, *The Inside Struggle, 1936–1939* (New York: Simon & Schuster, 1954), pp. 449–450.
16. Ernest Gruening, *Many Battles: The Autobiography of Ernest Gruening* (New York: Liveright, 1973), p. 283.

Chapter 6

1. U.S. Army, Alaska, *The Army's Role in the Building of Alaska*, Pamphlet 360-5, April 1, 1969 (Headquarters, U.S. Army, Alaska, 1969), p. 74 (hereafter cited as USARAL Pamphlet 360-5).
2. *Ibid.*, p. 70.
3. *Ibid.*, p. 71.
4. *Ibid.*
5. Claus-M. Naske, *An Interpretative History of Alaskan Statehood* (Anchorage: Alaska Northwest Publishing Company, 1973), p. 56.
6. USARAL Pamphlet 360-5, p. 73.
7. *Ibid.*, p. 74.
8. Naske, *An Interpretative History*, pp. 56–57; USARAL Pamphlet 360-5, p. 74.
9. Samuel Eliot Morison, *History of United States Naval Operations in World War II*, vol. III, *Coral Sea* (Boston: Little, Brown & Co., 1962), pp. 163–165.
10. Brian Garfield, *The Thousand-Mile War: World War II in Alaska and the Aleutians* (Garden City, N.Y.: Doubleday, 1969), p. 12.
11. Morison, p. 75.
12. *Ibid.*, pp. 3–7.
13. *Ibid.*, pp. 17–28.

14. *Ibid.*, pp. 7, 25.
15. *Ibid.*, pp. 180–181.
16. *Ibid.*, pp. 169, 181.
17. *Ibid.*, p. 183.
18. *Ibid.*, vol. 3, p. 4.
19. *Ibid.*, p. 5.
20. *Ibid.*, pp. 7–8.
21. *Ibid.*, pp. 12–13.
22. Garfield, pp. 146–147.
23. *Ibid.*, pp. 149–150.
24. USARAL Pamphlet 360-5, p. 90; Garfield, pp. 150–151.
25. Claus-M. Naske, "The Alcan: Its Impact on Alaska," *The Northern Engineer*, VIII, 1 (Spring 1976), 12–18.
26. Deane R. Brandon, "War Planes to Russia," *Alaska Magazine* (May 1976), pp. 14–17.
27. Garfield, pp. 153–155.
28. Morison, *Naval Operations,* vol. VII, p. 17.
29. *Ibid.*, p. 22; Garfield, pp. 178–179.
30. Garfield, pp. 251–252.
31. *Ibid.*, p. 256.
32. *Ibid.*
33. Morison, *Naval Operations,* vol. VII, pp. 54, 57–59.
34. *Ibid.*, pp. 59–60.
35. *Ibid.*, pp. 63–64.
36. USARAL Pamphlet 360-5, p. 96.
37. George W. Rogers, *The Future of Alaska: Economic Consequences of Statehood* (Baltimore: The Johns Hopkins Press, 1962), p. 95.
38. USARAL Pamphlet 360-5, pp. 68, 70–74, 85–89, 97–98.
39. *New York Times*, March 13, 1949, p. 26; March 16, 1949, p. 13.
40. *Ibid.*, March 19, 1949, p. 7.
41. *Ibid.*
42. *Ibid.*
43. *Ibid.*, March 21, 1949, p. 9.
44. *Ibid.*, March 26, 1959, p. 7; January 3, 1959, p. 92.
45. *Ibid.*, June 25, 1950, p. 15; June 26, 1950, p. 18.
46. Brent R. Bowen, "Defense Spending in Alaska," *Alaska Review of Business and Economic Conditions* (Fairbanks: Institute of Social, Economic, and Government Research, July 1971), p. 4.
47. *New York Times*, June 25, 1950, p. 15.
48. *Ibid.*, June 27, 1950, p. 37.
49. *Ibid.*, June 25, 1950, p. 15; June 26, 1950, p. 18; June 27, 1950, p. 37.
50. *Ibid.*, August 31, 1952, pp. 1–4.
51. *Ibid.*, November 2, 1952, p. 14.
52. *Ibid.*, January 6, 1954, p. 59; July 27, 1954, p. 12.
53. Naske, *An Interpretative History,* p. 168.

Chapter 7

1. Ted C. Hinckley, *The Americanization of Alaska* (Palo Alto, Cal.: Pacific Books, Publishers, 1972), pp. 41–42.
2. *Speech of William H. Seward, at Sitka, August 12, 1869* (Washington, D.C.: Philip & Solomons, 1869), pp. 15–16.
3. Jack E. Eblen, *The First and Second United States Empires: Governors and Territorial Government, 1784–1912* (Pittsburgh: University of Pittsburgh Press, 1968), pp. 151, 8.
4. James D. Richardson, ed., *A Compilation of the Messages and Papers of the Presidents* (New York: Bureau of National Literature, 1897–1922), XV, 7019–7020.
5. Claus-M. Naske, *An Interpretative History of Alaskan Statehood* (Anchorage: Alaska Northwest Publishing Company, 1973), p. 7.
6. George Washington Spicer, *The Constitutional Status and Government of Alaska* (Balti-

more: Johns Hopkins University Press, 1927), pp. 27–32; Marcos E. Kirnevan, "Alaska and Hawaii: From Territoriality to Statehood," *California Law Review*, XXXVIII (1950), 279.

7. Robert H. Wiebe, *The Search for Order, 1877–1920* (New York: Hill and Wang, 1967), p. 288.
8. Naske, pp. 8–9.
9. Territorial Senate, *Senate Journal*, 1915, pp. 4–5, 95; *Alaska Daily Empire*, March 31, 1915 (hereafter *ADE*); *Senate Journal*, 1915, pp. 100, 150.
10. *Senate Journal*, 1915, pp. 98, 100.
11. *ADE*, April 9, 13, 1915; *Senate Journal*, 1915, pp. 137, 192–193.
12. Jeannette Paddock Nichols, *Alaska: A History of its Administration, Exploitation, and Industrial Development during its First Half Century under the Rule of the United States* (New York: Russell and Russell, 1963), pp. 293–294.
13. *ADE*, March 31, 1915; *Daily Alaska Dispatch*, April 1, 1915 (hereafter *DAD*).
14. 64th Cong., 1st sess., H. R. 6887, January 4, 1916.
15. U.S. Congress, *Congressional Record*, 64th Cong., 1st sess., p. A1520.
16. James Wickersham, "The Forty Ninth Star," *Collier's*, August 6, 1910, p. 17.
17. *The Forty Ninth Star* (Valdez), December 4, 1915.
18. *Ibid.*, February 19; March 4, 1916.
19. Naske, p. 37.
20. 64th Cong., 1st sess., H.R. 13978.
21. Naske, pp. 38–39.
22. *Ibid.*, p. 39.
23. James A. Wickersham, *A Bibliography of Alaskan Literature, 1724–1924* (Cordova, Alaska: *Cordova Daily Times*, 1927), pp. 260, 256; *Jessen's Weekly*, May 2, 1947.
24. *DAD*, September 1, 1916.
25. *Alaska Monthly*, June 1906, p. 80.
26. W. F. Beers, Jr., "The Government of Alaska," *Alaska Yukon Magazine* (1908), p. 373.
27. Hugh A. Johnson and Harold T. Jorgenson, *The Land Resources of Alaska* (New York: University Publishers, 1963), pp. 202–203; *ADE*, February 16, 1917.
28. *ADE*, July 13, 1921.
29. *Ketchikan Alaska Chronicle*, January 6, 1923; *Anchorage Daily Times*, June 11, 1919 (hereafter *ADT*); *ADE*, December 8, 1921; January 7, April 29, 1922.
30. *ADT*, June 11, 1919.
31. *Fairbanks Daily News-Miner*, March 2, 1922.
32. *ADE*, April 29, August 15, 1922.
33. Naske, pp. 40–42.
34. *Ibid.*, p. 43.
35. U.S. Congress, House, Committee on the Territories, *Reapportionment of the Alaska Legislature: Hearings on H.R. 8114*, 68th Cong., 1st sess., pp. 1, 3.
36. *ADE*, February 41, June 16, 1925; *Daily Alaska Empire* (hereafter *DAE*), April 19, 1933.
37. *DAE*, November 6, 1929; January 28, February 17, 1930.
38. Naske, p. 52.
39. Author's interview with Sister Marie Therese, Dimond's eldest daughter, Trinity College, Washington, D.C., April 20, 1975.
40. *Ibid.*
41. Naske, p. 53.
42. Ernest Gruening, *The State of Alaska* (New York: Random House, 1969), p. 316.
43. Ernest Gruening, *Many Battles: The Autobiography of Ernest Gruening* (New York: Liveright, 1973), pp. 3–87, 210–228.
44. Naske, pp. 55–56.
45. *ADT*, September 2, 1939.
46. *DAE*, December 6, 1939.
47. *DAE*, Progress Edition, March 23, 1941.
48. "Statehood, Should We Have It Now?" *Alaska Life*, February 1941, p. 2.
49. Alaska Legislature, *House Journal*, 1941, pp. 192, 233; 1943, pp. 212, 309, 337; *Senate Journal*, 1941, p. 174; 1943, p. 293.
50. Naske, p. 60.
51. 78th Cong., 1st sess., S. 951, April 2, 1943.
52. Naske, pp. 60–61.
53. 78th Cong., 1st sess., H.R. 3768, December 2, 1943.
54. *Jessen's Weekly*, January 5, 1945; U.S. Congress, Senate, Committee on Interior and

Insular Affairs, *Rescinding Certain Orders of the Secretary of the Interior Establishing Indian Reservations in the Territory of Alaska: Report to Accompany S. J. Res. 162*, 80th Cong., 2nd sess., Rpt. 1366, pp. 5–7; U.S. Congress, Senate, Committee on Interior and Insular Affairs, *Alaska Statehood: Hearings on S. 50*; 83rd Cong., 2nd sess., January 20–February 24, p. 204.

55. Dean Sherman, "The Statehood Question," *Alaska Life*, June 1944, pp. 15–18.
56. Naske, p. 69.
57. *Ibid.*, pp. 68–78.
58. Naske, "103,350,000 Acres," *The Alaska Journal*, Autumn 1972, pp. 2–13.
59. *Ibid.*
60. *Ibid.*
61. Naske, *Alaskan Statehood*, pp. 90, 96.
62. *Ibid.*, pp. 105, 113.
63. Naske, "103,350,000 Acres," pp. 2–13.
64. Naske, *Alaskan Statehood*, pp. 113–121.
65. *Ibid.*, pp. 143, 151.
66. Naske, "103,350,000 Acres," pp. 2–13.

Chapter 8

1. "The 49th State," *Time*, July 14, 1958, p. 16.
2. Mary Lee Council to E. L. Bartlett, July 12, 1958, ELB Papers, Statehood File, box 2, folder Alaska Statehood Committee, 1958–59, University of Alaska Archives, Fairbanks, Alaska.
3. *FDNM*, Aug. 14, 9, 25, 1958; Robert B. Atwood, "Alaska's Struggle for Statehood," *State Government* (Autumn 1958), p. 208.
4. Murray to Ernest Gruening, July 9, 1958, Alaska Historical Library, Juneau, Alaska.
5. *FDNM*, July 16, 19, 1958; George Sundborg to E. L. Bartlett, July 4, 1958, Private Papers, Vide Bartlett.
6. *ADT*, July 15, 24, August 20, 1958; Donald R. Moberg, "The 1958 Election in Alaska," *Western Political Quarterly*, XII (1959), 259–260.
7. *FDNM*, Aug. 19, 25, 1958; *DAE*, July 13, Aug. 26, 1958.
8. "Statehood Primary Election Results," Alaska Historical Library, Juneau.
9. *Ibid.*
10. *FDNM*, Aug. 2, Nov. 4, 28, 1958; "Fred and the 49th," *Time*, November 24, 1958; Moberg, pp. 260–262; *DAE*, Dec. 1, 1958.
11. "Alaska Official Returns of the Special Statehood Referendum Election, August 26, 1958, and the General Election, November 25, 1958," copy in author's files.
12. Thomas B. Stewart to E. L. Bartlett, May 25, 1957, "Minutes of the Meeting of the Alaska Statehood Committee," March 7–8, 1958; "Minutes of Meeting, Executive Committee of the Alaska Statehood Committee," July 12–13, 1958; "Contract Amendment," ELB Papers, Statehood File, box 12, folder correspondence, general, May, 1957, box 2, folder Alaska Statehood Committee, 1958–1959.
13. *FDNM*, Jan. 3, 2, 1959.
14. *Congressional Record*, 86th Cong., 1st sess., p. 8737.
15. U.S. Congress, House, Subcommittee on Territorial and Insular Affairs, *Alaska Omnibus Bill: Hearings on H. R. 6091 and H. R. 6112*, 86th Cong., 1st sess., pp. 25–36, 55–56; U.S. Congress, Senate, Committee on Interior and Insular Affairs, *Alaska Omnibus Bill: Hearings on S. 1541*, 86th Cong., 1st sess.
16. *Hearings on H. R. 6091*, pp. 67–73; *Congressional Record*, 86th Cong., 1st sess., p. 9473; *Hearings on S. 1541*, p. 11.
17. *Hearings on H. R. 6091*, p. 45; *Hearings on S. 1541*, pp. 10–11.
18. *Hearings on H. R. 6091*, pp. 61–78.
19. *Hearings on S. 1541*, p. 11; *Hearings on H. R. 6091*, pp. 26–35.
20. *Hearings on H. R. 6091*, pp. 27–39; *ADT*, Mar. 25, 1959.
21. *Hearings on H. R. 6091*, pp. 56–58; *USC*, 1958 ed., title 23, sec. 103.
22. *Hearings on S. 1541*, pp. 5–8, 74.
23. *ADT*, May 11, 1959; *Hearings on H. R. 6091*, pp. 79–80.
24. Alaska, *Session Laws*, 1959, pp. 89–104; *ADT*, Apr. 21, 28; May 11, 1959.
25. 86th Cong., 1st sess., H. R. 7120, May 14, 1959; *ADT*, May 28, 1959; *Congressional*

Record, 86th Cong., 1st sess., pp. 9470, 9480, 9482–9484; *ADT,* June 15, 1959; E. L. Bartlett to Hugh Wade, June 4, 1959, ELB Papers, Alaska Statehood File, folder 1959–62; Omnibus Act, 1959, May–June.

Chapter 9

1. State of Alaska, *Constitution,* Article 10, sec. 1.
2. *Ibid.*
3. *Ibid.,* Article 8; Department of Education, Division of State Libraries, *Alaska Blue Book* (Juneau, 1973), p. 148.
4. State of Alaska, *Constitution,* Article 8, sec. 15.
5. Claus-M. Naske, *An Interpretative History of Alaskan Statehood* (Anchorage: Alaska Northwest Publishing Company, 1973), p. 142.
6. Author's interview with Hugh J. Wade, December 30, 1976, Anchorage, Alaska.
7. Department of Education, Division of State Libraries, *Alaska Blue Book,* 1975, ed. by Elaine Mitchell, 2nd ed. (Juneau, 1975), pp. 196–197.
8. State of Alaska, Department of Economic Enterprise, *Alaska Statistical Review* (Juneau, December 1972), pp. 15–16.
9. Patrick O'Donovan, "The Forty-Ninth Star on the U.S. Flag," *London Observer,* July 13, 1958.
10. Author's interview with Bert Faulkner, August 11, 1969, Juneau, Alaska.
11. "Message of Governor William A. Egan to the Second Session, First Alaska State Legislature, Recommending Appropriations for Fiscal Year 1961," in *State of Alaska, Budget Document 1960–1961* (January 27, 1960), pp. 1–4.
12. Ray J. Schrick, "Alaska's Ordeal," *Wall Street Journal,* March 16, 1960.
13. *Ibid.*
14. "Main Trails and Bypaths," *Alaska Sportsman,* January 1960, p. 7; Schrick, "Alaska's Ordeal."
15. "Main Trails and Bypaths," p. 7.
16. "Message of Governor William A. Egan to the Second Session," pp. 1–4.
17. *Ibid.,* pp. 7, 20; Alaska State Planning Commission, *State of Alaska Capital Improvement Program 1960–1966,* January 29, 1960, pp. C-4–C-7.
18. State of Alaska, Department of Economic Development, Industrial Development Division, *Alaska Statistical Review, 1968* (Juneau, April 1969), pp. 3, 23, 28, 56; "Bob" Bartlett, "Big Gains in Fish, Timber," *FDNM,* March 17, 1966, p. AA3.
19. Herman E. Slotnick, "The 1960 Election in Alaska," *The Western Political Quarterly,* March 1961, p. 300.
20. Thomas A. Morehouse and Gordon S. Harrison, *An Electoral Profile of Alaska* (Fairbanks: Institute of Social, Economic and Government Research, 1973), pp. 2–3.
21. Jan Juran and Daniel Raff, "Theodore F. Stevens, Republican Senator from Alaska," *Ralph Nader Congress Project: Citizens Look at Congress,* p. 8; Tom Brown, *Oil on Ice: Alaskan Wilderness at the Crossroads* (San Francisco and New York: Sierra Club, 1971), pp. 42–43.
22. State of Alaska, Office of the Governor, "Alaska Earthquake Disaster Damage Report" (Preliminary), April 4, 1964, in author's files.
23. *Washington Daily News,* March 30, 1964.
24. *Ibid.; Washington Post,* March 31, 1964.
25. *Washington Post,* March 31, 1964.
26. E. L. "Bob" Bartlett Press Release, April 3, 1964, in author's files.
27. E. L. Bartlett to Clinton B. Anderson, April 11, 1964, in author's files; *FDNM,* May 20, 1964; Public Law 88-451; 88th Cong., S. 2881, August 19, 1964.
28. Brookings Institution, Advanced Study Program, in association with the Legislative Council of the State of Alaska, "Conference on the Future of Alaska," Fall 1969.
29. *Ibid.*
30. *Ibid.*
31. *Ibid.*
32. *Ibid.*
33. *Ibid.*
34. *Planning Guidelines for the State of Alaska,* prepared for the Office of the Governor, State of Alaska, by Stanford Research Institute, Menlo Park, California, December 1969.

35. Capital Site Selection Committee, *Information for Participants.*
36. *Alaska Review,* a monthly television program funded by the Alaska legislature and the Alaska Humanities Forum.
37. *Ibid.*
38. *Ketchikan Daily News,* January 15, 1977.
39. Hammond campaign brochure, in author's files.
40. *Ibid.*
41. The Alaska Public Forum, Alaska Growth Policy Council, *Mid-Year Report, March, 1977.*
42. State of Alaska, Department of Revenue, *Alaska '75: Facing the Crunch.*
43. Federal-State Land Use Planning Commission for Alaska, *Interim Report to the President, Congress, and the State of Alaska,* May 1976, pp. 1, 12.
44. Senator Mike Gravel reports to Alaskans, July 1978, Newsletter.
45. Senator Ted Stevens, Newsletter, June 1978.
46. *FDNM,* October 14, 1978.
47. *All-Alaska Weekly,* December 22, 1978.

Chapter 10

1. Robert D. Arnold et al., *Alaska Natives and the Land,* Federal Field Committee for Development Planning in Alaska (Washington, D.C.: Government Printing Office, 1968), pp. 19–22.
2. William R. Hunt, *Arctic Passage* (New York: Charles Scribner's Sons, 1975), pp. 117, 132–133, 122.
3. George W. Rogers, *The Future of Alaska: Economic Consequences of Statehood* (Baltimore: The Johns Hopkins University Press, 1962), p. 89.
4. Bobby Dave Lain, "North of Fifty-Three: Army, Treasury Department, and Navy Administration of Alaska, 1867–1884" (Ph.D. diss., University of Texas at Austin, 1974), pp. 121–156.
5. U.S. Congress, House, Committee on the Territories, *Civil Government for Alaska: Report to Accompany S. 153,* 48th Cong., 1st sess., 1884, H. R. 476, p. 2.
6. George W. Rogers and Richard A. Cooley, *Alaska's Population and Economy: Regional Growth, Development and Future Outlook,* vol. 2, *Statistical Handbook* (College, Alaska: Institute of Social, Economic, and Government Research, 1963), p. 7.
7. *Civil Government for Alaska,* 1884.
8. *Ibid.,* p. 91.
9. *Ibid.*
10. Robert D. Arnold et al., *Alaska Native Land Claims* (Anchorage: Alaska Native Foundation, 1976), p. 83.
11. *Ibid.*
12. Ernest Gruening, *State of Alaska,* 2nd ed. (New York: Random House, 1968), pp. 355–381.
13. Senate Report 92-405, p. 91.
14. Stanton H. Patty, "A Conference with the Tanana Chiefs," *The Alaska Journal,* Spring 1971, pp. 2–10.
15. *Ibid.,* p. 11.
16. *Ibid.,* p. 18.
17. Senate Report No. 92-405, p. 91; 44 Stat. 629.
18. 48 Stat. 984.
19. 49 Stat. 1250, sec. 2.
20. Gruening, pp. 364–365.
21. *Ibid.,* p. 367; Arnold, *Alaska Native Land Claims,* pp. 86–87.
22. Arnold, *Alaska Native Land Claims,* p. 88.
23. Gruening, p. 370.
24. Senate Report No. 92-405, p. 93.
25. *Ibid.*
26. Arnold, *Alaska Native Land Claims,* pp. 85, 88–89, 91.
27. Senate Report No. 92-405, p. 94.
28. Paul Brooks, *The Pursuit of Wilderness* (Boston: Houghton Mifflin Co., 1971), pp. 60, 62–63.
29. *Ibid.,* p. 66.

30. *Ibid.*
31. *Ibid.*, p. 67.
32. *Ibid.*, pp. 68–69.
33. *Ibid.*, p. 72.
34. Arnold, *Alaska Native Land Claims*, pp. 95–96; Brooks, pp. 72–73.
35. Arnold, *Alaska Native Land Claims*, p. 100.
36. Senate Report No. 92-405, p. 96.
37. *Ibid.*, pp. 96–97.
38. Mary Clay Berry, *The Alaska Pipeline: The Politics of Oil and Native Land Claims* (Bloomington, Ind.: Indiana University Press, 1975), pp. 34–35.
39. *Ibid.*, p. 37.
40. *Ibid.*
41. Brooks, pp. 78–90.
42. *Ibid.*, pp. 91–92.
43. *Ibid.*, p. 92.
44. Senate Report No. 92-405, p. 96.
45. *Ibid.*; Berry, p. 44.
46. Arnold, *Alaska Native Land Claims*, pp. 103–105.
47. *Ibid.*
48. *Ibid.*, pp. 106–107.
49. Berry, p. 47.
50. *Ibid.*, p. 48.
51. *Ibid.*, p. 49.
52. *Ibid.*, pp. 48–49.
53. *Ibid.*, p. 50.
54. *Ibid.*
55. *Ibid.*, p. 51.
56. Arnold, *Alaska Native Land Claims*, p. 119.
57. *Ibid.*, p. 120.
58. U.S. Congress, Senate, 90th Cong., 2nd sess., *Alaska Native Land Claims*, Hearings Before the Committee on Interior and Insular Affairs on S. 2906, S. 1964, S. 2690, and S. 2020 (Washington, D.C.: Government Printing Office, 1968), pp. 441, 189, 237.
59. *Ibid.*, pp. 45–46, 289–290, 371–372.
60. Arnold, *Alaska Native Land Claims*, p. 123.
61. *Ibid.*, pp. 123–125.
62. Berry, pp. 60–61.
63. Arnold, *Alaska Native Land Claims*, p. 126.
64. Berry, p. 62.
65. Arnold, *Alaska Native Land Claims*, p. 132.
66. Berry, p. 65.
67. *Ibid.*, pp. 67–68.
68. *Ibid.*, p. 69.
69. *Ibid.*
70. *Ibid.*, pp. 76–77.
71. *Ibid.*, p. 80.
72. *Ibid.*, p. 81.
73. *Ibid.*, pp. 102–103.
74. *Ibid.*, pp. 117–118, 121.
75. Arnold, *Alaska Native Land Claims*, p. 134.
76. *Ibid.*
77. *Ibid.*, pp. 135–136.
78. *Ibid.*, p. 137.
79. *Ibid.*, pp. 139–140.
80. *Ibid.*, pp. 141–142.
81. *Ibid.*
82. *Ibid.*, pp. 146–147.
83. *Ibid.*
84. Berry, pp. 240–241; Arnold, *Alaska Native Land Claims*, pp. 148–149.
85. Arnold, *Alaska Native Land Claims*, p. 150.
86. *Ibid.*, pp. 150–151.
87. *Ibid.*, p. 152.

88. Berry, p. 250.
89. *Ibid.*, p. 251.
90. *Ibid.*, pp. 252–254.
91. Rosemary Shinohara and Virginia McKinney, "Natives Taking Leadership in Business Community," *Alaska Industry*, January 1976, p. 37.
92. *Ibid.*, pp. 39–40.
93. *Ibid.*, p. 37.
94. *Ibid.*, pp. 37–38.
95. *Ibid.*, p. 38.
96. *Ibid.*; *Alaska Magazine*, June 1976, p. 45.
97. *Alaska Magazine*, June 1976, pp. 41–42.
98. *Ibid.*, pp. 42–43.
99. *Ibid.*, pp. 43–45.
100. *Ibid.*, p. 45.
101. *Ibid.*, pp. 45–47, 53.
102. *Ibid.*, p. 53.
103. *Ibid.*, pp. 53–54.
104. *Ibid.*, p. 54.
105. Virginia McKinney, "Native Regional Firms Enter New, Post-pipeline Era," *Alaska Industry*, January 1977, pp. 29–32.
106. Chapter 19, SLA, 1976; Chapter 240, SLA, 1976.
107. PL 94-204, 94th Cong., sess. 1, 1469, January 2, 1976.

Chapter 11

1. William R. Hunt, "Notes on the History of North Slope Oil," *Alaska Magazine*, February 1970, pp. 8–10.
2. *Ibid.*
3. *Ibid.*
4. Ted A. Armstrong, "Alaskan Oil," *The Oil and Gas Journal*, August 22, 1966, pp. 95–96; *Alaska Sportsman*, September 1969, p. 20.
5. Hunt, "History of North Slope Oil," pp. 8–10.
6. Armstrong, "Alaskan Oil," p. 96; Memorandum from director, Naval Petroleum Reserves, November 26, 1952, RG 57, Records of John C. Reed, Staff Geologist for Territories and Island Possessions, Correspondence with Navy, 6.3, National Archives.
7. Armstrong, "Alaskan Oil," p. 96.
8. *Ibid.*
9. *Ibid.*
10. *Ibid.*
11. *Ibid.*
12. *Ibid.*, p. 91.
13. *Ibid.*
14. *Ibid.*, pp. 77, 81.
15. *Ibid.*, p. 86.
16. *Ibid.*, pp. 82–83.
17. *FDNM*, January 16, 18, 1968.
18. *Ibid.*; Tom Brown, *Oil on Ice: Alaskan Wilderness at the Crossroads* (New York and San Francisco: Sierra Club, 1971), p. 27.
19. Brown, p. 27.
20. *FDNM*, June 26, 1968.
21. Brown, p. 29.
22. *FDNM*, August 22, 1968.
23. Brown, pp. 42–45.
24. *Ibid.*, pp. 45–46.
25. Hugh G. Gallagher, *Etok: A Story of Eskimo Power* (New York: G. P. Putnam's Sons, 1974), p. 181.
26. *Ibid.*, pp. 181–182.
27. Mary Clay Berry, *The Alaska Pipeline: The Politics of Oil and Native Land Claims*

(Bloomington: Indiana University Press, 1975), pp. 99–100.

28. Gallagher, p. 182.
29. Brookings Institution, Advanced Study Program, in association with the Legislative Council of the State of Alaska, "Conference on the Future of Alaska," Fall 1969.
30. *Ibid.*
31. Berry, p. 102.
32. *Ibid.*, p. 104; "Special Pipeline Report," *Alaska Construction and Oil*, September 1975, p. 5.
33. Berry, p. 105.
34. *Ibid.*, p. 106.
35. *Ibid.*
36. *Ibid.*, pp. 106–107.
37. *Ibid.*, p. 108.
38. *Ibid.*, pp. 108–109.
39. *Ibid.*, pp. 109–110.
40. *Ibid.*
41. *Ibid.*, p. 111.
42. *Ibid.*, pp. 111–112.
43. *Ibid.*, p. 113.
44. *Ibid.*
45. *Ibid.*, pp. 115–116.
46. *Ibid.*, pp. 116–117.
47. *Ibid.*, pp. 117–118.
48. *Ibid.*, p. 118.
49. *Ibid.*, pp. 118–121.
50. Brown, pp. 86–91.
51. "Special Pipeline Report," p. 8.
52. *Ibid.*
53. *Ibid.*; Mark Wheeler, *half baked alaska* (Ketchikan, Alaska: Mark Wheeler, Publisher, 1972), p. 103.
54. Berry, p. 215.
55. *Ibid.*, pp. 215–216.
56. Thomas A. Morehouse and Gordon Scott Harrison, "State Government and Economic Development in Alaska," *Alaska Public Policy*, ed. Gordon Scott Harrison (College, Alaska: Institute of Social, Economic, and Government Research, University of Alaska, 1971), p. 35.
57. "Special Pipeline Report," p. 32; Berry, p. 217.
58. Berry, pp. 222–223.
59. *Ibid.*, pp. 226–227.
60. *Ibid.*, pp. 229–230.
61. *Ibid.*, p. 230.
62. *Newsweek*, January 23, 1973, p. 52.
63. *Alaska Industry* (June 1972), p. 17.
64. Robert G. Knox, "Pipeline Progress Report: Road Construction Gets Off to Early Start," *Alaska Industry* (June 1974), pp. 48–49.
65. *Ibid.*
66. *Ibid.*
67. *Ibid.*, pp. 50–51.
68. Mary Clare Langan, "The Boom Is Still Awaited," *Alaska Industry* (August 1974), pp. 39–40; *Fairbanks North Star Borough Pipeline Impact Office Report No. One*, July 11, 1974.
69. *Alaska Industry* (March 1975), pp. 33–34.
70. *Ibid.*, June 1975, pp. 39–40.
71. *Ibid.*, December 1975, p. 40.
72. *FDNM*, June 20, 21, 1977.
73. *Ibid.*, June 20, 1978.
74. *Ibid.*, July 9, 1977.
75. *Ibid.*, June 20, 1978.
76. *Ibid.*
77. *Ibid.*, June 8, 1978.
78. *Ibid.*
79. Thomas A. Morehouse, "Petroleum Development in Alaska," *Review of Business and*

Economic Conditions (University of Alaska, March 1977), p. 15.

80. *FDNM*, July 18, 1977.

Chapter 13

1. *FDNM*, June 7, 1978.

APPENDICES

Dates in Alaska/U.S. History

40,000–9,000 B.C.   The Peopling of the New World Via the Bering Sea Land Bridge

Dates in Alaska History		*Dates in U.S. History*
Vitus Bering sent by Peter the Great to explore North Pacific	1725	Colonists and Indians fight and first case reported of scalping by colonists, who were paid £100 for each scalp.
Vitus Bering sails through Bering Strait	1728	Jews of New York build the first synagogue in America.
Bering's second expedition, with George Wilhelm Steller, the first naturalist to visit Alaska	1733	Savannah, the first settlement in Georgia, is established by Oglethorpe; it is the 13th colony.
Aleksei Chirikov, with Bering expedition, sights land on July 15; Alaska is discovered	1741	"Negro Conspiracy" in New York: 11 Negroes burned at the stake, 18 others hanged, along with four white men.
First scientific report on the North Pacific fur seal (Steller)	1742	War of Jenkin's Ear, Battle of Bloody Swamp; Spanish defeated.
Concentrated hunting of sea otter by Russians	1743–63	
Juan Perez is ordered by Spain to explore West Coast; discovers Prince of Wales Island, Dixon Sound	1774	Declaration of Rights passed by 1st Continental Congress at Philadelphia.
Captain James Cook expedition to search for Northwest Passage	1776	The colonies formally declare independence from England.
Cook reaches King Island, Norton Sound, Unalaska	1778	Treaty of Alliance signed by Continental Congress and France.
Aleksandr Baranov establishes Russian post known today as Old Sitka; a trade charter is granted to the Russian-American Company	1779	Captain John Paul Jones captures the British man-of-war *Scrapis* during the Revolutionary War.
Gregory Shelikhov establishes first white settlement at Three Saints Bay, Kodiak	1784	Birth of Zachary Taylor, 12th U.S. president.

continued

Dates in Alaska History		Dates in U.S. History
Gerassim Pribilof discovers the rookeries on the islands now known as the Pribilofs	1786	First steamboat built in America.
George Vancouver leaves England to explore the coast; Alejandro Malaspina explores the northwest coast for Spain	1791	Vermont becomes the 14th state to join the Union.
Gregory Shelikhov granted a monopoly of furs in Alaska by Catherine II	1792	Bill of Rights goes into effect.
The first vessel built in northwestern America by Baranov at Voskressenski on Kenai	1794	Whiskey Rebellion takes place in Pennsylvania over excise tax on whiskey.
First Russian Orthodox Church established in Kodiak	1795	Birth of James K. Polk, 11th U.S. president.
The Tlingits massacre the Russians at Sitka; a few survive	1802	U.S. Military Academy opens on July 4th.
Yurii Lisiansky sails to Canton with the first Russian cargo of furs to be sent directly to China	1805	Jefferson inaugurated for a second term as president.
Russian-American Company given exclusive trading rights; no foreigners allowed in Russian America	1821	Santa Fe Trail is opened by William Becknell; spurs commerce in the Southwest.
Russian exploration of mainland; discovery of the Nushagak and Kuskokwim, Yukon and Koyukuk Rivers	1824–42	
Father Veniaminov moved to Sitka, consecrated as bishop in 1840	1834	The United States Congress establishes the Department of Indian Affairs.
Diocese formed; Bishop Innokentii Veniaminov given permission to use native languages in the liturgy	1840	James Fenimore Cooper publishes *The Pathfinder*.
Edward Stoeckl assigned to the secretariat of the Russian legation to the U.S.	1841	The first wagons arrive in California via the Oregon Trail.
Fort Yukon established	1847	First Mormon settlers arrive in Utah.
Cathedral of St. Michael dedicated at New Archangel (Sitka)	1848	Gold is discovered at Sutter's Mill in California, which had been sold to Sutter by the Russians.
Russian explorer-trappers find the first oil seeps in Cook Inlet	1853	The U.S. makes the Gadsden Purchase, in which it buys New Mexico and part of Arizona from Mexico.
Coal mining at Coal Harbor on the Kenai Peninsula carried on to supply steamers	1857	The Dred Scott decision is passed by the U.S. Supreme Court; the court rules that Negroes are not citizens of the U.S.
Stoeckl returns to U.S. from St. Petersburg with authority to negotiate the sale of Alaska	1859	The Comstock Lode is discovered in Nevada, the largest silver strike ever made in the U.S.
Gold discovered on the Stikine River near Telegraph Creek	1861	The Civil War starts with the shelling of Fort Sumter by the Confederacy.
Western Union Telegraph Company prepares to put a telegraph line across Alaska and Siberia	1865	The Civil War ends with the surrender of General Lee to General Grant.

Dates in Alaska History		Dates in U.S. History
U.S. purchase of Alaska from Russia; Pribilof Islands placed under jurisdiction of secretary of the treasury; fur seal population stabilized	1867	Credit Mobilier scandal breaks and political bribes by free gifts of company stock are exposed.
Alaska designated as the Department of Alaska under Brevet Major General Jefferson C. Davis, U.S. Army	1868	President Johnson acquitted in the impeachment proceedings.
	1869	The Transcontinental Railroad is completed at Promontory Point, Utah, connecting the East with the West.
Sitka Times, first newspaper in Alaska, published	1869–70	
Gold discovered near Sitka and in British Columbia near Cassiar	1872	The first mail order house in U.S. established— Montgomery Ward and Company.
Prospecting takes place near Dawson; George Halt is the first white man to cross the Chilkoot Pass	1874	The Greenback Party is organized mainly by farmers in favor of inflation of the currency.
Gold discovered south of Juneau at Windham Bay	1876	General George Custer and 265 men of the 7th Cavalry are killed by Sioux Indians in Montana.
U.S. troops withdrawn from Alaska	1877	Rutherford B. Hayes becomes the 19th president of the U.S.
A school opens at Sitka—to become Sheldon Jackson Junior College	1878	Thomas Edison is granted a patent on the phonograph.
Richard Harris and Joseph Juneau discover gold on Gastineau Channel where Juneau was founded	1880	The National Farmers' Alliance is organized to oppose unfavorable legislation aimed at farmers.
Treadwell claim staked—by 1885 the most prominent mine in Alaska	1881	President Garfield assassinated in Washington, D.C.
First commercial herring fishing begins at Killisnoo; first two central Alaska salmon canneries are built	1882	First law passed by Congress to limit immigration into the U.S.
Organic act passed by Congress; $15,000 appropriated to educate Indian children	1884	"Bob" M. LaFollette elected to Congress from the state of Wisconsin.
Dr. C. H. Townsend suggests the introduction of reindeer into Alaska	1885	Ulysses S. Grant dies at the age of 63.
A boundary survey is started by Dr. W. H. Dall of the U.S. and Dr. George Dawson of Canada	1888	Epidemic of yellow fever breaks out in Jacksonville, Florida; over 400 persons die.
Large corporate salmon canneries begin to appear	1890	
Dr. Sheldon Jackson explores the Arctic coast, introduces reindeer into Alaska	1890–92	Treaty with Great Britain regarding the Bering Sea seal fisheries.

continued

Dates in Alaska History		Dates in U.S. History
First oil claims staked in Cook Inlet area	1891	Basketball invented by Dr. James Naismith, an instructor at the YMCA.
Gold discovered on Mastadon Creek; Circle City founded	1894	Chinese Exclusion Treaty signed to exclude Chinese from the U.S.
Dawson City founded at mouth of Klondike River; gold discovered on Bonanza Creek	1896	*Plessy v. Ferguson* case establishes the separate but equal doctrine that legalizes segregation.
First shipment of fresh halibut sent south from Juneau	1897	Henry Ford builds his first car.
Klondike gold rush	1897–1900	
Skagway becomes largest city in Alaska because of Chilkoot Pass trail into Klondike; work is started on White Pass and Yukon Railroad—completed 1900; Congress appropriates money for telegraph from Seattle to Sitka; Nome gold rush begins	1898	Spanish-American War breaks out.
Local government organized in Nome	1899	Peace treaty to end the Spanish-American War signed by the president.
Civil code for Alaska passed, dividing state into three judicial districts with judges at Sitka, Eagle, and St. Michael; capital moved to Juneau	1900	Mrs. Carry Nation starts her campaign against liquor.
Alaska-Canada border settled as it is today	1903	Orville and Wilbur Wright successfully fly a heavier than air machine.
Tanana railroad built; telegraph from Fairbanks to Valdez built; Alaska Road Commission established under army jurisdiction	1905	President Theodore Roosevelt and Vice President Charles Fairbanks inaugurated for a second term.
Alaska authorized to send voteless delegate to Congress	1906	San Francisco earthquake.
Gold discovered at Ruby; Richardson trail established with regular stage service; Tongass National Forest, largest U.S. forest, created by presidential proclamation	1907	Congress passes legislation to limit campaign contributions by corporations.
First cold storage plant built at Ketchikan	1908	Smoking by women in public made illegal in New York City.
International agreement between U.S., Great Britain, Canada, Russia, and Japan to control fur seal fisheries; sea otters placed under complete protection	1911	Supreme Court requires that Standard Oil Company be dissolved.
Copper River and Northwestern Railroad in operation, serving Kennecott Copper Mine	1911–38	
Territorial status for Alaska provides for legislature; Mount Kenai explodes, forming Valley of Ten Thousand Smokes	1912	The *Titanic* strikes an iceberg and sinks—with a loss of 1502 lives.

Dates in Alaska History		Dates in U.S. History
First territorial legislature	1913	The 17th Amendment is passed by Congress, establishing the popular election of U.S. senators.
Surveying for Alaska Railroad begun—construction authorized by Congress; city of Anchorage begun as a construction campsite	1914	World War I starts in Europe.
First bill for Alaska statehood introduced in Congress	1916	Mexican bandit Francisco "Pancho" Villa attacks Columbus, New Mexico, and the U.S. Army pursues Villa into Mexico.
Treadwell Mine complex cave-in	1917	U.S. declares war on Germany.
Alaska Agricultural College and School of Mines created by Congress as a land-grant college	1918	Sedition Act passed by Congress to limit opposition to the war effort.
Anchorage city government organized	1920	Warren Harding and the Republicans sweep into White House and Congress.
Territorial College and School of Mines opened	1922	19th Amendment passes Congress, allowing women the right to vote.
President Warren E. Harding comes to Alaska to drive the last spike in the Alaska Railroad	1923	Vice President Calvin Coolidge becomes president at the death of Warren Harding.
Parts of Alaska mapped and surveyed by Navy	1929–34	
Matanuska Valley Project established	1935	The CIO (Congress of Industrial Organizations) organized by John L. Lewis.
Fort Richardson established; construction started on Elmendorf Air Force Base	1940	The selective service enacts the first peacetime draft for the army.
Alaska Juneau Gold Mine shut down	1944	D-Day in Europe: Allies land on the Normandy beach in the largest combined attack in the history of warfare.
Alaska Command established—the first unified command of the U.S. staffed jointly by army, air force, and navy officers	1947	Marshall Plan is first announced by Secretary of State George Marshall to help war-torn Europe rebuild.
Oil well drilled near Eureka on Glen Highway—beginning of Alaska's modern oil history; first plywood operations begun at Juneau; first big Alaskan pulp mill opened at Ketchikan	1953	An armistice is signed by the North Korean government and the U.S. to end hostilities.
Alaskans elect delegates to a constitutional convention	1955	AFL and CIO merge into the largest labor organization in U.S. history.
Constitutional convention at University of Alaska	1955–56	
Territorial voters adopt the constitution, send two senators and one representative to Washington under the Tennessee Plan	1956	President Eisenhower wins re-election by a wide margin.

continued

Dates in Alaska History		Dates in U.S. History
Statehood measure is passed, President Eisenhower signs statehood bill	1958	*USS Nautilus*, a nuclear-powered submarine, makes the first undersea crossing at the North Pole.
Statehood proclaimed, state constitution in effect; Sitka pulp mill opened	1959	Hawaii becomes the 50th state.
Good Friday earthquake	1964	The Civil Rights Act of 1964 signed by President Johnson.
Fairbanks flood	1967	U.S. troops in Viet Nam number almost one-half million by end of year.
Oil pumped from a well at Prudhoe Bay on North Slope	1968	Dr. Martin Luther King, Jr., is shot and killed in Memphis, Tennessee.
North Slope oil lease sale	1969	Richard Nixon becomes president of a divided country.
Congress approves Alaska Native Land Claims Settlement Act	1971	Richard M. Nixon calls for "New American Revolution" in domestic policy and proposes family assistance payments and revenue sharing.
Trans-Alaska Pipeline receives final approval and construction begins	1974	August 9. President Nixon resigns his office in disgrace.
Population, labor force increases with construction of pipeline; Alaska gross product soars to $5.8 billion, double that of 1973	1975	Final collapse of the South Vietnamese government.
Voters select Willow area near Anchorage for new capital site	1976	Democrat Jimmy Carter of Georgia elected President of the United States.
Completion of the Trans-Alaska Pipeline from Prudhoe Bay to Valdez; shipment of first oil by tanker from Valdez to Puget Sound	1977	At the opening of the year, the Democratic party stands in command of the country, beginning a post-Vietnam and post-Watergate phase of power.

Prepared by Dan Rodey, social studies teacher, West Valley High School, Fairbanks, Alaska.

Appendix B
Alaska Population Statistics

POPULATION OF ALASKA'S MAJOR TOWNS AND CITIES
1900-1970

Place	1900	1920	1940	1950	1960	1970	1977 (est.)
Kenai	290	332	303	321	778	3,533	5,223
Nome	12,488	852	1,559	1,876	2,316	2,488	2,585
Fairbanks	—	1,155	3,455	5,771	13,311	14,771	30,462
Anchorage	—	1,856	4,229	11,254	44,237	48,029	175,603*
Seward	—	652	949	2,114	1,891	1,587	1,823
Kodiak	341	374	864	1,710	2,628	3,798	4,960
Cordova	—	955	938	1,165	1,125	1,164	2,406
Valdez	315	466	529	554	555	1,005	8,253
Juneau	1,864	3,058	5,729	5,956	6,797	6,050	19,193†
Ketchikan	459	2,458	4,695	5,305	6,483	6,994	11,262†
Sitka	1,396	1,175	1,987	1,985	3,237	3,370	7,100†
Wrangell	868	821	1,162	1,263	1,315	2,029	3,152
Petersburg	—	879	1,323	1,619	1,502	2,042	2,126
Barrow	—	—	—	—	—	—	2,307
Bethel	—	—	—	—	—	—	3,004
Kotzebue	—	—	—	—	—	—	2,431

*Municipality   †City and Borough

DISTRIBUTION OF TOTAL ALASKA POPULATION BY SIZE OF PLACE
1950-1970

Size of Place	1950 Number of Places	Population	Percent of Total Population	1960 Number of Places	Population	Percent of Total Population	1970 Number of Places	Population	Percent of Total Population
Places of less than 1,000	—	79,394	61.7	—	116,446	51.5	—	117,017	39.0
1,000-1,500	3	3,575	2.8	10	12,444	5.5	13	15,170	5.1
1,500-2,000	4	7,190	5.6	4	7,032	3.1	4	6,918	2.3
2,000-2,500	2	4,222	3.3	2	4,478	2.0	7	15,765	5.2
2,500-5,000	2	5,976	4.6	2	5,865	2.6	6	21,355	7.1
5,000-10,000	3	17,032	13.2	3	22,354	9.9	6	43,268	14.4
10,000-25,000	1	11,254	8.7	1	13,311	5.9	2	32,860	10.9
25,000 or more	—	—	—	1	44,237	19.6	1	48,029	16.0

Sources: *U.S. Bureau of Census, Alaska Department of Commerce and Economic Development, Department of Community and Regional Affairs.*

ALASKA'S POPULATION BY REGION
1880-1975

Year	Total Alaska	Southeast	Southcentral	Southwest	Interior	Northwest
1880	33,426	7,748	4,352	13,914	2,568	4,844
1890	32,052	8,038	6,112	12,071	2,333	3,498
1900	63,592	14,350	10,000	13,000	5,600	20,642
1910	64,356	15,216	12,900	12,049	13,064	11,127
1920	55,036	17,402	11,173	11,541	7,964	6,956
1930	59,278	19,304	11,880	12,118	8,246	7,730
1940	72,524	25,241	14,881	12,846	10,345	9,211
1950	128,643	28,203	50,093	17,715	23,008	9,624
1960	226,167	35,403	108,851	21,001	49,128	11,784
1970	300,382	42,565	162,001	26,491	56,479	12,846
1971	312,930	43,349	174,609	26,650	54,977	13,345
1972	324,281	44,772	182,954	26,765	56,797	12,993
1973	330,365	43,417	188,698	29,040	56,593	12,617
1974	351,159	50,232	194,569	28,165	63,151	15,042
1975	404,634	50,438	229,492	28,428	78,614	17,662

Source: *Alaska Department of Labor.*

MAJOR COMPONENTS OF ALASKA'S POPULATION GROWTH
1880-1970

Year	Alaska	Native	Non-Native	Military
1880	33,426	32,996	430	—
1890	32,052	25,354	4,298	—
1900	63,592	29,542	30,450	—
1910	64,356	25,331	36,400	—
1920	55,036	26,558	28,228	250
1930	59,278	29,983	29,045	250
1940	72,524	32,458	39,566	500
1950	128,643	33,863	74,373	20,407
1960	226,167	43,081	150,394	32,692
1967	277,906	52,000	192,227	33,679
1970	300,382	50,554	219,828	30,000

ESTIMATED COMPONENTS OF NET CHANGE IN ALASKA'S POPULATION
1950-1975

Year	Total Population	Net Change	Net Civilian Migration	Natural Increase	Net Military Migration
1950	138,000	—	—	—	—
1955	221,000	83,000	34,900	24,100	24,000
1960	226,000	5,000	11,100	31,900	(15,800
1965	265,000	39,000	4,000	34,500	500
1970	300,382	37,382	14,972	25,410	(3,000
1975	404,634	104,252	75,297	28,955	(6,100

Source: Estimate from *Alaska Regional Population and Employment*, G. W. Rogers.
Source Note: Unless otherwise noted, all population statistics for 1960 and prior years from G. W. Rogers and R.A. Cooley, *Alaska's Population and Economy* and Alaska Department of Labor.

Source of Alaska Population Statistics: *Alaska Blue Book, 1977.*

General Fund Revenues

FISCAL YEARS 1965–1976
(in Thousands of Dollars)

	1965	1966	1967	1968	1969	1970	1971	1972	1973	1974	1975	1976
Taxes	$ 36,616	$ 43,782	$ 48,027	$ 50,922	$ 61,331	$ 74,234	$ 83,629	$ 89,138	$ 96,436	$109,400	$185,136	$578,023
Business Licenses, Fees and Permits	1,528	1,792	1,789	1,832	2,118	2,573	2,709	2,822	3,247	4,172	3,550	4,659
Non-business Licenses, Fees and Permits	3,011	4,491	4,451	4,741	5,196	5,803	6,175	6,239	6,509	6,939	10,486	11,981
Charges and Other Miscellaneous Revenues	6,613	8,665	9,171	10,740	12,032	50,406	109,028	112,318	91,980	33,399	17,298	19,342
Receipts from Other Lands	7,969	14,127	14,386	35,232	22,248	923,792	30,251	27,734	33,149	—	—	—
Alaska Court System	915	892	857	971	1,110	1,255	1,388	1,534	814	—	—	—
Federal Land and Resources	9,555	7,907	8,290	8,269	8,611	9,129	9,737	8,952	7,748	—	—	—
Transfers from Other Funds	—	—	—	—	—	—	—	—	—	—	—	—
Federal Transitional Grants	16,500	4,790	—	—	—	—	—	—	—	—	—	—
Federal Reimbursement and Grants	66,805	64,628	79,204	61,717	73,449	76,513	110,529	124,157	145,579	—	—	—
Governmental Revenue	—	—	—	—	—	—	—	—	—	8,064	11,104	7,568
Fines and Forfeitures	—	—	—	—	—	—	—	—	—	9,526	3,956	3,352
Miscellaneous Operating Accounts	—	—	—	—	—	—	—	—	—	—	102,139	80,566
Federal Grants	—	—	—	—	—	—	—	—	—	141,313	186,205	240,702
Other Grants	—	—	—	—	—	—	—	—	—	—	18,629	10,791
Interagency Receipts	—	—	—	—	—	—	—	—	—	25,084	49,984	55,489
Other Restricted Misc. Revenues	—	—	—	—	—	—	—	—	—	—	—	5,356
Miscellaneous Revenue	—	—	—	—	—	—	—	—	—	95,250	—	—
Other Program Augmentation	1,471	1,485	2,333	3,204	2,024	2,453	2,545	3,342	—	—	—	—
Totals	$150,987	$152,564	$168,507	$177,628	$188,119	$1,146,220	$355,991	$376,236	$385,462	$424,577	$588,491	$1,017,834

Source: *State of Alaska Annual Financial Reports and Supplements.*

Source of General Fund Revenues Statement: *Alaska Blue Book, 1977.*

Appendix D
Governors of Alaska

Aleksandr Andreevich Baranov	1790–1818
Leonti Andreanovich Hagemeister	Jan.–Oct. 1818
Semen Ivanovich Yanovski	1818–1820
Matvei I. Muraviev	1820–1825
Peter Egorovich Chistiakov	1825–1830
Baron F. P. Wrangell	1830–1835
Ivan Antonovich Kupreanov	1835–1840
Adolph Karlovich Etolin	1840–1845
Michael D. Tebenkof	1845–1850
Nikolai Y. Rosenberg	1850–1853
Alexander Ilich Rudakof	1853–1854
Stephen Vasili Voevodski	1854–1859
Ivan V. Furuhelm	1859–1863
Prince Dmitri Maksoutov	1863–1867
Brevet Major General Jefferson C. Davis	1867–1868
Captain W. H. Dennison (U.S. Army)	1868–1869
Captain G. K. Brady (U.S. Army)	1869–1870
Major J. C. Tidball	1870–1877

[U.S. troops were withdrawn in 1877, leaving M. C. Berry, customs collector, the only federal official in Alaska, 1877–1879.]

Captain L. S. Beardslee (U.S. Navy), Sloop *Jamestown*	1879–1880

Henry Glass (U.S. Navy), assumed command from Beardslee in 1880.

Edward P. Lull (U.S. Navy), the *Wachusett*	1880–1881
Lt. Commander Henry E. Nichols (U.S. Navy), the *Pinta*	1881–1884

John H. Kinkead, appointed by President Arthur, July 4, 1884–May 7, 1885.

Alfred P. Swineford, appointed by President Cleveland, May 7, 1885–April 20, 1889.

Lyman E. Knapp, appointed by President Harrison, April 20, 1889–June 18, 1893.

James Sheakley, appointed by President Cleveland, June 18, 1893–June 23, 1897.

John G. Brady, appointed by President Roosevelt, June 23, 1897–March 2, 1906.

Wilford B. Hoggatt, appointed by President Roosevelt, March 2, 1906–May 20, 1909.

Walter E. Clark, appointed by President Taft, May 20, 1909–April 18, 1913.

John F. A. Strong, appointed by President Wilson, April 18, 1913–April 12, 1918.

Thomas Riggs, Jr., appointed by President Wilson, April 12, 1918–June 16, 1925.

George A. Parks, appointed by President Coolidge, June 16, 1925–April 19, 1933.

John W. Troy, appointed by President Roosevelt, April 19, 1933–December 6, 1939.

Ernest Gruening, appointed by President Roosevelt, reappointed by President Truman, December 6, 1939–April 10, 1953.

B. Frank Heintzleman, appointed by President Eisenhower, April 10, 1953–January 3, 1957, resigned, and Waino Hendrickson became acting governor.

Mike Stepovich, appointed by President Eisenhower, April 8, 1957, resigned August 9, 1958, to run for U.S. Senate seat. Waino Hendrickson once again became acting governor.

William A. Egan, elected, January 3, 1959–December 5, 1966.

Walter J. Hickel, elected, December 5, 1966–January 29, 1969, resigned, appointed secretary of the interior by President Nixon.

Keith H. Miller, succeeded Hickel, January 29, 1969–December 5, 1970.

William A. Egan, elected, December 5, 1970–December 5, 1974.

Jay S. Hammond, elected, December 5, 1974–present.

Appendix E
Secretaries of the Territory

The office of surveyor-general was established in 1897. The holder of the office also acted as ex-officio secretary of the territory.

W. J. Hills	1897–1901
William L. Diston	1902–1912

The first territorial legislature convened in 1913. A joint resolution was adopted, addressed to Congress, calling for the establishment of the territorial offices of secretary and attorney general.

Charles E. Davidson	1913–1918
Robert J. Sommers	1919–1921
Karl Theile	1922–1932
Edward W. Griffin	1933–1938
E. L. "Bob" Bartlett	1939–1944
Lew M. Williams	1944–1951
Joseph W. Kehoe	1951–1952

| Burke Riley | 1952–1953 |
| Waino E. Hendrickson | 1953–1959 |

Attorneys General of the Territory

George Grigsby	1917–1918
Gerry C. Murphy	1919–1921
John Rustgard	1922–1932
James S. Truitt	1933–1940
Henry Roden	1941–1944
Ralph J. Rivers	1945–1948
J. Gerald Williams	1949–1959

The office of territorial treasurer was established by the first territorial legislature in 1913.

Walstein G. Smith	1913–1933
Oscar G. Olsen	1934–1948
Henry Roden	1949–1954
Hugh J. Wade	1955–1959

In 1970, the office of secretary of Alaska was changed by constitutional amendment to that of lieutenant governor of Alaska.

Hugh J. Wade	elected	January 3, 1959–December 5, 1966
Keith Miller	elected	December 5, 1966–January 29, 1969
Robert W. Ward	succession	January 29, 1969–December 5, 1970
H. A. Boucher	elected	December 5, 1970–December 5, 1974
Lowell Thomas, Jr.	elected	December 5, 1974–present

Appendix F
Delegates to Congress

In 1906 Congress authorized Alaska to send a voteless delegate to the House of Representatives. The following individuals served in that capacity:

Voteless Delegates

Frank H. Waskey	1906–1907
Thomas Cale	1907–1909
James Wickersham	1909–1917
Charles A. Sulzer	1917 (contested election)
James Wickersham	1918 (seated as delegate)

Charles A. Sulzer	1919 (elected, died before taking office)
George Grigsby	1919 (appointed)
James Wickersham	1921 (seated as delegate, having contested the 1919 election and resulting appointment)
Dan A. Sutherland	1921–1930
James Wickersham	1931–1933
Anthony J. Dimond	1933–1944
E. L. "Bob" Bartlett	1944–1958

Tennessee Plan Delegation

Senators:

| Ernest Gruening | 1956–1958 |
| William A. Egan | 1956–1958 |

Representative:

| Ralph J. Rivers | 1956–1958 |

Alaska's Congressional Delegation
(statehood proclaimed, January 3, 1959)

U.S. Senators:

E. L. "Bob" Bartlett	1959–1968 (died in office, December 11, 1968)
Ernest Gruening	1959–1968
Mike Gravel	1968–present
Theodore F. Stevens	December 11, 1968–present (appointed to E. L. "Bob" Bartlett's vacant seat, elected 1972–present)

Representatives:

Ralph J. Rivers	1959–1966
Howard Pollock	1966–1970
Nicholas Begich	1970–1972

(On October 16, 1972, Begich boarded a small plane to continue his campaign for reelection. The plane took off from Anchorage, bound for Juneau, and disappeared. Thirty-nine days of intensive air, land, and sea search revealed no trace of the aircraft, its passengers, or its pilot.)

| Don Young | 1973–present |

Appendix G
Federal District Judges for Alaska Before Statehood in 1958

First Judicial District (seated at Juneau)

Judge	Date of Appointment
Ward McAllister, Jr.	July 5, 1884
Edward J. Dawne	August 28, 1885
Lafayette Dawson	December 3, 1885
John H. Keatley	August 25, 1888
John S. Bugbee	December 7, 1889
Warren Truitt	January 15, 1892
Arthur K. Delaney	November 8, 1895
Charles S. Johnson	July 28, 1897
Melville C. Brown	April 1, 1900
Royal A. Gunnison	December 3, 1904
Thomas R. Lyons	May 4, 1909
Robert W. Jennings	May 6, 1913
Thomas M. Reed	August 16, 1921
Justin W. Harding	January 15, 1929
George F. Alexander	July 18, 1933
George W. Folta	May 7, 1947

Second Judicial Division (seated at St. Michael, later moved to Nome)

Arthur H. Noyes	June 6, 1900
Alfred S. Moore	April 27, 1902
Cornelius D. Murane	July 5, 1910
John Tucker Randolph	October 7, 1913
William A. Holzheimer	November 1, 1917
G. J. Lomen	February 16, 1926
Lester O. Gore	June 28, 1932
J. H. S. Morison	June 28, 1934
Joseph W. Kehoe	December 18, 1944
Joseph Earl Cooper (recess appointment)	July 17, 1952
Walter H. Hodge	March 2, 1954

Third Judicial Division (seated at Valdez, later moved to Anchorage)

Judge	Date of Appointment
James Wickersham	June 6, 1900
Silas H. Reed	November 6, 1907
Edward E. Cushman	May 18, 1909

Peter D. Overfield (transferred from Fourth Judicial Division)	Unknown
Frederick M. Brown	June 17, 1913
Elmer E. Ritchie	August 16, 1921
E. Coke Hill	February 14, 1927
Cecil H. Clegg (transferred from Fourth Judicial Division)	June 16, 1932
Simon Hellenthal	June 27, 1934
Anthony J. Dimond	January 3, 1945

Fourth Judicial Division (seated at Eagle, later moved to Anchorage)

Peter D. Overfield	March 3, 1909
Frederic E. Fuller	August 16, 1912
Charles E. Bunnell	January 15, 1915
Cecil H. Clegg	November 9, 1921
E. Coke Hill (transferred from Third Judicial Division)	May 3, 1932
Harry E. Pratt	June 21, 1935
Vernon D. Forbes	August 26, 1954

Appendix H
Important Placer Gold Discoveries

Russian River, 1849	Port Clarence, 1899
Stikine, 1862	Kougarok, 1899
Windham Bay, 1869	Fairhaven, 1899
Sumdum Bay, 1870	Koyukuk, 1899
Cassiar, B.C., 1871	Nizina, 1902
JUNEAU, 1880	Koyuk, 1902–1915
Fortymile, 1886	FAIRBANKS, 1902
Yakutat, 1887	Valdez Creek, 1903
Lituya, 1887	Bonnifield, 1903
Resurrection, 1888	Kantishna, 1905
Rampart, 1893	Yentna, 1905
Birch Creek (Circle), 1893	Richardson, 1906
Seventymile, 1895	Chandalar, 1906
KLONDIKE, 1896	Innoko, 1906
Yakataga, 1898	Ruby (Poorman), 1907

Atlin, B.C., 1898

Porcupine, 1898

Chistochina, 1898

Shungnak, 1898

NOME, 1898

Manley Hot Springs, 1898

Council, 1898

Bonanza (Ungalik), 1899

Solomon, 1899

Bluff, 1899

Aniak, 1907

Melozitna, 1907

Iditarod, 1909

Kiana, 1909

Hughes (Indian River), 1910

Nelchina, 1912

Chisana (Shushana), 1912

Marshall, 1913

Livengood (Tolovana), 1914

Goodnews Bay, 1900–1928

Source: Dr. Ernest Wolff, Director, Mineral Research Laboratory, University of Alaska, Fairbanks, Alaska, 1978.

Index

Persons and Places

Subjects

Guggenheim Brothers, 84; "Guggs," 86
Gulf-British Petroleum Consortium, 240

Haida Indians, 14, 196; location and language, 14, 16; village self-government, 199; land claims suit, 202, 203
Haines-Fairbanks military petroleum pipeline, 129, 130
Haines cut-off, 129
Haul road, 244, 246, 247; winter, 177, 239, 246; "Hickel Highway," 177, 239, 246; North Slope, 257
Havenstrite Oil Company, 235
Hawaii, 142; military importance of, 111
Health care, 163
Heartland defense concept, 124, 126
Hercules air transports, 239, 255
"Hickel Highway": see Haul road
Highways: see Alaska-Canada Military Highway; Roads
H.M.S. Osprey (warship), 61
Home rule, 86, 87, 134, 141, 143; limited, 91; Wickersham and, 135; and sectionalism, 137
Homestead Act, 78
Homesteading: difficulty of, 173; Indian opposition to, 199–200
Homestead laws, 198
Housing, 125, 126, 127, 128
Housing industry: native regional corporations and, 228
Howard-Wheeler Act, 201
Hudson's Bay Company, 14, 233, 267
Humble Oil and Refining Company, 236, 237, 241, 247, 248
Hunters: first migration of, 11; and land bill, 193
Hunting, native: coastal Indians, 15–16, Athapaskans, 17, Eskimos, 23, 24; Project Chariot and, 205–206
Hunting rights, 207
Hutchinson, Kohl & Co., 58, 61

I-boats, 120, 121
Icebreakers, 248
Ice bridge (Yukon River), 252
Independent party, 188
Indian claims, 197; see also Native claims; Native lands
Indian Claims Commission Act, 203, 215
Indian hunting rights, 207; see also Native Alaskans
Indian Reorganization Act of 1934, 107, 201
Indians, 13–17, 136, 267; language of, 13–14; tools of, 14–15; social structure, 16; religion, 16–17; Ingalik, 19; Tanaina, 18; Yuit, 22; Nez Perce, 61; diet, 93, 107; Chilkat, trade monopoly, 197; death and disease, 200; Copper River, 216; see also Native Alaskans
Insular Cases, 85, 134

International migratory bird treaty, 207
Inupiat Paitot, 208
Iwo Jima, 121

Jackson native settlement bill, 220–221
Jade mining claims, 228
Japan current, 9, 21
Japanese in World War II: fear of, invasion, 110–111; attack on Dutch Harbor, 114–115; occupation of Attu, Adak, and Kiska, 115; Aleutian operation, 115–117; air attack (July 20, 1942), 117; evacuation of Kiska, 121–122
Japanese investment groups, 174–175
Japanese oil companies, 251
Japanese salmon fishing, 175
Japanese steel, 242
Japan oil market, 264
Joint Federal-State Land Use Planning Commission, 192, 223–224; first recommendations, 225; and Omnibus Act, 231
"Jones Act" (U.S. Maritime Act of 1920), 90–91, 92, 146–147
J. P. Morgan and Company, 84
Judges, 79, 88, 89
Judicial council, 168
Judicial districts, 79
Junyo (carrier), 114

Katalla oil field, 234
Kennicott Copper Company, 84
Ketchikan Alaska Chronicle, 140, 145
Kiska Island: occupation force, 115; American bombing of, 121; invasion of, 122; see also World War II
Kodiak crab and salmon canneries, 179–181
Koniag, Inc., 228–229
Korean War, 151

Labor: Russians, 37; Aleuts, 39; creole, 51; in canneries, 62, 93–94; wages, 81, 90, 126–127; strikes, 126, 128; seasonal employment, 128–129; pipeline jobs and wages, 257–259; non-native, for salmon packing, 269
Land: native selection process, 192; natives' need for, 210–211; distribution of, 224; withdrawals for natives, 198
Land claims task force, 215
Land freeze, 192, 214, 215, 242, 244, 245, 246; effect on state land selection, 172; and oil and gas leasing, 216, 218; effect on native cause, 217
Land grants, 136, 149, 151, 152, 154–155
Landing Force Attu, 121
Land legislation, 194
Land lease boom (oil), 236, 239, 240; see also Oil
Land-use planning commission, 222
Land-use planning controversy, 192–193
Langer-McCarran bill, 145

Maps